D1030454

HISTORY
OF
THE FEDERAL COURTS

HISTORY
OF
THE FEDERAL COURTS

by

ERWIN C. SURRENCY
Director, Law Library
Professor of Law
University of Georgia School of Law

1987
OCEANA PUBLICATIONS, INC.
New York • London • Rome

Library of Congress Cataloging-in-Publication Data

Surrency, Erwin C.
    History of the federal courts.

    Includes index.
    1. Courts—United States—History.   I. Title.
I. Title.
KF8719.S97   1987   347.73'2'09   87-5673
ISBN 0-379-20855-5   347.307109

Manufactured in the United States of America

TABLE OF CONTENTS

TABLE OF CASES

FOREWORD

It is with some trepidation that this volume, which has consumed so many years of the author's life, is finally published. Many factors contribute to this uneasiness. The subject matter of this book is so broad and the literature so vast, a thorough examination of all legal sources including decisions, statutes, attorney general opinions, congressional reports, local histories and legal texts was impossible. Even if one could examine all the literature, read all reported decisions and distill them, it remains a difficult task to present in full a complete history of the federal courts. In this context, the author cannot resist posing the question: do all these reported cases contribute to any greater understanding of the development of the court system or are each but a grain of sand that collectively constitute the beach?

Another reason for this trepidation is that so much has been omitted which could be included. One area of law which is exclusively federal is the bankruptcy law, yet, because of the limitation in space, this subject had to be omitted. Certainly, Charles Warren, BANKRUPTCY IN UNITED STATES HISTORY (1935), an excellent book, should be updated. The gradual growth in supporting staff for judges has impacted the administration of justice in many ways which have not been documented either in decisions or other sources. This development is only sketchily referenced here.

Many conclusions that are made can be challenged by a finding that practices other than those described in this book prevail in certain judicial districts. The author is painfully aware that law is not applied equally throughout the United States, for judges and lawyers exhibit a propensity for finding reasons to circumvent certain decisions and, indeed, unpopular laws, with sufficient legal justification. During the Vietnam War, federal judges who were opposed to the war found ways to circumvent the draft act by allowing exemptions. This was true during the Civil War as well! Such separate trends do not detract from legal doctrines but are an important aspect of the legal story. How certain procedural devices were developed is hidden in the unwritten practices of the courts. One Circuit Court of Appeals required the entire record to be printed whereas another required the parties jointly to print only the parts of the record necessary to the appeal. Such practices may have been prescribed in rules or left to local knowledge. These examples may seem trivial, but in time, the operation of the courts is affected by administrative practices.

The courts are ongoing institutions which appear to change very little; yet, change they do! The jurisdiction and practices of the courts, especially the federal courts, have expanded rather slowly during the two centuries of their existence. The jurisdiction dictates what cases will come before the courts, and its rules or procedure govern how and what issues the court will resolve. This is the thread that connects the thousands of decisions made by the courts. Changes in nuances are difficult to detect, but in time, differences become apparent. Increased jurisdiction is not due exclusively to additional laws but may in part be explained by an ever increasing role of the federal courts, a factor which cannot be documented with precision. At times, this increased role is fostered by actions of the state courts. Following the enactment of the Immigration Act of 1924 (43 Stat. 153), state courts discontinued considering petitions for naturalization which resulted in the federal courts assuming this burden. This type of change is impossible to document.

An even more difficult task is to trace the origin of a particular legal doctrine. Legal history shows that law is often preceded by the establishment of a custom that may become the basis of a uniform practice and later be given a higher status denoted as law. Just when and how each legal rule passes through this evolution often cannot be clearly resolved. The development of the office of chief judge can only be explained by a gradual accretion of authority, whether by a strong personality or a response to very real daily demand, until in time, it is recognized in statutes. Even then, some chief judges shy away from exercising the authority of these offices. Perhaps the curious will be aroused to expand our knowledge through a more detailed examination of archival sources of the role of individual judges. Only through such sources will one find the administrative determinations the judges made which impacted the functioning of their courts and the development of American law.

Traditionally, the histories of courts have focused on one of three themes: 1) the organization; 2) the famous cases decided by the courts; or 3) biographical sketches of the judges. Hopefully, this book takes a new tact, focusing on the development of the structure of the federal courts, including their procedural jurisdiction, rather than upon the substantive law which they apply. It is a synthesis of many sources, and hopefully, it has captured the continued growth of the federal courts as institutions. An attempt has been made to convey a feeling for the procedure used in the federal courts — with the full realization that the full complexities of procedure cannot be compressed. The steps required to get a case before the United States Supreme Court in the Nineteenth Century are not nearly as glamorous as ascertaining the implications of the latest decision defining some constitutional issue, yet procedure is important to the legal craftsman. How successful the author has been in explaining these procedural changes will be revealed in debates over his contribution.

In undertaking such an extensive work over so many years, an author becomes indebted to many individuals. Members of my staff both at Temple University and the University of Georgia during that period have contributed by locating materials that had long been forgotten in legal literature. Jose Rodriguez and Margaret "Peggy" Durkin have had to blow the dust off many long forgotten tomes. But chiefly the author is indebted to Miss Jennifer Lynn Houser — research assistant, critic, and mentor. Without her encouragement, the author would have given up the struggle of completing this work many times. She has graded each chapter, but her grades will be kept confidential. My colleague, Professor Ronald Carlson, has read portions of the manuscript and given valuable suggestions. Ms. Katrina DeFoor has been the reluctant secretary, taking a manuscript all marked up with often illegible notations from which she prepared a manuscript. Howard J. Shifke has read portions of this manuscript and searched out some information for the author. Dean J. Ralph Beaird has given his support. With wifely pride, Ida Surrency has followed closely the progress of the manuscript over the dinner table, encouraging at times and exhorting on many occasions. Although not a direct participant in writing this book, her support was invaluable. Finally, Deborah L. Dance gave one last review of the manuscript. To all, my many thanks for their individual contributions!

Erwin C. Surrency   June 30, 1986
Athens, Georgia

Chapter 1
PRELUDE

The Constitution of the United States provided for a Supreme Court and such inferior courts as Congress should establish. The Constitutional Convention in 1787 had settled the issue that there could be federal courts separate from the existing state courts, but had not mandated federal trial courts. The Convention gave little consideration to the shape the system was to assume. The First Congress under the Constitution was faced with the duty of establishing the judicial system as authorized by the Constitution. This opportunity was unique, as this was the first time in history that a judicial system could be established for a new nation without the heavy hand of tradition dictating the form of its structure. Since there were no previous federal courts other than the Court of Appeals under the Confederation, the Congress had to create them, name them, and define their jurisdiction. The state governments established during the Revolution were not afforded this opportunity of establishing a new judicial system, but in most instances, the existing judicial system was continued with a change in personnel, and perhaps new titles were adopted and some changes in structure. But where were those charged with establishing the federal courts to turn for guidance?

The authors of the First Judiciary Act came from states with an established judicial system that had in many cases been functioning for over a century. Several of these individuals had been involved in restructuring the judicial system in their own states, making changes in jurisdiction and powers of the colonial courts. One concern was the need to separate the judicial functions from the executive, for in the Royal Colonies, the governor was the chancellor, probate judge, and chief judge in the courts of appeals. When the members of the Congressional Committee drafted the First Judiciary Act, this experience of establishing the judicial systems in the states provided some guidance in establishing the federal courts.

Another model was the English courts. These drafters incorporated some of the features of the English courts with which they were familiar. One such feature built into this new system was the requirement that the Justice of the Supreme Court travel throughout this country to hold a circuit court. All the states' systems, with few exceptions, required the judges to ride the circuit as was the custom in England, where the judges went on assizes or circuit to try cases. In the federal system, this was accomplished by creating the circuit courts which were the major trial courts in the federal system and originally presided over by two justices; later this was reduced to one member of the Supreme Court and the judge from the district court. The belief that the justices of the Supreme Court should hold a trial court throughout the country was so strongly held that this was to be a central feature of the federal system. The vestige of this was to remain to the present date. This was one of the most controversial and unfortunate features of the federal system.

A justification for the circuit system was the argument that the justices represented the central government as the English judges on assizes represent the king. This was a method of bringing the reality of the national government to the attention of the citizens living at some distance from the federal capital. In a sense, the circuit system provided an opportunity for representatives of the federal government to go out into the states and observe events, reporting their observations to the President. George Washington wrote to each justice as they began their first circuit, that "many things may occur . . . which it would be useful should be known", and he invited the justices to communicate such information directly to him.[1] Doubtless the justices informally conveyed information to the President about the condition of the country.

On circuit, the justices provided a convenient group of officials to perform other services for the federal government. In 1792, Congress attempted to take advantage of this by requiring the justices to examine claims for pensions. In that year, certain acts of the Continental Congress pertaining to pensions were suspended, and the statute provided that the circuit courts would consider the applications of those individuals who applied to be placed upon the pension list for services rendered during the Revolution.[2] The judges of the circuit court were required to examine the evidence, including the nature of the wound or disability, and ascertain the degree of such disability and transmit the results of the inquiry to the Secretary of War. The Secretary of War had the authority to overrule the justices.[3] The justices objected to this duty because the act subjected their decision to review by the Secretary of War who was a member of the Executive Branch. In their view, this infringed on the newly established concept of separation of functions between the three branches of government. The justices addressed letters to President Washington objecting to this procedure. One claimant petitioned the Supreme Court for a mandamus to direct the circuit court to proceed on his petition, and the Court took the motion under advisement but never reached a decision.[4] At its next session, Congress repealed the provision of the statute requiring the justices to examine pension claims and authorized the district court judge to appoint commissioners for this purpose.[5] This episode ended any attempt to involve the justices in performing extra judicial duties of this nature.

Another characteristic of the federal courts envisioned by the First Judiciary Act was the multiple judge trial court. The only single judge court created was the district court which, as originally conceived, exercised limited jurisdiction over such matters as revenue, admiralty, and minor crimes. All other matters went to the circuit court which was held by a justice of the Supreme Court and the district court judge. No statute ever required the two judges to sit together, and there is evidence that if either of the judges had to disqualify himself, the other would try the cases. Otherwise, when the justice was available, they held court concurrently. This court had often been confused with the Circuit Court of Appeals created over a century later, which was truly an appellate court. The disappearance of any differences in jurisdiction of the circuit and district courts until the two were merged in 1911 is another trend in this history of the judicial system. During the century of their coexistence, the jurisdiction of the two courts overlapped.

At first, the appellate function in the federal court system was limited by the technicalities in the writ of error, which confined the court to consider matters of law, and the writ of appeals, which brought up issues of facts and law.[6] But these distinctions were eroded, first by Congress and then a gradual lessening of these differences in the courts. The appellate function, as practiced in the federal and state courts, has evolved from a review of very technical and narrow issues to one practically reexamining the complete trial of the cause.

Another historical change was the extension of the jurisdiction of the federal courts. The limited number of types of causes within federal jurisdiction at the beginning of the Nineteenth Century began to expand, but this was a function of the change in complexity of society and the need for federal intervention. With the omnipresence of the federal courts in all aspects of state law during the final decades of the Twentieth Century, it is difficult to appreciate that until 1875, the federal courts were limited in their jurisdiction. In that year, Congress gave to the federal courts complete federal jurisdiction as defined in the Constitution. This is not to say that before 1875 the federal courts did not consider and decide important cases of national concern, but this statute did make it possible to apply the Constitution to many other areas than envisioned when the federal courts were first established. The claim of constitutional privilege when a case is judicially reviewed by a federal court afforded greater opportunity of declaring federal and state statutes unconstitutional.

The courts established under the First Judiciary Act were not the only ones needed by a growing nation. Congress established courts by necessity in the territories, and specialized courts were established for limited purposes; some have become permanent fixtures of the federal judicial system. Very early in the Nineteenth Century, the Supreme Court of the United States recognized a difference between these two groups of courts and designated one group as Constitutional Courts, or Article III courts, and the other as Legislative Courts, or Article I courts.[7] The Legislative Courts were those created under other provisions of the Constitution, especially Article I. The judges of these legislative courts did not enjoy life tenure or a permanent salary, and they were given only special jurisdiction. This dichotomy has long been accepted in American Constitutional Law, but the distinction between the Legislative and

Constitutional Courts is not at all clear. The matters which each court may hear provide little basis for distinguishing between the tribunals. Both Constitutional Courts and Legislative Courts may hear issues of "public rights" — matters that are "inherently judicial" but may be determined by the Executive or Legislative branches.[8] Among the courts operating outside of the Article III Constitutional Courts were Territorial Courts and courts of special jurisdiction such as the Tax Court. Congress has created several courts of limited jurisdiction which were recognized as Constitutional Courts.[9] In 1970, Congress became more aware of the different roles the two groups served as evidenced by the legislation which classified the courts in the District of Columbia as those established under either Article III or Article I.[10] Before then, the courts had been grouped as "superior" and "inferior" courts.

The federal courts were a constant concern to the Congress, which legislated on their jurisdiction and structure frequently! These statutes regulated many aspects of the administration of the courts in considerable detail from terms, details of procedure, location of clerk's offices, and other details. Gradually, over two centuries, the federal courts obtained more autonomy over these matters. After 1945, another concern was the administration of the courts, and more supporting staff for the federal judges was provided. When establishing new courts, the administrative aspects of the courts are given greater consideration than at any previous period. To understand these changes in the structure and jurisdiction of the federal courts contributes to a better understanding of the federal judiciary than merely examining their judicial decisions. The administrative decisions of individual judges have greatly shaped the development of the federal courts, and provide a better understanding of these bodies as institutions.

The history of the federal judiciary properly begins in 1789 with the passage of the First Judiciary Act, but before that, the federal government had exercised judicial functions under the Articles of Confederation, and a national court was organized under this provision. This experiment furnished experience for the guidance of the Founding Fathers and should be remembered for this reason.

FOOTNOTES TO CHAPTER 1

1. Julius Goebel, Jr., HISTORY OF THE SUPREME COURT; vol. 1, ANTE-CEDENTS AND BEGINNINGS TO 1801 (1971), p.555.

2. Act of March 23, 1792, sec. 2, 1 STAT. 244.

3. Act of March 23, 1792, sec. 4, 1 STAT. 244.

4. Hayburn's Case, 2 Dall. 409 (U.S. 1792).

5. Act of February 28, 1793, sec. 1, 1 STAT. 324.

6. Justice Miller, "Judicial Reforms", 2 U.S. JURIST 1 (Jan. 1872).

7. American & Ocean Insurance Co.'s v. 356 Bales of Cotton, 1 Pet. 511, 546 (U.S. 1828).

8. Northern Pipeline Construction Co. v. Marathon Pipe Line Co. et al, 458 U.S. 50, 67-68, 50 USLW 4892 (1982); Wilber G. Katz, "Federal Legislative Courts", 43 HARV. L. REV. 894 (1930).

9. Act of July 28, 1953, sec. 1, 67 STAT. 226, 28 U.S.C. 171, declaring the Court of Claims to be a constitutional court. Act of August 25, 1958, sec. 1, 72 STAT. 848, 28 U.S.C. 211, declaring the Court of Customs and Patent Appeals to be a constitutional court. The designation of these courts as constitutional courts was recognized by the Supreme Court in Glidden Co. v. Zdanok, 370 U.S. 530 (1962).

10. Act of July 29, 1970, sec. 111, 84 STAT. 475.

Chapter 2
FEDERAL COURTS UNDER THE ARTICLES OF CONFEDERATION

Under the Articles of Confederation, Congress received the authority to establish or designate the courts to try disputes in four areas.[1] The first such jurisdiction was the authority to appoint courts for the trial of piracies and felonies committed on the high seas. It is questionable if this clause gave the central government the authority to establish courts for this purpose, but the question never arose. By an ordinance passed on April 5, 1781, Congress provided that a person charged with any of the above crimes should be tried according to the course of common law in courts consisting of the "Justices of the Supreme or Superior courts of judicature and the judge of the court of admiralty". The governors were authorized to commission any one of the judges of the state courts of admiralty if there were two or more judges to join in the performance of this duty. The ordinance adopted the same punishment for felonies committed upon the sea, as for those committed on land.[2] Later, this ordinance was amended to require the judge of the Court of Admiralty to be a member of the court.[3]

A problem which had plagued the colonies was overlapping claims to western lands. This was not a serious problem until the decades preceding the Revolution when settlers spread out into areas west of the Allegheny Mountains. To resolve the claims of both the states and individuals under conflicting grants, the Articles established an elaborate procedure. To settle the claims among the states, each member of the Confederation was required to appoint a panel of three individuals. The commissioner of each state who was a party to the dispute was to strike the names alternately from the entire panel until the list was reduced to thirteen. At this point, in the presence of Congress, seven to nine names were to be drawn by lots, and this commission was to hear and settle the controversy. If a state did not appear, the secretary of the Congress would act for the absent commissioner. The findings of the commissioners were final and conclusive. The decision was to be transmitted to Congress "and lodged among the acts of Congress for the security of the parties concerned". Only one case proceeded to trial under this provision and that was the case between Pennsylvania and Connecticut. The decision was rendered in favor of Pennsylvania on December 30, 1782.[4] Panels were convened for two other cases but the boundaries were settled amicably without a hearing.[5]

Obviously, conflicting claims would arise between individuals who claimed the same property under grants from different states. Congress could resolve this group of claims by using the same procedure as that used in settling disputes between states. As far as is known, no dispute was brought to Congress under this provision.

The fourth area of jurisdiction exercised by the Continental Congress was over appeals in all cases of captures and prizes. Acting under this clause even before the Articles went into effect, Congress established a Court of Appeals in Prize Cases which heard a number of cases which were to have later ramifications. This was the only court established by the central government.

The impetus for the creation of this court came from George Washington. In November, 1755, Washington forwarded to the Continental Congress a copy of the Massachusetts Act establishing a prize court along with the suggestion that Congress establish a court for prizes taken by ships commissioned by it. A committee was appointed to consider this letter, and the idea was extensively debated. Finally, a resolution was adopted allowing appeals to Congress provided they be demanded within five days and the appeals lodged with the secretary within forty days of judgment. The term "appeal" was a technical procedure requiring the submission of the documents associated with the cases to the court for examination. The party making the appeal was required to give security to prosecute it. The resolution further provided that the appeal should be heard in Congress within 20 days. All suits were to commence in the newly established admiralty courts in the states. Acting on this suggestion, several of the states established admiralty courts, but these states limited the appeals to Congress to those cases involving vessels commissioned by the Confederation.[6]

The first case to be heard under this appellate procedure was the *Schooner Thistle*. Congress attempted to hear this case, but eventually referred it to a committee which reversed the condemnation of the vessel. Beginning at this point, all cases were referred to a committee. Later, the resolution referred a case to a "committee on appeals" without naming the members.[7]

In 1777, Congress appointed a standing committee of five members to hear appeals brought against sentences passed in the courts of admiralty. The following named individuals were chosen as members of this committee, many of whom became known in later years as judges: James Wilson of Pennsylvania; Jonathan D. Sergeant of New Jersey; William Ellery of Rhode Island; Samuel Chase of Maryland; and Roger Sherman of Connecticut.[8]

The committee was discharged the following year because Congress felt that it was too large to function properly. Another committee was appointed with the same number of individuals, any three of which were authorized to hear an appeal. Congress authorized this committee to appoint a register.[9] The personnel on the committee changed frequently, but this did not seem to be injurious to its work.

Congress did not consider establishing a court to hear appeals from the state admiralty courts until January 15, 1780. The ordinance provided for a court consisting of three judges commissioned by Congress, any two of whom could hold the court. The trials were to be conducted according "to the usage of Nations and not by Jury". The debates do not reveal any reason for this provision, for there would be no need for a trial in an appellate court. The judges were required to hold the first session of court as soon as possible in Philadelphia, and then at such places as they should judge conducive to the public good, provided they did not sit farther southward than Williamsburg, Virginia, and farther eastward than Hartford, Connecticut. The first judges were George Wythe from Virginia, William Paca of Maryland, and Titus Hosmer of Connecticut. Mr. Wythe declined the office and Cyrus Griffin of Virginia was appointed in his place.[10] Thus, the first federal court was constituted. Both Paca and Griffin would become the first judges of the United States District Courts for the states of their residency.

In December, 1784, the court informed Congress that all matters pending before it had been concluded. This letter was referred to a committee that recommended the court be continued, but this resolution was rejected. However, the salaries of the judges were suspended. In June 1786, Congress authorized the court to hear certain appeals made to Congress from New York. The final case handled by the court was the case of the *Sloop Chester* on an appeal from the Court of Admiralty of South Carolina.

The weakness inherent in this judicial system was the fact that the court depended upon state officers to enforce its decisions, which they were unwilling to do. In at least one case, the state officers refused to carry out these orders. Congress recommended to the State "to make laws authorizing and directing the courts of admiralty therein established . . . to carry into full and speedy execution the final decrees of the Court of Appeals".[11]

One of the most interesting cases brought before the court was the case of the *Sloop Active*.[12] The excitement and drama generated by his case cannot be fully recaptured in this short account of its history. Gideon Olmsted, a Connecticut fisherman, was captured with three others by the British and taken to Jamaica. Olmsted and his crew recaptured the ship, and off the coast of New Jersey, a vessel commissioned by Pennsylvania captured the Active. The question of whether this was a lawful prize was tried before the Pennsylvania Admiralty Court, which decided that the capture of the Sloop Active was lawful, and ordered it to be sold and the proceeds divided among the captives. Olmsted took an appeal to the Court of Appeals in Cases of Capture which upheld his position. This incident infuriated George Ross, Judge of the Pennsylvania Court of Admiralty, who felt that the Court of Appeals had no authority to examine the facts in the case in view of the Pennsylvania act setting up the Court of

Admiralty, which provided for a trial by jury whose findings should be final. The Court of Appeals took every step it could to enforce its decision, but without avail. The matter was considered by Congress which concluded that the court had the authority to examine the facts of the case. However, the Pennsylvania Admiralty Court continued to ignore the confederation authorities.

Olmsted continued to pursue his legal rights, and in 1790, he won a suit by default against the estate of Judge Ross. Ross' estate then proceeded against the estate of the signer of the bond of indemnity. When this suit came before Chief Justice Thomas McKean of the Pennsylvania Supreme Court, he refused to sustain the suit, thus ruling against Olmsted.[13] Olmsted quietly awaited the turn of events and in 1795, the Supreme Court decided the case of *Penhollow v. Doane*,[14] holding that the district courts of the United States had the power to carry into effect the decrees of the Court of Appeals in Cases of Capture. Olmsted presented himself before Judge Richard Peters of the United States District Court of Pennsylvania and asked for a decree against the estate of the security. McKean had become Governor of Pennsylvania, and the action of Olmsted aroused the governor's wrath because of the apparent inattention paid to his decision as chief justice. The Governor ordered that the money in dispute be paid into the state treasury. No decree was entered by Judge Peters because he viewed the case as a source of conflict between the state of Pennsylvania and the United States. Olmsted, in 1808, applied to the United States Supreme Court for a writ of mandamus against Judge Peters, and it was granted.[15] Judge Peters issued the necessary writs, but it was necessary to serve them. The state turned out the militia to protect the executors of the estate, but the United States marshal was clever enough to serve the writs without being observed by the militia. The commander of the troops and several of his officers, as well as the militia, were arrested for obstructing federal justice and were tried and sentenced. Thus, in the end, the jurisdiction of the Court of Appeals in Cases of Capture was upheld.

The committees of Congress decided 49 cases and the Court of Appeals decided 11.[16] The court wrote opinions in eight cases which were published in Dallas' reports.[17] Finally, in 1792, the Congress of the government under the Constitution provided that the records of this court were to be deposited with the clerk of the Supreme Court.[18]

The judicial experiences under the Articles of Confederation were like all other aspects of this government, "a shadow without the substance". The experience of this court in trying to enforce its own decrees was a lesson not lost on the drafters of the Constitution.[19] This lack of enforcement power was commented upon in legal circles during the first decades of the Nineteenth Century. The Court of Appeals in Prize Cases has passed into oblivion, and rarely is it mentioned as the first national court.

FOOTNOTES TO CHAPTER 2

1. Articles of Confederation, Article 9.

2. Ordinance of April 5, 1781, JOURNAL CONTINENTAL CONGRESS, v.19, p.354.

3. Ordinance of March 4, 1783, JOURNAL CONTINENTAL CONGRESS, v.24, p.164.

4. J.C. Bancroft Davis, "Federal Courts prior to the adoption of the Constitution," 131 U.S. (Appendix) p.liv-lviii; John C. Hogan, "The Court of Appeals in Cases of Capture," 33 ORE. L. REV. 95 (1954). For the dispute between New York and Connecticut, which proceeded to the point of selecting the agents, *see* Julius Goebel, Jr., THE LAW PRACTICE OF ALEXANDER HAMILTON (1964), v.1, p.545-564.

5. Franklin Jameson, "The Predecessor of the Supreme Court," in J. Franklin Jameson, ESSAYS IN THE CONSTITUTIONAL HISTORY OF THE UNITED STATES (1889), p.3.

6. Davis, *supra,* note 4, p.xix, xx. A fuller account is Henry J. Bourguignon, THE FIRST FEDERAL COURT; THE FEDERAL APPELLATE PRIZE COURT OF THE AMERICAN REVOLUTION (1977).

7. Davis, *supra,* note 4, p.xxiii.

8. Davis, *supra,* note 4, p.xxiii.

9. Davis, *supra,* note 4, p.xxiii-xxiv.

10. Davis, *supra,* note 4, p.xxv, 16; JOURNAL CONTINENTAL CONGRESS 61-62.

11. JOURNAL CONTINENTAL CONGRESS, v.16, p.61.

12. This series of cases has been the subject of numerous articles, but the most thorough and the account relied upon in this case is Carson, "The Case of the Sloop Active," 7 GREEN BAG 17 (1895). See Henry J. Bourguignon, THE FIRST FEDERAL COURT (1977), p.101.

13. Russell et al v. Rittenhouse, 2 Dallas 160 (1792).

14. Penhollow v. Doane, 3 Dallas 54 (1795).

15. United States v. Peters, 5 Cranch. 115 (U.S. 1801).

16. Davis, *supra,* note 4, p.xxxv. The list of all cases considered by the court begins on this page.

17. 2 Dallas 1-42.

18. Act of May 9, 1792, 1 STAT. 279.

19. Joseph Story, COMMENTARIES ON THE CONSTITUTION OF THE UNITED STATES (4th ed., 1873), v.1, pp.155, 172.

Chapter 3

THE ESTABLISHMENT
OF THE FEDERAL COURTS

When the members of the Constitutional Convention assembled in Philadelphia in 1787, apparently a consensus existed among the delegates that there should be a system of federal courts. In examining the debates, it is interesting to note that the structure and power of the federal courts received limited attention. The delegates had to determine first whether there should be federal courts, what jurisdiction these courts should exercise, how the judges were to be appointed, and what their tenure should be. The debates on the structure of the new government centered around two plans: the Virginia plan and the New Jersey plan.

Both plans provided for trial and appellate courts. Although the idea of the United States Supreme Court was accepted, some delegates questioned the need for inferior courts, as it was suggested that the state courts could handle the jurisdiction which would be assigned to these courts. The resolution establishing a national judiciary with inferior courts was temporarily adopted.[1]

However, a strong sentiment for the elimination of the lower federal courts developed. On June 5, 1787, John Rutledge from South Carolina moved to reconsider the original decision of establishing lower federal courts, for he felt that review by the Supreme Court was sufficient to protect the interests of the federal government. Some delegates opposed the establishment of inferior courts because of the cost of supporting such a system. Other delegates expressed their concern that the states would "revolt" at such encroachments as inferior federal courts. This motion was carried by five states against four states, with two states divided. James Madison moved for the adoption of a resolution establishing a Supreme Court, leaving to Congress the question of establishing inferior courts.[2] Thus, the final version of the United States Constitution authorized the establishment of a Supreme Court and deferred to the discretion of Congress the issue of inferior courts.

There was a clear agreement that a federal court should exercise the jurisdiction formerly exercised by the courts under the Articles of Confederation which included cases of piracy and other felonies committed on the high seas and prize cases. All the plans introduced extended this jurisdiction.

The Virginia plan, introduced by Governor Randolph of Virginia, provided that the courts would have jurisdiction in cases where foreigners and citizens of other states were interested, and in cases involving national revenue. Further, impeachment cases were to be tried in the federal courts as well as cases involving national peace and harmony. The New Jersey plan, introduced by William Patterson, would have omitted the impeachment jurisdiction, but added cases involving construction of treaties. Later, this treaty clause was broadened to include jurisdiction in cases arising under the laws and treaties of the United States.[3]

The method of appointment of judges aroused more debate as several plans were discussed. Some delegates thought that the national legislature should have the power of appointment, but it was finally agreed that the President would have the power of appointment subject to the approval of the Senate. When this question was being discussed, the arguments must have become acrimonious for it was at this point that Benjamin Franklin arose to tell his famous story of how judges were chosen in Scotland. There, so he related, the judges were nominated by the lawyers "who always selected the ablest of the profession in order to get rid of him, and share his practice."[4]

The experience of the colonial period in relation to the tenure of judges was not forgotten by the members of this convention. The Declaration of Independence itself had indicted King George III for making judges dependent on his will through their tenure during good behavior. The Constitutional Convention therefore adopted life tenure, which was the norm for state judges following the Revolution. The life tenure for federal judges has been a unique feature of the federal system, although since then attempts have been made to establish a term for judicial appointments.

It remained for the first Congress to act upon this constitutional mandate and to determine if there should be inferior courts and the extent of their jurisdiction. Federal court organization was established by the Judiciary Act of 1789, a work mainly attributed to Oliver Ellsworth, later Chief Justice of the United States.[5] The Act recognized that the Supreme Court was mandated by the Constitution by the opening statement that the court would "consist of a chief justice and five associate justices" whereas the sections establishing the district courts and the circuit courts began by stating "that there be a court called a district court."[6] The Supreme Court met at the seat of the government in two sessions, beginning on the first Monday in February and August. The Constitution did not mandate that this court be an appellate court, but it did give the court certain original jurisdiction. The Judiciary Act of 1789 supplied this omission by authorizing a review of the decisions of the circuit courts by the writ of error where the amount involved exceeded $2,000.[7] The original jurisdiction of the court as given in the Constitution was restated.

The First Congress provided for the establishment of inferior or trial courts by establishing the Circuit Courts and the District Courts. The establishment of the federal courts alongside of state courts was a unique experience in judicial history up to this period, for in no other country had a dual system been established.

The existing states at that time, with the exception of Kentucky and Maine, then a district of Massachusetts, were organized into three circuits — the Eastern, Southern and Middle Circuits. Each state constituted a district, and in each district the district courts were held in one or two cities at stated terms by the district court judges. The circuit court was held by two justices of the Supreme Court and the district court judge in at least one location in each state. The Circuit Court of Appeals of a later date should not be confused with the circuit courts. It was the circuit organization requiring the justices of the Supreme Court to preside in a trial court which caused the greatest dissatisfaction with the federal system at its inception. The modification of this circuit organization was the subject of much controversy in the Nineteenth Century.

The first justices of the Supreme Court were of the opinion that they could not be commissioned as judges of an appellate and inferior court because they saw a conflict between their duties as appellate judges passing upon questions decided by their colleagues as trial judges. They argued that this constituted a conflict which would undermine the confidence in the Supreme Court.[8] In 1803, the question was raised whether the judges of the Supreme Court could sit as circuit judges although they were not being appointed as such by a distinct commission. The court concluded that "it is sufficient to observe the practice and acquiescence under it for a period of several years, commencing with the organization of the judicial system, affords an irresistable answer, and had indeed fixed the construction". The court concluded that the tradition was "too strong and obstinate to be shaken or controlled".[9]

The jurisdiction of the circuit court extended to all matters triable under the federal statutes and not reserved exclusively to the district courts, including all major federal crimes except those committed on the high seas. Appellate jurisdiction from decisions of the district court, along with exclusive jurisdiction in diversity of citizenship cases where the amount exceeded $500, was vested in the circuit courts.[10] Other matters were assigned to this court by later statutes.

In each state, including Kentucky and Maine, a district court presided over by a district judge was established. This court was given jurisdiction of crimes in which the punishment did not exceed thirty stripes, nor a fine over $100, nor a term of imprisonment of six months. These courts had exclusive jurisdiction in admiralty and seizures under the imports, navigation, or trade statutes, or of seizures on land for the violation of the federal statutes. The district courts had concurrent jurisdiction with the circuit courts when an alien sued for a tort in violation of the law of nations or treaty, or where the federal government itself sued and the amount equalled $100 or less, or suits against consuls.[11]

Because of the pattern established in 1789, the geographical jurisdiction of district courts has been conterminous with state boundaries since that date. However, there have been a few exceptions. For example, the

District Court for the Western District of Arkansas,[12] the District Court of Kansas,[13] and the District Court for the Northern District of Texas,[14] all exercised criminal jurisdiction in certain parts of the Indian Territory, beyond the boundaries of their states. The District Court of Wyoming exercises jurisdiction today over the Yellowstone Park, including those portions of the Park in Montana and Idaho.[15]

The beautiful symmetry of this system whereby a district court was created in each state and assigned to a circuit was never fully realized. The Judiciary Act of 1789 gave the District Courts for Maine and Kentucky the jurisdiction of a circuit court, and in these states, the district courts were the sole federal courts.[16] At no period before 1866 were all the districts included in a circuit. The system never functioned as originally established.

It is rather easy to focus on those sections of the Judiciary Act of 1789 establishing the structure of the court or providing for the appointment of court officials and the oath that they must take. However, the jurisdictional sections of the act are significant as many of these sections have passed into the present judicial code. One obvious example is Section 25 providing for review by the writ of error by the Supreme Court of decisions of the highest state courts where questions of the validity of a federal statute or treaty were decided adversely. This section was drawn rather narrowly, but has since been expanded. The jurisdiction granted to the district and circuit courts under this First Judiciary Act remains vested in the district courts today, although greatly expanded. It is difficult to understand many of the jurisdictional provisions, for many times terms are used in a technical sense. The Act speaks of an appeal from the district court to the circuit courts in admiralty cases and a review of the decisions of the circuit courts by the Supreme Court by a writ of error.[17] These two terms are used in a technical meaning which has long since lost its connotations in practice. The changes that were made can easily be overlooked and go unappreciated because previous practices are not known. At the time the statute was drafted, only a court of chancery could require the production of books generally of accounts or other writings by a party to the suit but this authority is specifically given to judges in trials at common law.[18] Some of the provisions require close reading to fathom all of the Act's implications. An examination of the section defining the procedure before the Supreme Court will be found to contain all the elements and steps of practice in that court until displaced by the gradual substitution of the writ of certiorari.[19] These requirements are not set forth in the order that they will naturally be complied with. Some of the practices which are generally accepted at the present were originally established by this act. All evidence was required to be given before a jury in open court unless there was some compelling reason to take testimony by depositions.[20] The contribution of this section to our judicial system can be easily underestimated until the fact is considered that procedures followed in other English and American courts provided for the taking of testimony by depositions and a decision by a panel of judges at the trial level. Although the Judiciary Act of 1789 did establish the federal courts, its significance exceeds this basic accomplishment.

FOOTNOTES TO CHAPTER 3

1. Max Farrand, ed., THE RECORDS OF THE FEDERAL CONVENTION OF 1787 (1966), v.1, p.119.

2. Farrand, *supra,* note 1, v.1, p.124-125; John P. Frank, "Historical Basis of the Federal Judicial System," 13 L. & CONTEMP. PROB. 3, 10 (1948).

3. Farrand, *supra,* note 1, v.1, p.39.

4. Farrand, *supra,* note 1, v.1, p.120.

5. Act of September 24, 1780, 1 STAT. 73; John J. Parker, "The Federal Judicial System," 14 F.R.D. 361. For a complete history of the passage of this bill, see the classic article by Charles Warren, "New Light on the History of the Federal Judiciary Act of 1789," 37 HARV. L. REV. 49 (1923).

6. Act of September 24, 1789, sec. 1, 3, 1 STAT. 73.

7. Act of September 24, 1789, sec. 22, 1 STAT. 84.

8. Joseph Story, COMMENTARIES ON THE CONSTITUTION OF THE UNITED STATES (4th ed. by Thomas Cooley, 1873), v.2, p.387 where the letter of the justices is reproduced.

9. Stuart v. Laird, 1 Cranch. 299 (U.S. 1803).

10. Act of September 24, 1789, sec. 11, 1 STAT. 79.

11. Act of September 24, 1789, sec. 9, 1 STAT. 77.

12. Act of June 17, 1844, 5 STAT. 680.

13. Act of January 6, 1883, 22 STAT. 400.

14. Act of January 6, 1883, 22 STAT. 400.

15. Act of June 25, 1948, sec. 131, 62 STAT. 895.

16. Act of September 24, 1789, sec. 11, 1 STAT. 79.

17. Act of September 24, 1789, sec. 22, 1 STAT. 84.

18. Act of September 24, 1789, sec. 15, 1 STAT. 82.

19. Act of September 24, 1789, sec. 22, 1 STAT. 84.

20. Act of September 24, 1789, sec. 30, 1 STAT. 88.

Chapter 4

THE JUDICIARY ACT OF 1801 AND ITS AFTERMATH

The most controversial act affecting the federal courts and the only one which is popularly known to every student is the Judiciary Act of 1801. Very often, this statute is referred to as the "Midnight Judges Act" because, allegedly, President Adams sat up into the wee hours of his last day in office signing the commissions for the newly appointed judges. It is true that President Adams acted in unseemly haste, but the statute itself was not one which was hastily drafted and enacted after his defeat in the elections of November, 1800. The need for some change in the federal system had been recognized and had been incorporated much earlier into bills considered by Congress. Certainly the defeat of the Federalist Party in the previous election gave cause for their favorable vote in Congress, but the changes made in the structure of the courts had been urged during the previous decade.

From the time the Judiciary Act of 1789 was approved until the middle decades of the next century, there were a number of proposals designed in some way to relieve the justices of traveling to preside in the circuit courts. Since traveling in the United States in the Nineteenth Century was not undertaken with any degree of luxury or ease, it was often impossible for the justices to hold the circuit court as required by the law, which gave rise to complaints by them.

As early as August 9, 1792, the justices of the Supreme Court forwarded to the President a petition to be presented to Congress. The justices complained of the amount of travel that was required of them and the fact that they were called upon to correct judgments which they rendered in the circuit courts on the Supreme Court. They argued that "it appeared to be a general and well-founded opinion, that the act when passed was to be considered rather as introducing a temporary expedient than a permanent system, and that it would be revised as soon as a period of greater leisure should arrive." They asked the earnest consideration of a change, but declined to give any detailed proposal for such change.[1] George Washington, as President, was convinced that the circuit duty would be abolished, for he assured Thomas Johnson, who was appointed as an associate justice of the Supreme Court, that "these disagreeable tours" would be eliminated. He stated "that an opinion prevails pretty generally among the judges, as well as others who have turned their minds to the subject, against the expediency of continuing the Circuit of the Associate Justice".[2]

Prior to this petition, however, the Congress had asked the Attorney General, Edmund Randolph, to report on proposals for reform of the Federal Judicial System. Randolph's report of December 27, 1790 presented a newly proposed judiciary act with commentary. He discussed in some detail the jurisdiction of the federal courts and the advantages or disadvantages of any changes. The first suggestion was that the district court and the circuit court be continued with the same jurisdiction, but that the latter court be held by the judges of the district court.[3] After examining the issue of the justices remaining on the circuit courts, he concluded that: "Inferior Courts ought to be distinct bodies from the Supreme Court." Furthermore, the justice of the Supreme Court "must be a master of the common law in all instances, a chancellor, a civilian, a federal jurist, and skilled in the laws of each State."[4]

The Attorney General examined the jurisdictional questions and recommended that the federal courts be given exclusive jurisdiction in all federal questions and in certain other circumstances. However, the federal courts did not receive this grant of authority for over one hundred years.

In 1793, Congress ameliorated the travel burdens of the justices by providing that one justice and one district court judge would be sufficient for holding sessions of the circuit court.[5] The necessity of this act is questionable, for the Act of 1789 provided that any two of the three judges would constitute a quorum. An examination of the minutes of the Circuit Court for Pennsylvania, for example, indicated that rarely was more than one justice of the Supreme Court in attendance.[6]

Several bills were introduced into Congress to incorporate some of Randolph's proposals, but it was not until 1801 that Congress finally enacted a statute that sought to change the circuit system and clarify some other jurisdictional problems. The most controversial part of the Judiciary Act of 1801 was the creation of the office of circuit court judge.[7] President John Adams appointed the judges authorized by this Act, and hence, set the stage for the charge that he and his fellow Federalists had sought to perpetuate their political party in the judiciary after their defeats at the polls the previous November.

It is difficult to appreciate or to understand the passions that the passage of this Act generated. Many of the newly-elected Congressmen strongly denounced this Act with such descriptions of the judiciary as "a hospital for decayed politicians". The Judiciary Act of 1801 was perceived as an attempt to increase the power of the Federal Government at the expense of the states. Under an expanded judiciary, the cost to the Federal Government would increase, necessitating increases in taxes.[8] The newly elected Republicans did not view the Judiciary Act of 1801 as a necessary reform of the federal court system.

The most controversial feature of the Judiciary Act of 1801 was the creation of circuit court judgeships, which relieved the justices of the Supreme Court from attending these courts. The states were organized in six circuits; in five of them, three judges would have been appointed. The Sixth Circuit was unusual, however. Only one circuit judge would be appointed there and the district court judges of that circuit would join him in holding the circuit court. As the position of the district court judge came vacant in the Sixth Circuit, only circuit court judges would be appointed. Strangely, in effect, this abolished the district courts in the states of Kentucky and Tennessee, which had only recently been admitted to the Union.[9]

The criticism of the Jeffersonian opponents of this Act was that the size of the federal judiciary was increased substantially. At this time, there were seventeen district court judges and six justices of the Supreme Court, a total of twenty-three judges in the federal system. The Act of 1801 created sixteen new judgeships, but provided that when judgeships on the three district courts and one place on the Supreme Court became vacant, these positions would not be filled, thus increasing the total number of federal judges to thirty-five. The Act created four new district courts by dividing three states into two districts and creating a district court for the District of Columbia, but in none of these districts did the Act provide for additional judges. For example, the judge of the United States District Court for Maryland would preside in the District Court for the District of Potomac, which included portions of Maryland, the District of Columbia, and Northern Virginia. The sessions of this court were held in Alexandria, Virginia.

The strongest arguments against the establishment of the circuit courts was the fact that they were created to perpetuate the Federalists in office. Adams contributed to this perception by his appointment of Federalists. Among those receiving appointments to the new post were Charles Lee, formerly Attorney General in the Adams' administration, and Oliver Wolcott, who had been the Secretary of Treasury. Jared Ingersoll and Philip Barton Key were ardent Federalist partisans. Elijah Paine and Ray Greene, members of the United States Senate, and William H. Hill and Jacob Read, members of the House of Representatives, left to take places on the district court. One authority concluded "it is not surprising, therefore, that factional feelings among the Republicans ran high and severe criticism was meeted out to the courts."[10]

The Judiciary Act of 1801 significantly increased the number of court officials. Each of the states of New Jersey, Maryland, Virginia, and North Carolina were divided into two or more districts and a clerk was appointed in each district. In addition, the judges of the circuit court could appoint a clerk in each one of the twenty-nine districts in which the circuit courts were held.[11] A marshal and a district attorney were authorized in each of the districts in which the district courts were held. If the Act of 1801 did not increase significantly the number of federal judges, it did increase the number of court personnel and was the basis of the complaint that it increased the size of the federal courts. It would be interesting to know how many of these positions were filled by John Adams before he retired as President.

John Adams appointed all of the judges created for the circuit courts except for the judges in the Fifth Circuit who did not accept the commission. It is interesting to note that Thomas Jefferson filled these vacant positions.[12] Sessions of these newly established circuit courts were held, and business was conducted under this statute.[13]

The most significant change made by the Judiciary Act of 1801 was the extension of the jurisdiction of the federal courts to all cases arising under the Constitution or federal laws — a power which, because of the subsequent repeal of the Act, was not to be given again to the federal courts until the latter part of the century.[14] The repeal of this section was to confine the courts to matters specifically granted to it. The sections on removal of cases from state courts were extended to include all federal questions. Provisions were made in the Act for the removal of suits brought in the state courts involving federal questions where the defendant had not received personal service.[15] The political followers of Thomas Jefferson viewed this provision as an expansion of the federal courts at the expense of the state courts, resulting in easy access to the federal judiciary, which was contrary to their views on the sovereignty of the states.

The federal courts had cognizance of cases involving disputed titles to property claimed under grants from different states. However, this was expressed in more detail in the Act of 1801. The circuit courts were given jurisdiction over disputes arising over the titles to property under grants from different states regardless of value. The plaintiff in the state court could require the defendant to specify under which state he claimed the property, and, if the title was derived from a different state, then the plaintiff could remove the suit into federal court. The defendant possessed the same right. Neither party on removal could rely upon any other title than that claimed for the purpose of removal.[16]

Most authorities agree that the Judiciary Act of 1801 was not drafted by the Federalists after they learned of the extent of their political defeat in the election of 1800. Rather, the Act was an attempt to introduce needed reforms that had been urged during the first decades of the existence of the federal courts, but they were generous in creating new clerks, marshals and district attorneys. However, the newly elected members of the Jeffersonian Party saw it otherwise. In their view, this Act was a conspiracy to enlarge the number of federal judges and to expand the jurisdiction of the Federal Courts at the expense of the State Courts. The abolishment of the circuit riding duties of the Justices of the Supreme Court was not a needed reform in the minds of the new majority. Jurisdiction over all controversies arising under the Constitution and federal laws were contemplated by the Constitution, but had not been specifically granted to the federal courts.

As soon as the Seventh Congress convened in 1801, Thomas Jefferson, in his first annual message, stated that the recent Judiciary Act would "present" itself for the contemplation of Congress.[17] He laid before Congress a statement of the cases decided in the federal courts since they were established and the number of cases then pending in the different states.

The debate over the repeal of the Judiciary Act of 1801 began on January 6, 1802 in the Senate when John Breckinridge (1760-1806) of Kentucky proposed a resolution to accomplish this. These debates were considered of such contemporary importance that they were published in two separate editions.[18] The assumption behind some of the arguments advanced by Senator Breckinridge and others was the belief that matters such as excise tax, which had constituted about 800 cases in the federal courts since their founding, would disappear as the new administration trimmed the activities of the federal government and reduced taxes. From statistics, it was concluded that the number of federal cases did not justify an increase in the size of the federal courts, but some members of Congress pointed to discrepancies in these reports, especially the returns from some courts that omitted pending cases. Because of the requirement that justices of the Supreme Court hold the circuit courts, those supporting the Act of 1801 argued that the selection of a justice required "a character for the bench, . . . less the learning of a judge than the agility of a post-boy". When the argument was advanced that under the Constitution the judge holding life tenure could not be legislated out of his office, such a suggestion was not well received by the more democratic minded Congressmen. What property right, they asked, did a federal judge have in his office? The answer to this question for them was none. Accusations were made that Adams had "an immoderate thirst for executive patronage" but the opposition to repeal pointed out that the administration of Jefferson rewarded its friends. Finally, the Act of 1801 was repealed by a narrow vote in the Senate and by nearly a two to one vote in the House. The new Act was signed by the President on March 8, 1802.[19]

However, the repeal of the Judiciary Act of 1801 did not lay to rest the need to give the justices some respite from their circuit duties. Although Presidents Madison and Monroe made no specific recommendations of how a modification of the courts should be accomplished, President Monroe certainly urged that the justices of the Supreme Court be relieved of their circuit duties.[20] Other presidents suggested the need for reorganizing the judicial system, but Andrew Jackson in all of his annual messages expressed the need for a uniform federal court system throughout the nation.[21] Abraham Lincoln in his first annual address made some proposals for the reorganization of the courts. He was opposed to adding judges to the Supreme Court in sufficient numbers to accommodate all parts of the country with the circuit courts, but he suggested that "Circuit Courts are useful or they are not useful. If useful, no State should be denied them; if not useful, no state should have them". This logic led to his proposal that circuit courts be provided for all states or abolished.[22]

Lincoln proposed that the justices be assigned to as many circuits as possible and independent circuit judges be provided for the other circuits. As an alternative, he suggested the Supreme Court judges be relieved from the circuit courts and that circuit judges be provided. The final alternative he proposed was to leave the judicial function to the district courts and an independent Supreme Court.

One of the unfortunate results of the repeal of the Act of 1801 was the creation of a precedent against similar reform. Time and time again, the members of Congress would use the repeal as an argument against any change. In 1825, when Congress was again considering abolishing the requirement of the justices riding the circuit, one Senator described the Act of 1801 in the following terms:

> The fact that the Act of 1801 was found so little adapted to the interest of sentiments of the American people, as to call from them at once, in terms too loud and strong to be resisted or denied, an imperious demand for its repeal. A repeal was as promptly acceded to by the councils of the nation, and a newly created host of judges stripped of their salaries, their offices, and their honors, before time had been given them to enjoy, or even taste the delicious flavor of the dainties which had been placed before them — to warm the seats on which they had been placed, or to be warmed by the ermines with which they had been enshrouded.[23]

The Judiciary Act of 1801, contrary to popular understanding, did not repeal the Judiciary Act of 1789. The changes made in the federal courts were more structural than procedural. In fact, the jurisdiction of the district courts remained as defined in the Judiciary Act of 1789, whereas, the jurisdiction of the circuit court was redefined and expanded. Another feature of the Judiciary Act of 1801 was the establishment of a district court in the only organized territory. Indiana would have been incorporated into the District of Ohio, and if this precedent had been followed in the future, each territory would have had a federal court together with the territorial courts.

Although the Judiciary Act of 1801 was repealed, it continued to have a life of its own. In providing for the government of the District of Columbia in 1801, a circuit court was established which had "all the powers by law vested in the circuit courts and judges of the circuit courts of the United States."[24] This reference was to the circuit courts established under the Judiciary Act of 1801, and to the extent that it defined the jurisdiction of the circuit court, this statute remained in effect until that court was abolished in 1860.

The Judiciary Act of 1801 was repealed in 1802, but that judiciary statute made some changes in the federal courts. The circuit system was reestablished, but the justices of the Supreme Court were provided some relief in that the court only met for one term each year in February at the seat of the government rather than for the previously required two terms.[25]

Several other issues relating to the work of the justices were addressed. Certification as a method of judicial review by the Supreme Court of issues of law in the event of disagreement between the justice and the district court judge sitting as the circuit court was introduced. The opinions of the justice of the Supreme Court sitting in a circuit court would become the opinion of the court in the event of review by the writs of error or appeal to the Supreme Court.[26] The other provisions of the statute of 1802 were directed toward restructuring the districts and changing terms of both the district and circuit courts. The Judiciary Act of 1802 did not entirely reestablish the federal courts as they existed under the Act of 1789. As with the Act of 1801, in no way did the Act of 1802 materially change the Judiciary Act of 1789.

FOOTNOTES TO CHAPTER 4

1. Petition of the Justices, 1792, 1 AMER. STATE PAPERS, Misc. 52.

2. Leonard Baker, "The Circuit Riding Justices," 1977 YEARBOOK SUPREME COURT HISTORICAL SOCIETY, p.63.

3. 1 AMER. STATE PAPERS, Misc. 29.

4. 1 AMER. STATE PAPERS, Misc. 23.

5. Act of March 2, 1793, 1 STAT. 334.

6. Act of September 24, 1793, sec. 4, 1 STAT. 74.

7. Erwin C. Surrency, "The Judiciary Act of 1801," 2 AMER. J. LEG. HIST. 53.

8. The account of this controversy is included in all texts on this period.

9. Act of February 13, 1801, sec. 6 & 7, 2 STAT. 90.

10. William S. Carpenter, JUDICIAL TENURE IN THE UNITED STATES (1918), p.89.

11. Act of February 13, 1801, sec. 7 & 26, 2 STAT. 90, 97.

12. Surrency, *supra,* note 7, p. 54.

13. Erwin C. Surrency, "Federal District Court Judges and the History of Their Courts," 40 F.R.D. 272 (1966).

14. Act of February 13, 1801, sec. 11, 2 STAT. 92; Charles Warren, "Federal Criminal Laws and the State Courts," 38 HARV. L. REV. 562 (1925).

15. One author has suggested that this was in answer to some of the state statutes which allowed suits against defendants who had not been personally served. Kathryn Turner, "Federalist Policy and the Judiciary Act of 1801," 22 WM. & MARY Q. 1, 28 (1965).

16. Act of February 13, 1801, sec. 14, 2 STAT. 93.

17. James D. Richardson, A COMPILATION OF THE MESSAGES AND PAPERS OF THE PRESIDENTS, 1789-1897 (1896), v.1, p.331.

18. DEBATES IN THE SENATE OF THE UNITED STATES ON THE JUDICIARY, DURING THE FIRST SESSION OF THE SEVENTH CONGRESS. (Philadelphia, for E. Bronson, 1802); DEBATES IN THE CONGRESS OF THE UNITED STATES ON THE BILL FOR REPEALING THE LAW "FOR THE MORE CONVENIENT ORGANIZATION OF THE COURTS OF THE UNITED STATES." (Albany, Collier & Stockwell, 1802). There may have been another printing of this volume for a copy is shown to have been published in Albany by Whiting, Leavenworth and Whiting, 1802.

19. Max Farrand, "The Judiciary Act of 1801," 5 AMER. HIST. REV. 682 (1900). Act of March 8, 1802, 2 STAT. 132.

20. James D. Richardson, A COMPILATION OF THE MESSAGES AND PAPERS OF THE PRESIDENTS 1789-1902 (1904), v.1, p.573; v.2, p.248.

21. Richardson, *supra* note 17, v.1, pp.461, 558, 605; v.3, pp.117-177.

22. *Ibid,* v.5, p.49.

23. 8 Benton's ABRIDGMENT OF THE DEBATES OF CONGRESS 160-161. For similar sentiments, see Benjamin Robbins Curtis, JURISDICTION, PRACTICE AND PECULIAR JURISPRUDENCE OF THE COURTS OF THE UNITED STATES (1880), p.95.

24. Act of February 27, 1801, sec. 3, 2 STAT. 105.

25. Act of April 24, 1802, sec. 1, 2 STAT. 156.

26. Act of April 29, 1802, sec. 5, 2 STAT. 158.

Chapter 5

CIRCUIT DUTY BY THE JUSTICES

One of the more colorful aspects of the history of the American judiciary concerned circuit riding by judges and lawyers as they traveled from one court session to another. Beginning with the Judiciary Act of 1789, the justices of the Supreme Court had to travel to hold the circuit court with the district court judge of the district in which the circuit court was held. The district court judge, likewise, had to travel to different cities in the state for purposes of holding court.

In assigning justices to the Supreme Court for the purpose of holding the circuit courts, the states were organized into circuits by the various judiciary acts. Under the Judiciary Act of 1789, there were three circuits designated as the Southern, Middle, and Eastern Circuits. No specific provision was made for the assignment of justices to the circuits as it is evident that Congress expected the members of the Supreme Court to decide who would go on which circuit.[1]

In 1802, six circuits, the same number as formed by the ill-fated Act of 1801, were created, embracing all the states then in the Union with the exception of Kentucky, Tennessee, Ohio, and also Maine, which was then a part of Massachusetts, but not yet a state.[2] Each of these circuits was designated by number. The Act specially allotted the justices of the Supreme Court to the various circuits, but provided that after the next appointment to the bench, the Court was to allot its members to the circuits and enter such allotment as an order of the court. This changed the previous practice of different justices holding terms of the circuit court, and thereafter, it has become customary that a justice remain the circuit justice for the same circuit during his tenure on the bench.

Thereafter, Congress intervened twice by making assignments of the justices to the circuits, but their motives for this action in at least one case is not clear. In 1802, Congress assigned the justice of the Supreme Court presiding in the Third Circuit, William Patterson, who was a resident of New Jersey, to the Second Circuit. To the Third Circuit, Congress assigned the senior associate justice, Bushrod Washington, who resided within the Fifth Circuit.[3] When Patterson died in 1806, he was succeeded on the court by H. Brockholst Livingston, who resided in New York. Since Congress had required that the associate justice residing in the Third Circuit hold the court in the Second Circuit, this had to be rectified in 1808.[4] Livingston was already holding the courts in that circuit and it was probably felt that Congress ought to clear up this statutory inconsistency. This is the last time that Congress assigned by statute an associate justice to a particular circuit. During most of the early decades of the Nineteenth Century, justices were assigned to the circuit in which they lived and once assigned, generally remained in that circuit until they left the court.[5] It was the custom during the first half of the century to appoint individuals to the Supreme Court who were residents of the circuit which became vacant.

The Judiciary Act of 1802, authorizing the court to assign themselves to the circuit, permitted the President of the United States to make such an allotment which "shall be binding until another allotment shall be made".[6] Apparently, the only time that a President exercised this authority was when Abraham Lincoln did so by an executive order of October 29, 1862.[7] The reason given for this unusual step was that three appointments had been made to the court and no allotment of the members had been made.

To hold these circuit courts required the justices to travel many miles each year. In 1838, Secretary of State John Forsythe reported to the Senate the number of cases pending in the circuit courts and the number of miles traveled by the justices during the course of the year. According to this report, Chief Justice Roger B. Taney traveled a total of 458 miles in holding the terms of the courts in his circuit.[8] Most of the justices, however, averaged a total of 2,000 miles annually, but Justice McKinley of Alabama traveled a total of 10,000 miles during the course of the year.[9]

Justice John C. McKinley of Alabama was assigned to the Ninth Circuit, which included Alabama, Mississippi, Louisiana and Arkansas. This circuit was established in 1837,[10] and terms of the circuit courts, as established by Congress, were held in the following locations: Little Rock, Arkansas, on the fourth Monday in March; Mobile, Alabama, on the second Monday of April; Jackson, Mississippi, on the first Monday in May; New Orleans, Louisiana, on the third Monday in May; and Huntsville, Alabama, on the first Monday in June. In the fall, the terms of the circuit courts were held in New Orleans, Jackson, and Mobile. One year later, the term of the Circuit Court at Huntsville was abolished.[11] Justice McKinley wrote that to hold the circuit court he had to travel by boat from Little Rock, Arkansas, through New Orleans to Mobile, Alabama, a distance of approximately 850 miles. To get to Jackson, Mississippi, he reported that he had to travel from Mobile back through New Orleans and then, up to Vicksburg, Mississippi, by water, and then by stage to Jackson, a distance of 800 miles. He then returned to New Orleans, a city through which he had passed three times, to preside at the term of the circuit court in that city.

Justice McKinley's situation may have been extreme in comparison to the other justices, but the difficulties were similar. Justice John McLean of Ohio traveled a total of 2,500 miles by public conveyances. He wrote that in May, 1837, the mud was so deep in Indiana that it was impossible for a carriage of any description to pass. The mails and passengers were conveyed in common wagons.[12] Justice Philip P. Barbour of Virginia reported that he traveled 1,498 miles in holding the circuit courts in North Carolina and Virginia.[13]

The Supreme Court justices riding the circuits have generally been neglected by their biographers, though quite a few of the justices commented on these experiences. Justice William Cushing equipped himself well for traveling, possessing a four wheel carriage packed with groceries, books and other conveniences in addition to his traveling coach. His wife and servant accompanied him on his travels.[14]

Chief Justice John Marshall left a few insights of his difficulties on circuit. While dressing for his first term of court in Raleigh, North Carolina, he discovered that the pair of pants he intended to wear into court had not been packed, and he had to wear the clothes in which he had traveled. Another problem the circuit justices had was gauging the amount of time the cases would take. The Chief Justice, while in Norfolk, wrote his wife, Polly, and stated that he could not come home as soon as he had expected because the case he was hearing took longer than he had anticipated — an excuse known to every lawyer.[15]

Probably the most notorious adventure of a justice of the Supreme Court on circuit was the assault on Justice Stephen J. Field on August 14, 1889. Field was on his way to hold the Circuit Court in San Francisco when he was attacked by a husband in a divorce suit. The attacker was shot by the deputy marshal, who had been sent along with Field on the train trip for the justice's protection. Because of this incident, both Field and his guard were arrested for murder, but later the charges were dropped.[16] This incident has been the subject of numerous books and articles.

As one would naturally expect, the different justices on circuit reacted to the conditions of travel in different ways. It is said that Justice John Catron had been accustomed to camping out and carousing and that he did not find his condition unbearable.[17] Justice John McLean (1785-1861) participated extensively in social activities while on circuit, whereas Justice Taney kept to himself largely because of his health.[18] Other justices participated in different degrees in the local social events. The opening of the court with an important guest was a significant local event. One of the arguments often advanced for continuing circuit duty by the justices was that this brought the federal government to the local public. As the country grew, this argument had less merit.

When the justices first began to hold the circuit courts, it became customary for the justice to deliver a charge to the grand jury to explain the federal laws and other policies of the government. Many of these charges were published in newspapers and often dealt with political subjects. Justice Samuel Chase (1741-1811) gave, by all accounts, an intemperate charge to the grand jury on May 2, 1803 against "mobocracy", for which he was later impeached. Justice John McLean (1785-1861) urged the strict enforcement of the neutrality laws against those participating in filibustering expeditions into Canada.[19] Roger B. Taney (1777-1864) announced when he held the Circuit Court in Maryland on April 30, 1836 that he would not deliver such a charge to the grand jury. He thought that the public was aware of the laws of the United States, and hence, the federal criminal law constituted such a small part of the criminal jurisprudence, the action of the grand jury was limited.[20] The justices continued to deliver charges to the grand jury on the opening of the court occasionally, but the importance of the charge decreased with the passing years.

Although usually only two weeks were allotted to the justices of the Supreme Court to conduct the business of each circuit court, they were able to conduct a large amount of business. Between 1827 and 1831, the Circuit Court in Ohio was in session for periods from ten to nineteen days, during which time the circuit justice made final disposition of the majority of the cases. The docket of the Circuit Court for West Tennessee was the heaviest, and during the same period, the court was in session from sixteen to thirty-two days and disposed of 58 to 153 cases each term.[21] It is not certain whether a justice of the Supreme Court would try a few of the cases and then go on, leaving the district court judge to finish all other cases on the docket.

An 1823 petition from the bar of the City of Nashville, Tennessee, indicated that the circuit courts were not held as often as prescribed by statute. The petition stated that only one half of the required number of terms of the circuit courts had been held for the Western District of Tennessee since its establishment in 1807. In 1819, 170 suits were pending on the dockets of the courts; in 1820, 152; 1821, 202; 1822, 148; 1823, 185; and in 1824, 161. Some of these suits had been accumulating for years for lack of a qualified court.[22]

The Act of 1838 established the terms of the newly reorganized Seventh Circuit. Congress declared it to be the duty of the justice to attend at least one term annually in his circuit. In the absence of a justice, the district judge could "adjourn the cause to the succeeding term of the circuit court."[23] In 1844, a statute provided that the justice of the Supreme Court need not attend but one term annually of each of the circuit courts in his circuit, but the justice was to designate the term he would attend, taking into consideration the nature and importance of the business pending therein and public convenience. When the justice attended the circuit court, appeals and writs of error from the district court and those cases specially reserved by the district court judge were given priority. In the final section of the 1844 Act was a declaration that the statute did not prohibit the justice from attending other terms whenever the interests of the public demanded his presence.[24]

It has always been a matter of speculation as to how often the justices of the Supreme Court held the circuit court sessions. It is certain that the justices held these sessions during the first decades of the Nineteenth Century, and were conscientious in meeting this obligation. Many factors probably influenced the justices in performing this duty, among them the distance they were required to travel. If the circuit court were held close to home, the justice frequently handled his circuit duties as Joseph Story did in Massachusetts. However, it is equally clear that he did not visit the Circuit Court in New Hampshire, Maine, and Rhode Island as frequently as that in Massachusetts. It is equally clear that by the middle part of the century, the service on the Supreme Court became demanding as the number of cases on the docket of the Supreme Court increased. One point is clear, however, and that is that the circuit system, as originally envisioned, did not work in practice after the country expanded beyond the Mississippi River.

It is significant that by 1860, Congress gradually, in statutes designating the terms of the federal courts, provided for the district and circuit courts to sit simultaneously. It was only after 1860 that there was any campaign mounted to merge these courts into one.

Inadvertently, Congress relieved the justices of the Supreme Court of the absolute necessity of holding the circuit court in 1802. The Judiciary Act of 1802, which repealed the infamous Judiciary Act of 1801, provided "that when only one of the judges hereby directed to hold the Circuit Courts, shall attend, such Circuit Court may be held by the judge so attending".[25] Thus, from the beginning of the new century, the need for a justice of the Supreme Court to preside as a circuit court judge was minimized. The judges of the district courts came to preside over the majority of trials in the federal courts, whether in the circuit or district court.

The Commission to Revise and Codify the Criminal Laws of the United States, in its Report in 1899, recommended the merger of the district and circuit courts, for it estimated that the circuit court judges who had been appointed in 1869 were busily engaged on the new Circuit Courts of Appeals. It was estimated that 80% of the sessions of the circuit court were held by the district court judge. In the report of the same Commission two years later, of the 904 days of actual sessions of the circuit court, the district court judges held 535 days, not quite the percentage they had estimated earlier.[26] The report concluded "as both courts are commonly held at the same time and place, we have the incongruity of two courts exercising the jurisdiction concurrently as to the same matters and exclusive as to others, with two dockets, two journals, two clerks, and two juries, but with a single judge".[27]

Just how much influence the justices of the Supreme Court had on the administration of the Federal Circuit Court probably varied from justice to justice, for the further away the circuit, the less influence he could possibly have unless he lived in that circuit. There is evidence that Chief Justice Samuel Chase did exercise considerable influence in the Fourth Circuit. In 1868, he was quoted saying, "it is only as a Circuit Judge that the Chief Justice or any other Justice of the Supreme Court has, individually, any considerable power".[28]

At times the justice and the local district judge were at odds, which caused some interruptions in the courts. When Philip K. Lawrence was appointed as district judge in Louisiana, he removed the clerk and appointed another in his place. The incumbent clerk challenged this removal, and since Justice McKinley took the position that the incumbent clerk could not be removed, this impasse prevented any business being conducted in the circuit court during that session. The Supreme Court later held that the clerk could be removed.[29]

Definitely, by the end of the Civil War, it must have been the exception for a justice to preside in the circuit court. This fact may explain why Congress in statutes designating the terms of the federal courts enacted after 1860, provided for both the district and circuit courts to sit simultaneously. After the establishment of the Circuit Courts of Appeals in 1891, with judges specifically designated for that court, the circuit courts were definitely held by the district court judge, and occasionally by the circuit judge. For the fiscal year ending June 30, 1901, no justice held a session of the circuit court.[30] In 1911, any pretense of the justice being required to preside in the circuit courts was ended by the amalgamation of the district and circuit courts.

The work of the justices of the Supreme Court on circuit was rather accurately and succinctly summarized by John C. Rose (1861-1927), judge on the United States Court of Appeals for the Fourth Circuit (1922-1927): "The conditions under which circuit work had to be done were very trying. As a rule, the Supreme Court Justices heartily disliked it. There was a doubt as to whether under a strict construction of the Constitution a Justice of the Supreme Court could be required to sit in an inferior tribunal."[31] The latter point was never seriously argued during the early decades of the Nineteenth Century. In the existing political climate, John Marshall and his colleagues would not dare advance such an argument.

FOOTNOTES TO CHAPTER 5

1. Act of September 24, 1789, sec. 4, 1 STAT. 74.
2. Act of April 29, 1802, sec. 4, 2 STAT. 157.
3. Act of March 3, 1803, 2 STAT. 244.
4. Act of March 9, 1808, 2 STAT. 471.
5. Justices assigned to the circuit under the Judiciary Act of 1802:

    First   - William Cushing
    Second   - Bushrod Washington
    Third   - William Patterson
    Fourth   - Samuel Chase
    Fifth   - John Marshall
    Sixth   - Alfred Moore

Whether these justices actually held circuit courts in the assigned circuit is not clear.

6. Act of April 29, 1802, sec. 5, 2 STAT. 158.
7. James D. Richardson, A COMPILATION OF THE MESSAGES AND PAPERS OF THE PRESIDENTS, 1789-1902 (1904), v.6, p.123. The assignments made by Lincoln were as follows:

    First   - Nathan Clifford
    Second   - Samuel Nelson
    Third   - Robert C. Grier
    Fourth   - Roger B. Taney
    Fifth   - James M. Wayne
    Sixth   - John Catron
    Seventh - Noah H. Swayne
    Eighth   - David Davis
    Ninth   - Samuel F. Miller

8. S. Doc. No. 50, 25th Cong. 3d sess. Vol. II, p.32. The mileage reported by each of the Justices is as follows: Roger B. Taney, 458; Henry Baldwin, 2,000; James M. Wayne, 2,370; Philip P. Barbour, 1,498; Joseph Story, 1,896; Smith Thompson, 2,590; John McLean, 2,500; John Catron, 3,464; John McKinley, 10,000.
9. S. Doc. No. 50, 25th Cong. 3d sess. Vol. II, p.39.
10. Act of March 3, 1837, 5 STAT. 176.
11. A year later, the term of the Circuit Court at Huntsville was abolished. Act of February 22, 1838, 5 STAT. 210.
12. S. Doc. No. 50, 25th Cong. 3d sess. Vol. II, pp.36-37.
13. S. Doc. No. 50, 25th Cong. 3d sess. Vol. II, p.39.
14. Henry Flanders, THE LIVES AND TIMES OF THE CHIEF JUSTICES OF THE SUPREME COURT OF THE UNITED STATES (1881), v.2, p.38.
15. Frances Norton Mason, MY DEAREST POLLY; LETTERS OF CHIEF JUSTICE JOHN MARSHALL (1961), pp.152, 246.
16. This incident in the life of Stephen J. Field has been the subject of many accounts. See Carl Brent Swisher, STEPHEN J. FIEDL, CRAFTSMAN OF THE LAW (1930), p.321.
17. Carl B. Swisher, HISTORY OF THE SUPREME COURT: THE TANEY YEARS 1836-1864 (1974), p.265.
18. *Ibid*, p.263.
19. 30 Fed. Case. 1018 (CCD. Ohio 1839).
20. 30 Fed. Cas. 998 (CCD. Md. 1836).
21. S. Doc. No. 229, 25th Cong. 3d sess. Vol. III. A similar study of the dockets of the state courts would be interesting for comparison of the amount of business conducted.
22. Ex. Doc. No. 29, 18th Cong. 2d sess. Vol. II.
23. Act of March 10, 1838, 5 STAT. 215.

24. Act of June 17, 1844, 5 STAT. 676.

25. Act of April 29, 1802, sec. 4, 2 STAT. 158.

26. Letter from the Attorney General transmitting a report of the Commission to Review and Codify the Criminal and Penal Laws of the United States, 57th Cong. 1st sess. doc. no. 68, p.40.

27. A letter from the Attorney General, 56 Cong. 1st sess. doc. no. 49, p.4.

28. Peter Graham Fish, THE POLITICS OF FEDERAL JUDICIAL ADMINIS-TRATION (1973), quoted on p.9.

29. Ex parte Henner, 13 Pet. 225 (1839).

30. S. Doc. No. 68, 57th Cong. 1st sess. (1901), p.11.

31. John C. Rose, JURISDICTION AND PROCEDURE OF THE FEDERAL COURTS (3d ed., 1926), p.90.

Chapter 6

ORGANIZATION OF THE CIRCUITS

The organization of the states into circuits was basic to the functioning of the federal courts, for it was clearly envisioned by the authors of the first Judiciary Act that the justices would have the responsibility of presiding in the major federal trial court. The geographical realities made such a system impractical. To overcome some of the difficulties of travel and the great distances involved, the number of justices required at a session of the circuit court was reduced from two to one during the first decade of the federal courts. Congress recognized that it would be impossible for the justices to preside in all the circuit courts, and probably for that reason, some judicial districts were either omitted from the circuit system or the circuit court held a single session in a state in which all cases would be tried. Omission of a state from a circuit appears to have caused more discontent within the sections of the country concerned, than did the holding of the sessions of a circuit court in one city within the judicial district or state.

Efforts were made in the pre-Civil War years of coping with the ever increasing workload of the circuit courts, the conflicting demands of the business of the Supreme Court, and the political demands by either incorporating the states into the existing circuits and making provisions for a circuit court, or by giving the district court judge such authority.

Many alternatives were considered. One such step was the appointment of the circuit judges in 1869, which made the circuits the geographical limits of their authority. The next change in the nature of the circuit occurred when the Circuit Courts of Appeals were established, and each circuit took on the role it now enjoys in the organization of that court.

Until the establishment of the Circuit Court of Appeals in 1891, the organization of the circuits was for the sole purpose of assigning the justices to a given geographical region of the country for the purpose of holding the circuit courts. The geographical jurisdiction of these courts extended only to the state or the judicial district in which it was organized. The proper title of this court was the Circuit Court for the Northern District of Georgia. With the increase in the number of appeals, a realignment of the circuits became necessary, but even here, the grouping of states was cause for some controversy. To detach one state from one circuit and attach it to another was cause of complaint, for it could be argued that one state had more in common with those states in that circuit as far as legal problems were concerned, than it did with the proposed grouping, or that the old circuit was more familiar with the peculiar legal problems of the state than the new circuit. The need to organize the states into circuits was real, and hence, was an important aspect of the history of the federal courts.

The Judiciary Act of 1789 created three circuits designated as the Southern, Middle, and Eastern Circuits for the purpose of holding circuit courts.[1] The states of Rhode Island and North Carolina, when admitted to the Union after the adoption of the Constitution, were assigned to one of the existing circuits.[2]

The ill-fated Act of 1801 divided the country into six circuits and for the first time, designated them by numbers, a practice which has continued to the present day.[3] When the Act of 1801 was repealed in 1802, the reorganization of the circuits was necessary. The Act of 1802 organized the country into six circuits, again designating them by numbers. The states of Maine, Kentucky and Tennessee were excluded from this reorganization of the circuits.[4] It was an accepted feature of the organization of the federal courts that some district courts had full federal jurisdiction. When the reorganization of the circuits was made in 1862, and Congress attempted to abolish all district courts exercising the jurisdiction of circuit courts, some judicial districts were omitted from this statute and the district court in those few districts was the exclusive federal forum.[5]

After 1802, all the newly admitted states clamored to be included in a circuit. Responding to this demand, Congress created the Seventh Circuit in 1807, to consist of the states of Tennessee, Kentucky and Ohio.[6] A seventh judge was added to the Supreme Court to preside in this circuit. After the passage of this act, all the states in the Union were then included in a circuit, but not all judicial districts were included. All cases within the jurisdiction of the circuit court were transferred from the district courts when they were incorporated into a circuit. This statute was unique in that it required the justice to live within that circuit establishing a trend of appointing individuals from a circuit to vacancies on the Supreme Court.

The Seventh Circuit soon became the largest geographical circuit with the heaviest case load. The population of the circuit when it was organized was approximately one and a half million, whereas it was six million in 1860. As estimated in 1836, approximately seventeen hundred cases were pending in the circuit courts from the three states constituting the circuit. The next highest circuit was the first with a caseload of 130.[7] Lincoln commented in his first address to Congress that "During the long and brilliant judicial career of Judge McLean his circuit grew into an empire — altogether too large for any one judge to give the courts therein more than a nominal attendance".[8] He used that fact to inform the Congress that "the country generally has outgrown our present judicial system".

Between 1807 and 1820, five new states were admitted to the Union, and for each state a district court was established with circuit court jurisdiction. In 1820, Maine was admitted to the Union and was added to the First Circuit.[9] Since the area encompassing the present state of Maine was never a federal territory, but rather a part of the state of Massachusetts, it already had been served by a district court which had the full federal jurisdiction that had been established by the Judiciary Act of 1789 and not by the customary territorial courts.

With the increased number of new states established in what was then considered the western part of the United States, the inhabitants considered themselves as being discriminated against by their exclusion from the circuit organization. Several of the legislatures of the newly established states petitioned to be included in a circuit, but Congress failed to act. One of the reasons Congress did not extend the circuit organization of these new states was a question as to what would be the best structure. The old proposals to create circuit judges, as was done under the Judiciary Act of 1801, was again debated, but rejected. Another proposal was to appoint judges with the same authority as a justice to these newly established circuits, but not appoint them to the Supreme Court. The representatives from the western states objected to this proposal because they felt that such an organization was discriminatory in that some states would be visited by the justices of the Supreme Court and others would not. The western states preferred to increase the size of the Supreme Court, and in 1826, a bill was introduced to create new circuits and add three new justices to the Supreme Court, bringing the total to ten. Generally, the eastern states were opposed to this measure because they felt it would dilute the authority of the Supreme Court.[10] Further, it was felt that the Supreme Court could not function effectively with an enlarged membership. And so it went with Congress in each of its sessions, attempting in some way, to agree upon a satisfactory judicial organization by expanding the circuit system in some form, to those states newly admitted to the Union.

Another issue introduced into this debate over the reorganization of the circuits was the concept of judicial representation. This issue arose because of the perception of the western states that the Supreme Court was deciding some issues based upon their own political views.[11] When two new circuits were created in 1837, John Catron of Tennessee represented the new Eighth Circuit and John McKinley of Alabama was appointed to the Ninth Circuit. It was customary for most of the Nineteenth Century for the President to appoint someone from that circuit to the Supreme Court. Lincoln was reluctant to fill the vacancies created by the death of Justice Peter Vivian Daniel and John McLean, and the resignation of Justice Archibald Campbell, because they presided in Southern circuits.

In his first annual message to Congress, December 3, 1861, Lincoln stated that he had "forborne" making nominations to fill these vacancies because two of the judges represented circuits overrun by revolt and "if successors were appointed in the same localities, they could not now serve upon their circuits; and many of the most competent men there probably would not take the personal hazard of accepting to serve, even here, upon the Supreme bench". Lincoln was reluctant to throw all the appointments to the North "thus disabling myself from doing justice to the South on the return of peace".[12]

No other changes were made in the organization of the circuits after 1807 until 1837. By that date, nine new states had been admitted to the Union and district courts were established in every state, each exercising the jurisdiction of a circuit court. In 1837, after a decade of debate, Congress passed an Act creating two new circuits, the Eighth and Ninth Circuits.[13] All twenty-six states, then members of the Union, were assigned to a circuit. In the states of Louisiana and Alabama, where the states had been divided into two districts, one of these district courts continued to exercise full federal jurisdiction of both the district and circuit courts. In the other districts of the same state, a judge would hold a circuit court with the justice of the Supreme Court. At no time were states that were organized into two or more districts divided between different circuits.

In 1842, Alabama and Louisiana were detached from the Ninth Circuit and were designated as the Fifth Circuit.[14] The states of Virginia and North Carolina, comprising the Fifth Circuit under the former act, were assigned either to the Fourth or the Sixth Circuit. The reason for this reorganization of the Fifth Circuit was for the purpose of relieving the workload of the Ninth Circuit under Justice John McKinley (1780-1852) who had petitioned Congress, asking for an alteration in the judicial circuits.[15] The Supreme Court was directed to assign the justices. Since Justice Peter V. Daniel (1784-1860) presided in the Fifth Circuit and had been appointed to the Court by the Democratic President, Martin Van Buren, in the final months of his administration, it did not upset the new Congress to have him travel from his home in Virginia into this area.[16] The new Fifth Circuit consisted of Alabama and Louisiana, marking the only time that a circuit did not consist of states who had a common boundary.

In 1861, the Civil War broke out, and the justices suspended holding the circuit courts in the Southern states. In 1862, the circuits were reorganized and the states which had been admitted since the last arrangement of the circuits, were now assigned to the circuits.[17] The number of justices of the Supreme Court was not increased; only the circuits were enlarged. By this shuffling of states, the number of circuits in the South were reduced for the obvious reasons. A new circuit embracing California, Nevada and Oregon was organized and designated as the Tenth Circuit.[18] A justice was added to the Supreme Court to preside in that circuit.

The Tenth Circuit was abolished in 1866, and all the states that were then in the Union were allotted among nine circuits.[19] The old Tenth Circuit was designated as the Ninth and the state of Nevada was added to it. The Third through the Seventh Circuits took the final form that they were to keep to the present, except for the Fifth which was divided in 1981. As new states were admitted to the Union after 1866, they were assigned to either the Eighth or Ninth Circuits, until these circuits became very large.

At the time the Eighth Circuit was divided in 1929, it consisted of thirteen states, by far the largest in geographical size. The statute of 1866 was noted for decreasing the size of the Supreme Court, from ten to seven, but this was reversed by Congress in 1869.[20]

In 1869, the circuits took on a new significance. In that year, Congress created the office of circuit court judge, who had the same powers as the justices of the Supreme Court when functioning as a circuit judge.[21] For the first time, judges were selected and appointed to roam the circuits. This did not relieve the justices of their statutory obligation to attend the circuits.

In 1891, with the establishment of the Circuit Court of Appeals, the circuits became the geographical areas of the new appellate courts. Because these appellate forums were defined by the same geographical boundaries, the courts were referred to as Circuit Courts of Appeals. The circuit court, which was predominately a trial court, continued to exist until 1911. This use of the term "circuit" led to some confusion between the two courts.

No significant changes were made in the boundaries of the circuits until 1929, when the Tenth Circuit was created from the Eighth Circuit.[22] The Eighth Circuit had become rather large because from 1866 to 1929, as new states were admitted to the Union, they were assigned to either the Eighth or Ninth Circuits, which led to the former circuits becoming rather large. The struggle to divide the Eighth Circuit had a long genesis.

As early as 1889, the Attorney General had suggested that some division of the Eighth Circuit was necessary, which at that time, consisted of nine states embracing twelve judicial districts divided into twenty-five divisions. The Attorney General stated that, "It is, of course, necessary to say that no circuit judge can hold the circuit courts as contemplated by the present system in all of these districts".[23] This recommendation was acted upon and a bill was introduced in the Senate in 1891 to redistribute the states among ten circuits.[24] The failure of this bill may be found in the radical realignment of the states. Only the First and Second Circuits kept their existing and historic organization. Maryland would have been added to the Third Circuit and the Fourth would have consisted of Virginia, Kentucky, West Virginia and Ohio.

In the meanwhile, the states west of the Mississippi River continued to grow, and inevitably, the caseload of the only two complete circuits west of the Mississippi increased as well. A possible division of the existing Eighth Circuit continued to be examined. In 1916, a plan was proposed to organize a Tenth Circuit by separating the states of Tennessee from the Sixth Circuit and Arkansas from the Eighth Circuit, and joining the state of Oklahoma, plus the districts for the Northern District of Alabama and Mississippi.[25] Memphis, Tennessee, was designated as the seat for this proposed court. But no reason was given for this proposed organization, other than the ease of getting to Memphis. The opposition to this bill was great. The Attorney General pointed out that the Eighth Circuit had a number of cases on appeal from the Oklahoma courts involving suits to cancel conveyances of Indian allotments, alleged to have been made in violation of the restrictions imposed by Congress, plus disputes of suits growing out of the question of who owned the riparian rights under the Oklahoma River. There certainly was opposition to having two districts in a state in different circuits.

In 1928, a rearrangement of the states within the circuits was proposed. The First would have included all the New England states, and the Second would have included New York only. Georgia would have been assigned to the Fourth, and Arkansas would have been added to the Fifth. The states west of the Mississippi would have been divided between the Eighth, Ninth, and Tenth Circuits. Some specious arguments were advanced against any realignment of the states. The president of the Utah State Bar Association, objected to the separation of Utah from the Eighth Circuit "because of the interpretation of various questions of law by this circuit (Eighth) and which have become established in this state."[26] The same objection was raised against placing Arkansas in the Fifth Circuit, taking it out of the existing Eighth. The argument was "If Arkansas is put into the fifth circuit, the judges there will have to learn Arkansas law, and in the learning will no doubt make many mistakes, some of which will be prejudicial to the people living in Missouri."[27] Other proposals would have simply divided the Eighth Circuit into two other circuits. However, the plan of dividing the Eighth into only two circuits creating the Tenth, was finally adopted. This was the last time Congress considered any plans to reorganize all the circuits.

In the middle decades of this century, proposals were made to divide the Fifth and Ninth Circuits.[28] Both circuits were extremely large geographically and the number of judges exceeded twenty, making a session *en banc* difficult. Various pressure groups opposed the division of either circuit for numerous reasons, including some that were strictly personal. Many of the landmark civil rights cases had been decided in the Fifth Circuit, and some opposed the division of that circuit because of fear that a new court would be too conservative. In 1980, the Fifth Circuit was divided and included the states of Texas, Arkansas, and Mississippi. Alabama, Georgia, and Florida constituted the newly created Eleventh Circuit.[29] The new court officially began operation in October, 1981. Probably the circuits will undergo additional modification in future years, as the work of the courts continue to grow.

FOOTNOTES TO CHAPTER 6

1. Act of September 24, 1789, sec. 4, 1 STAT. 74.

2. Act of June 4, 1790, 1 STAT. 126 attached North Carolina to the Southern Circuit. Act of June 23, 1790, 1 STAT. 128 attached Rhode Island to the Eastern Circuit.

3. Act of February 13, 1801, sec. 6, 2 STAT. 90.

4. Act of April 29, 1802, sec. 4, 2 STAT. 157.

5. Alfred Conkling, A TREATISE ON THE ORGANIZATION, JURISDICTION AND PRACTICE OF THE COURTS OF THE UNITED STATES (4th ed., 1864), p.264.

6. Act of February 24, 1807, 2 STAT. 420-421.

7. REG. OF DEBATES 19th Cong. June 19, 1826, p.1047. The average case load given by the speaker was:

    First   - 130
    Second   - 130
    Third   - 110
    Fourth   - 57
    Fifth   - 70
    Sixth   - 100
    Seventh - 1700

No source for these figures are given.

8. James D. Richardson, A COMPILATION OF THE MESSAGES AND PAPERS OF THE PRESIDENTS (1904), v.6, p.49.

9. Act of March 30, 1820, 3 STAT. 554.

10. Curtis Nettels, "The Mississippi Valley and the Federal Judiciary, 1807-1837," 12 MISS. V. HIST. REV. 214 (1925).

11. *Ibid,* p.217.

12. Richardson, supra, note 8, v.6, p.49.

13. Act of March 3, 1837, 5 STAT. 176.

14. Act of August 16, 1842, 5 STAT. 507.

15. Carl B. Swisher, HISTORY OF THE SUPREME COURT, THE TANEY PERIOD 1836-64 (1974), p.256.

16. Justice Philip Barbour died February 24, 1841. The Democrat controlled Senate confirmed Daniel as an associate justice on March 2d, a record.

17. Act of July 15, 1862, 12 STAT. 576.

18. Act of March 3, 1863, 12 STAT. 794.

19. Act of July 23, 1866, 14 STAT. 209.

20. Act of April 10, 1869, sec. 2, 16 STAT. 44.

21. Act of April 10, 1869, sec. 2, 16 STAT. 44.

22. Act of February 28, 1929, 45 STAT. 1347.

23. Note: 24 AMER. L. REV. 133 (1890).

24. S. Rept. No. 2179, 51st Cong. 2d sess. Reprinted in Bernard D. Reams and Charles R. Haworth, CONGRESS AND THE COURTS; A LEGISLATIVE HISTORY (1978), v.3, p.4551.

25. H.R. Rept. 825, 64th Cong. 1st sess. (1916).

26. Hearings before the Committee on the Judiciary, House of Representatives, 70th Cong., 1st sess. serial 23, p.21.

27. *Ibid,* p.21.

28. Report of the Judicial Conference, H.R. Doc. No. 475, 83d Cong. 2d sess., p.3.

29. Act of October 14, 1980, P.L. 96-452, 94 STAT. 1994.

Chapter 7

CIRCUIT COURT JUDGES

After the repeal of the Act of 1801, several attempts were made to provide judges for the circuit courts and organize all such courts the same.[1] Several congressional committees studied the problem and made recommendations which were nearly always rejected. A few members of Congress made speeches against the existing system, centering their criticism on the requirement that justices of the Supreme Court were required to hold the circuit courts, which, as in the Ninteenth Century, they increasingly ceased to do. Nevertheless, a majority of the members of Congress defended the system with eloquency, and doubtless many members of the Bar supported them. Why there should have been such strong opposition to relieving the justices of the Supreme Court of this circuit duty by the appointment of judges for this purpose is difficult to explain.

The benefits of the organization of the judicial system of that period were described in glowing terms by the Senator from Kentucky, Isham Talbot, who was also a lawyer. He spoke of how the present system was organized in 1789 "framed in so much wisdom and experience — sanctioned by such names as the Congress in the United States of that period enrolled in the catalogue of its members." The Senator praised the fact that this was modeled after the British System where the justices of Westminister Hall had original and appellate jurisdiction and sat in all parts of the kingdom to hold the courts in *nisi prius,* a system which "has never yet been held as a blemish, much less of fatal error in the organization of the British Courts."[2] The speaker thought there was an advantage to have the justices ride the circuits as they would visit the states of the Union and preserve "sentiments and feelings connected, in some degree, with the just pride, the sovereignty, the constitutional independence." He felt if relieved of circuit duty, the justices would become national in their attitude, a thing which some of the states had reason to dread. Certain states had been severely attacked "and, after a feeble and ineffectual struggle, have been successively vanquished in the contest; have contended without aid or cooperation from their sister states." The contention of the speaker was that the proposed amendment would deny these states equal rights under the Constitution.[3]

A different opinion was presented by a lawyer from Mississippi in 1849 when he observed that since the Act of 1789, "patchwork expedients have continued to mar and deform the structure, till the whole machine has become rickety, disjointed, and impractical."[4]

In 1823, the Committee on the Judiciary of the Senate rendered a report which emphasized that, in its opinion, "some change would be necessary in the organization of the federal courts." At that time there were twenty-seven district courts: one in each of the states, and two each in New York, Pennsylvania, and Virginia. Obviously, in the opinion of the Committee, it was impossible for the seven judges on the Supreme Court to hold circuit court in many distant places. The report offered two solutions: one, increase the number of justices on the Supreme Court and include the recently admitted Western states in the new circuits; or two, adopt the same measure as included in the Act of 1801. The committee, however, was of the opinion that the latter proposal should not be adopted until the first had been given a trial.[5]

The Senate Committee on the Judiciary rendered another report in 1829 on the judicial system with observations about certain reforms.[6] The report began with the comment that after a casual survey of the system, the committee could not discover any motive to continue the circuit system. The Committee reviewed the fact that states had been omitted from the circuit organization since the Act of 1789. The report observed that since 1807, seven states were admitted, and the district courts in all but one of these (Maine, which was attached to the First Circuit) were given circuit court jurisdiciton. In other words, only one federal court was established in these states exercising federal jurisdiction, whereas, in the other states, two federal trial courts, the district court and the circuit court were functioning. One of the serious defects of such a system, as this report indicates, was the fact that appeals could be taken to the Supreme Court from a circuit court where the amount in controversy exceeded $2,000. However, an appeal could be taken from the district court to the circuit court where the amount exceeded $50 or in an admiralty or maritime case where the amount exceeded $300. The committee felt this created injustices, for in those states where no circuit court was established, all decisions under $2,000 were left to the fiat of one man — the district court judge — from whose decisions there could be no appeal. This theme, that the decisions of one district court judge were final, whereas in the majority of districts, these decisions were subject to review, was a recurring one.

The committee suggested that Congress could reorganize the system by adopting one of the following proposals. Under the first of the committee's proposals, the present system would be continued, but new circuits would be created presided over by additional Supreme Court justices. The new circuits would embrace the new states. A second plan would be to create circuit judges for the new areas, but these judges would not be members of the Supreme Court. However, as vacancies should occur on the court, these judges would be elevated to that court. This, in effect, would have resulted in creating a court for the training of the justices of the Supreme Court, an idea which had merit. A third plan was to revive the system of 1801. Under the fourth plan, as proposed by the Committee, three district court judges would hold the circuit courts, and thus the justices of the Supreme Court would be relieved of this duty. The fifth proposal was a variation of several of the above proposals. Under this plan, the states which were not then included in a circuit would be organized within new circuits, and judges would be appointed to preside over these new circuits who would not be members of the Supreme Court. The justices of the Supreme Court would continue to hold the circuit courts in the existing circuits, but these circuits would not be extended. The Committee did not make a recommendation as to which plan Congress should adopt. The reorganization of the circuits was frequently discussed, but no solution was adopted, so the search for an answer went on.

In 1853, Congress, by resolution, requested Attorney General Caleb Cushing to furnish Congress with an opinion suggesting the organization of the federal judicial system.[7] Cushing reviewed the proposals suggested by others from time to time. He recommended the organization of the country into nine circuits, with the circuit courts retaining the jurisdiction they then exercised. A circuit judge would be appointed to assist the Supreme Court justices in holding the circuit courts. The Attorney General thought the addition of judicial personnel would invoke the least change in the system of the federal courts. He concluded his opinion with the observation that the "existing judicial organization is altogether insufficient for the obvious necessities of the people even of the present United States."[8]

The proposal of Caleb Cushing was adopted by Congress in 1869, for in that year, the office of circuit judge was created.[9] A circuit judge was to be appointed for each of the nine existing circuits. They possessed the same powers as the associate justice of the Supreme Court sitting as a circuit court judge. The creation of these new judgeships was dictated by a perceived need to relieve the congestion of work that only the circuit court judge could perform.

At this time, the circuit courts could be held by one of three judges: a Supreme Court justice, a district court judge or a newly established circuit court judge. Whether the creation of a circuit judge changed the nature of these circuit courts is debatable. Nearly four decades later, a justice of the Supreme Court, Henry Billings Brown (1836-1913), observed that this section "put an end to the superiority of the Circuit Courts" reasoning that if "a court possesses both original and appellate jurisdiction, it is pretty sure to become either an appellate court, or a court of first instance."[10] The circuit court had a primary trial role and its appellate function was limited. For this reason, it was a natural development for the court to become a trial court, if it had not become such a forum before 1869.

The creation of the office of circuit judge did not disassociate the justices of the Supreme Court from this trial court. The Act required the justices to go on circuit once every two years. Congress was not yet willing to relieve the justice of the circuit duty. This provision was described as "preposterous." The justice was engaged at the Supreme Court from October until May. "Allowing the usual time of vacation the statute requires of the Circuit Justice in the three remaining months of each year duties which he could not possibly perform in thrice that time."[11]

This was not the first time Congress had created a circuit court with a separate circuit judge. Congress recognized that it would be impossible for a justice of the Supreme Court to travel to California when that state was admitted in 1850 to hold the circuit court and then return to Washington for the sessions of the Supreme Court. In 1856, a circuit court was established in California with the same jurisdiction as the other courts of this designation, but with one difference.[12] The President was authorized to appoint a circuit judge to preside in this circuit, and to that position, Matthew Hall McAllister was appointed. When Judge McAllister resigned in 1862, the court was abolished. One can only speculate that strong feelings existed that this plan discriminated against California.

To overcome this objection, California and Oregon were organized as the Tenth Circuit in 1863, and a tenth justice was added to the Supreme Court.[13] It is obvious that the Congress did not expect this justice to be in Washington very often, for it authorized payment of an additional sum for traveling "for each year in which he may actually attend a session of the Supreme Court of the United States." Four years later, the number of justices was reduced from ten to seven, and this ended the apparent attempt to have a judge with the same authority as a justice of the Supreme Court, but who was not expected to be a part of the high court.[14]

It is difficult to define the role of the circuit judge in the judicial system. Obviously, the office was created to assume some of the functions of the justices of the Supreme Court acting as circuit judges, and for this reason, he would preside in the circuit courts. The decisions of the Supreme Court stressed that circuit judges had the same authority as justices of the Supreme Court when presiding in the circuit court.[15] From the correspondence of several justices, it appears that certain cases were reserved for them to handle.[16] Although no statute required the justice to hear certain cases in the circuit courts, the Act of 1844 did indicate that the justice of the Supreme Court would give preference to "appeals and writs of error from the district court, questions of law arising upon statement of fact agreed by the parties or specially reserved by the district judge, and cases at law and in equity of peculiar interest or difficulty."[17] Where the district court judge had an interest in the case, the circuit court judge could preside.[18] All of these provisions certainly gave some guide as to what cases would be reserved for the attention of the justice or the circuit judge when he came on circuit.

It would have made sense if the circuit judge, when traveling to distant parts of his circuit, reserved for his consideration types of cases which the district court could not finally resolve: chiefly, the few appellate cases which would come from the district court to the circuit court. The circuit court had appellate jurisdiction in civil actions where the matter exceeded $50 and in bankruptcy cases. Under the Act of 1879, the circuit court heard on a writ of error all criminal cases from the district court where the sentence was imprisonment or where the fine exceeded $300.[19] During the period of 1869-1891, it is doubtful whether criminal cases on appeal were reserved for the circuit judge as a routine practice. One survey in 1889 indicated that no particular type of case was reserved for the circuit judge in many circuits.[20] A justice of the Supreme Court observed that the office was created to hear appeals in admiralty cases.[21] This would hardly be true in areas other than Louisiana and the eastern seaboard.

One significant difference in the power of the circuit judge over the district court judge was in the appointment of receivers in bankruptcy. When appointed by the circuit judge, the receiver's commission ran the entire circuit, whereas the commission issued by the district court was limited to that district. This same rule was probably applicable to warrants and other documents issued by the circuit judge. After creating the office of circuit judge, Congress did not legislate further on his duties, except to give him the authority to act in the place of a disabled district judge or designate another judge to do so.[22]

Congress has not changed the requirement that two judges preside over the circuit court, although from the beginning, the circuit court could be held by a single judge, whether it was the district court judge or the justice of the Supreme Court, or later, the circuit judge. When the composition of a circuit court, presided over by the district court judge, was challenged in 1808, Chief Justice Marshall upheld the practice.[23] The practices established in each circuit as to what cases would be reserved for the circuit court where two judges would preside is not clear.

The creation of the circuit judge did not solve any of the problems of the federal courts, nor did it meet the chief objections raised by the critics. It was obvious that the circuit judge could not perform the duties required by the provisions of the statute. "The only thing he can do is to exercise his jurisdiction in a few spots here and there. He wings his flight across a broad expanse and dips down in a few favored localities."[24] Most of the work of the circuit court was performed by the district court judge. By 1889, his decisions were final in cases under $5,000, railway reorganization cases and criminal cases. The lack of review was viewed as a fatal flaw. However, the term circuit judge has survived, for this is the statutory title of a member of the United States Court of Appeals.

FOOTNOTES TO CHAPTER 7

1. For a complete discussion of all the efforts made in Congress from 1798 to 1891, *see* Felix Frankfurtherand James M. Landis, THE BUSINESS OF THE SUPREME COURT, A STUDY IN THE FEDERAL JUDICIAL SYSTEM. (New York, 1928), p.4-102.

2. Benton's ABRIDGMENT OF THE DEBATES OF CONGRESS v.8, p.160.

3. *Ibid,* v.8, p.165.

4. House Misc. Doc. 17, 31st Cong. 1st sess., Vol. I, December 31, 1849.

5. Reports of Committees, No. 105, 17th Cong. 2d sess., Vol. II.

6. S. Doc. No. 50, 20th Cong. 2d sess., January 26, 1829.

7. 6 Op. Atty. Gen. U.S. 271, February 4, 1854; Senate Exec. Doc. 41, 33d Cong. 1st sess., Vol. VIII, March 2, 1854.

8. 6 Op. Atty. Gen. U.S. 284, February 4, 1854. We are informed by the editors of the AMERICAN LAW REVIEW that a bill to reorganize the circuit court failed of passage in 1866. The bill provided that the district judges were to perform all duties of a circuit judge at nisi prius, and the circuit justice with the district judge was to hear appeals. The editorial argues that the "direct and indirect benefits derived from them infinitely outweigh any real objections which can be urged against the practice.... The discipline, even if each judge try but half a dozen criminal and patent cases a year, more than repays him for the trouble and inconvenience; and the consequent mingling and association with the bar all over the circuit keeps up an acquaintance and understanding between it and the bench which we should be sorry to see lessen." 1 AMER. L. REV. 207 (1866).

9. Act of April 10, 1869, 16 STAT. 44.

10. Henry B. Brown, "The New Judicial Code," 73 CENT. L. J. 279 (1911).

11. Walter B. Hill, "The Federal Judicial System," 12 A.B.A. REPT. 289, 302 (1889).

12. Act of March 2, 1855, 10 STAT. 631; Act of April 30, 1856, 11 STAT. 6.

13. Act of March 3, 1863, 12 STAT. 794.

14. Act of July 23, 1866, 14 STAT. 209.

15. New England Marine Insurance Co. v. Dunham, 11 Wall. 1, 21 (U.S. 1870); Wallace v. Loomis, 97 U.S. 146, 157 (1877).

16. Benjamin R. Curtis, Jr., A MEMOIR OF BENJAMIN ROBBINS CURTIS (1879) vol. 1, p.249-254, Judge, United States District Court for Maine. Arthur Ware stated in a letter to Justice Curtis: "There has been one admiralty appeal entered that will be ready for hearing at next term; and this is all that I know of which cannot be disposed of without your presence."

17. Act of June 17, 1844, sec. 2, 5 STAT. 676.

18. Act of March 3, 1821, 3 STAT. 643.

19. Act of March 3, 1879, 20 STAT. 354.

20. Hill, *supra,* note 11, p.303.

21. Brown, *supra,* note 10, p.277.

22. Wallace v. Loomis, 97 U.S. 146 (1877). Act of March 3, 1871, sec. 3, 16 STAT. 494.

23. Pollard and Pickett v. Dwight, 4 Cranch 421 (U.S. 1808).

24. Hill, *supra,* note 11, p.289, 302.

Chapter 8
CIRCUIT COURT OF APPEALS

Historians have acknowledged that the Civil War affected the growth of the nation in many ways, and with this growth came a parallel increase in the business of the federal courts. Federal statutes enforcing federal policies increased the number of cases in the courts.[1] To add further to the increasing number of cases, Congress extended the jurisdiction of the courts by the Act of 1875 to all rights arising under the Constitution.[2] This statute had a profound impact on the federal courts, changing their jurisdiction from a limited one to one embracing all federal rights. These new statutes and the growth in the case loads of the federal courts caused the Supreme Court to be inundated with cases, resulting in a caseload it was ill-equipped to handle.[3]

Congress submitted numerous proposals to relieve the Supreme Court. However, not everyone thought that the Supreme Court needed any type of relief. Judge Albert C. Cox of the United States District Court of the Northern District of New York suggested that the Court itself could eliminate its backlog by abstaining from doing circuit duty and by extending the length of the annual sessions which was then twenty-six weeks.[4]

Several proposals had been advanced to relieve the Supreme Court.[5] One suggestion was to allow the Court to sit in panels of three, but the Court would sit *en banc* when considering cases involving the construction of the Constitution, the validity of a statute or treaty, or appeals from the state supreme court.[6] The other major proposal was to establish an intermediate appellate court. This latter suggestion had been a popular theme, and bills had been introduced by Senator Stephen A. Douglas (1813-1861) of Illinois in 1854 and by Senator Ira Harris (1802-1875) from New York in 1863 to establish such courts.[7] A group of eleven district court judges meeting in a convocation in 1865 had recommended the establishment of an intermediate appellate court to relieve the burden of the Supreme Court justices.[8] Senator David Davis, a senator from Illinois and previously an associate justice of the Supreme Court of the United States, introduced a bill in 1882 which would have established a court of appeals to consist of the justices of the Supreme Court when available, the circuit judges, and two district judges sitting in rotation. All cases would first go from the district and circuit courts to the court of appeals and on to the Supreme Court. Nothing in the act would have prevented an appeal from the court of appeals to the Supreme Court.[9] This bill was known as the Davis Bill and was widely discussed and debated during this period but not enacted. The Supreme Court is indebted to its former colleague for his interest in relieving the court of some of its burdens.

When former Senator A. H. Garland became Attorney General in 1885, he began to urge upon Congress the creation of an intermediate appellate court. He recommended several changes in the Davis Bill, including the merging of the district and circuit courts. He proposed the appointment of additional judges to the court of appeals so that it would consist of three judges with the provision that the district court judge could be called upon in the event of interest in a particular case or lack of attendance of the judge of the court of appeals. Garland proposed that the appeals from the District of Columbia and the territorial courts be limited to federal questions. Garland repeated his recommendations in subsequent annual reports.[10]

To get this bill passed through Congress, Senator William Evart (1818-1901) of New York, and a distinguished member of the bar, had to make several compromises with past traditions. He accepted the idea of adding one more circuit judge in those circuits and made optional the previous requirement that the justice of the Supreme Court preside when attending these courts.[11] Realistically, few members of Congress expected the justices of the Supreme Court to play a significant role in these courts in view of their own workload, or the fact that any review of any case would have involved a justice.

In establishing the Circuit Courts of Appeals, no adjustments were made in the organization of the circuits.[12] However, the statute did have an unusual feature of directing the Supreme Court to assign the territories to the existing circuits. The territories in New Mexico, Oklahoma and Utah were added to the Eighth Circuit, and the territories of Alaska and Arizona were added to the Ninth Circuit by order of the Court. In 1901, the territory of Hawaii was assigned to the Ninth Circuit.[13] In other statutes, new courts, such as those established in the Indian Territory, were assigned to the circuits.[14] The jurisdictional amounts needed to bring a case to the Circuit Courts of Appeals were clarified.[15] In the Judicial Code of 1911, these territories were assigned to the circuits, and the authority of the Supreme Court to make this assignment was abolished.[16]

The judges of the Circuit Courts of Appeals consisted of the circuit judge appointed under the Act of 1869, the associate justice of the Supreme Court assigned to that circuit, or a district court judge. One of the first orders of business of the newly created circuit court of appeals was to provide a method of selecting the district court judges to serve. In the majority of the circuits, it was provided by rule of court that the district judges would serve in rotation according to their seniority by commission. In some circuits, the district court judge was designated by special assignment. It soon became apparent that the district court judge had his own work to accomplish, and hence, did not have a great deal of time to devote to duties on the appellate court.

When an appeal was taken from the district court, the litigant would not want the district court judge who rendered the decision in the court below to sit in the case on appeal, and hence, another difficulty arose. Another district court judge had to be called up out of rotation to hear a single appeal, thus taking him away from his own court. District court judges may be assigned presently to sit on the court of appeals, but this is done with much less frequency than during the early decades. During the decades before 1940, panels consisting entirely of three district court judges were common.[17]

When the Circuit Courts of Appeal were established, there was some agitation to authorize three judges in each circuit, but Congress was reluctant to add these new judicial positions. However, Congress provided for an additional circuit judge in each circuit with the establishment of the Circuit Court of Appeals. With these additional judges, all circuits had two judges except the Second, which began with three judges.[18] By 1911, three circuits had four judges, the Fourth Circuit consisted of only two judges, and all the other circuits had three. A third judge was added to the Fourth Circuit in 1922. After the addition of the Third Circuit judge, district court judges were needed only in the event of a vacancy or the disqualification of a judge.

Additional judges have been appointed to the court of appeals; in 1948 the First and Fourth were the only circuits with three judges.[19] The Eighth and Ninth Circuits had seven, while all the others had six, except the Tenth, which had four judges. Since the enactment of the Judicial Code of 1948, the number of judges on these courts has continued to increase.

The Circuit Courts of Appeals now sit in panels of three judges except to consider petitions for rehearing or other important issues which are done *en banc.* The custom of the court sitting in panels of three was, in a limited sense, established by statute. The court was originally constituted by assignment of three judges from among the justices of the Supreme Court, district court judges, and the circuit court judges. The Judicial Code of 1911 stated that "there shall be in each circuit a circuit court of appeals, which shall consist of three judges, of whom two shall constitute a quorum."[20] Even at that date, three circuits, the Second, the Seventh and the Eighth, had four judges. The question which naturally arose was whether these courts would sit as a panel of four.[21] In those circuits where there were more than three circuit judges, the courts could sit in panels of three.

The practice of all the circuit court judges sitting as a panel was challenged, but the Supreme Court stated that it was permissible for all the judges to sit. It was pointed out that the statutes required "the court" to perform such administrative functions as establishing rules and regulations, appointments of the clerks, and fixing of the times when the court should be held.[22] No compelling reason could be advanced for not allowing all members of the court to sit as a panel to hear an appeal. The Circuit Court of Appeals for the Third Circuit had promulgated rules in

the 1930's which provided that three judges would sit, whether they be
circuit judges or district court judges, except in those situations "which the
court by special order directs to be heard by the court *en banc*."[23] As late
as 1936, no other circuit court of appeals had such a rule.[24] The Judiciary
Code of 1948 made it clear that the circuit judges could sit in divisions "in
such order and in such times, as the court directs."[25] This section
authorized divisions of not more than three judges unless a hearing was
ordered by the entire court. After more than half a century, the authority
of the circuit court of appeals to sit in panels of three to hear appeals and
make final decisions was finally established.

The Act of 1891 abolished the appellate jurisdiction of the circuit
courts over appeals from the district courts, and directed all such appeals
to the circuit court of appeals within their circuits. In matters where vital
federal questions were involved, Congress felt that an appeal directly from
the district and circuit courts should be taken to the Supreme Court.
Included were questions of the constitutionality of statutes or the validity
of a treaty. In all other cases, the appeal was taken from the district or
circuit court to the Circuit Court of Appeals where the appeal was
described as "final."

This term "final" was introduced to make it clear that there were no
existing rights of an appeal to the Supreme Court of the United States
except those given by statute. The term "final" was dropped in the
Judiciary Code of 1948. The Circuit Court of Appeals' judgments were
final in diversity cases and all matters of patents, admiralty, revenue cases
and criminal law. The court could certify a question to the Supreme Court
for its instruction or the Supreme Court could grant certiorari and bring
the case up for a full review. The trend since 1891 has been to enlarge the
jurisdiction of the Circuit Court of Appeals.

This process of expanding the jurisdiction of the Circuit Courts of
Appeals began in 1895 with the statute that permitted an appeal where an
injunction was granted or refused.[26] This was followed in frequent
succession by other statutes often allowing appeals in limited areas. A
major transfer of jurisdiction of an area which was a prodigious source of
federal litigation occurred in 1916 when appeals arising under the various
railroad safety and other railroad regulatory statutes were directed to the
circuit courts of appeals rather than to the Supreme Court.[27] In the
previous year, the decisions of the courts of appeals were made final in
bankruptcy matters. During this era, Congress departed from allowing
strictly judicial review to authorizing the circuit courts to modify or set
aside decisions of such agencies as the Federal Trade Commission, the
Interstate Commerce Commission and other federal agencies.[28] At a later
time, it was the courts of appeals to which the National Labor Relations
Board applied to have its orders enforced.[29] All these increases in
functions and jurisdiction gave the courts an increased number of cases.

As the possibility of appeals to the Supreme Court lessened, their decisions became final on many federal questions.

A most significant statute on this path of increased jurisdiction was the Judges Act of 1925, which broadly increased the matters in which the judgments of the courts of appeals were final.[30]

The statute of 1891 authorized the Circuit Court of Appeals to certify a question to the Supreme Court. The statute itself seems to give the circuit court of appeals wide discretion to certify "questions or propositions of law concerning which it desires the instruction of that court for its proper decision."[31] This process was originally created to avoid the conflicts in the circuit courts between the two judges, the justice of the Supreme Court and the district court judge. Such divisions apparently could not happen with three judges on the Circuit Court of Appeals. It was suggested that the reason certification was included was the fact that the Circuit Court of Appeals would consist of two circuit judges and one district judge; hence, two judges of equal rank could disagree.[32] It was the practice in several circuits, with the consent of the parties, to permit a panel of two circuit judges to hear the appeal. However, this authority to certify cases has been used sparingly since the establishment of the courts.

The statute establishing the Circuit Court of Appeals provided that the first session of each court was to be held on the second Monday in January, 1891, and thereafter as fixed by the courts.[33] This was impossible, for the statute was not finally passed and approved until March, so an amendment was necessary authorizing the first session of these courts to be held on the third Tuesday in June, 1891.[34]

The justices of the Supreme Court spread out over the country to open the sessions of the new circuit courts of appeals as mandated by the statute. The opening ceremonies on June 16, 1891, in some courts were rather short, while others had elaborate speeches by the justices or by members of the bar. In all of the speeches, the justices stressed that the purpose of the new courts was to relieve the burden on the Supreme Court of the United States.[35] This organizational day was taken up with the appointment of clerks, marshals and other court officials, but more importantly, the adoption of the rules of court. These rules were based upon those suggested by the Supreme Court, but were very soon amended by the opening of the regular term in the fall of 1891. In the Second Circuit, special rules governing appeals in admiralty were adopted and the court announced that admiralty cases would be given priority.[36]

In initiating these courts, the Supreme Court originally drew up a set of proposed rules for the courts of appeals. One rule provided that "the practice shall be the same as in the supreme court of the United States, as far as the same shall be applicable."[37] This rule was continued in all the circuits for a good many years. These courts were empowered to establish rules for the conduct of their business.[38] Exercising this power over a period of time, great variations began to appear in the practice of the courts, and the question arose whether the Supreme Court could prescribe uniform rules as it was doing for the district courts. One authority argued that by accepting the original rules, the circuit courts of appeals recognized the authority of the Supreme Court to prescribe rules of practice for them.[39] However, this position was denied.

In the early 1960's, during the flurry of revising all the rules of procedure of all the federal courts under the chairmanship of Albert B. Maris, a circuit judge on the Court of Appeals for the Third Circuit, the Supreme Court's authority to prescribe uniform rules for appellate procedure was challenged. The Court clearly had the authority to prescribe rules of civil and criminal procedure up to the filing of the notice of the appeal and the docketing of the appeal and filing of the record in the court of appeals.[40] The Judicial Conference of the United States had considered the problems of diversity in the appellate procedure and had recommended in 1964 a draft of an act to extend the rule making power of the Supreme Court.[41] By this date, the practice in the various courts of appeals varied considerably to the disadvantage of those litigants who would often appear in several circuits.

An advisory committee on appellate rules under the chairmanship of E. Barnett Prettyman, a senior judge in the Court of Appeals in the District of Columbia, proposed a uniform set of rules.[42] The rules introduced some unique innovations, the chief one being a prehearing conference. The court was authorized to direct the attorneys to appear before the court or a judge "to consider the simplifications of the issues and such other matters as may aid in the disposition of proceedings by the court."[43] The rules recognized the technological advances in the art of printing and permitted the preparation of the record or brief by any "copying process capable of producing a clear black image on white paper."[44] Instead of a separate appendix containing the record as it applied in the Fourth Circuit, the new rules opted for a joint appendix in which the appellant would indicate those portions of the record he intended to print with the option for the appellant to indicate additional parts of the record he wanted included. The rules clarified the rehearing *en banc* stating that "a hearing or rehearing *en banc* is not favored and ordinarily would not be ordered except" when considered necessary by the entire court for uniformity or where the question involved was of exceptional importance.[45] The significance of the rule was the establishment of the uniformity in appellate procedure among all the appellate courts. As one commentator stated, the "new appellate rules are not revolutionary."[46]

The local courts of appeals were free to adopt supplementary rules, chiefly governing admissions to the bar of the court and other administrative details. More recently, each circuit has had to adopt rules governing procedures involving complaints against federal judges and implementing the reporting procedures.

At the time of the organization of the Circuit Court of Appeals, the issue was raised of whether the judges should wear gowns. It was reported that some newspapers developed opposition to the practice because this was not in keeping with "our Republican simplicity."[47] It was later reported that the judges of the Seventh Circuit at its October term in 1891 wore gowns. At this session, Justice Harlan presided. It was reported that this was the first time any bench of judges in Illinois was clad in gowns.[48] The custom of the judges on the Circuit Courts of Appeals to wear gowns was probably influenced by the justice of the Supreme Court, where the custom was well entrenched.

When first established, the circuit court of appeals held its sessions in one location in the circuit, but beginning in 1902, a trend was established for sessions of the court to be held in several cities. The first court affected by such a requirement was the Fifth Circuit. The Court of Appeals for the Fifth Circuit originally held sessions in New Orleans, but in 1902, the court was authorized to sit in Atlanta where it could hear appeals from the courts in Georgia.[49] This statute gave it authority to hold sessions in other cities within the circuit, but apparently the court did not take advantage of this authority, for an act was passed shortly thereafter requiring sessions of this court to be held in Fort Worth, Texas.[50] Later acts required sessions of this court to be held in Montgomery[51] and Jacksonville.[52] The number of cities in which the courts in the other circuits were held was increased and at present, the Courts of Appeals for the Fourth, Fifth, Eighth, Ninth and Tenth Circuits hold sessions in several cities within their circuits. The rules of these courts specify in which cities the courts will sit.

Generally, when the court sat in a given city within a state, it was for the purpose of hearing appeals from the district courts in that state. However, in 1904, an exception was made to this rule by permitting appeals from the District Court at Beaumont, Texas, to be taken to New Orleans rather than Fort Worth.[53] The reason given for this was that it was more convenient for parties to go to New Orleans from Beaumont than to Fort Worth. Inexplicably, this statute was later repealed. Under present practice, the courts of appeals hold sessions in a more convenient city than that city in which the clerk's office is located. In the Ninth Circuit, the attorney must file a request for such a hearing and the court will assign the hearing in another place from where the court is generally held.[54]

The act establishing the Circuit Court of Appeals, did not relieve the circuit judges of their duty to sit in the circuit courts. With the increase of business of the circuit courts of appeals, they gradually began to leave the business of the circuit court to the district court judge. A number of exigencies forced this change. Each year, the business of the circuit courts of appeals grew steadily and the judges had less time to attend the circuit courts. One author used the example of the Eighth Circuit in which the court sat in St. Louis, St. Paul, Cheyenne and Denver, which required the three judges to be in continuous session the year around. With a limited number of judges, there was a natural reluctance to be placed in a position of having to disqualify oneself upon an appeal because of presiding in the trial court. No objection was raised by the bar "to criticize the growing tendency of the circuit judges to confine their labors to that court."[55] Since most of the burden had been shifted to the district court judge, it made little sense to continue the circuit courts which were finally abolished in 1911.

It is not surprising that attempts were made to abolish the Circuit Court of Appeals and reestablish the dominance of the Supreme Court, but the seriousness of these attempts is difficult to gauge. It was argued that these courts did not command the same respect as the Supreme Court, and the old argument of conflicts in the decisions of these circuits was again raised. This is a perennial argument which will never be laid to rest nor will it be possible to resolve. However, the opinion was expressed that since two circuit judges and one district court judge usually constituted a panel, all of whom were local residents, the judges would not decide cases impartially because of their social and professional connections. The proposal was made that as a measure of relief for the Supreme Court, a court under the Supreme Court should be established to decide all patent, trademarks, copyrights and unfair competition appeals. Other than this one editorial, no serious effort was ever made in Congress to abolish or to substitute another organization for these courts.[36]

Since its creation, the tendency has been to give jurisdiction to the Circuit Court of Appeals over matters which normally would have gone directly to the Supreme Court. Over a period of time, a direct appeal from the district court to the Supreme Court has been limited so that today this jurisdiction can rarely be invoked. One cannot boast that he will take his case to the Supreme Court, for such an approach is blocked both by statute and by the pressure of numbers of cases.

The Judicial Code of 1948 changed the names of these courts from the Circuit Courts of Appeals to the Courts of Appeals for a given circuit, e.g., from the First Circuit Court of Appeals to the United States Court of Appeals for the First Circuit.

The courts of appeals have played a significant role in the development of federal jurisprudence as increasingly, more federal cases are finally determined by the judges of these courts. Their role in this unfolding drama is a matter of controversy upon which no consensus will ever be reached. As is true with all institutions, each circuit developed a personality all its own. This was due in part to the personalities and power of the judges who sat on the court and their philosophies of their roles as well as the location within the country.[57] In the middle of the Twentieth Century, the Courts of Appeals for the Second and Third Circuits were considered as the strongest benches in the country. The triumvirate of Learned Hand, Thomas W. Swann, and Augustus Hand were well known. At the same time on the Third Circuit were John Biggs, Albert M. Máris and Herbert F. Goodrich, the latter two considered as authorities in the area of conflicts of laws. At the same time, John M. Parker in the Fourth Circuit was recognized for his contributions to the administration of the federal courts as well as some significant decisions in the area of Indian law. These two circuits were emerging from a bad reputation given to the Second Circuit by the resignation of Martin T. Mantom in 1939 under a cloud of misconduct.[58] In the Third Circuit, John Warren Davis had received bribes for swinging decisions and using his colleague, Joseph Buffington, who had become helpless and senile, to provide the second and majority vote. The First and Fourth Circuit Courts of Appeals were known for their collegiality. This appraisal does not do justice to the many judges who worked diligently in meeting their responsibilities. There can be no doubt that the courts of appeals have significantly shaped American law.

FOOTNOTES TO CHAPTER 8

1. For a list of these acts extending the jurisdiction of the federal courts, *see* Felix Frankfurter and James M. Landis, THE BUSINESS OF THE SUPREME COURT, A STUDY IN THE FEDERAL JUDICIAL SYSTEM (1928), p.61 Footnotes 20 through 22.

2. Act of March 3, 1875, 18 STAT. 470.

3. The Supreme Court had 82 cases on its docket at the end of its term in 1843 and five years later in 1848, 250 cases were pending. 7 WESTERN L.J. 299 (1849). The following is a list of numbers of cases at the beginning of each term of the Supreme Court of the United States:

> Oct. T. 1884 - 1315 cases
> Oct. T. 1885 - 1340 cases
> Oct. T. 1886 - 1396 cases
> Oct. T. 1887 - 1427 cases
> Oct. T. 1888 - 1536 cases
> Oct. T. 1889 - 1635 cases
> Oct. T. 1890 - 1800 cases

See the ANNUAL REPORTS OF THE ATTORNEY GENERAL for the years mentioned and 140 U.S. 707.

4. Note, 23 AMER. L. REV. 427 (1889); Samuel Maxwell, "Relief of the United States Supreme Court," 23 AMER. L. REV. 958 (1889).

5. These various proposals are discussed by Walter B. Hill, "The Federal Judicial System," 12 A.B.A. REPT. 289 (1889).

6. *Ibid,* p.308.

7. ATT'Y GEN. ANN. REP. 1885, p.41.

8. Donald O. Dewey, "Hoosier Justice: The Journal of David McDonald 1864-1868," 62 INDIANA MAG. OF HISTORY 209 (1966).

9. The text of the Davis bill is found in ATT'Y GEN. ANN. REP. 1885, p.37.

10. ATT'Y GEN. ANN. REP. 1886-1887, p.xv.

11. The legislative history of the statute is given in Felix Frankfurter and James M. Landis, THE BUSINESS OF THE SUPREME COURT (1928), p.98.

12. Act of March 2, 1891, 26 STAT. 827.

13. 139 U.S. 707; 186 U.S. 625.

14. Act of February 8, 1896, 29 STAT. 6.

15. Act of June 6, 1900, sec. 504, 31 STAT. 414.

16. Act of March 3, 1911, 36 STAT. 11.

17. Frank O. Loveland, THE APPELLATE JURISDICTION OF THE FEDERAL COURTS (1911), p.17; *See* Peters v. Hanger, 136 Fed. 181 (C.A. 4th, 1905).

18. The Second Circuit judge was created by Act of March 3, 1887, 24 STAT. 492.

19. Act of March 3, 1887, 24 STAT. 492.

20. Act of March 3, 1911, sec. 117, 36 STAT. 1131.

21. "Federal Circuit Court of Appeals - Their Impractical Organization," 69 CENT. L. J. 217 (1909).

22. Textile Mills Securities Corp. v. Commissioners of Internal Revenue, 314 U.S. 326, 329 (1941).

23. Rule cited in Textile Mills Securities Corp. v. Commissioners of Internal Revenue, 314 U.S. 326, 327-28, note 3 (1941).

24. These rules are found in Nathan April, A GUIDE TO FEDERAL APPELLATE PROCEDURE (1936). The rule in question is not included.

25. Judicial Code of 1948, Title 28, sec. 46. This had been proposed in Congress on other occasions. S. Rept. 1246, 77th Cong., 1st sess.

26. Act of February 18, 1895, 28 STAT. 666.

27. Act of January 28, 1915, sec. 4, 38 STAT. 804; Act of September 6, 1916, sec. 3, 39 STAT. 727.

28. Act of March 3, 1891, sec. 6, 26 STAT. 828; Act of January 28, 1915, sec. 2, 38 STAT. 803 and other statutes.

29. Act of July 5, 1935, sec. 10, 49 STAT. 454.

30. Act of February 13, 1925, 43 STAT. 936.

31. Act of March 2, 1891, sec. 6, 26 STAT. 828; William L. Murfree, "Jurisdiction and Practice of the Federal Courts of Appeals," 26 AMER. L. REV. 544 (1892).

32. Forsyth v. City of Hammond, 166 U.S. 506 (1897).

33. In the JUDICIAL CODE OF 1911, the terms of the Circuit Court were set by statute, but the JUDICIAL CODE OF 1948 returned the authority to the Court of Appeals to establish these dates by rule of court.

34. Resolution of March 3, 1891, 26 STAT. 1116.

35. The record of these proceedings are found in volume 1 through 9 of the U.S. APPEALS REPORTS.

36. 2 U.S. APP. 714.

37. Rule 8, 47 Fed. v.

38. These rules were originally published in the FEDERAL REPORTER, volume 47. However, later reprinting of these volumes omitted these rules.

39. Charles E. Clark, "Power of the Supreme Court to Make Rules of Appellate Procedure," 49 HARV. L. REV. 1314 (1936).

40. H.R. Rept. No. 2153, 89th Cong. 2d sess. 1966 U.S. CODE CONG. & ADM. NEWS 4173.

41. Act of November 6, 1966, PL. 89-773, 80 STAT. 1323.

42. The proposed rules with comments of the Committee are found in 34 F.R.D. 263 (1964).

43. Proposed Rule 33, 34 F.R.D. 263, 309 (1964).

44. Proposed Rule 32, 34 F.R.D. 263, 308 (1964).

45. Proposed Rule 35, 34 F.R.D. 263, 310 (1964).

46. Bernard J. Ward, "The Federal Rules of Appellate Procedure," 54 A.B.A.J. 661 (1968); Sherman L. Cohen, "The Proposed Federal Rules of Appellate Procedure," 54 Geo. L. Rev. 441 (1966).

47. Note, 26 AMER. L. REV. 116 (1892).

48. Note, 26 AMER. L. REV. 410 (1892).

49. Act of June 30, 1902, 32 STAT. 548.

50. Act of December 18, 1902, 32 STAT. 756.

51. Act of January 30, 1903, 32 STAT. 784.

52. 28 U.S.C. (1948) 48; Senate Rep. 1559, 80th Cong. 2d sess.

53. Act of March 4, 1904, 33 STAT. 59.

54. Rules, Court of Appeals, 9th Circuit, Rule 4(3) (1968).

55. James Love Hopkins, THE FEDERAL JUDICIAL CODE AND THE JUDICIARY (3d ed., 1926), p.15.

56. "The United States Appellate Courts," 2 LAW NOTES 29 (May 1898).

57. NATIONAL L.J., v.5, No. 34 (May 2, 1983), pp. 1, 24-28; J. Woodford Howard, Jr., COURTS OF APPEALS IN THE FEDERAL JUDICIAL SYSTEM (1981).

58. Joseph Borkin, THE CORRUPT JUDGE (1966), p.23, 95.

Chapter 9

THE DISTRICT COURTS

The district courts at the time of their establishment were one of two sets of trial courts in the Federal Judicial System, and the only ones with a permanently assigned judge and a staff consisting of a clerk and marshal. However, their jurisdiction was limited to minor civil and criminal matters. The court's jurisdiction over admiralty and revenue cases was exclusive.[1] All other matters were vested in the circuit courts. As one author has commented, "The division of the federal caseload *jurisdiction* between the circuit courts and the district courts was then like a pie, with the district courts having a very small slice and the circuit courts having the larger share."[2] However, the dual system of trial courts was not established in all the existing states, and from the Judiciary Act of 1789 until the creation of the circuit judges in 1869, the district court could be the exclusive federal court in a particular judicial district. At times, the district court held in one part of a judicial district could have greater powers than the same court held in another part of the same district. These inconsistencies became more glaring by the end of the Nineteenth Century.

Immediately following the enactment of the Judiciary Act of 1789, the jurisdiction of the district court was expanded. In 1790, the district court was given jurisdiction over certain questions arising under the patent laws[3], and in 1800, a similar jurisdiction was given over bankruptcy cases.[4] However, the understanding of many lawyers before 1911 was that the district court was primarily a criminal court. This perception was created when, by an Act of 1842, the district courts were given concurrent jurisdiction with the circuit court over crimes which were non-capital in their punishment.[5] Apparently, it was the custom of the district court judge by the closing decades of the Nineteenth Century to try criminal cases in the district courts and most if not all of the civil cases in the circuit courts.[6] This practice had become possible for the Judiciary Act of 1802 authorized the district court judge to preside in the circuit court in the absence of the justice. The Supreme Court, as early as 1808, recognized the power of either of the two judges to preside in the circuit court alone.[7]

Under the Judiciary Act of 1789, an appeal could be taken from the district court to the circuit court held in the same district where the amount exceeded $50 in civil suits or $300 in admiralty suits.[8] A criminal case from the district court was not subject to review in the circuit court until 1879.[9]

The dual system of trial courts was not established in each state, and until 1911, when the circuit and district courts were merged, the district courts, especially in the new states, exercised the jurisdiction of a circuit court. The organization and jurisdiction of these courts were not nationally uniform. This trend was established under the First Judiciary Act of 1789 when the district courts in Kentucky and Maine were left out of the circuit organization and these courts were the exclusive federal courts in those states. Under this statute, appeals from the court in Kentucky went directly to the Supreme Court. Because Maine was a part of Massachusetts at that time, an appeal was taken from the District Court in Maine to the Circuit Court in Massachusetts under the same regulations as appeals from other district courts. It is not clear whether all cases were first taken on appeal to the Circuit Court in Boston or only those matters properly within the jurisdiction of a district court.[10] Maine was made a part of the First Circuit in 1820, and a circuit court was established in that state.[11]

Where the district court was the exclusive federal forum in a few states, appeals were directed to a circuit court held in another judicial district. An appeal could be taken from the District Court of the Northern District of New York to the Circuit Court in the Southern District of the same state from the creation of the district in 1814 until 1826.[12] In practice, this permitted a writ of error or appeal from the Northern District to the Southern District in matters that would normally go from a district court to a circuit court. The normal review of the circuit court went to the Supreme Court.

A similar pattern of appeals existed in Alabama when the state was divided into two districts. An appeal was taken from the District Court for the Northern District of Alabama from its creation in 1824[13] to the Circuit Court in the Southern District until an appeal in all civil cases directly to the Supreme Court was provided in 1842.[14] Since the same judge sat in both districts of Alabama, his jurisdiction was greater in the Northern District than in the Southern District, but unlike the situation in New York, he did not have another district court judge review his decisions. This pattern of appeals from a district court to a circuit court not held in the same district was not used after 1842.

If the pattern in Alabama sounds absurd, the situation in the Western District of Pennsylvania was even more so. In 1837, the circuit court jurisdiction of the District Court in Pittsburgh was abolished, but when the same judge held the District Court in Williamsport, Pennsylvania, he exercised circuit court jurisdiction and appeals were taken from his decision there to the Supreme Court of the United States.[15]

Where the district court exercised the jurisdiction of a circuit court, an appeal could be taken to the Supreme Court of the United States but only when the amount involved exceeded $2,000. The decision of a federal district court judge was final when the amount involved was less than $2,000 where he exercised the function of a circuit judge, but in other districts where he presided in the district court only, the jurisdictional amount for review in the circuit court was $500. This difference in appellate review was viewed as a weakness. In fact, it was suggested that district court exercise of circuit court jurisdiction was unconstitutional for the organization of a district court with full federal jurisdiction did not accord the new states equal treatment under the Constitution.[16]

The opening sessions of the district courts did not attract as much attention as did the first session of the circuit court. The visit of the justice from the Supreme Court was an important local event.

The expectations of some of the leaders of the bar that the creation of the circuit court judges in 1869 would preserve the dual system was not realized. In practice, rarely after this date would the circuit judge or the justice preside in these courts. The American Bar Association began its campaign in 1894 to abolish the circuit courts and legislation for this purpose was introduced into Congress but failed to pass. It was not until the adoption of the Judicial Code of 1911 that these courts were abolished and the district courts became the only trial court in the federal system. Why such a system of dual courts should exist at all may be ascribed to the usual inertia of the groups who have vested interests in such institutions.[17]

The Judiciary Act of 1789 made each state into a single district with several of the district courts sitting in different cities within the state. One of the innovations of the Judiciary Act of 1801 was the division of New Jersey, Virginia, and Maryland into two districts and North Carolina into three districts. A separate judge was not appointed for these divisions, but this organization was a means to provide another location for the sessions of the court with a clerk in both locations for the convenience of litigants.[18] When the Judiciary Act of 1801 was repealed, the division of North Carolina into three districts and Tennessee into two districts for the purpose of holding the district court was kept.[19] A clerk was appointed in each district in North Carolina, but no provision was made for the appointment of an additional district judge, district attorney or marshal. The Act did not restrict in any respect the return of process or the place of trial as was done in later acts. For the two districts of Tennessee, the appointment of a clerk, a district attorney and a marshal for each of these districts was authorized. In 1838, the third district was created in Tennessee which did require that all suits be brought in the district where the defendants resided or could be found.[20] It is not clear why Congress made these provisions other than for convenience of litigants.

In 1823, South Carolina was divided into two districts for the purpose of holding the district court.[21] In later acts providing for the terms of the circuit court, the court was described as "the Circuit Court for the District of South Carolina." When the question arose of whether the circuit court was confined to these same districts, it was decided that the circuit court constituted the entire state of South Carolina whereas the district court was divided into two districts.[22]

The first division of a state into two districts with a separate judge in each was made in New York in 1814,[23] followed by Pennsylvania in 1818[24] and Virginia in 1819.[25] This organization was made because of the long distances the litigants had to travel to attend the sessions of the federal courts. The business of each of the courts in each of these districts was thought to be sufficient for one judge. As new districts were created, they were named for their general location within the state — Eastern and Western Districts or Northern and Southern Districts.

The creation of two districts in Arkansas was for a unique purpose. Here in 1851, the state was divided into two districts. The new Western District of Arkansas was given jurisdiction over parts of the Indian Territory. This was the first time that a District Court was given jurisdiction of cases arising outside the boundaries of the state.[26] This was the court made famous in western literature by Judge Isaac C. Parker (1838-1896). Parker was a controversial judge and has been described as a great trial judge by no less an authority than Wigmore, but by others, he was described in less flattering terms.[27] He was known popularly as the "hanging judge." Between 1875 and 1895, 344 defendants were tried for capital offenses in this court of which 83 were hung. Many of the famous outlaws of the period, including Bell Starr, and members of the Buck gang, were defendants in this court. Judge Parker has been the subject of several biographies with such engrossing titles as HELL ON THE BORDERS and HE HANGED THEM HIGH.[28] The experiences with this court led to the establishment of territorial courts in the Indian Territory as well as appeals in criminal cases.[29] The jurisdiction of the United States District Court for the Western District of Arkansas over the Indian Territory was finally terminated in 1895, and since then, a district court has not exercised jurisdiction beyond the boundary of the state except for the District Court of Wyoming.[30]

The creation of new districts was brought about by a number of reasons, but chiefly for the convenience of litigants. Several of the state legislatures petitioned Congress for the division of their states to form a second district. The legislature of Texas desired such a division because of the inconvenience and the expense of attending the District Court at Galveston for the citizens of the farther reaches of their state. They desired an additional district and provision for the holding of the court in at least two places in each district, a reasonable request for a state that large.[31] Congress granted this request in 1857 by creating the Eastern and Western districts in Texas, and provisions were made for convening the courts in two places in each of those two districts.[32]

The combination of maritime business and the distance to travel made imperative the creation of another district in Florida to handle the extensive maritime problems arising in the waters south of Florida. In 1853, the value of the vessels and wrecks in these waters exceeded two million dollars.[33] The Southern District was created in 1847 to have geographical jurisdiction covering the area lying south of the line from east to west, north of Charlotte Harbor.[34] This area was sparsely settled, having less than 3,000 inhabitants, exclusive of Indians in the area. Nearly all the settlers lived in Key West. The judge of the Southern District would reside in Key West exercising the same jurisdiction as that assigned to the District Court of Kentucky under the Act of 1789; namely, full federal jurisdiction. For regular judicial purposes, sessions were held in May and November, but for purposes of admiralty and maritime jurisdiction, the court was open at all times. Until a judge could be appointed, the judge of the Northern District would exercise jurisdiction in the Southern District. [35]

The first judge appointed to this court was William Marvin, a native of New York who must have found the climate congenial as have many others from that state. Judge Marvin served as judge until 1863 and later as the Provisional Governor of the state. He became an expert on the law of salvage so that he authored a book on the subject in which he frequently refers to practices in his court. [36]

A great many vessels were destroyed on the reefs in those waters which attracted a group known as wreckers who would perform salvage operations. At first, this business was based in the Bahama Islands until Congress prohibited the carrying of wrecked goods to a foreign place in 1825, four years after Florida became a territory of the United States. [37] The wreckers were accused of all types of misconduct including piracy, concealment of salvaged goods, deception in regard to channels and reefs, and connivance with lighthouse keepers to purposely dim the light to lure vessels onto the reefs. [38] These activities were reported in the popular contemporary periodical, *Harper's Magazine.* When the court in the Southern District was created, one of the additional duties assigned the judge was the authority to grant licenses to ships engaged in salvage operations in the area. He was especially ordered to see that the ships were properly and sufficiently fitted and equipped for the business of saving property and that the master was trustworthy and innocent of any fraud and misconduct in relation to any property that had been shipwrecked on the coast. [39] Judge Marvin in his book notes that the wreckers had been traditionally rewarded "with greater liberality" than in other courts of the United States or the High Court of Admiralty of England. [40] Several cases are summarized from his court showing the fees allowed for these operations.

The court in the Southern District was held by the Union forces throughout the entire Civil War, probably the only federal court in the South that continued to function without interruption. The Confederate Congress had created a special admiralty court to replace this federal court, but the Confederate judge appointed to hold the court was never able to exercise his jurisdiction. [41]

Since the middle of the Twentieth Century, the practice of appointing additional judges in a district has been the accepted practice rather than dividing the states into further districts. The Judicial Conference of the United States has generally opposed further division of states. [42] However, in 1962 a third district was created in Florida, [43] and in 1966, California was divided into four districts. [44] In the same year, Congress took unusual steps by merging the two districts of South Carolina into one district. The last state to be reorganized was Louisiana, when in 1971, its two judicial districts were divided into three. [45]

When Congress provided for the holding of the district or circuit courts in two or more locations within a district, many problems of administration presented themselves. Was the jury to be selected from the entire district or from the area close to the place where the term of court was held? In which city would the case be tried? To solve some of these problems, in 1836, the Northern District of New York was divided into divisions for the trial of "all issues of fact, triable by a jury." [46] This act grouped the counties into divisions designated as the Northern, Eastern, and Western Divisions of the Northern District. This is the first organization of a judicial district by divisions. A cause of action which arose in the Northern or Eastern Division was triable in the circuit court held in Albany, and the causes of action arising in the Western Division were triable in Canadaigua. However, this did not regulate the venue of transitory actions or the transfer of cases for good cause. It cannot be assumed, however, that all states have been so divided. The pattern of division was not used again until after 1859 when an Iowa district was made into divisions. [47] Since then, it has been used in a number of judicial districts.

Generally, court divisions have been known by the names of the cities in which the court for that division is held, although some are named for points of the compass. Only in two states have divisions been numbered. [48]

Congress continued to legislate on the establishment of new divisions within a district, the division of a state into more districts, and the reorganization of divisions within a district on an individual basis. It is evident that in the middle part of the Twentieth Century, Congress began to look upon the federal courts comprehensively rather than focusing on an individual judicial district. In 1978, the Judicial Conference adopted a policy statement that changes within the geographical configuration of judicial districts should not be made without a strong showing of need. Congress has adhered to the policy of seeking the conference's approval as well as that of all affected parties and of making these changes in a comprehensive bill. [49]

Associated in the public's conception of a court is the courtroom in which its sessions are held. Until the middle of the Nineteenth Century, no general provisions were made for the erection of courthouses in any of the judicial districts, for the federal government relied "upon the liberality of the local governments for the accommodation of the national courts." [50] The sessions of the circuit and district courts were held in public buildings belonging to the state, county or city where they sat. However, if any of these facilities were denied to them, it was the responsibility of the marshal under the direction of the courts to provide a suitable room at the expense of the United States, provided that he did "not incur an expense of more than twenty dollars in any one year for furniture, or fifty dollars for rent of building and making improvements thereon, without first submitting a statement and estimates to the Secretary of the Interior, and getting his instructions in the premises." [51] The minutes of the courts were often vague as to where the court actually met. On April 25, 1791, the Circuit Court for Georgia met at "the Courthouse," in Savannah, without further identification. [52] This was probably the county courthouse.

In the territories, land was set aside for a courthouse. As early as 1824, Congress provided for a quarter section in each county of the territories to be set aside for establishment of seats of justice and that the sale of this property would be used for erecting such public buildings. [53] In 1832, a thousand acres were given to the Territory of Arkansas to sell to pay the cost of constructing a courthouse and jail in Little Rock. [54]

Congress clearly established the principle that courtrooms would be located in the customs houses which were apparently some of the first public buildings constructed by the federal government. In 1854, the Secretary of the Treasury was authorized to construct a building "for the accommodation of the custom-house, post-office, and United States courts" in Milwaukee, Wisconsin, "to cost not more than fifty thousand dollars," and for the same governmental offices and steamboat inspector's building in New Haven, Connecticut; Newark, New Jersey; and several other cities, those buildings not to cost more than $88,000. [55] These buildings were not to be constructed until the land was purchased and the states relinquished the right to tax the property. These funds were administered by the Collectors of the Customs, who supervised construction of the buildings. [56] One can assume that the Treasury rented necessary quarters for the courts until public buildings were available. However, in the latter part of the century, it was common for Congress to authorize sessions of the United States District Courts in specified cities, provided accommodations were furnished without cost to the government. [57] It would be interesting to have more details on the courtrooms in which the federal courts were held.

The district courts obtained the status of the only trial court in 1911 when the circuit courts were abolished and all federal trial functions were vested in the district courts. This was a long overdue recognition that the district court judge appointed for the purpose of holding the district court and assisting in the circuit court had become the only federal trial judge. The other federal judges of the Supreme Court and the Circuit Court of Appeals had ceased any pretense of presiding in a trial court. After this merger of the two trial courts by the Judicial Code of 1911, the emphasis shifts from structure to less interesting but equally important problems of jurisdiction, number of judges and other related questions.

FOOTNOTES TO CHAPTER 9

1. Act of September 24, 1789, sec. 9, 1 STAT. 76.
2. Mary K. Bonsteel Tachu, FEDERAL COURTS IN THE EARLY REPUBLIC: KENTUCKY 1789-1816 (1978), p.19.
3. Act of April 10, 1790, sec. 5, 1 STAT. 111; Act of February 21, 1793, 1 STAT. 323.
4. Act of April 4, 1800, 2 STAT. 21.
5. Act of August 23, 1842, 5 STAT. 517.
6. Robert W. Breckus, "The Judicial Code of United States with some incidental observations on its application to Hawaii," 22 YALE L. J. 453, 457 (1913).
7. Pollard v. Dwight, 4 Cranch 421, 429 (1808).
8. Act of September 24, 1789, sec. 21, 22, 1 STAT. 83, 84; Act of March 3, 1803, 2 STAT. 244.
9. United States v. Wonson, 1 Gall. 5, 28 Fed.Cas. 745 (D. Mass., 1812); United States v. Haynes, 2 McLean 155, 26 Fed.Cas. 240 (D. Ohio, 1840); McLellan v. United States, 1 Gall. 227, 16 Fed.Cas. 292 (D. Mass., 1812); Act of March 3, 1879, 20 STAT. 354.
10. Act of September 24, 1789, sec. 21, 22, 1 STAT. 83.
11. Act of March 3, 1820, 3 STAT. 544.
12. Act of April 9, 1814, 3 STAT, 120; Act of May 22, 1826, 4 STAT. 192.
13. Act of February 22, 1838, 5 STAT. 210.
14. Act of August 4, 1842, 5 STAT. 504.
15. Act of March 3, 1837, 5 STAT. 177.
16. This is suggested by Justice Story in Martin v. Hunter's Lessee, 1 Wheat. 304 (U.S. 1816).
17. The efforts to abolish these courts is detailed in Felix Frankfurter and James M. Landis, THE BUSINESS OF THE SUPREME COURT: A STUDY IN THE FEDERAL JUDICIAL SYSTEM (1928), p.130-135.
18. Act of February 13, 1801, sec. 21, 2 STAT. 96.
19. Act of April 29, 1802, sec. 7, 16, 2 STAT. 162, 165.
20. Act of June 18, 1838, 5 STAT. 249; Act of January 18, 1839, 5 STAT. 313.
21. Act of February 21, 1823, 3 STAT. 726.
22. Barrett v. United States, 169 U.S. 218 (1897).
23. Act of April 9, 1814, 3 STAT. 120.
24. Act of April 20, 1818, 3 STAT. 462.
25. Act of February 4, 1819, 3 STAT. 478.
26. Act of March 3, 1851, 9 STAT. 594.
27. Harry P. Daily, "Isaac C. Parker, One of the Greatest American Trial Judges," 35 PROC. BAR ASSOC. OF ARK. 88, 97 (1932). *See,* Hudson v. Parker, 156 U.S. 277 (1895).
28. S.W. Harman, HELL ON THE BORDER (1953) and Homer Croy, HE HANGED THEM HIGH (1952).
29. Act of March 1, 1889, 25 STAT. 783; Act of February 6, 1889, sec. 6, 25 STAT. 656; Act of March 3, 1891, sec. 13, 26 STAT. 829.
30. Act of March 1, 1895, 28 STAT. 693.
31. Petition of Legislature of Georgia, 1845. House Doc. 121, 29th Cong. 1st sess. Vol. IV. Petition of Legislature of Texas, 1850. Senate Misc. Doc. 102, 31st Cong. 1st sess. Vol. I.
32. Act of February 21, 1857, 11 STAT. 164.
33. William Marvin, A TREATISE ON THE LAW OF WRECK AND SALVAGE (1858), p.2.
34. Act of February 23, 1847, 9 STAT. 131.
35. Act of February 23, 1847, 9 STAT. 132.
36. Marvin, *supra,* note 33.

37. Act of March 3, 1825, 4 STAT. 132.

38. "Key West and Salvage in 1850," 8 FLA. HIST. Q. 47, 62 (1929).

39. Act of February 23, 1847, sec. 3, 9 STAT. 131.

40. Marvin, *supra,* note 33, p.211.

41. William M. Robinson, Jr., JUSTICE IN GREY (Cambridge, Mass. 1941), pp.299-308.

42. Henry P. Chandler, "Some major advances in the Federal Judicial System, 1922-1947," 31 F.R.D. 343.

43. Act of July 30, 1962, 76 STAT. 247.

44. Act of March 18, 1966, sec. 2, 80 STAT. 75.

45. Act of December 18, 1971, sec. 3, 85 STAT. 741.

46. Act of July 7, 1838, 5 STAT. 295.

47. Act of March 3, 1859, 11 STAT. 437.

48. Kansas, Act of June 9, 1890, 26 STAT. 129, all divisions abolished by Act of August 27, 1949, 63 STAT. 666; Minnesota, Act of April 26, 1890, 26 STAT. 72.

49. *See* H.R. Rept. 98-1062, 98th Cong. 1984.

50. Alfred Conkling, TREATISE ON THE ORGANIZATION, JURISDICTION AND PRACTICE OF THE COURTS OF THE UNITED STATES (4th ed., 1864), p.198.

51. Act of February 26, 1853, sec. 2, 10 STAT. 165.

52. Minute Book, U.S. Circuit Court for Georgia, April 25, 1791.

53. Act of May 26, 1824, 4 STAT. 50.

54. Act of June 15, 1832, 4 STAT. 531.

55. Act of August 4, 1854, sec. 2, 10 STAT. 571.

56. Act of June 12, 1858, sec. 17, 11 STAT. 327.

57. An additional term of the Circuit Court could be held in Florence, South Carolina provided suitable accommodations were furnished without expense to the government. Act of May 10, 1900, 31 STAT. 174 was typical of a number of acts of that period.

Chapter 10

JUDICIAL LEGISLATION

For over a century, Congress was content to legislate for the federal courts in a piecemeal fashion. It was not until the adoption of the REVISED STATUTES in 1874 when all of the statutes pertaining to the courts including the statutes on procedure were collected in one title that so many glaring inconsistencies were revealed. During this period, the single most important issue was the release of the justices from circuit duties and the adjustment of the jurisdiction of the circuit courts. A considerable amount of energy was expended on prescribing the terms of the court, in the cities in which they would meet, and, if the congressional delegation was fortunate enough, the creation of a new district so that additional judges could be authorized. Because of other historical events, and the amount of time Congress devoted to private claims, consideration of the courts was pushed into the background.

In 1869, Congress appointed commissioners for the purpose of compiling all the federal statutes. This commission for the first time organized the statutes pertaining to the courts and made some detailed observations on the various sections which were proposed. Congress was dissatisfied with the report because it was perceived that the commissioners had exceeded their authority by revising the laws rather than presenting the statutes as enacted. However, the organization as proposed by the commissioners was incorporated into the REVISED STATUTES. [1]

Statutes relating to the federal courts were consolidated in the REVISED STATUTES OF 1874 as Title 13. However, these statutes were merely compiled and no attempt was made to remove inconsistencies or to change any of their basic provisions. An examination of the sections of the REVISED STATUTES reveals the uneven organization of the district courts, for some had varying numbers of court officials and special functions assigned to certain district court judges. Even the sections governing procedure were in conflict. It made no sense that an appeal could be taken from the supreme court of one territory to the Supreme Court of the United States where the amount exceeded $1,000, while from another territory, the amount needed to exceed $2,000. [2] During the Nineteenth Century, Congress had legislated individually for each of the courts, and, for this reason, disparities developed in organization of the district courts. For example, seventy of the judicial districts had a single clerk with deputies, but in eight districts, the number of clerks varied from three to six. [3] In practice, this meant that each clerk acted independently of his counterpart in the same district. The Judicial Code of 1911 made provision for one clerk in each district with deputies appointed by the clerk with the approval of the district judge. [4] The consolidation of the laws applicable to the court had shown many of these disparities and some had been remedied in subsequent statutes.

The establishment of the Circuit Courts of Appeals, in 1891, did not resolve all the problems of the functioning of the federal courts. Questions relating to the number of judges and other court officers, the non-uniformity of procedure, and the merger of the two trial courts continued to be debated by lawyers and legislators. To resolve some of these problems, in 1899, Congress directed the Commission revising the criminal and penal statutes to codify the laws relating to the jurisdiction and practice of the federal courts.[5] The Commission to Revise and Codify the Criminal and Penal Laws was created in 1897, consisting of three commissioners, appointed by the President, who were to revise the criminal laws under the direction of the Attorney General.[6] Two years later, this Commission was charged with the responsibility of revising the laws relating to the federal judiciary. A report was sent to Congress in 1901 which was later used as the basis for the Judicial Code enacted in 1911.[7] However, in the interim, the Commission was charged with drafting a revision of the entire federal law. The Commission was directed to finish its work and make a final report by 1906, which it accomplished. The work of this Commission formed the basis for the act signed into law on March 3, 1911, known as the Judicial Code of 1911.[8]

The most significant change brought about by the Judicial Code of 1911 was the abolition of the circuit courts. The district courts became the only court of the federal system exercising all jurisdiction defined in the statutes. This was a major reform which simplified the federal system over the protest of some of the leaders of the bar.[9]

The need for a merger of the two courts had long been obvious. One justice of the Supreme Court observed that "[i]t had been customary in all, except possibly a few of the largest districts, for the district judge to take up cases from both courts indiscriminately, and it was impossible for one not acquainted with federal jurisdiction, to tell in which court he was at the moment administering justice, although separate dockets and journals kept by separate clerks were provided for each."[10] The Commission to Revise and Codify the Criminal Laws of the United States in its Report in 1899 recommended the merger of the district and circuit courts, for the circuit court judges who had been appointed in 1869 were busily engaged on the new Circuit Court of Appeals. It was estimated that 80% of the sessions of the circuit courts were held by the district court judge. In a Report of the same Commission two years later, of the 904 days of actual sessions of the circuit courts, the district court judges held 535 days, which was not quite the percentage they had previously estimated.[11] The Report concluded, "as both courts commonly sit at the same time and place, we have the incongruity of two courts exercising a jurisdiction concurrent as to some matters and exclusive as to others, with two dockets, two journals, and two clerks, but with a single judge." [12] The justification for the two trial courts had long since ceased to exist.

No attempt was made in the Judicial Code to clarify or expand the jurisdiction of the federal courts except in one limited area. The amount involved for diversity jurisdiction was raised from $2,000 to $3,000. The Circuit Court of Appeals was given final appellate jurisdiction in all criminal cases and appellate jurisdiction from an interlocutory order refusing to grant or dissolve the temporary injunctions. [13]

The Judicial Code of 1911 did not include sections on pleading, evidence or habeas corpus. This was in accordance with the policy of Congress not to attempt too much at one time; these sections were reserved for later action. [14]

One of the duties which the new circuit judges came to perform after 1869 was the appointment of receivers, who found that property was in several different locations in the United States. Since the appointment by a district judge only ran to the district in which he was located, the appointment by a circuit judge extended his control to the geographical limits of the circuit. If there was property outside of this circuit, it was necessary for the judge to consult with the judge of that circuit. Judge Don A. Parde of the Fifth Circuit protested the lack of control of all property, and a provision was enacted giving the receiver control of all property regardless of where it was located. A provision was allowed for an objection to be made to the appointment. [15]

The enactment of the Judicial Code retained some provisions which had outlasted their usefulness. For example, a right to trial by jury in the Supreme Court of the United States was preserved, although such hearings had not been held in over a century. Another section stated an elementary principle of law that "[s]uits in equity shall not be sustained in any court in the United States in any case where a plain, adequate, and complete remedy may be had at law." [16] The statutes enacted during the Civil War governing seizures of property intended to be employed "in aiding, abetting, or promoting any insurrection against the Government of the United States" were preserved in the new Code. [17]

The Judicial Code of 1911 established a special function for the justices of the Supreme Court to issue extraordinary writs. The need for this provision arose when the Attorney General of the state of Minnesota was imprisoned for contempt in disobeying an order of the Circuit Court of the United States enjoining him from continuing certain criminal prosecutions under state statutes. [18] There were numerous examples of conflicts arising where state officials were prohibited from proceeding in their duties by injunctions issued by the federal courts. To prevent this, the Judiciary Act prohibited any judge from granting an interlocutory injunction suspending or restraining the enforcement of any state statute on the basis of its alleged constitutionality. If there was a possibility of irreparable damage, application could be made to any justice of the Supreme Court or to any of the other federal judges for a temporary restraining order. Such orders would remain effective for only a short period of time. A direct appeal could be taken to the Supreme Court of the United States from the order granting or denying such an application. [19]

The Judicial Code of 1911 was the first time Congress had considered a single piece of legislation applying to all federal courts since the Judiciary Act of 1789. It was generally agreed that the new Code was an improvement over the "mass of related but undigested congressional enactments" pertaining to the courts. [20] Yet the Code did little more than address the problem of organization of the courts. Such a complete revision and consolidation of the statutes, in the opinion of many, was long overdue. There were certainly objections to sections within the Act from many leaders of the bar and from legislators who wanted to introduce other reforms. The Code by no means included all the statutory provisions relating to the courts, including those governing court officials, or procedural statutes which could only be found in other sources. Individual problems of the courts were addressed in separate subsequent statutes.

For the first two decades of the Twentieth Century, the merits of a recompilation of the laws of the United States, including the laws governing the courts, were extensively debated. However, the myth that the REVISED STATUTES OF 1874 was a failure was so ingrained that little progress was made against those who did not wish to examine the merits of compiling the laws or the problems such a work engendered. Finally, Congress was able to prepare the UNITED STATES CODE first published in 1926. The laws pertaining to the judiciary were incorporated in Title 28 which was much more comprehensive than the Judicial Code of 1911. The chapters on evidence, procedures, court officers and other topics were included in that title. New numerical designations were assigned to the sections in Title 28, but the old designations to the Judicial Code of 1911 were given as well. For a number of years, after 1926, courts continued to refer to the Judicial Code of 1911 and often to both statutory sources. Organizationally, Title 28 followed the outline of the Judicial Code.

The joint committee established by Congress to oversee the incorporation of the newly enacted statutes in the UNITED STATES CODE worked diligently to incorporate all of the new laws. By 1940, the arrangement of the materials within Title 28 became confusing and the need for a revision was obvious.

In 1944, the House Committee on Revision of the Laws began consideration of Title 28, and an advisory committee was established consisting of legislators, judges and members of the bar. The proposed statute was reviewed extensively by a committee of the Judicial Conference under the chairmanship of Judge Albert B. Maris of the Third Circuit. [21] Another federal judge who made significant contributions was Judge John

J. Parker, Chief Judge of the Fourth Circuit. Both of these judges had attained reputations for their interest and work in improving the functioning of the federal courts.

The new Title 28 of the Code was adopted in 1948 and was generally hailed as a constructive piece of legislation.[22] The new title was the first major review of the judicial statutes since 1911. For this reason, many statutes were consolidated and obsolete materials omitted. Congress had granted to the Supreme Court power to prescribe rules of procedure, and hence, this had made many sections of former laws which were included in all contemporary editions of the UNITED STATES CODE obsolete. Although technically this was not designated as a "code," it was comprehensive and for all practical purposes contained all the laws pertaining to the federal courts.

The new title made several significant changes. One of its unique features was granting to the federal courts the authority to set by rule the times for holding terms of court. Traditionally, since the First Judiciary Act of 1789, Congress had regulated the terms of all federal courts by prescribing the times and places where such terms were to be held. The magnitude of this task is indicated by the fact that between 1789 and 1845, ten acts were passed regulating the times and meetings of the Circuit Courts of New York, nine acts to regulate the terms of the Circuit Courts of Massachusetts, and four acts regulating the Circuit Court of Delaware. Only two courts had been granted the authority at some period during the Nineteenth Century to prescribe the times for their terms.[23] After 1930, Congress gave several courts this authority.

Permitting the federal courts to establish their own terms ended a great many procedural problems. The rules of the court provided that certain motions had to be filed within so many days following the end of the term of court. It was an accepted principle that any court had control over its own judgments during the term they were entered, but this control ceased upon expiration of the term. The court could retain control by a standing order or special order. These principles applied to a motion for new trials, preparation of a bill of exceptions, and the issuance of a writ of error.[24] In those situations in bygone eras, when terms were limited to fourteen days and the court could finish all work within that time, these rules made some sense. However, with the expansion of the business of the court, the terms extended much beyond the normal two week period. For this reason, it became more difficult to determine whether the rules were complied with. Judges could often forget to enter an order terminating the term or the necessary orders extending the time for completing certain orders.[25]

The Judicial Code gave the federal courts other additional powers which they had previously lacked. Prior to this time, a federal court might dismiss an action, but it had no authority to vest another federal court with jurisdiction unless the parties themselves instituted a new suit. The courts for the first time were empowered with the authority to transfer any case to a more convenient forum even though the venue was proper.[26] The revisor's note substantiated the need for this provision by referring to *Baltimore & Ohio Railroad Company v. Kepner.*[27]

The federal courts had frequently suffered the humiliating experience of having a disappointed suitor in their court try to reverse the results of his loss by bringing an action in the state courts.[28] The federal courts were powerless to intervene. Although stated in the negative, the federal courts were granted the power for the first time to enjoin proceedings in a state court by an injunction "where necessary in aid of its jurisdiction, or to protect or effectuate its judgments."[29]

The method of selecting federal jurors had been determined by the laws of the state in which the federal court was located. The Judicial Code of 1948 prescribed uniform standards for the selection of jurors in the federal courts at the recommendation of the Judicial Conference of the United States.[30]

A review of the revisor's notes to Title 28 reveals omissions of many phrases which were surplusage or the substitution of new procedures, such as payment of salaries by the Administrative Office of the Courts or the payment of the salaries of the members of the Supreme Court by the marshal of that court rather than by the Department of Justice. Phrases were added to bring the original statutes into conformity with other sections of the Code. These numerous changes are rather minor in one sense, but important in accurately reflecting the administrative changes made in the law. Provisions were incorporated into Title 28 which were found in other titles of the Code. For example, the "federal courts" of the District of Columbia were brought within this title to emphasize their equality with other federal courts of the same level. The attempt to incorporate the Tax Court within this title failed. The work on the new title was thorough and fundamental, and, as a result of this careful revision, Title 28 was probably the most technically correct collection of judicial statutes of any existing statutory compilation. None other was as concise and exhaustive.

Although the Judicial Code of 1948 has received great praise, a few critics have noted its failure to redistribute the judicial power between the federal and the state courts. Such a herculean task would have been virtually impossible, as a similar project undertaken by the American Law Institute proved.[31] Such is virtually the only substantive criticism of the 1948 Judicial Code in existing literature.[32]

The Judicial Code of 1948 was characterized as disappointing in its coverage.[33] This authority found that the Code was merely a statement and rearrangement of the old matters and that it failed to include other "important jurisdictional grants" as are found in a number of other major acts, such as the Federal Employers' Liability Act or the Securities Act. The few changes of substance were "slight in character." It is correct that a number of special grants of jurisdiction are found in other titles of the UNITED STATES CODE, but to characterize the changes made as being "slight" is to ignore the inestimable changes in language which brought all sections into conformity.

Since 1948, the judicial title has grown not only with amendments but with new materials, such as chapters on the immunities of foreign states, review of orders of federal agencies, and others. After a separation of a quarter of a century, sections applying to the Department of Justice were incorporated in 1966 into this title.[34] Title 28 continues to expand as new adjuncts to the administration of justice are added. The proven advantage of Title 28 is that any amendments can be immediately compared to the existing law, and its need or impact can be more readily determined.

FOOTNOTES TO CHAPTER 10

1. Act of June 27, 1866, 14 STAT. 74.

2. Felix Frankfurter and James M. Landis, THE BUSINESS OF THE SUPREME COURT: A STUDY IN THE FEDERAL JUDICIAL SYSTEM (1928), p.144, fn. 174.

3. S. Rept. No. 388, 61st Cong. 2d sess. p.31. The number of clerks listed were as follows:

> Eastern District, Arkansas, 3 clerks
> Eastern District, Kentucky, 6 clerks
> Western District, Kentucky, 4 clerks
> Western District, Missouri, 4 clerks
> Eastern District, North Carolina, 5 clerks
> Western District, North Carolina, 4 clerks
> Western District, Virginia, 4 clerks
> Western District, Wisconsin, 3 clerks

4. Act of March 3, 1911, sec. 124, 125, 36 STAT. 1132.

5. Act of March 3, 1899, 30 STAT. 1116.

6. Act of June 4, 1897, 30 STAT. 58.

7. Act of March 3, 1899, 30 STAT. 1116; Senate Doc. 68, 57th Cong. 1st sess.

8. Act of March 3, 1911, 36 STAT. 1087.

9. Frankfurter and Landis, *supra,* note 2, p.133.

10. Henry Billings Brown, "The New Federal Judicial Code," 73 CENT. L. J. 279 (1911). This same article is found in 36 REPT. A.B.A. 339 (1911). Brown was a former justice on the Supreme Court.

11. Letter from the Attorney General transmitting A Report of the Commission to Revise and Codify the Criminal and Penal Laws of the United States, 57th Cong. 1st sess., doc. no. 68, p.40.

12. S. Doc. No. 68, 57th Cong. 1st sess., p.2.

13. Jacob Trieber, "The New Federal Judicial Code," 46 AMER. L. REV. 704 (1912).

14. Brown, *supra,* note 10.

15. J.S. Sexton, "The Judicial Code," 7 Proc. Miss. S. Bar Assoc. 99 (1912).

16. Act of March 3, 1911, 36 STAT. 1087, 1163.

17. Act of March 3, 1911, sec. 46, 47, 36 STAT. 1100.

18. Ex parte Young, 209 U.S. 123 (1907).

19. Sexton, *supra,* note 15, p.100.

20. *Ibid,* p.102.

21. H.R. Rept. No. 308, 80th Cong., 1st sess., p.3.

22. Act of June 25, 1948, 62 STAT. 869.

23. The District Court of Illinois was given authority to make all rules for regulation of its terms; Act of March 3, 1851, 9 STAT. 636; similar power granted Circuit Court in the District of Columbia, Act of February 7, 1857, 11 STAT. 158.

24. Michigan Insurance Bank v. Eldred, 143 U.S. 293 (1891); O'Connell v. United States, 253 U.S. 142 (1919).

25. *See* Greyerbiehl v. Hughes Electric Co., 294 Fed. 802 (1923).

26. Act of June 25, 1948, Title 28, sec. 1404(a), 62 STAT. 937.

27. Baltimore & Ohio R. Co. v. Kepner, 314 U.S. 44 (1941).

28. Toucey v. New York Life Insurance Co., 314 U.S. 118 (1941).

29. Act of June 25, 1948, sec. 2283, 62. STAT. 968.

30. H.R. Rept. No. 308, 80th Cong., 1st sess., p.6.

31. The work of the American Law Institute was introduced into Congress but failed of passage although approved by the PROCEEDINGS JUDICIAL CONFERENCE OF THE UNITED STATES (1971), p.79.

32. Herbert Wechsler, "Federal Jurisdiction and the Revision of the Judicial Code," 13 L. & CONTEMP. PROBLEMS 216 (1948). Also, *see* adverse comment in Charles Alan Wright, FEDERAL PRACTICE AND PROCEDURE, v.13 (1975), p.29 for other adverse comments.

33. Moore's Federal Practice, v.13 (2d ed., 1982), sec. 0.61.

34. Act of September 6, 1966, 80 STAT. 611.

Chapter 11

ADMINISTRATIVE CHANGES
IN THE FEDERAL COURTS

Between the enactments of the Judicial Code of 1911 and the judicial Title 28 of the UNITED STATES CODE in 1948, three changes of great consequence were made in the administration of the federal courts. The first of these was the establishment of the Judicial Conference of the United States, followed two decades later by the second change, the creation of the Administrative Office of the Courts. Third, after years of cajoling by the organized bar and other interested parties, the Supreme Court was given the authority to prescribe rules governing procedure in the district courts and later, to govern appellate procedure.[1] These three innovations were responsible for beginning a trend which has unified the administration of the federal courts and ended atomistic tendencies of the federal judges.

During this same period, Congress enacted numerous statutes adding federal judges and organizing new districts and divisions within districts. No basic changes were made in the structure of the federal courts other than transferring jurisdiction from the Supreme Court to the courts of appeals and the enactment of statutes creating new federal questions which would increase the number of cases coming to the federal courts.

The federal district courts enjoyed complete independence in the conduct of their business and in the appointment of staff from their creation in 1789 until 1922. The judges appointed and removed the clerks and other officers of the court.[2] The judges were solely responsible for the administration of each court, and how well this function was performed depended upon them. If the judge made an error in law, this could be corrected on appeal, provided one was taken, but a judge who did not dispose of the business of his court, or permitted slovenly practices in the clerk's and marshal's offices could not be disciplined in any way. If the circuit functions of the justices of the Supreme Court had developed in the same way as the judges on assizes in England, perhaps this oversight would have brought about a more centralized judicial system earlier. No consensus could be reached in Congress on many issues pertaining to the proper organization of the courts including the circuit system. Federal judges would often point out needs of the courts, and these letters would be printed, but no legislation was forthcoming. Occasionally, a few of the federal judges would meet as a group to discuss the business of the courts, but any recommendation had to be forwarded to a member of Congress for legislative enactment.

Such a group of eleven district court judges met on July 12, 1865 at the Cataract House in Niagara Falls, New York. The two items on the agenda of the "Judicial Convocation" were salaries and the creation of an intermediate Court of Errors. This group drew up recommendations and placed them in the hands of members of Congress.[3] Perhaps federal judges in other regions organized similar informal conferences, but no formal structure was authorized for either better supervision of the court officials or the input of judges concerning the functioning of the federal judiciary until 1922.

Judicial Conference of the United States

In 1922, at the urging of Chief Justice Taft, who was interested in judicial administration, Congress established the Judicial Conference of the United States.[4] The statute authorized the Chief Justice of the United States to summon annually to Washington the senior judges of the United States Courts of Appeals for each circuit to make a comprehensive survey of the condition of business in the courts, prepare plans for the temporary assignments of the judges to districts in which they were needed, and make suggestions to the various courts "as may seem in the interest of uniformity and expedition of business."[5]

Since its establishment, the Judicial Conference of the United States has made numerous studies that have resulted in recommendations to Congress which have brought about necessary changes in substantive and procedural laws. During its first decades, the Conference concerned itself with the need for additional judges, urging the district courts to control and expedite cases in their courts and the improvement of the statistical reports filed by the courts. Chief Justices Taft and Hughes encouraged the senior circuit judge to take whatever steps were necessary to prevent delays in the district courts although they had no statutory authority to take any action. However, action by the Conference or the Chief Justice was often persuasive and the conditions were generally remedied.[6]

Another issue that needed resolving was whether the Conference could make recommendations for legislation directly to Congress, although this was done in 1931 when extensive changes were recommended for the Bankruptcy Act. The Conference also expressed opposition to a bill limiting the authority of the federal judge to comment on evidence produced at trial. The authority to make such recommendations was enacted expressly in the Judiciary Code of 1948.[7]

Originally, only the chief judges of the Courts of Appeals for each circuit attended the Judicial Conference of the United States, but this act has been amended to authorize the attendance of the Chief Judge of the Court of Claims and one district court judge from each circuit chosen by the judges at the Judicial Conference of the Circuit.[8] Later amendments have authorized representation from the specialized courts.[9] The Conference has been charged with carrying on a continuous study of the operation and effect of the general rules of practice and procedure. In addition, the Conference must approve the rules adopted by the courts of appeals. [10] The Conference makes recommendations for legislation needed in the federal courts.

Administrative Office of the Courts

Until 1939, funding for the administration and supplies of the federal courts came from the budget of the Department of Justice. Even the report of the Judicial Conference of the United States was submitted to the Attorney General of the United States who incorporated it into his annual report. When the Conference recommended the appointment of additional judges, the Attorney General joined in its recommendation if he approved of the judges so named. Such an arrangement was the source of friction and acrimonious misunderstandings between the courts and officials in the Justice Department. The federal judges were resentful of this dependence.

Fiscal supervision of the courts originated when the supervision of the accounts of the clerks and the marshals was transferred to the Department of Justice upon its creation in 1870. [11] For some years thereafter, the appropriations for both the courts and the Department of Justice were grouped under the heading "Judiciary" in the Appropriation Acts until such time as this was changed to the Department of Justice.

The Judicial Conference considered various proposals to transfer the control of budgets and other administrative matters into the courts almost from its inception. From the idea of appropriating the necessary budgets and placing the responsibility for expenditures in the hands of the clerks of the Circuit Courts of Appeals after their creation, this proposal and others received elaboration by the chief judges of the circuits. Controversy over the court packing plan in 1937 unfortunately cooled the enthusiasm of the Chief Justice toward any suggestions coming from the Attorney General who had zealously supported this plan to appoint additional judges to the bench when they reached a certain age. However, another forceful individual who was the president of the American Bar Association at that time gave his support to the bill and actively worked for its adoption. Arthur T. Vanderbilt of New Jersey, a dynamic leader in the efforts to improve the administration of justice, encouraged and lobbied for the enactment of a bill to make the Judiciary a separate branch of government in practice as it had been in theory. [12] In 1939, the Administrative Office of the United States Courts was created to supervise the administration of the courts.

This office furnishes the courts with the necessary supplies and aids in the central control of the courts through the preparation of statistics as to the status of dockets, including the number of cases filed and other facts. These statistics had taken on significant substance as a measure of the performance of the courts and the justification for the appointment of new judges and other personnel. The office has also been a strong influence in attaining an efficient administration within the courts.[13] Such court officers as the clerks, marshals and referees in bankruptcy are supervised by this office.

The primary function of the Administrative Office of the Courts was to prepare and submit the budget estimate for the federal courts, bypassing the Bureau of the Budget, the office which ordinarily received expenditure estimates, and sending it directly to Congress. The director was appointed by the Judicial Conference, but he was responsible for appointment of all subordinates in the office. Like every other governmental body, its duties have grown.

Since the successful establishment of this office, it has been a model for similar organization in the states, and through this influence, the office has had its greatest impact on judicial administration in this country.

Circuit Conference

The statute of 1939 creating the Administrative Office of the Courts created two new bodies on the circuit level — the Circuit Conference and the Circuit Council. In considering whether to place control of the work of the federal courts in the hands of the Judicial Conference of the United States or the Supreme Court, Chief Justice Hughes and other leaders in the federal judiciary urged that the decisions relating to the work of the judges should be made at the circuit level, by other judges, rather than by an administrative officer. The creation of the circuit conference and circuit council was done with the expectation that the work of the federal courts would be managed more expeditiously and that judges would be prodded into deciding cases without delay.

The chief judge, formerly known as the senior circuit judge, was authorized to call all the judges including the district court judges to an annual conference to discuss the business of the courts in that circuit and to devise "ways and means of improving the administration of justice within the circuit."[14] Members of the bar could be invited to participate in the programs.

A number of such conferences had been called previously and had met regularly for a number of years prior to 1939.[15] One of the first such circuit conferences had been held in the Fourth Circuit continuously since 1931 under the leadership of Judge John J. Parker. Chief Justice Hughes had attended several of these conferences as circuit justice and was impressed with the chance that such a meeting afforded the participants to exchange views about the workings of the federal courts.[16] The Judicial Conference of the Courts had approved such conferences in the Sixth and the Eighth Circuits, but little is known of their activities since no published reports are available. By 1939, Chief Justice Hughes and other members of the federal bench were convinced of the value of such conferences and urged their establishment.

The primary accomplishment of these conferences was the opportunity afforded the judges of discussing the administration of the courts in their circuits, providing a forum for the exchange of views. Some chief judges were slow to embrace this opportunity to call such conferences, for the statutory authorization was not mandatory. The alacrity with which these conferences were convened depended upon the leadership of the chief judge. One authority has summarized the accomplishments of the conferences rather accurately:

> Success depended on the chief judge. If he had, as some did, an 'ever-lasting enthusiasm' for the conferences, they came off well. If not, they proved less than satisfactory.[17]

During these conferences in several circuits, all the judges met separately in an executive session to consider judicial business without the attendance of the lawyers who participated in the conference. All judges are required to attend unless excused by the chief judge, but this is more honored in the breach than in the observance.

Along with the authorization to annually convene a circuit conference, the judges of the courts of appeals were constituted as a judicial council to meet and consider the business of the circuit. The council was given the authority to issue all necessary orders for the effective and expeditious administration of the business of the courts within its circuit.[18] The district court judges were enjoined "promptly to carry out the directions of the council as to the administration of the business of their respective courts." From this beginning, the duties and powers of the circuit judicial council have expanded while other powers have gradually been assumed for the lack of another forum in which they could be resolved.

The concept of a judicial council was not embraced enthusiastically by the federal judges. Judge John Biggs, Jr., chief judge of the Third Circuit, was led to state in 1961, that:

> One of the areas in which Congress is inclined to be critical of the judiciary, and I think with some reason, is the failure of some of the Judicial Councils of the Circuits to fulfill the functions which Congress intended they should fulfill.[19]

The decision in the case of *Chandler v. Judicial Council* clearly shows the division among judges as to the extent that the council can or should control the flow of work in the district courts.[20] This debate has continued without resolution.

One of the flaws perceived in the organization of the council was the lack of representation of the district court judges. Any suggestions for improvement in the work of the trial courts should come from the trial bench rather than from the appellate court judges who review a very limited amount of the work performed on the trial level. A consultation role for the trial judges was viewed as insufficient for any meaningful changes in the flow of work. In some circuits, the district court judges organized an informal council, such as the one established in 1948 known as the Ninth Circuit District Judges Association. Such associations were organized in other circuits, but these organizations have escaped any mention in the literature. On a national scale the judges organized the National Conference of Federal Trial Judges which met annually.[21] In 1980, the composition of the circuit council was changed to include the chief judge and a number of both circuit judges and district court judges as determined by all active judges within the circuit.[22] It is a growing perception that since the establishment of the Administrative Office of the Courts, Congress has tended to pass on to the Judiciary control over its operations. Now,

> Councils may pass on issues running the gamut from decisions on the most mundane housekeeping details to critical cases of judicial misbehavior on which the judiciary's reputation hangs.[23]

Chief Judges

An office that evolved and came to be statutorily recognized in the Judicial Title of 1948 was the Chief Judge. The administrative aspect of running a court was not a significant issue during the Nineteenth Century when the districts were presided over by a single judge, who was responsible for the appointment of all subordinate court officials and was literally answerable to no one. The number of court officials, such as the clerk, was authorized by statute and the power of appointment vested in the circuit judge, who was a justice of the Supreme Court, or in the district judge. Deputies could generally be appointed without specific statutory authorization, and paid from fees generated by the court. The dockets of the court and other administrative matters would be controlled by the judge, who generally had no experience in this area. For this reason, clerks were left to run their own offices without the supervision of the judge. There can be little doubt that Congress envisioned in the First Judiciary Act that the justice of the Supreme Court would preside at the sessions of the circuit courts and because of his rank, would take an active role in the administration of the federal trial courts. In every statute of the Nineteenth Century, the justices were given precedence over all other judges. It is possible that had this system unfolded as envisioned, the justices of the Supreme Court would have developed into administrators of the local federal courts and would have provided the necessary contacts among the members of the federal bench.

Since the Supreme Court from its establishment consisted of six members, it was necessary to have a presiding justice with certain administrative powers. For this reason, the office of Chief Justice of the United States was established, though its duties were left largely undefined.

Since 1789, additional administrative functions, other than presiding at the sessions of the court, have become part of that office. This office was developed by the prestige of the incumbents, through traditions and from statutes that have added administrative functions. Not only is the chief justice responsible for the daily operation of the staff of the court and for functioning as a working member in deciding cases, he must preside in the Judicial Conference and appoint its committees. He influences the programs of that organization and the Judicial Center. These are two offices through which the chief justice influences the functioning of the federal courts. He has contacts with the chief judges of the circuits on a wide range of problems, and assigns judges to other courts. His advice is sought by members of Congress, as well as by state and federal judges.[24] The successors of John Jay and John Marshall now exercise a broad range of powers. Minimal attention has been given to how each chief justice exercised that office.

Little need existed for a similar office in the lower federal courts until the establishment of the Circuit Courts of Appeals in 1891 and the later addition of several judges on the district courts. Upon the establishment of the Circuit Courts of Appeals, the statute provided that the judge senior in commission would preside.[25] It would be of great interest to learn how through custom the senior circuit judge began to manage the assignment of cases and judges to panels and other such administrative functions, including the supervision of court personnel. Much depended upon the strength and personality of the senior circuit judge. The recognition of the senior circuit judge in the statute establishing the Judicial Conference gave these officers a stronger role in the administration of their own court and the district courts within their circuits. When the bench of the several Circuit Courts of Appeals consisted of as few as four members, the judges could agree among themselves on the distribution of work, but with any increase in the number of judges, such consensus became improbable. The need for an administrative judge was recognized by a 1934 statute which provided that when the senior circuit judge was "unable because of illness or other cause to exercise any power given or to perform any duty imposed by law," the next judge in seniority of commission would act in this capacity.[26] No enumeration of duties referred to in this statute was included, and neither is any specific reason given for its enactment. In all probability, some judges failed to assume this function because of some perceived defect in previous practice. The title of senior circuit judge was changed in 1948 to chief judge, but the only duty imposed was that he would "have precedence and preside at any session of the court" which he attended.[27] The other duties referred to in the statute included those that had become associated with the office by tradition in each circuit or imposed by statute. Today, the chief judge is responsible for controlling the court's budget, providing office accommodations for court personnel, developing new techniques to improve the functioning of the court, and responding to requests of judicial agencies such as the Administrative Office of the Courts.

In 1903, when a second judge was added to the District Courts in Minnesota and the Southern District of New York, the statute provided that in Minnesota the senior circuit judge would make all assignments of cases, whereas nothing was said about the same functions in the Southern District of New York.[28] Obviously, the administration of the court was not of great concern to those responsible for drafting the statute. The pattern was established that in some districts where a second judge was added, Congress would provide that judges may agree among themselves upon the division of business and assignment of cases for trial and if they did not, then the senior circuit judge of the circuit should make all necessary orders for the assignment of cases.[29] In the Judicial Code of 1911, these provisions were made applicable to all "districts having more than one district judge."[30] In 1939, the circuit judicial council was organized "for the purpose of considering the state of the business of the courts and advising ways and means of improving the administration of justice."[31] This council assumed a role in the assignment of work where the judges could not agree among themselves.

The position of chief judge in a multi-judge district court received statutory recognition in the Judicial Title of 1948.[32] The revisors of the code noted that they were employing this term "in view of the great increase of administrative duties of such judge."[33] Since that formalization of this office in 1948, although it may have existed in practice before, the duties have given the chief judges great influence within their districts. The chief judge may be equal among other district judges, but through this office he can influence the functioning of the court over which he presides.

The District Court for the District of Columbia has always been among the largest in the number of judges, and for that reason, it was the first district court in the federal system which had a presiding judge. A statute of 1863 had designated a chief justice in the Supreme Court for the District of Columbia which later became the district court.[34] When the title of the Supreme Court of the District of Columbia was changed to the District Court for the District of Columbia in 1936, the title "chief justice" was continued in use until 1948.[35] The first occasion in which the chief justice or chief judge was given a statutory duty to assign a judge to a specific type of case was in 1928, when a justice in the Supreme Court of the District of Columbia was assigned to sit in condemnation cases and when not sitting there, could be assigned to other cases.[36] Subsequent statutes defining this office have not been as explicit.

Judicial Administration in the Last Half of the Twentieth Century

After 1950, the functioning of the federal courts received greater scrutiny from Congress and to a lesser degree, from the legal profession. After Earl Warren became Chief Justice in 1954, he began to deliver what he termed the state of the judiciary messages before the annual meetings of the American Law Institute.[37] This was a gradual development, but his successor in office, Warren Burger, used the same forum to speak out on the needs of the federal courts. With Warren's interest and encouragement, conferences were organized to deliberate upon the same theme. One of the earliest conferences on the federal courts was held in 1956 and known as the Attorney General's Conference on Court Congestion. Numerous hearings have been conducted by the Judiciary Committees of Congress. As a result of all this attention, after 1960, a number of supporting staff and institutions were added, and the administrative practices were streamlined.

No single event was responsible for these dramatic changes, except for a general realization that the growing number of cases had to be handled by some other means than the mere addition of judges to the bench. The Judicial Conference played a significant role in urging changes by suggesting various programs for keeping abreast of the dockets. In fact, the chief judges of circuits in the private proceedings of the Judicial Conference were critical of certain judges who failed to administer the courts in which they presided effectively. The many innovations brought about in streamlining procedure are too numerous to be considered in detail, but it should be noted that often many of these changes were conceived and put into practice by a local federal district court before the practice became accepted nationally. Such was the case with the six-member jury.[38]

One of the perceived needs was for education of the newly appointed federal district court judges to familiarize them with problems of judicial administration. A first step was taken in 1958 when sentencing institutes in each circuit were authorized under the auspices of the Judicial Conference of the United States.[39] The purpose of these conferences was to study and formulate objectives, standards, and policies for sentencing those convicted under the federal criminal laws. The chief judge of each circuit was authorized to invite the judges of the district courts to attend under such conditions as would not delay the work of the courts. Several of these institutes were held and their proceedings published.[40] These conferences have contributed immeasurably to the better administration of the criminal law, acquainting the judges with the problems of parole, probation and penology, subjects with which so few judges as lawyers are familiar. A number of private groups organized other educational programs for newly appointed federal judges until this function was taken over by a Judicial Center.

Gradually, following the decade of 1960, it became plain to many judges, including Chief Justice Earl Warren, that improvements in the functioning of the federal courts could be brought about only through study and analysis of various proposals, a task that the busy federal courts could not undertake. If the federal courts were to keep up with their ever increasing dockets, other measures, including more effective managerial techniques, would have to be applied to the handling of trials. Merely adding more judges had not proven efficacious in reducing the backlog of cases.[41] The committee of the Judicial Conference which had sponsored conferences for newly appointed federal judges developed the idea of a center for the study of the operations of the federal courts.

In 1967, President Johnson recommended the establishment of the Federal Judicial Center for the purpose of promoting a more effective federal judicial system through a program of research, planning and education. It is rather significant that this proposal was included in his "Message on Crime in America." At that time, the federal courts were immersed in the federalization of all criminal laws and were inundated with criminal appeals. The proposal of the Center was warmly supported by Congress because it was felt that the Center could study and develop administrative techniques to control the tremendous increase in the business of the courts.[42] The Center was established in 1967 under the chairmanship of retired Justice Tom C. Clark.[43]

A number of reasons dictated the establishment of the Center separate from the Administrative Office of the Courts. Originally, the Administrative Office was expected to undertake studies which would lead to the more effective performance of the courts, but unfortunately, for many reasons, this never materialized. The promoters of the Center wanted objective evaluations of proposals which they argued could not come from an agency so closely involved in working relations with all branches of the judiciary.[44] Although some educational programs for court personnel had been sponsored by the Administrative Office, more were needed and have since become a regular feature of the work of the Center.[45] Much of the work done has not been dramatic; nonetheless, the Center's persistent study of limited aspects of the operations in the courts has resulted in immeasurable improvements in court management and the professionalization of the supporting staff. The studies conducted by the Center have influenced the rules and the development of the sentencing commission. Nothing is more prosaic than court reporting until one realizes the extent that courts and litigants depend upon it.[46] A study of this subject helped to modernize the court practices. From this work by the Center, state courts have profited as well.

The supporting staff for the federal judges has been augmented significantly since 1959. In that year, the district court judges were authorized to appoint law clerks without getting permission of the chief judge of the circuit.[47] In justification for law clerks, the Judicial Conference trotted out the statistics on the increase in the number of cases in the federal courts claiming that the availability of clerks would aid the judge in handling more cases. In 1970, the position of circuit executive was established to relieve the chief judge of each circuit of the burdens of the day-to-day management of the business of the court.[48] The control of budgeting and accounting procedures of any growing organization is an onerous task which the circuit executive assumed. Good management practices, so the theory holds, require statistics which the circuit executive was required to gather. The circuit executive is appointed by the Circuit Judicial Council from among candidates who have been certified.

In the following years, the chief justice of the United States was authorized to appoint an administrative assistant to relieve him of some administrative chores.[49] In 1982, each of the Courts of Appeals was authorized to appoint staff assistants and staff attorneys whose duties were left undefined.[50] In the Ninth Circuit, the staff attorneys were used to screen briefs and classify the subject matter of each so that the same types of cases would be assigned to the same panel of the court for consideration.[51] Prior to this, the Courts of Appeals had been permitted in the Appropriations Act to appoint a senior law clerk who performed many of these functions. Several of these positions were put into practice long before they were authorized by statute by using existing staff positions, such as using a position for a guard to create an archivist, although the courts did not have this authority.[52]

The judges of the Nineteenth Century would be envious of the supporting staff which has been furnished to the judges in the last decades of the Twentieth Century. Dictating opinions is a far cry from writing them out in longhand; having law clerks scramble off to ever enlarging law libraries to do the laborious tasks of "finding" the law is a relief from a jejune task; having quarters in a building designed to be a courthouse rather than quarters grudgingly furnished by some other agency is more prestigious. All these changes have been the products of the administrative changes brought about since 1922. To borrow an advertising phrase, Yes, the federal courts have come a long way! But one might wonder if the federal courts are not becoming overburdened with staff, requiring more time in supervision to the detriment of deciding cases, which is the perceived function of the courts.

In the opinion of many observers, the authority of the Supreme Court of the United States to prescribe rules to govern procedure in civil and criminal cases in the trial courts was the significant event in the history of the federal courts. As a result of this act, the practice and procedure in the numerous federal judicial districts has become uniform and no longer depends upon the vagaries of the local judge's interpretation of the commingling of local and federal practices. The federal courts had at last cast off dependency on the local legal system.

The last remaining tie of the federal courts to the practices of the states was the selection of jury panels which was severed in 1968. The First Judiciary Act provided that jurors would be selected "in each State . . . according to the mode of forming juries therein now practised (sic), so far as the laws are the same shall render such designation practicable." The judge could designate that jurors would be selected "from such parts of the

district . . . so as not to incur an unnecessary expense, or unduly to burden
the citizens of any part of the district with such services."[53] These
standards remained virtually unchanged throughout the entire Nineteenth
Century. However, Congress did legislate and prescribe various details for
different districts. For example, the circuit or district courts in North
Carolina could order a grand or petit jury to attend any special term.[54]
Other judges were given special authority to deal with other aspects of jury
selection. Because the federal courts had such freedom in making the
selection of panels over a period of time, each established its own method
of selecting names. A common method was the use of the "key men"
method whereby citizens of the community who were thought to have
extensive contacts would provide the names of prospective jurors.[55] In
1968, the jury system was completely changed to meet the ever increasing
standards formulated by the Supreme Court in its decisions.[56] Under this
statute, the names of prospective jurors were to be randomly selected from
persons on the voting lists who met certain objective standards.

As the number of cases filed in the federal courts was significantly
increasing after 1970, other solutions were sought to reduce their numbers.
A committee was appointed to address the workload of the Supreme
Court.[57] The most controversial proposal of the committee was the
creation of a National Court of Appeals which would review cases coming
to the Supreme Court. Another commission was appointed to study the
appellate system, and this commission's chief recommendation was a
division of the Fifth and Ninth Circuits.[58]

Frequent studies were made by Congressional committees on the
needs of the federal judiciary: additional judges, enhancing the authority
of the magistrate system in the federal courts, streamlining judicial
administration by reorganizing the specialized courts, as well as other
measures.[59] All of these hearings and studies have resulted in numerous
volumes containing many proposed changes which have yet to be enacted
into law. More changes were made in the structure, practices and
personnel of the courts after 1950 than at any other period in judicial
history. After this mid-point of the Twentieth Century, the courts were
gradually changed from a leisurely paced operation to a more streamlined
and highly structured organization where the workload became more
demanding. This was a period of great change and transition for the
courts.

FOOTNOTES TO CHAPTER 11

1. Henry P. Chandler, "Some Major Advances in the Federal Judicial System," 31 F.R.D. 309, 321 (1963).

2. *Ibid,* p.309, 314.

3. Donald O. Dewey, "Hoosier Justice: The Journal of David McDonald: 1864-1868," 62 INDIANA MAG. OF HISTORY 209 (1966).

4. Act of September 14, 1922, sec. 2, 42 STAT. 838.

5. Act of September 14, 1922, sec. 2, 42 STAT. 838.

6. Chandler, *supra,* note 1, p.309, 348.

7. *Ibid,* p.309, 354.

8. Act of July 9, 1956, sec. 1(d), 70 STAT. 497.

9. Act of September 19, 1961, 75 STAT. 356.

10. Act of July 11, 1958, 72 STAT. 356.

11. Act of June 22, 1870, sec. 15, 16 STAT. 164.

12. Chandler, *supra,* note 1, p.309, 367.

13. Act of August 7, 1939, 53 STAT. 1224.

14. Act of August 7, 1939, sec. 307, 53 STAT. 1224.

15. John W. Oliver, "Reflections on the History of Circuit Judicial Councils and Circuit Judicial Conferences," 64 F.R.D. 214, 217 (1975).

16. Chandler, *supra,* note 1, p.309, 385.

17. Peter Graham Fish, THE POLITICS OF FEDERAL JUDICIAL ADMINIS-TRATION (1973), p.341.

18. Act of August 7, 1939, sec. 306, 53 STAT. 1224.

19. John Biggs, Jr., "Some Observations on Judicial Administration," 29 F.R.D. 464, 468 (1962); J. Edward Lumbard, "The Place of the Federal Judicial Councils in the Administration of the Courts," 47 A.B.A.J.169 (1961).

20. Chandler v. Judicial Council of the Tenth Circuit, 398 U.S. 74 (1970).

21. Oliver, *supra,* note 15, p.214, 220.

22. Act of October 15, 1980, 94 STAT. 2035.

23. Fish, *supra,* note 17, p.398.

24. These duties are fully discussed in S. Rept. No. 92-616, 92d Cong. 2d sess., reprinted in 1972 U.S. CODE CONG. & ADM. NEWS 1977.

25. Act of March 3, 1891, sec. 3, 26 STAT. 827.

26. Act of May 23, 1934, 48 STAT. 796.

27. Act of June 25, 1948, sec. 45, 62 STAT. 871.

28. Minnesota, Act of February 4, 1903, 32 STAT. 795; New York, Act of February 9, 1903, 32 STAT. 795.

29. The following acts provided for the district judges to agree among themselves on division of work: Nebraska, Act of February 27, 1907, 34 STAT. 997; California, Northern District, Act of March 2, 1907, 34 STAT. 1253; Oregon and Western District of Washington, Act of March 2, 1907, 35 STAT. 686.

30. Act of March 3, 1911, sec. 23, 36 STAT. 1090.

31. Act of August 7, 1939, sec. 307, 53 STAT. 1224.

32. S. Rept. No. 1559, 80th Cong. 2d sess.

33. Revisor's comment on sec. 136, Sen. Rept. 1559, 80th Cong. 2d sess.; Act of June 25, 1948, sec. 136, 62 STAT. 897.

34. When the Supreme Court was created in 1863, it consisted of four judges, one of whom was designated as Chief Justice. Act of March 3, 1863, 12 STAT. 763.

35. Act of June 25, 1936, 49 STAT. 1921.

36. Act of December 20, 1928, 45 STAT. 1056.

37. The speeches are generally found in the PROCEEDINGS of the American Law Institute and other publications including 25 F.R.D. 213 (1960).

38. Edward J. Devitt, "The Six Man Jury in Federal Court," 53 F.R.D. 273 (1972).

39. Act of August 25, 1958, 72 STAT. 845.

40. *See* 27 F.R.D. 287 (1961); 30 F.R.D. 185 (1962).

41. This thought has been expressed in many ways in many places, but see 1967 U.S. CODE CONG. & ADM. NEWS 2404.

42. S. Rept. No. 781, 90th Cong. 1st sess., 1967 U.S. CODE CONG. & ADM. NEWS 2404.

43. Act of December 20, 1967, 81 STAT. 1907.

44. 1967 U.S. CODE CONG. & ADM. NEWS 2410-2411.

45. *See* "Reports of the Conferences for District Court Judges," conducted by the Federal Judicial Center, February 11-14, 1974, 64 F.R.D.225 (1975).

46. J.M. Greenwood, et al., A COMPARATIVE EVALUATION OF STENO-GRAPHIC AND AUDIOTAPE METHODS FOR THE UNITED STATES DISTRICT COURT REPORTING (1983).

47. Act of September 1, 1959, PL 86-221, 73 STAT. 452.

48. Act of January 5, 1971, PL 91-647, 84 STAT. 1907; 1970 U.S. CODE CONG. & ADM. NEWS 5876.

49. Act of March 1, 1972, PL 92-238, 31, 86 STAT. 46; 1972 U.S. CODE CONG. & ADM. NEWS 1977.

50. Act of April 2, 1982, PL 97-164, 120, 96 STAT. 34.

51. Judicial Conference, Second Circuit, 1984, 106 F.R.D. 163.

52. 1982 U.S. CODE CONG. & ADM. NEWS 27.

53. Act of September 24, 1789, sec. 29, 1 STAT. 88.

54. Act of June 4, 1872, sec. 4, 17 STAT. 215.

55. H.R. Rept. No. 1076, 90th Cong. 2d sess., p. 3; Judicial Conference of the United States, REPORT, OPERATION OF THE JURY SYSTEM, 42 F.R.D. 353 (1967).

56. Act of March 27, 1968, 82 STAT. 53.

57. "Report of the Study on the Caseload of the Supreme Court," 57 F.R.D. 573 (1972). This committee was known as the Freund Committee after the Chairman, Professor Paul A. Freund.

58. Act of October 13, 1972, 86 STAT. 807; "COMMISSION ON REVISION OF THE FEDERAL COURT APPELLATE SYSTEM" (1973), 62 F.R.D. 223 (1974).

59. Myron H. Bright, "The Changing Nature of the Federal Appeals Process in the 1970's," 65 F.R.D. 469 (1975).

Chapter 12

GROWTH OF FEDERAL JURISDICTION

For the lawyer, jurisdiction is an important issue as this governs what controversies are brought into which courts and determines whether the litigation can proceed in the federal or state courts. Jurisdiction often shapes the issues considered by the judges. The fact that the amount involved in diversity cases was $500 or more obscures the result that certain disputes involving matters where no monetary value could be attached were excluded, including such issues as divorce, adoption and crimes. The jurisdiction of the federal courts has expanded since their establishment in 1789.

The jurisdiction of the federal courts as defined in Article III, section 2 of the Constitution extends to all cases arising under the Constitution and the laws and treaties of the United States, to all cases of admiralty, to controversies where the United States is a party, and to controversies between one or more states or between citizens of the same state claiming lands under grants from other states. The Supreme Court of the United States was given original jurisdiction in suits against ambassadors and in all actions where a state was a party.

The jurisdiction conferred by the Judiciary Act of 1789 upon the newly established federal courts was not the complete federal jurisdiction as defined in the Constitution. A broad jurisdiction was conferred upon the courts in the ill-fated Judiciary Act of 1801, which was repealed very shortly after its enactment. Because the act was only in effect for a few months, it has not been determined if any federal court took jurisdiction under this provision.[1] It was not until 1875 that the courts were given complete constitutional jurisdiction. The significance of the failure to have this jurisdiction as defined by the Constitution can be explained by the fact that the federal courts had only those powers given to them by statute. They were embarrassed to find that in absence of a statute, they could not punish for the simple act of interfering with the federal survey of public lands.[2] This defect had to be supplied by statute. In numerous early decisions, the Supreme Court stressed the fact that the federal courts, especially the circuit court, had a "limited jurisdiction. . . . And the fair presumption is . . . that a cause is without its jurisdiction till the contrary appears."[3]

The first Judiciary Act of 1789 conferred jurisdiction on the district courts for all crimes committed in the district or upon the high seas where the punishment did not exceed whipping, a fine of $100 or a term of imprisonment not exceeding six months. The district courts had exclusive jurisdiction in all seizures under the revenue laws of the United States and in admiralty cases. Civil jurisdiction in cases brought by the government was limited to matters exceeding $100.[4]

The circuit court was given jurisdiction over all crimes except for those criminal acts which were reserved for the district court. Suits in equity were conferred upon the circuit courts. Further, the circuit courts were given jurisdiction where the amount in controversy was in excess of $500, as well as when the United States was a plaintiff or when an alien or citizen of another state was a party. The diversity of citizenship cases has been the source of much controversy, for it is argued that it has brought many cases into the federal courts which more properly belong in the state courts. The accepted rationale for this diversity jurisdiction is that the federal courts were tribunals presumed to be free from local influence. This theory was specifically mentioned in at least one decision of the Supreme Court, and this reasoning has been accepted in the literature on the subject.[5] Whether this concern was directed at the state courts or the state legislatures cannot be determined. One authority has concluded that the feeling abroad at the time of the establishment of the federal government was that the federal courts "would be strong courts, creditors' courts, business men's courts."[6] All attempts to repeal the diversity jurisdiction have been met with strong opposition and, therefore, have failed.[7]

An area of jurisdiction which has lost its importance covers disputes over land titles issued by two different states. Such disputes were frequent in the Eighteenth Century and resulted from overlapping claims to the same area by different states. The original boundaries of the colonies as established by the English government overlapped, and, for that reason, two or more states would have claims in the same area and each would grant lands in the disputed areas. The Articles of Confederation provided for a means of settling such disputes by the Continental Congress, and it was not unexpected that this jurisdiction would be vested in the circuit courts by the Constitution.[8] Such disputes continued well into the Nineteenth Century as new territories or states were created from existing territories. These disputes were replaced by litigation arising from the various dispositions of the federal lands.

The circuit courts were given the authority to review the decisions of the district courts by writ of error when the matter in controversy exceeded $50 and by writ of appeal in admiralty and maritime cases where the amount exceeded $300. In time, these cases were reserved for the justice when he came out on circuit. The printed opinions of the federal courts other than those of the Supreme Court in cases other than admiralty were also cases considered by the justices.

Another aspect of the jurisdiction of the circuit courts was the right to remove cases from the state courts into the federal courts when the latter had jurisdiction and the amount exceeded the value of $500, exclusive of costs. This right could be exercised only by the defendant by posting sufficient bail with the state court, and the state judge was required to accept this security for his entering copies of "the process against him" in the circuit court.[9] The state court could proceed no further in the case. It was certainly logical that should the plaintiff bring his suit in the state court, he should abide by the action of that forum.[10] Under no circumstances was the state court to allow a reduction in the amount claimed to keep the case from being removed.[11] To exercise his option, the defendant had to be a resident of a different state or an alien. The court decided early that where several defendants had the right to remove a cause, some having appeared and others having not, those who had appeared could not alone remove the cause.[12] This was later permitted by statute. Again, removal of causes from state to federal courts began with a limited application but later expanded. The authors of the Judiciary Act of 1789 believed that diversity jurisdiction would be more effective if these cases were removed by the defendant if the plaintiff had commenced them in a state court.

Obviously, conflicts in jurisdiction between the two trial courts of the federal system arose. At least one suit in the Supreme Court had to make it clear that the circuit courts had no original jurisdiction in suits for penalties and forfeitures arising under the laws of the United States, for this jurisdiction was exclusive with the district courts.[13] One would wonder why there are not more cases reporting conflicts in jurisdiction between the two federal trial courts. The answer may be found in the fact that there were no separate judges for these courts and when Congress created such judges in 1869, there were too few in number to handle all the business of the circuit courts. Many of the difficulties which normally would have arisen by the existence of two trial courts with overlapping jurisdiction were obliterated by the fact that the district court judge held the terms of the circuit court.

In contrasting the jurisdiction of the United States district and circuit courts, it is apparent that the latter courts were considered by the authors of the Judiciary Act of 1789 as the chief trial courts in the federal system.[14] However, this distinction began to erode almost immediately as Congress began to give the judges of the district courts the authority to act on certain matters before the justice of the Supreme Court (who was the circuit court judge) arrived for a term of court, or by assigning concurrent jurisdiction to the two courts over the same matter. Between 1789 and 1911, when the circuit courts were abolished, the differences between the two courts eroded until it became obvious that only one trial court was desirable.

From the beginning, the federal courts required that their jurisdiction be limited to precisely those matters defined in the statutes. This led to a description of the federal courts as being "inferior courts," a contemporary legal term that had a technical meaning. In one of its earliest cases, the Supreme Court decided that the federal courts were not inferior courts in the common law sense, "nor are its proceedings subject to the scrutiny of those narrow rules, which the caution or jealousy, of the Courts at Westminister, long applied to Courts of that denomination. . . ."[15] The jurisdiction was limited in the sense that it could not be assumed that the court had jurisdiction of a matter, as would a court of unlimited jurisdiction. The plaintiff must clearly state the jurisdiction invoked; this has continued to be a requirement of pleading.[16] It is to the credit of the federal courts in the Nineteenth Century that they did not, by judicial interpretation, seek to exercise the full range of federal jurisdiction granted by the Constitution, but rather recognized Congress' power to grant and withhold matters from their jurisdiction. The federal courts in the Nineteenth Century did not have the benefit of the academic juris-prudents urging an expansion of jurisdiction.

As Congress enacted new laws, jurisdiction was specifically conferred upon the federal courts. The various copyright acts conferred jurisdiction upon the circuit courts, as did the First Bankruptcy Act.[17] New penalties were frequently defined under such statutes as the Post Office Acts during the Nineteenth Century which added to the caseload of the federal courts. These specific grants of jurisdiction arising under rights created by federal laws resulted, in time, in a large number of miscellaneous statutes, all involving different requirements for jurisdictional amounts, service and venue. A number of these statutes granted concurrent jurisdiction to both the circuit and district courts. It would be tedious to recite all of the individual statutes defining many types of criminal omissions or new areas governed by federal statutes which added to the cases coming into the federal courts. The focus here is on those broader additions to the jurisdictions of the courts.

One of the most interesting chapters of this early period involved the attempt of the federal government to confer jurisdiction, usually in criminal matters, upon the state courts. In 1797, the state courts were given jurisdiction in matters involving collection of duties under the Revenue Acts and the remission of fines.[18] In 1806, certain county courts in Pennsylvania and New York were given jurisdiction over all complaints and prosecutions for fines, penalties and forfeitures arising under the Revenue Acts.[19] This jurisdiction did not extend to civil cases for collection of duties or bonds given for security in payment of duties.

The Post Office Act of 1799 gave the state courts concurrent jurisdiction with the federal courts over violations of that Act.[20] This jurisdiction was rejected in Virginia where the courts held that the state courts could not try an individual for the violation of an act made a crime by another jurisdiction.[21] Chief Justice Marshall stated later in the Supreme Court of the United States that "the courts of no country execute the penal laws of another."[22] This experiment of granting state courts concurrent jurisdiction was ended and not attempted thereafter.[23]

The dependence of the federal courts upon the states is not fully appreciated in the present century. Congress on numerous occasions drew upon the state statutes as the source of law for the federal courts. For example, the fees for the marshals were made the same as those for the sheriffs in the state.[24] By the latter decades of the Nineteenth Century, the federal courts had grown to full maturity with the necessary number of courts and other supporting administrative machinery; dependency on the states was no longer necessary.

Numerous federal statutes were enacted to aid in prosecuting the War of 1812. Several of the special revenue statutes added a unique venue requirement which has not been repeated. The official charged with the enforcement of this measure could recover all fines or other sums due the government in the district court unless the cause of the action or the complaint arose more than fifty miles from the city in which the federal courts normally met; then the action could be brought in the nearest state court.[25]

The War of 1812 had an impact upon the admiralty jurisdiction of the circuit and district courts due to the nature of naval warfare of that period. One of the accepted practices was to issue letters of marque and reprisal to owners of ships who then went out on the seas making prizes of the enemy's merchant ships. Whether a ship was a legitimate prize had to be determined in a court known as a prize court. The district courts were given jurisdiction in prize cases, and the circuit courts were given jurisdiction over the crime of piracy as defined by the law of nations.[26] The definition of piracy was extended to include robbery on the high seas, or in any roadstead where the tide ebbs and flows.[27] Later the district courts were given concurrent jurisdiction in these matters.[28]

The most significant expansion in the jurisdiction of the federal courts during this period was the extension of the removal statute. A conflict developed between the federal government and those states that did not wish to prosecute the war. Several states refused to enforce federal laws prohibiting exports to Europe and interfered with federal customs officials who sought to enforce the act. Because of this conflict, Congress conferred jurisdiction on the federal courts in actions taken against a federal officer for carrying out the provisions of the non-intercourse acts. Such action against a federal officer which had begun in the state courts could be removed by him to the circuit court regardless of the amount involved. These acts expired by their own limitations.[29] These and other cases under similar statutes which were carried to the federal courts are known as removal cases.

Other sources of federal jurisdiction were the various statutes dealing with slavery. Beginning in 1794, a ship that was fitted out for the purpose of trade or traffic in slaves was to be condemned in either the circuit or district courts. Any suit to recover forfeitures under this act could also be brought in either court. This act was extended over a period of time to include persons aiding or abetting the violations of the statutes or those who had a commercial interest in such acts.[30] A statute in 1820 extended the definition of piracy by including the act of landing on a foreign shore to seize negroes with the intent of making them slaves.[31]

Probably the most controversial statute dealing with slavery was the Fugitive Slave Law. This statute was not directed exclusively at those "held to labour" but included fugitives from justice.[32] However, the procedure for the recovery of those "held to labour" was different from that for other fugitives. The owner of a slave could seize or arrest the slave and take him before any federal or state judge, who, upon satisfactory proof, could give the claimant a certificate which would be sufficient warrant for the removal of the slave. Penalties were provided against any attempt at rescue. Only later did the federal statute make it clear that the owner could recover the value of the slave from any one who was responsible for the escape. The recovery could be sought in any court, federal or state, but slave owners probably felt that only in the federal courts could they successfully seek the recovery of their property, and it was for that reason, that these cases tended to come before the federal courts. Since there were few federal judges available for a summary proceeding, the commissioner was authorized to make such determinations.[33] This statute gave rise to the Dred Scott decision and many others, plus innumerable scholarly studies.[34] The jurisdiction of the federal courts under statutes attempting to end the slave trade has been ignored when considering the workload of the judges.

The different types of federal jurisdictional statutes had various impacts on federal courts located in different parts of the country. The extension of the admiralty jurisdiction to the navigable rivers and the great lakes brought cases involving steamboats into the federal courts in the central part of the United States. As the Indians moved farther West, the federal courts in the East found that they had fewer problems arising under the Indian laws. The statutes enacted in 1790 and expanded by several acts until 1834 regulating trade with the Indians and punishing certain defined offenses against the Indians were enforced in the federal courts.[35] These laws extended to non-Indians but not to crimes committed by Indians against other members of the same tribe.[36]

Generally, the different tribes were left to govern themselves and punish members of their own tribes for offenses committed by them. At the time of the Civil War, the federal government reserved jurisdiction of Indian affairs when states were admitted into the Union. This trend started with the admission of Kansas in 1861.[37] Jurisdiction was further extended by the Major Crimes Act of 1885 which made certain crimes committed by an Indian punishable in the federal courts rather than in the tribal courts.[38] Another profligate source of Indian litigation was the General Allotment Act adopted two years later which permitted the allocation of property to individual Indians who could then dispose of it as they wished.[39] Some jurisdiction of Indian crimes was returned to the state court, but this tale of jurisdiction over the Indians is contorted in such a way as would only be elucidated by detailed study.[40] The Major Crimes Act did not significantly increase the number of cases before the federal courts, but the General Allotment Act was a rich mine of litigation for the federal courts in Oklahoma.

The next major extension of federal jurisdiction was the Force Bill of 1833.[41] South Carolina had passed an act interfering with the collection of revenue and providing for action in the courts of that state to enforce these statutes. Congress replied with the Force Act, providing that the federal courts would have jurisdiction in all cases arising under the Revenue Act. The Force Act also provided that any person injured because of acts done under a statute of the United States for the protection of the revenue or collection of the duty should be entitled to maintain a suit in the circuit court without regard to the amount involved. Another section provided for the removal to the federal courts of all suits against any officer accused of acts done under the revenue laws. The result of these statutes was to give to the federal courts jurisdiction over all officers acting under federal authority. These statutes started a trend which has expanded in subsequent decades.

The Civil War gave rise to numerous problems, and Congress passed a number of statutes to implement the war effort, including confiscation acts and extension of protection to acts performed under color of the federal law. As a result, the federal courts experienced an increase in the number of cases filed. In addition to the several statutes passed in support of the war effort, Congress began to expand the causes which could be removed from the state courts to the federal courts by the defendant where some federal immunity was asserted or where the defendant was exposed to local prejudice against national authority.[42] An Act of 1863 permitted the removal to the federal courts of actions brought in the state courts against an official claiming to have acted under the authority of the President or a statute of Congress.[43] The Force Act was restated and slightly extended. Removal rights were granted in suits involving recently enacted civil rights.[44] A few of the other acts that permitted removal granted corporations other than banking corporations, organized under a law of the United States, the right to remove any suits against them.[45] The same right was granted to common carriers in actions for loss or damage to goods caused by the hostilities of the Civil War.[46] Probably because of the emotions generated by the Civil War, an Act of 1867 provided for removal where there was diversity of citizenship and the sum exceeded $500. The petition could be filed by either party and had to include an affidavit as to the existence of prejudice in the local state courts.[47] Another statute of the same period permitted the removal of a cause where one or more of several defendants was a citizen of another state or an alien, if it appeared to the court that it could make final judgment in the case without the presence of the defendants that would not join in the removal.[48]

Up to this period, for a person to assert any other rights given by federal law not covered by the Force Act or the removal statutes, the suitor had to first claim these rights in the state courts, then, if unsuccessful, appeal to the Supreme Court of the United States.[49] Congress had not granted the federal courts their full potential jurisdiction given under the Constitution. In 1875, Congress sought to consolidate some of the special acts involving the jurisdiction of the federal courts and to state some of the principles, especially those dealing with removal statutes, in more general language.[50]

This series of removal statutes enacted between 1864 and 1875 created certain illogical inconsistencies in the jurisdiction of the circuit courts. The statute of 1866 took away the court's jurisdiction of cases brought against revenue agents unless the parties could establish diversity of citizenship, but these same cases could be removed to the circuit courts from the state courts upon the petition of the defendant irrespective of the citizenship of the parties.[51] At least one contemporary writer was critical of the statute which permitted one of a group of defendants to remove the suit.[52]

Another confusion introduced by these statutes was the extension of the time within which the defendant could exercise this right of removal. The original Judiciary Act of 1789 required the defendant to petition the state court at the time of his first appearance. The removal statutes enacted in this period were inconsistent on this point and made it possible for the defendant to petition the circuit court first; under several of these statutes he could exercise this right any time before trial.[53] The act restated many of the previous statutory provisions governing jurisdiction, but in some instances, it expanded the jurisdiction. Diversity cases were permitted to be brought or removed to any district in which the defendant was an inhabitant, or in which he could be found at the time of serving process. The Supreme Court later held that this permitted removal suits against any corporation in every district in which it was doing business.[54] The federal courts were directed not to proceed with any cases which did not "really and substantially" involve a controversy within their jurisdiction or where the parties "improperly or collusively" joined to give them jurisdiction.[55]

The most significant section of the statute of 1875 was that which gave the federal courts original jurisdiction concurrent with the state courts in all matters exceeding $500, exclusive of costs arising under the Constitution, laws of the United States or treaties. The effect of this statute was to give a person claiming a right under the federal Constitution or laws the option of initiating his suit in federal or state court.

The existing records do not give a clue as to the reason for the enactment of this important jurisdictional statute in 1875, for the bill aroused little debate in Congress. This statute could have been enacted to eliminate the confusion created by these various removal statutes, and, since effectuating the policy of these laws, could have been accomplished best by conferring on the federal courts full jurisdiction as defined in the Constitution, a step which Congress had resisted up to this date. During Reconstruction, Congress was in an expansive mood which would not again be so strong until the latter half of the Twentieth Century. All of these reasons are matters of speculation.

Few contemporary observers appreciated the full implication of this section of the act as greatly expanding the jurisdiction by making it possible to initiate a suit in the federal courts where a federal right was claimed.[56] Most of the early decisions applying this section involved the question of what constituted a controversy arising under the laws of the United States. Texts on federal practice merely recited the fact that the circuit courts had jurisdiction "concurrently with the courts of the several states, of all suits at common law or in equity," where the matter involved more than $2,000.[57] Another writer points out that this statute made two important changes in the jurisdictional requirements of the Judiciary Act of 1789. By the terms of the Judiciary Act of 1789, jurisdiction was conferred on the federal courts where the suit was between the citizen of the state where the suit was brought and a citizen of another state.[58] Under the new statute, neither party had to be a citizen of the forum state. Furthermore, a suit arising under the Constitution and laws of the United States was sufficient to confer jurisdiction on the federal courts. The fact that this lecture was written by a circuit judge may explain his recognition of the changes made by this statute.

Another significant piece of legislation enacted during the post-Civil War era, and one whose full impact was not to be felt for a century, was the Civil Rights Act of 1871.[59] Several statutes passed earlier had defined certain acts which violated the right to franchise, but the act of 1871 was broader in that it punished conspiracies to deprive an individual of certain rights. The statute of 1870 had extended the jurisdiction of the federal courts significantly, for any person who was "denied or cannot enforce in the courts or judicial tribunals of the State" any right secured under the several civil rights statutes could enforce these rights in the federal courts.[60] However, this statute was used sparingly during the Nineteenth Century. The judiciary raised questions of whether equity could be used to enforce political rights, but the judges recognized that the courts had little practical power to supervise action of state officers.[61]

After the mid-decade of the Twentieth Century, the Constitution was interpreted to apply the Bill of Rights to the states through the Fourteenth Amendment, which had the effect of expanding the rights enforceable in the federal courts against the states. In 1964, Congress enacted a comprehensive civil rights act and authorized the plaintiff to recover damages or any other relief providing for the protection of civil rights, including the right to vote.[62] The number of civil rights cases filed has significantly increased during the period from 1950 to 1980 from 142 cases to 12,944.[63]

This has enabled the federal courts to become supervisors of state institutions ranging from schools to penal institutions.

No period in American history has received the scholarly scrutiny as has the Civil War in Reconstruction periods. Some academic scholars have concluded that the Republican majority in Congress, who were responsible for these removal statutes and other pieces of legislation which extended jurisdiction of the federal courts, had a plan to "nationalize" the judiciary, which would serve the Republican goal. In support of this thesis, these historians point out that Congress expanded the jurisdiction of the federal courts by enacting the removal statutes, bankruptcy laws and many other Reconstruction statutes.[64] It is doubtful if the leaders in Congress had an overriding objective to "nationalize" the judiciary through the extension of the jurisdiction of the federal courts or whether they fully realized that this was the result of the enactment of these statutes. Statutes are generally enacted to meet some perceived need on the part of the legislators, whether the need arises from a court decision or some change that the individual Congressman wants enacted. The extension of the enforcement of all federal rights in the federal courts rather than in the state courts with an appeal to the United States Supreme Court was perceived as a more desirable procedure, certainly from a lawyer's perspective. This one section of the removal statutes gave to the federal courts full federal jurisdiction as defined in the Constitution.[65] The full implication of this statute was not appreciated or fully utilized for several decades.

No less an authority than Justice Frankfurter concluded that the developments "in the federal judiciary, which in retrospect seems revolutionary, received hardly a contemporary comment."[66] Generally, this statement is accurate, but at least one contemporary writer recognized the fact that by the enactment of the statute of 1875, "Congress has exhausted its power; and has conferred upon the federal courts all of the jurisdiction authorized by the Constitution."[67] The result of the statute was to give to the federal courts a wide range of new cases. They grew from "restricted tribunals of fair dealings between citizens of different states and became the primary and powerful reliances for vindicating every right given by the Constitution, the laws, and treaties of the United States."[68] Up to the enactment of the statute giving the federal courts their constitutional jurisdiction, Congress had apparently acted upon the theory that full jurisdiction was not necessary to the full "harmonious working of the system." As a result, only part of the jurisdiction was conferred upon the courts, and the remnant was reserved. This statute of 1875 may have changed a political philosophy as well as given the federal courts additional jurisdiction, the potential of which would not be fully utilized for several decades.[69]

In a sense, when the federal courts were given complete federal jurisdiction in 1875, they had obtained the jurisdiction to enforce any federal right. This statute was a turning point in the history of the jurisdiction of the federal courts, for they became free to accept jurisdiction of any claim or any right arising under a federal statute, whereas, before this date, the courts had to review the statute to determine if they had the jurisdiction. Since this statute, the growth in the business of the courts has been entirely due to Congressional legislation in new areas. When Congress enacts new rights or creates agencies, the powers of the court to review or decide certain issues may be limited, but this is not a limitation on the authority of the federal courts to hear matters arising under these statutes. The statute of 1875 was a watershed in the history of the jurisdiction of the federal courts. The history of the federal courts would have been much different if this grant of full federal jurisdiction had not been repeated in 1801.

During the last quarter of the Nineteenth Century, the federal courts were faced with an increasing number of cases resulting from the increased size of the country, several new federal statutes including the Act of 1875 and the Bankruptcy Act, an increase in the number of corporations, and many other factors. Congress became concerned with changing the organization and structure of the federal courts to enable them to cope with this increasing number. Beginning with the Act of 1887, an attack on this problem was mounted by restricting the jurisdiction of the courts. It is paradoxical that as the federal government was expanding into new areas, at the same time, attempts were being made to restrict the jurisdiction of the federal courts.

The Act of 1887 had a restricting influence on the federal courts. The jurisdictional amount in diversity cases was raised from $500 to $2,000. When the jurisprudential question of whether justice should be confined to cases over these amounts was raised, the reply was that all controversies under this amount were within the jurisdiction of the state courts. Suits could no longer be brought in the districts in which the defendant was found, but could be brought where he was a resident. Removal of a case from the state courts to the federal courts was limited to the defendant's privilege unless the plaintiff could show local prejudice. The status of "national banking associations established under the laws of the United States" was clarified. Such a corporation was considered a citizen of the state in which it was incorporated and not where it was doing business. Jurisdiction based solely upon the federal incorporation was in effect withdrawn from the federal courts by this provision.[70] This statute was an amendment to the Act of 1885.

This piece of legislation was considered by many members of the bar as wise in contracting the jurisdiction of the national courts.[71] The effects were felt by the courts, but any gain was offset by the Tucker Act of the same year which gave the federal courts concurrent jurisdiction with the Court of Claims upon all cases based on contracts with the government other than pension cases.[72] However, neither the statutes of 1885 or 1887 repealed all the removal statutes nor cleared up all the inconsistencies, although they went a long way in attempting to do so.

A dramatic increase in business of the federal courts came after World War I and, again, an even greater one, after World War II. It can be documented that between 1918 and 1921, the number of civil cases filed in the federal courts increased three-fold and the criminal cases approximately two and one-half times. Such acts as the Prohibition Act, the Mann Act, and statutes in support of the war efforts significantly increased the business of the federal courts.[73] Congress has continued to legislate in new areas which significantly increased the work of the federal courts. It has been suggested that Congress include an impact statement on the effects of the proposed laws on the work of the federal courts. Such a proposal has not been adopted by Congress. The revisors of the Judiciary Code of 1948 stated that they found 158 provisions in the various federal statutes enacted since the Judiciary Code of 1911 conferring jurisdiction on the federal courts.[74] No attempt was made to list all the statutes.

As the workload of the courts increased, various proposals were made to decrease the cases coming before the federal courts. One of the most obvious areas to curtail was that of the diversity jurisdiction cases. Diversity jurisdiction, which as late as 1950 constituted nearly one-third of the total number of cases in the federal courts, has often been criticized. Attempts have been made in Congress to repeal it, and the number of times these attempts have been made are lost in the congressional archives. Those who oppose the abolishment of the jurisdiction continue to argue that the "Founding Fathers" were concerned that local prejudices and interests would prevent non-residents from receiving justice in the local courts. Some would deny that this assumption was true. In 1951, a committee of the Judicial Conference of the United States considered diversity citizenship and recommended that it be "preserved in the interest of the commercial as well as the political fabric of the country."[75] Congress raised the $3,000 minimum established by the Judicial Code of 1911 to $10,000 in the Act of 1958.[76]

This same statute took other steps to limit the access of the federal courts. Corporations were declared to be citizens of the state of incorporation as well as the state in which they did business. The effect of this statute was to prevent the establishment of diversity jurisdiction when the corporation was doing business in that district and the other party was an inhabitant of the same district or state. The right to remove workmen's compensation cases from the state courts to the federal courts was abolished.[77] However, to no one's surprise, the increase in the amount required for diversity jurisdiction has not had a significant effect on reducing the number of cases brought in the courts.[78]

The acts since 1887 have tended to restrict somewhat the jurisdiction of the federal courts in the removal cases. The original Federal Employers

Liability Act gave concurrent jurisdiction to the state and federal courts. Two years later, Congress prohibited removal in such cases. Seamen's personal injury cases first brought in state courts were made nonremovable. If brought in the federal courts, jurisdiction was allowed, but jurisdiction was denied in suits against state officials for orders affecting public utility rates not interfering with interstate commerce.[79] Finally, for the purpose of preventing removal, a corporation was made a citizen of the state in which it did business. All these statutes have restricted jurisdiction but have not prevented the increase in the number of cases filed in the federal courts.

The factors which cause the federal courts to be popular forums in states vary. More often than not, these factors depend upon the respect held for the local courts. Some particular local statute may make it more attractive to bring a suit in the federal courts. The fact that Louisiana law allows a direct action against a tortfeasor's insurance company, which establishes diversity jurisdiction more easily than in other states, and that the federal courts are bound by the findings of the jury whereas the state courts are not, increased the popularity of the Louisiana federal courts for personal injury suits.[80] As the workload of the federal courts increases, future attempts will be made to restrict the cases coming to the courts either by removal or on the basis of diversity of citizenship.

FOOTNOTES TO CHAPTER 12

1. Act of February 13, 1801, 2 STAT. 89.

2. Act of May 29, 1830, 4 STAT. 417.

3. Turner v. Bank of North America, 4 Dall. 8, 11 (U.S. 1799); Kempe's Lessee v. Kennedy, 5 Cranch. 173 (U.S. 1809); Livingston v. Van Ingen, 1 Paine 45.

4. Act of September 24, 1789, sec. 9, 1 STAT. 76. One authority has reported that he cannot find a single complaint in contemporary literature of the assignment of admiralty jurisdiction to the federal government. John P. Frank, "Historical Bases of the Federal Judicial System," 13 L. & CONTEMP. PROB. 3, 9 (1948).

5. Gordon v. Longest, 16 Pet. 97, 104 (U.S. 1842).

6. Henry J. Friendly, "The Historic Basis of the Diversity Jurisdiction," 41 HARV. L. REV. 483, 498 (1928).

7. Robert W. Kastenmeier and Michael J. Remington, "Court Reform and Access to Justice: A Legislative Perspective," 16 HARV. J. LEG. 311 (1979).

8. Act of September 24, 1789, sec. 11, 1 STAT. 78. Town of Pawlet v. Clark, 9 Cranch. 292 (U.S. 1815); Colson v. Lewis, 2 Wheat. 377 (U.S. 1817).

9. Act of September 24, 1789, sec. 12, 1 STAT. 79.

10. Benjamin Robbins Curtis, JURISDICTION, PRACTICE, AND PECULIAR JURISPRUDENCE OF THE COURTS OF THE UNITED STATES (1880).

11. Kanouse v. Martin, 15 How. 197 (U.S. 1853).

12. Ward v. Arredondo, 1 Paine 410, 29 Fed. Cas. 167 (1825).

13. Ketland v. The Cassius, 2 Dall. 365 (U.S. 1796).

14. One author described the Circuit Courts as the "great courts of original jurisdiction." C.L. Bates, FEDERAL PROCEDURE AT LAW... (1908), v.2, p.492, sec. 655.

15. Turner v. Bank of North-America, 4 Dall. 8, 11 (U.S. 1799).

16. Turner v. Bank of North-America, 4 Dall. 8 (U.S. 1799).

17. *See* notes, 1 STAT. 78.

18. Act of March 3, 1797, sec. 2, 1 STAT. 506.

19. Act of March 8, 1806, 2 STAT. 354.

20. Act of March 3, 1797, 1 STAT. 506; Act of March 8, 1806, 2 STAT. 354.

21. Commonwealth v. Feely, 1 VA. CAS. 321 (1813). Court held that trial court had no jurisdiction without an opinion. Jackson v. Rose, 2 VA. CAS. 34 (1815).

22. The Antelope, 10 Wheat. 66, 122 (U.S. 1825).

23. Charles Warren, "Federal Criminal Laws and the State Courts," 38 HARV. L. REV. 545 (1925).

24. Act of May 8, 1792, sec. 3, 1 STAT. 276.

25. Act of July 24, 1813, sec. 10, 3 STAT. 47; Act of August 2, 1813, sec.5, 3 STAT. 73.

26. Act of March 3, 1819, sec. 5, 3 STAT. 513, made perpetual by Act of May 15, 1820, sec. 2, 3 STAT. 600.

27. Act of May 15, 1820, sec. 3, 3 STAT. 600.

28. Act of March 3, 1823, 3 STAT. 789.

29. Act of February 4, 1815, sec. 8, 3 STAT. 198; Act of March 3, 1815, sec. 6, 3 STAT. 233.

30. Act of March 22, 1794, 1 STAT. 347.

31. Act of May 15, 1820, sec. 4, 3 STAT. 600.

32. Act of February 12, 1793, 1 STAT. 302. Sections 3 and 4 apply to slaves.

33. Act of September 18, 1850, 9 STAT. 462.

34. For a review of this literature, *see* Reid, "Lessons of Lumpkin: A Review of Recent Literature on Law, Comity, and the Impending Crisis," 23 WM. & MARY L. REV. 571 (1982); Scott v. Sandford, 19 How. 393 (U.S. 1856).

35. Act of July 22, 1790, 1 STAT. 137; Act of March 1, 1793, 1 STAT. 1793; Act of March 30, 1802, 2 STAT. 139; Act of March 3, 1817, 3 STAT. 383; Act of June 30, 1834, 4 STAT. 729.

36. United States v. Rogers, 4 How. 567 (U.S. 1847).

37. Act of January 29, 1861, sec. 1, 12 STAT. 126.

38. Act of March 3, 1885, sec. 9, 23 STAT. 385.

39. Act of February 8, 1887, 24 STAT. 388.

40. Robert N. Clinton, "Development of Criminal Jurisdiction over Indian Lands: The Historical Perspective," 17 ARIZ. L. REV. 951 (1975).

41. Act of March 2, 1833, 4 STAT. 632.

42. Act of March 3, 1863, sec. 5, 12 STAT. 756.

43. Act of March 3, 1863, sec. 5, 12 STAT. 756.

44. For a list of these acts, *see* Felix Frankfurter and James M. Landis, THE BUSINESS OF THE SUPREME COURT, A STUDY IN THE FEDERAL JUDICIAL SYSTEM (1928), p. 61, note 22.

45. Act of July 27, 1868, 15 STAT. 227.

46. Act of January 22, 1869, 15 STAT. 267.

47. Act of March 2, 1867, 14 STAT. 558.

48. Act of July 27, 1866, 14 STAT. 306.

49. *The Moses Taylor,* 4 Wall. 411 (U.S. 1866).

50. Act of March 3, 1875, 18 STAT. 470.

51. Felix Frankfurter and James M. Landis, THE BUSINESS OF THE SUPREME COURT, A STUDY IN THE FEDERAL JUDICIAL SYSTEM (1928), p.61, fn. 22, which cites The Assessors v. Osbornes, 9 Wall. 567 (U.S. 1869).

52. Curtis, *supra,* note 10.

53. *See* Revisor's Notes, Revision of the United States Statutes as drafted by the Commissioners (1872), title XIII, The Department of Justice, sec. 113, p.74.

54. In *Ex Parte Schollenberger,* 96 U.S. 369 (1877), the Supreme Court allowed jurisdiction over an insurance company on the basis that the state law made the corporation consent to service and suit within the state.

55. Act of March 3, 1875, sec. 5, 18 STAT. 472.

56. A.I., "Our Federal Judiciary," 2 CENT. L. J. 551, 553 (1875), commented "Congress has exhausted its power; and has conferred upon the federal courts all the jurisdiction authorized by the constitution."

57. Roger Foster, A TREATISE ON PLEADING AND PRACTICE IN EQUITY IN THE COURTS OF THE UNITED STATES (1890), p.21.

58. Amos M. Thayer, JURISDICTION OF THE FEDERAL COURTS (2d ed., 1895), p.9.

59. Act of April 20, 1871, sec. 1, 17 STAT. 13.

60. REV. STAT. sec. 629(16); Act of April 9, 1866, sec. 3, 14 STAT. 27. The other statutes were the Act of May 31, 1870, 16 STAT. 140; Act of February 28, 1871, 16 STAT. 433. These statutes were refined in the REVISED STATUTES 1874.

61. Giles v. Harris, 189 U.S. 475, 486, 488 (1902).

62. Act of July 2, 1964, sec. 101, 78 STAT. 241.

63. Civil Rights cases filed:

1950	142
1960	280
1970	3,985
1980	12,944

These statistics are taken from the Annual Reports of the Administrative Office of the United States Courts.

64. Harold M. Hyman, A MORE PERFECT UNION: THE IMPACT OF THE CIVIL WAR AND RECONSTRUCTION ON THE CONSTITUTION (1973), p. 224;

William M. Wiecek, "The Reconstruction of Federal Judicial Power, 1863-1875," 13 AMER. J. LEG. HIST. 333 (1969).

65. Act of March 3, 1875, 18 STAT. 470.

66. Frankfurter and Landis, *supra,* note 51, p.65.

67. A. I., "Our Federal Judiciary," 2 CENT. L. J. 553 (1875).

68. Frankfurter and Landis, *supra,* note 51, p.65.

69. A.I., "Our Federal Judiciary," 2 CENT. L. J. 551 (1875).

70. Act of March 3, 1887, 24 STAT. 552. This statute was amended by Act of August 13, 1888, 25 STAT. 433.

71. Jacob Trieber, "The New Federal Judicial Code," 46 AMER. L. REV. 702, 711 (1912).

72. Frankfurter and Landis, *supra,* note 51, p.95; Act of March 3, 1887, 24 STAT. 505.

73. Henry P. Chandler, "Some Major Advances in the Federal Judicial System 1922-1947," 31 F.R.D. 309, 319 (1963).

74. U.S. CODE CONG. SERV. Tit. 28, pp. 1835, 1836.

75. 1958 U.S. CODE CONG. & ADM. NEWS 3114, 3119.

76. Act of March 3, 1911, sec. 24, 36 STAT. 1091; Act of July 25, 1958, 72 STAT. 415, PL 85-554; H. Rept. 97-808.

77. Act of July 25, 1958, 72 STAT. 415, PL 85-554.

78. 1958 U.S. CODE CONG. & ADM. NEWS 3114, 3123.

79. All these statutes are listed in 1958 U.S. CODE CONG. & ADM. NEWS 3125; Henry Campbell Black, A TREATISE ON THE LAW AND PRACTICE GOVERNING THE REMOVAL OF CAUSES FROM STATE COURTS TO FEDERAL COURTS (1898), p.11.

80. Erwin C. Surrency, "Federal District Court Judges and the History of Their Courts," 40 F.R.D. 139, 212 (1966).

Chapter 13

GROWTH OF FEDERAL CRIMINAL JURISDICTION

Basis for Federal Criminal Law

The First Congress had the difficult task of delineating the boundaries of authority between it and a group of state governments which had the advantage of established law. This difficulty is best illustrated in the area of criminal law, in which Congress had to consider defining offenses and punishments contrary to its laws, yet stay within the confines of its powers. The options for punishment were few because the penitentiary system was just being introduced in some states. In most states, the classical crimes were punished by hanging. Punishments such as the pillory and whipping-post as well as fines for minor criminal misconduct also were the norm. Whether the members of Congress realized the difficulties in adapting a criminal law system for a federal government with limited powers superimposed on a group of independent states is not certain.

The Constitution made it very clear that Congress would have the power to prescribe punishments for crimes committed within federal areas and to punish those guilty of counterfeiting securities and current coins of the United States. The Constitution granted Congress the authority to "define and punish" piracies and other felonies committed on the high seas as well as offenses against the law of nations. This is the only provision that clearly charges Congress with defining and punishing. Furthermore, the Constitution provided that Congress was "to make all Laws which shall be necessary and proper for carrying into Execution the foregoing Powers."[1] Alexander Hamilton, in the FEDERALIST PAPERS, recognized the Confederation's lack of authority to punish for the violation of laws.[2] For all of these reasons, the members of Congress were cognizant of their authority to punish any transgressions of the laws enacted by them.

One of the first acts considered by Congress was an act to regulate the collection of the duties imposed on ships and vessels. Here, for the first time, crimes against the United States which were punishable in the federal courts were defined. A master of vessels who neglected to make an entry or deliver his manifest to the appropriate authorities could be fined $500.[3] Various provisions of the act included crimes such as unloading at night without permission of the collector and forcibly resisting customs officers in the performance of their duties. The punishment provided for in the act was the payment of a $400 fine. The reason for imposing a set amount for all violations of this act is unknown. Bribery was recognized as a traditional common law offense, but the acts constituting bribery had to be specially defined by statute in England. This statute punished officials of the Customs Service for taking a bribe to connive at any false entry, and the fine ranged from $200 to $2,000 for each offense. Additionally, the statute prohibited individuals so convicted from holding an office "of trust or profit" under the United States.[4] This additional punishment was not imposed for similar crimes. In other words, it was a more serious offense for a government employee to take a bribe than for a civilian to offer or give a bribe.

Another basis for the enforcement of criminal penalties has been the situs of a crime. In 1790, the federal government owned very little property, but it did possess a number of military forts, arsenals and dockyards. The Constitution recognized this and provided for the acquisition of other buildings and a location for the capital. Congress was to have exclusive legislative authority over these acquisitions.[5] In any event, a comprehensive statute was needed to designate the punishments for these crimes. At its second session, Congress adopted "An Act for the Punishment of Certain Crimes against the United States" which set the penalties for these traditional crimes.[6] The crimes themselves, however, were not defined. For this purpose, recourse to the common law was necessary. The crimes in this act can be grouped under two headings, those against the federal government and those taking place on areas governed by the federal government. With the exception of those sections prescribing punishments for treason, counterfeiting and forgery, each clause defining the other crimes began with the introductory phrase, "that if any person or persons shall, within any fort, arsenal, dockyard, magazine or any other place or district of the country under the sole exclusive jurisdiction of the United States. . . ." Presence in one of these places became one of the elements of the crime which had to be specified in the indictment.

Capital punishment was prescribed for treason, murder, forgery, piracy and felonies committed on the high seas. Later, debasing the United States coins was added to the list of capital offenses.[7] Other punishments prescribed in the First Crimes Act include imprisonment, generally for seven years, payment of fines, and whipping. During the debate on the bill, one proposal was made to distinguish between counterfeiting and uttering (passing known counterfeited securities), which was a common law offense, the former being a capital offense and the latter carrying a lesser punishment. Objections were raised to the capital punishment provisions and the section pertaining to donation of the felon's body for dissection. In no other way does the record reveal the reasoning behind the formation of the First Crimes Act.[8]

Criminal jurisdiction was divided between the two federal courts, namely the district and the circuit courts. Under the Judiciary Act of 1789, the district court was limited to crimes for which the penalty did not exceed a whipping and a small fine, or a term of punishment not exceeding six months. An appeal could be taken from the district court to the circuit court. This distinction in criminal jurisdiction was abolished in 1842 when the district court was given concurrent jurisdiction with the circuit court in all criminal actions which were not capital offenses.[9] Some two decades later, one commentator observed that "indictments for all offenses . . . may be found indifferently either in the district or circuit court. . . ."[10] He further observed that the district attorney could move that the case be transmitted from one court to the other for trial, unless it involved a capital offense in which case it had to be transferred to the circuit court. By this date, the district court judge often served in both the circuit and district courts. The district court judge's dual capacity provided a basis for the general statement that prior to abolishment of the circuit courts in 1911, the district court was essentially a criminal court.

Federal Criminal Jurisdiction of the State Courts

The sessions of the federal courts were held in only two or three cities in each state in the early part of the Nineteenth Century, which made it both difficult and inconvenient to bring criminal charges under the federal law. Congress attempted to solve this problem by allowing states to exercise concurrent jurisdiction for violation of some criminal statutes. For example, the Carriage Tax Act of 1794 provided that ". . . fines, penalties and forfeitures, all or any of them, shall and may be sued for, and recovered, in any court of the United States, or before any magistrate, or state court, having competent jurisdiction."[11] The owner of a vessel or its captain could recover a penalty against a seaman who failed to report at a designated time "before any justice or justices of any state, city, town or county within the United States."[12] Other examples of situations in which penalties could be recovered in the state courts are found in the early federal statutes.[13]

Congress seemed to have been aware of the inconvenience caused by the limited locations for holding the federal courts, for in the Carriage Tax Act of 1794[14] it recognized that where any complaint arose "more than fifty miles distant from the nearest place by law established for the holding of a district court," recovery could be before any state court within that district. This same provision was included in a statute levying duties on foreign spirits, wine and tea.[15] Disputes involving wrongfully withheld seaman's wages were within the jurisdiction of the state courts when the "residence" of the federal district judge was more than three miles from the place, presumably, where the ship was docked.[16] As one authority noted, these statutes and others "were not couched in such imperative language as to impose *duties* upon the State Courts," but granted them the power to act.[17] The duties given to the State Courts in this group of statutes were in the nature of recovery of fines rather than punishment of offenders.

Beginning with the Fugitive Slave Act of 1793[18] and the Naturalization of Aliens Act of 1795[19], however, Congress expressly conferred duties on the state courts. These acts were followed by similar ones imposing duties on state courts to carry out federal statutes.

The first statute which clearly gave the state courts concurrent jurisdiction with the federal courts over federal crimes was the Post Office Act of 1799.[20] A number of crimes were defined, including delaying or embezzling letters, robbing or attempting to rob the mails, and counterfeiting a frank. The term of reference giving the state courts jurisdiction is a clear direction to the state courts in that the judges "shall take cognizance thereof, and proceed to judgment and execution as in other cases."[20A]

This assumption that the states would prosecute offenders of federal crimes may have been based upon certain experiences under the Articles of Confederation, where central government was given jurisdiction over crimes committed on the high seas. The Continental Congress by an ordinance granted this jurisdiction back to the states. Another reason advanced for assigning the state courts concurrent jurisdiction by the first Congresses was the "clearly preponderant sentiment against expansion of the federal courts."[21] The state courts, however, rejected this jurisdiction, for prosecuting and punishing individuals for violation of penal statutes.

In Virginia, the case of *Jackson v. Rose* decided that prosecution for violation of federal criminal law was vested exclusively in the federal courts by the Constitution, which provides that "the Judicial power of the United States shall be vested" in the federal courts.[22] This case canvasses all the arguments against the state courts exercising jurisdiction over federal criminal law. The court concluded that the state could not accept the obligation of trying federal criminal cases. The supreme courts in several other states adopted this view[23], as did Chief Justice Marshall, who declared, "the courts of no country execute the penal laws of another."[24]

Several justices had expressed as dicta in opinions that Congress could not delegate criminal jurisdiction to the state courts. In one opinion, Justice Story stated that "the whole judicial power of the United States should be, at all times, vested, either in an original or appellate form, in some courts created under its authority."[25] In 1842, in a case involving the Fugitive Slave Act of 1793, Justice Story stated that the Constitution

> does not point out any State functionaries or any State action to carry its provisions into effect. The States cannot, therefore, be compelled to enforce them; and it might well be deemed an unconstitutional exercise of the power of interpretation to insist that the States are bound to provide means to carry into effect the duties of the national government, nowhere delegated or intrusted to them by the Constitution.[26]

Although it became a clearly accepted Constitutional principle that the federal government could not require state courts to enforce its penal laws, the question arose under the full faith and credit doctrine of the Constitution whether the state courts of another jurisdiction could enforce penalties imposed under these penal laws. The Supreme Court distinguished remedial provisions of statutes which were in the nature of reimbursing or compensating the individual in the nature of damages from those which were penal in nature.[27] The state courts could enforce and entertain jurisdiction where the action was remedial. No state court would undertake to try a defendant charged with violation of a crime committed in another jurisdiction. Citing Blackstone's definition of crime as being local in nature, the Supreme Court reasoned that criminal jurisdiction was local as well, and, hence, "good faith and credit" did not require one state to try those who had violated the laws of another jurisdiction. The federal statutes giving criminal jurisdiction to the state officials were not immediately amended, and the Supreme Court indicated that the state officials "may" exercise the jurisdiction given them.[28] It was not until the REVISED STATUTES of 1874 that the "jurisdiction vested in the courts of the United States in the cases and proceedings hereinafter mentioned, shall be exclusive of the courts of the several states: First. Of all crimes and offenses cognizable under the authority of the United States."[29]

In several statutes, Congress made it clear that it did not intend to deprive the courts of the individual states of jurisdiction under certain criminal laws. In "[a]n act to punish frauds committed on the Bank of the United States," Congress declared that "nothing herein contained shall be construed to deprive the courts of the individual states of a jurisdiction under the laws of the several states over the offences declared punishable by this act."[30] A view of the records of local state courts reveals that some courts did indict and punish offenses against the federal laws.

Samuel Bayard edited and published in 1804 an abstract of the federal laws which placed duties on the judges and justices of the peace of the states. It reviewed the various acts of Congress which did and did not impose duties on this group of officers. This was a useful handbook on the federal criminal law of that period and the earliest text in which the federal criminal law is examined.

The theory that one sovereign will not punish an offender for the violation of the laws of another is seemingly contradictory, as is illustrated by the removal statutes which permit the removal into the federal courts of charges against federal officers. In 1815, Congress provided for removal into the federal courts of "any suit or prosecution . . . against any collector, naval officer, surveyor, inspector, or any other officer, civil or military, or any other person aiding or assisting . . . for any thing done, or omitted to be done, as an officer of the customs."[31] In 1833, the Force Act was adopted which extended the jurisdiction of the federal circuit courts over all cases under the revenue laws and provided for the removal from the state courts of "any . . . suit or prosecution . . . against any officer of the United States, or other person, for or on account of any act done under the revenue laws of the United States."[32] A stronger removal statute was enacted in 1863 which provided for removal from the state courts of any "civil or criminal" prosecution against federal officers for acts done under presidential authority.[33] All of these statutes resulted in a provision for trying state criminal prosecutions against federal officers in the federal courts. In 1880, a federal internal revenue officer indicted for murder in a state court removed the prosecution to the federal circuit court. The Supreme Court upheld the removal observing that the federal courts had adopted and applied "the laws of the State in civil cases, and [that] there is no more difficulty in administering the State's criminal law."[34] Those opposed to these removal statutes object to them on the basis that federal courts can try individuals for violating state criminal laws, yet state courts cannot try those indicted for violation of federal criminal statutes. This argument is answered by the observation that removal is limited to federal officials, and, certainly, the federal government has an interest in protecting those who act on its behalf.[35]

Adoption of State Criminal Law for Federal Areas

The First Congress immediately was faced with legislating for areas in which there was no organized state government to enforce the criminal laws of that state. For the territories, Congress adopted a policy of establishing a local legislative body to adopt laws applicable to the area. The organization of the District of Columbia presented a unique problem because Congress itself functioned as the state legislative body in prescribing laws for the District. The laws of Maryland and Virginia were continued in effect until displaced by Congressional enactments. For those lands federally owned, the states' laws were generally extended to those areas, known as federal enclaves, which included military ports, national parks and other federally owned lands. Jurisdiction over crimes committed in these areas is vested in the federal courts.

Congress attempted in several instances to avoid the difficulty of drafting a comprehensive criminal code by making the criminal laws of the state applicable. In 1790, Congress made it a crime to trade with the Indians without a license obtained from the President. This same act made offenses committed within the Indian territory punishable by the laws of the state in which the territory was contained, or, if the territory was not situated within a state, the state in which the offender was a citizen.[36] When the District of Columbia was established in 1801, Congress continued to impose the laws of Virginia and Maryland in those parts of the District originally within those states. For this reason, the criminal laws of those two states continued in effect until they were gradually modified by Congress.[37] In 1825, Congress for the first time made criminal acts in a federal enclave punishable under the laws of the state in which the enclave was located.[38]

In 1832, the question was certified to the Supreme Court whether this act of 1825 adopted the criminal law for the state at the time of its enactment or included any changes made in the law since 1832. The court limited its application of the act to those crimes defined in 1832, as it had done with the Conformity Act.[39] This view was dictated in the court's opinion because it would be unconstitutional for a state to legislate for the federal government. Because of this decision, cases arose where it was advantageous to be convicted in the federal courts because federal law provided for a lighter sentence than did the contemporary state law. Illustrative of this point is Judge John C. Rose's example of the "famous professional criminal" who snatched a satchel of a bank runner in the post office in Baltimore. The accused was convicted and sentenced to one year, which was the maximum penalty under federal law. Had he committed this offense outside the post office and the case been tried in the courts of Maryland, however, he could have been sentenced for fifteen years.[40] On the other hand, if the individual had been convicted of murder, he would have been worse off under federal law, which until 1897 imposed the death penalty. In the state court, the defendant might only have been convicted of murder in the second degree.

Theoretically, the federal courts, under the rationale of *United States v. Paul*, were to enforce a static criminal law in a federal enclave as defined by the state as it stood in 1825. The extent to which the federal judges adhered to this rule is difficult to ascertain. Further, the federal courts were of the opinion that this decision not only applied to the date of the enactment of the law, but also embraced only those places and buildings ceded to the United States before the passage of this act. One court refused to extend the act to the Customs House in New York City which was not ceded to the United States until 1865. It argued that construing this statute as applying to all future acquisitions of territory would produce some surprising results. The courts would be required "to revive a criminal code which has been defunct for forty years . . . Whipping and the pillory would, in some cases, have to be inflicted, for they were the penalties denounced by some of the State laws in force in 1825, for offences for which the laws of the United States provide no punishment."[41] To overcome the difficulty of punishment being frozen as it was defined in 1825 and its impact on federal areas ceded since that date, Congress provided for the application of the then current state laws in several successive statutes.[42]

The first act of 1866 may have been in response to the decision refusing to extend federal jurisdiction to the federal Customs House in New York. The Supreme Court took the position that once the territory was ceded to the federal government, the state government could in a subsequent act grant it exclusive criminal jurisdiction.[43] The issue was raised whether federal jurisdiction extended to those military reservations established in the territories which were later incorporated as states. It was resolved that those areas used as military bases would be free from any interference from the state "as would destroy or impair their effective use for purposes designated."[14] For all other uses, the state had to consent to the federal government's exclusive jurisdiction.

The Common Law of Crimes

The question was raised as early as 1798, only some eight years after the establishment of the federal courts, whether the federal courts could punish those crimes which were not defined by statute. The question was first raised in the Circuit Court for Pennsylvania; Justice Chase and Judge Peters were divided on the issue. Justice Chase was of the opinion that Congress had to define the offense by statute, whereas Judge Peters believed that a government had the power to preserve itself and that any act which aims at the subversion of a federal institution is a crime that is punishable by the federal courts.[45] It is not clear from the record whether the indictment was allowed to stand because the next justice who came to assist in the holding of the Circuit Court agreed with Judge Peters, which would have given a majority in favor of common law crimes in the federal government, or if the indictment was dropped.

Fourteen years later, the question was certified to the Supreme Court, and, in a very short opinion, the Court took the position that the federal courts had no common law jurisdiction in criminal cases. The Court's decision is based on the notion that this jurisdiction had not been exerted and that "the general acquiescence of legal men shews the prevalence of opinion in favor of the negative of the proposition."[46] The Court concluded that the federal government was one of limited powers and that the courts possessed no jurisdiction other than that given to them. The courts had the inherent power "to fine for contempt — imprison for contumacy — inforce the observance of order, etc."; however, the exercise of criminal jurisdiction in common law cases was not within their implied powers.[47] The question was again certified to the Court some four years later and was reaffirmed.[48] One historian has noted that the drafters of the First Judiciary Act clearly intended the federal courts to have jurisdiction "of all crimes and offences that shall be cognizable under the authority of the United States *and defined by the laws of the same.*"[49] This result was certainly consistent with the requirement in civil cases that the jurisdiction of the federal courts be limited to those matters granted by statute.

During this same period, several state courts were considering the question of whether they could punish for common law offenses. One author of the period argued against the state courts of Ohio having this inherent power.[50] The outcome of these decisions was that the United States would have no unwritten criminal code; all crimes must be defined by statute.

Criminal Law in Admiralty

At the time of the American Revolution, there was a well-defined body of criminal law in admiralty which was tried in special court of admiralty sessions upon indictment and before a petit jury.[51] These crimes included inciting to mutiny, striking an officer, stealing from the ship's stores, as well as other acts unique to seafarers. The question of whether the conferring of maritime jurisidiction on the federal courts included this group of crimes was raised early in the federal courts.

The Constitution extended the judicial power to "all cases" of admiralty and maritime jurisdiction. However, Congress has never completely conferred criminal jurisdiction in admiralty upon the federal courts. *United States v. Coolidge*[52] involved an indictment for the forceful rescue of a prize captured by an American cruiser. The offense clearly was under the maritime law, and hence, was thought to distinguish *Coolidge* from previous cases which held that there was no common law criminal jurisdiction. The Supreme Court did not distinguish the case and adhered to its former decision that common law criminal jurisdiction did not reside in the federal courts.

The District Court of Massachusetts subsequently held that it could not take jurisdiction of a murder committed on board an American vessel of war in Boston Harbor because the First Crime Act defined murder on ship board as being committed "upon the high seas, or in any river, haven, basin, or bay, out of the jurisdiction of any particular state."[53] The First Crime Act, in defining larceny on board ship, limited the crime to that committed aboard an American vessel on the high seas.[54] It was later found that in defining offenses within the maritime jurisdiction "there [were] approximately twenty different phrases used in defining the places within which as many different crimes [were] made cognizable by the courts of the United States."[55] In the Crimes Act of 1825, jurisdiction was extended to crimes committed aboard American vessels within the jurisdiction of a foreign state in the same manner as if committed on the high seas.[56] However, since Congress used the expression "upon the high seas, or in any river, haven, basin, or bay, out of the jurisdiction of any particular state" or some variation of this phrase in subsequent sections in the same act, this section never was construed as curing these variations.

The admiralty jurisdiction was extended in 1845 to embrace navigable waters of the country, but this did not affect jurisdiction over crime. The 1845 statute clearly was limited to matters of contracts and torts involving vessels over twenty tons on rivers and lakes. In one case, the question arose whether a crime committed aboard an American vessel on the Canadian side of the Detroit River was considered to be on the high seas, and the court responded in the affirmative.[57] Neither Congress nor the Supreme Court has evidenced any desire to extend criminal jurisdiction to crimes committed within the waters of a state which are considered maritime for other purposes.

Extension of Federal Criminal Law Through the
Interstate Commerce Clause

Until the Civil War, the power of Congress to punish individuals for criminal conduct was limited to crimes against the laws of the United States and those committed in the areas which were controlled by the federal government. Interstate commerce took on a greater significance in the life of the country in the decade following the Civil War and has caused the number of federal crimes to multiply. This new flexibility in transportation made it possible for an individual in one state to perform an act that was criminal in another, yet escape punishment, or to commit an act which was harmful to society, yet avoid punishment because a particular state did not recognize that act as criminal.

Asserting its newly found authority over interstate commerce, Congress, in 1866, provided a penalty for the transportation of explosives on vessels carrying passengers.[58] Next, in 1872, Congress adopted a statute prohibiting the use of the mails for the promotion of lotteries[59] and, a few years later, the circulation of obscene literature. The constitutionality of these statutes was never challenged for the obvious reason that during this period a criminal case could not be appealed. Congress did not utilize its power under the commerce clause again until 1895 when it adopted a statute making it an offense to send lottery tickets in interstate commerce.[60] Obviously, there were those who doubted Congress' authority to act under the commerce clause to define crimes. However, when the power of Congress was considered by the Supreme Court, it was upheld.[61]

During the opening decades of the Twentieth Century, Congress began to pass a series of acts enforcing prohibition. The Criminal Code of 1911 made it a violation to deliver liquor to a person other than the one to whom it was addressed. Other sections of the Code prescribed penalties for violations relating to the shipment of spirits. Additionally, it was a crime to send liquor through the mail.[62] The experiment of prohibition provided an increase in the number of criminal cases tried in the federal courts.

The most famous statute based upon the regulation of interstate commerce was the Mann Act of 1910, which prohibited the transportation of young women across the state lines for immoral purposes.[63] When this statute was challenged in the Supreme Court of the United States, the constitutionality of those decisions upholding the statutes defining crimes under the interstate commerce clause was affirmed. The court stated "that we are one people; and the powers reserved to the States and those conferred on the Nation are adapted to be exercised . . . to promote the general welfare, material and moral."[64] This often expressed concept of "one people" has formed the basis for cooperation among federal and state agencies in police work. Since the Mann Act, Congress has passed a number of criminal statutes, including the famour Lindberg Kidnapping Act. It is significant that the Penal Code of 1909 has a section entitled

"Offenses against foreign and interstate commerce," which was introduced for the first time.[65]

Another trend contributing to the number of criminal cases in the federal courts was the multiplication of the number of petty crimes consisting of violations of regulations prescribed by certain officials governing government property, especially in the national parks. In 1890, the Secretary of Interior was empowered to prescribe regulations governing the use of the Yellowstone National Park.[66] Commissioners were authorized to adjudicate these cases with an appeal to the District Court of Wyoming.

Another statute provided for a fine of $100 and not more than $5,000 or imprisonment for a term not to exceed five years for the violation of "any regulation of the War Department that has been made for the prosecution of such mine, torpedo, fortification or harbor-defense system."[67] Because these crimes appear to have been limited to certain district courts, their general impact on federal criminal law has been minimized.

Codification of Federal Criminal Law

Congress enacted criminal statutes without any uniformity in punishment or definition for similar types of activities, such as perjury. The first crimes defined by Congress were violations of the Customs Act, which were followed by many statutes of a similar nature. The First Crime Act was the first comprehensive criminal statute which formed a basis for punishment of the classical crimes committed within the criminal jurisdiction of the federal government. In 1825, Congress again adopted a criminal act which provided punishments for many crimes within the admiralty jurisdiction, such as attacking any vessel with intent to plunder, or crimes against any persons of the high seas.[68] This was not a comprehensive criminal code, although among its provisions were definitions of several different forms of forgery. This statute was reported to have been drafted by Joseph Story, then a member of the Supreme Court.[69] These two statutes, of 1790 and 1825, represent the only statutes in the nature of a penal code passed by Congress during the Nineteenth Century. All other statutes respecting crimes were passed from time to time as needed to supplement existing law or to narrow the scope of broad statutes.

At the urging of Edward Livingston, a single effort was made to adopt a comprehensive penal code. Livingston had made an international reputation for himself by developing a comprehensive model criminal code in Louisiana which was widely recognized for its sanguine approach to rationalizing and organizing criminal law. As a member of the House of Representatives, Livingston secured the printing of A SYSTEM OF PENAL LAW FOR THE UNITED STATES OF AMERICA, which, some modifications, was identical to the criminal code he had prepared for Louisiana. The code was too complex for the existing mood of Congress. It included crimes which were at that time considered unnecessary, such as the threat of violence to any member of Congress with an intent to influence his official conduct or to make an assault on him in consequence of anything he may have said or done.[70] The penalty for this crime was a fine of not less than $100 nor more than $500. The most unique feature of the code was the abolition of the death penalty. Other crimes found in this code were probably not applicable to any system of criminal justice administered by the federal courts. After becoming a United States senator, Livingston introduced a bill on March 3, 1831 urging the adoption of his code. Because Livingston resigned his position in the Senate, his bill received no further consideration. During the Nineteenth Century, Congress gave no further thought to a revision of the criminal law.[71]

Alfred Conkling, a judge in the District Court for the Northern District of New York, observed in his treatise on federal practice published in 1864 that "[t]he Criminal Code of the United States is, in several respects, defective, and stands much in need of a thorough revision." Judge Conkling noted that the Crimes Act of 1825 repealed all prior acts inconsistent with its provisions, but that determining which parts of the act of 1790 were repealed was "a task of some difficulty" — truly an understatement.[72]

When Congress authorized a revision of the statutes of 1866, which resulted in the adoption of the REVISED STATUTES (1874), the revisors took advantage of the opportunity to make a few modest changes in the criminal law. Their basic objective was to collect and organize the statutes of a permanent and general nature and to eliminate inconsistent provisions, but not to make any major revisions. The degree to which the revisors adhered to their objectives has been a matter of dispute. Nevertheless, several minor changes in the criminal law were recommended. The first was establishing a distinction between a felony and a misdemeanor, terms which frequently had been used inconsistently in federal statutes. For example, those who violated the provisions of the act establishing the Treasury were deemed guilty of a "high misdemeanor," subject to a fine and incapable of holding any office under the United States.[73] No attempt was made to establish any distinction between these terms.

A felony was defined as any crime punishable by death or imprisonment at hard labor. All other crimes were characterized as misdemeanors. An attempt was made to clear up the many statutes defining the crime of accessory which, as the revisors pointed out, was defined thirteen times in the Crimes Act of 1825. The definitions of several crimes which varied in different acts were consolidated. These constituted the only proposals for changes to be made in the criminal law, but even these were rejected by Congress.

The Attorney General of the United States had on several occasions urged a revision of the United States laws. In 1897, Congress appointed a commission "to revise and codify [under the direction of the Attorney General] the criminal and penal laws of the United States."[74] The duties of the Commission to Revise and Codify the Criminal and Penal Laws of the United States was extended by Congress at various times. In 1898, the commission was to prepare a short code of criminal procedure.[75] The next year, the commission was asked to codify the laws concerning the jurisdiction and practice of the courts of the United States, including removal and transfer of causes.[76]

In the introduction to its report proposing a criminal code in 1901, the Commission called the attention of Congress to the imperfect condition of the criminal law of the federal government. It pointed out that in the REVISED STATUTES OF 1874 the title "crimes" consisted of 228 sections. The criminal code of Alabama, for example, contained 1,332 sections, of which 762 related to procedure, while 570 were devoted to definitions or punishments of crime. The Commission added, "it may be stated with confidence that no State of the Union retains the system of penal laws which was in force three-quarters of a century ago; and this is equally true of the leading nations of Europe."[77] Illustrative of how the criminal law was dated is the crime of murder. Prior to 1897, there were no degrees of murder, and the only punishment was the death penalty. In 1897, the jury was permitted to return a guilty verdict for murder, but could recommend guilty "without capital punishment." In this event, the defendant was sentenced to life in prison.[78] The Criminal Code of 1909 introduced degrees in murder as had been done in all the states earlier in the Nineteenth Century.

The Commission's report recommended the combination of different offenses and the expansion of others. Its principal additions were sections covering offenses against the postal service and offenses against foreign and interstate commerce. The Commission to Revise and Codify the Criminal and Penal Laws found it impossible to consolidate the great many misdemeanors defined in the non-criminal statutes. The commissioners argued that the penal provisions of such statutes such as those relating to customs, pensions and the post office were found to be closely connected with the non-penal provisions, so that their separation was "a task of serious difficulty."[79] They argued that to undertake the consolidation of these many penal statutes would involve a general revision of all the statutes.[80] Whether it was because of this observation or some other reason, in the same year, Congress authorized the Commission to revise all laws.[81]

The Commission for the Codification and Revision of the Laws was directed to make its final report to Congress on or before December 15, 1906; thereafter, the Commission was terminated. The Commission submitted to Congress "a work of great magnitude, covering 1,900 pages and embracing 9,000 sections of proposed legislation, which covered the entire field of permanent and general laws of the United States."[82] The work of the Commission was passed on to a Special Joint Committee on the Revision of the Laws. The Committee felt that it did not have the opportunity to study the proposed alterations, so it undertook to present to Congress for its consideration the revision of the criminal law which was enacted as the Criminal Code of 1909.[83]

The Criminal Code of 1909 used the titles from the REVISED STATUTES OF 1874, but expanded their number. No sweeping changes were made, and it has been estimated that only ten new offenses were defined.[84]

The revision of the criminal law was a subject of continuous agitation, and it was not until 1948 that another revision was completed. This revision was the work of a Congressional committee assisted by an advisory committee that worked with the bench and bar. The revision accomplished, among other things, an adjustment of the penalties. For the first time, an attempt was made to eliminate the inequalities in punishments and to adopt uniform penalties for related offenses. The various sections were stripped of their verbose language, and sections were consolidated. The need for this is evidenced by a comparison of the previous laws with the revised ones.[85] Additionally, the crimes were arranged alphabetically rather than being grouped under headings as they had been in previous revisions. This statute became Title 18 of the UNITED STATES CODE.

In 1966, Congress established the National Commission on Reform of Federal Criminal Laws to undertake the task of completely revising the criminal law. The Commission prepared a comprehensive bill which both revised existing law and attempted to clarify a number of nebulous areas.[86] In 1973, the code was introduced as the first bill in the 94th Congress, replacing Title 18 of the UNITED STATES CODE. It immediately drew protests from a number of special interest groups who felt it was detrimental to individual rights. These groups did concede, however, that the code was a vast improvement over the existing criminal law. The bill was revised several times as it was introduced in succeeding Congresses. In the 98th Congress (1983-1984), the proposals were separated into individual bills.

The proposed code addressed two chief concerns, other than redefining different crimes and adjusting penalties. The first was the geographical jurisdiction of the federal laws. The jurisdiction of the federal government over crimes was generally made explicit in each statute or section defining a crime. The second concern, often expressed in literature, was the fact that an individual could be prosecuted by both the federal and state governments for criminal conduct relating to the same set of facts. The frequency of this occurrence was a matter of some controversy. The code, however, proposed solutions to this problem of double prosecution.

The drafters attempted to address matters of criminal defense and to clarify the law of criminal responsibility, including mental illness. A great deal of attention was given by congressional committees to the provisions of this code, and continuous efforts were made after 1973 to enact these recommendations into law. These efforts were successful in 1984 by the enactment of a substantial portion of the proposed code. Included among the portions adopted were those providing for appeals for sentences imposed by the trial court and the establishment, in the Judiciary branch, of the United States Sentencing Commission. The United States Sentencing Commission was charged with the duty of establishing guidelines by which the judges were to govern imposition of the sentences.[87] Only time will determine the effectiveness of these two innovations in ending the apparent provision of unequal sentences for the same crime. Among other innovations made by this statute were harmonizing the penalties for similar crimes, modifying parole practices, strengthening the use of forfeitures in many crimes, and clarifying the law relating to the insanity pleas. These are only a few of the changes made by the statute, but surely other provisions will prove equally important over the next decades.

The growth in the number of crimes prosecuted in the federal courts has been observed on different occasions throughout the Twentieth Century. One former federal district attorney reminisces that in 1896 the federal criminal courts had:

> small calendars to deal with; there was now and then a national bank defalcation; there were a certain number of counterfeiting cases; there were a few cases of fraud in obtaining pensions; there were the usual number of cases of larceny by post office employees; there were semi-occasional cases of offences against custom laws; there were a few cases of moon-shining. . . , and now and then there would be a case of some offence upon the high seas brought in for trial.[88]

He then proceeds to discuss the new crimes developed mostly under the interstate commerce power of the Constitution. Statistics show that there was a near tripling of the number of criminal cases filed in the federal courts between the fiscal years 1918 and 1921, chiefly due to the criminal cases arising under the Prohibition Act.

Another factor which contributed to the steady growth of federal criminal cases was the creation of agencies responsible for developing cases against those violating specific laws, ranging from the Federal Bureau of Investigation Treasury Agents to the office of the Immigration and Naturalization Service. With the exception of game enforcement, states rarely have special policing bodies to enforce specified statutes. General law enforcement on the state levels is left to local sheriffs and police forces.

When viewing the entire span of the federal criminal law, one is impressed by the hesitant start made by the first Congress in its attempt to involve the state courts in the enforcement of federal criminal law. During most of the Nineteenth Century, there was strong opposition to the increased strengthening of the federal courts. The Civil War appears to have instilled a new nationalism which was reflected in the federal courts when they took over prosecuting violations of the law by their own officers. Congress abandoned its effort to involve the state courts. The legislation in support of the national efforts in World War I and World War II provided the next major impetus to this growth.

Another result of this criminal caseload after World War II was an increase in the number of individuals employed by the United States district attorneys and the professionalization of these subordinates in the sense that they became career prosecutors instead of following a short career in this capacity before becoming a defense attorney.

FOOTNOTES TO CHAPTER 13

1. U.S. Const. art. I, sec. 8, para. 6, 10, 17. One should not overlook the "necessary and proper" clause in para. 18.
2. FEDERALIST, no. 21.
3. Act of July 31, 1789, sec. 11, 1 STAT. 38.
4. Act of July 31, 1789, sec. 35, 1 STAT. 46.
5. U.S. Const. art. I, sec. 8, para. 17.
6. Act of April 30, 1790, 1 STAT. 112.
7. Act of April 2, 1792, sec. 19, 1 STAT. 250.
8. ANNALS OF CONGRESS (1834), v.1, pp.1520, 1521.
9. Act of August 23, 1842, sec. 3, 5 STAT. 517.
10. Alfred Conkling, A TREATISE ON THE ORGANIZATION, JURISDICTION AND PRACTICE OF THE COURTS OF THE UNITED STATES (4th ed. 1864), p.590.
11. Act of June 5, 1794, sec. 10, 1 STAT. 375.
12. Act of July 20, 1790, sec. 2, 1 STAT. 132.
13. Act of March 8, 1806, 2 STAT. 354; Act of April 21, 1808, 2 STAT. 489; Act of March 3, 1815, 3 STAT. 244.
14. Act of June 5, 1794, 1 STAT. 373.
15. Act of June 5, 1794, sec. 5, 1 STAT. 378.
16. Act of July 20, 1790, sec. 6, 1 STAT. 134.
17. Charles Warren, "Federal Criminal Laws and the State Courts," 38 HARV. L. REV. 545, 552 (1925).
18. Act of February 12, 1793, sec. 3, 1 STAT. 302.
19. Act of January 29, 1795, sec. 1, 1 STAT. 414.
20. Act of March 2, 1799, sec. 28, 1 STAT. 740.
20A. Act of March 2, 1799, sec. 28, 1 STAT. 741.
21. Warren, *supra,* note 17, p.545, 551.
22. 2 Va. Cas. 34, 39 (1815).
23. The cases are reviewed in Warren, "Federal Criminal Laws and the State Courts," 38 HARV. L. REV. 545, 577-580 (1925). United States v. Lathrop, 17 Johns.(N.Y.) 4 (1819) (an action to collect a penalty under a federal statute where the court refused to take jurisdiction); Ely v. Peck, 7 Conn. 239 (1828) (an action against a deserting seaman where a state court did not have jurisdiction under a federal statute); *See,* 1 Kent's Comm. 402.
24. The Antelope, 10 Wheat. 66, 123 (U.S. 1825).
25. Martin v. Hunter, 1 Wheat. 304, 331 (U.S. 1816).
26. Prigg v. Pennsylvania, 16 Pet. 539, 615-616 (U.S. 1842).
27. Huntington v. Attrill, 146 U.S. 657 (1892).
28. Prigg v. Pennsylvania, 16 Pet. 539, 622 (U.S. 1842).
29. REV. STAT. (1874) sec. 711.
30. Act of June 27, 1798, 1 STAT. 573; Act of February 24, 1807, 2 STAT. 423.
31. Act of February 4, 1815, sec. 8, 3 STAT. 198. This statute was limited to the period of the war with Great Britain and was extended to Act of March 3, 1817, 3 STAT. 396.
32. Act of March 2, 1833, sec. 2, 3, 4 STAT. 632.
33. Act of March 3, 1863, sec. 5, 12 STAT. 756.
34. Tennessee v. Davis, 100 U.S. 257, 271 (1879). *See* Allan B. Magruder, "Removal of Suits from State to Federal Courts," 13 AMER. L. REV. 434 (1879); Warren, *supra,* note 17, p.545, 584-593.
35. L.B. Schwartz, "Federal Criminal Jurisdiction and Prosecutors' Discretion," 13 L. & CONT. PROB. 64, 68 (1948), argues that these removal statutes have "exploded" the theory that one sovereign cannot punish for the violation of the criminal laws of another.
36. Act of July 22, 1790, sec. 5, 1 STAT. 138.

37. Act of February 27, 1801, sec. 1, 2 STAT. 103.

38. Act of March 3, 1825, sec. 3, 4 STAT. 115.

39. United States v. Paul, 6 Pet. 141 (U.S. 1932).

40. John C. Rose, JURISDICTION AND PROCEDURE OF THE FEDERAL COURTS (3d ed. 1926), p.113.

41. United States v. Barney, 5 Blatch. 294, 301 (S.D. N.Y. 1866).

42. Act of April 5, 1866, sec. 2, 14 STAT. 13; Act of July 7, 1898, sec.2, 30 STAT. 717; Act of March 4, 1909, sec. 289, 35 STAT. 1145; Act of June 15, 1933, 48 STAT. 152; Act of June 20, 1935, 49 STAT. 394; Act of June 6, 1940, 54 STAT. 234.

43. Benson v. United States, 146 U.S. 325 (1892).

44. Fort Leavenworth Railroad Co. v. Lowe, 114 U.S. 525, 541 (1884).

45. United States v. Worrall, 2 Dall. 384, 395 (U.S. Cir. Ct. Pa. 1798).

46. United States v. Hudson, 7 Cranch 32 (U.S. 1812).

47. United States v. Hudson, 7 Cranch 32, 34 (U.S. 1812).

48. United States v. Coolidge, 1 Wheat. 414 (U.S. 1816).

49. Charles Warren, "New Light on the History of the Federal Judiciary Act of 1789," 37 HARV. L. REV. 49, 73 (1923).

50. John Milton Goodenow, HISTORICAL SKETCHES OF THE PRINCIPLES AND MAXIMS OF AMERICAN JURISPRUDENCE (1819).

51. James Kent, COMMENTARIES ON AMERICAN LAW, v.1, p.360.

52. United States v. Coolidge, 1 Wheat. 414 (U.S. 1816).

53. United States v. Bevans, 3 Wheat. 336 (U.S. 1818).

54. Act of April 30, 1790, sec. 16, 1 STAT. 116; United States v. Morel, 26 Fed. Cas. 1310 (Cir. Ct. E.D. Pa. 1834).

55. REPORT OF THE COMMISSION TO REVISE AND CODIFY THE CRIMINAL AND PENAL LAWS OF THE UNITED STATES, 57 Cong., 1st sess., doc. no. 68, Pt. 2, p.XX.

56. Act of March 3, 1825, sec. 5, 4 STAT. 115.

57. United States v. Rodgers, 150 U.S. 249 (1893).

58. Act of July 25, 1866, sec. 5, 14 STAT. 227.

59. Act of June 8, 1872, sec. 79, 17 STAT. 294.

60. Act of March 2, 1895, sec. 1, 28 STAT. 963.

61. Lottery Case, Champion v. Ames, 188 U.S. 321 (1902).

62. Criminal Code 1911, Act of March 4, 1909, sec. 217, 238, 239, 240.

63. Act of June 25, 1910, 36 STAT. 825. *See,* Martin Conboy, "Federal Criminal Law," in LAW: A CENTURY OF PROGRESS 1835-1935, v.1, pp.295, 319 (1937).

64. Hoke v. United States, 227 U.S. 308, 322 (1912).

65. Act of March 4, 1909, 35 STAT. 1134.

66. Act of May 7, 1894, 28 STAT. 73. The Secretary of Interior continues to have authority to prescribe rules governing certain activities in the Park. His authority to proscribe acts in other National Parks with penalties attached has been extended.

67. Act of July 7, 1898, 30 STAT. 717. Became sec. 44, Criminal Code, 1909, 35 STAT. 1097. In this section, provision for violation of regulation of War Department was dropped.

68. Act of March 3, 1825, 4 STAT. 115.

69. REPORT OF THE COMMISSION TO REVISE AND CODIFY THE CRIMINAL AND PENAL LAWS OF THE UNITED STATES. Senate. 57th Cong., 1st sess., doc. no. 68, Pt. 2, p.III. This report does not indicate if the bill as prepared by Story was adopted or whether it was the basis of this Act.

70. Edward Livingston, A SYSTEM OF PENAL LAW FOR THE UNITED STATES OF AMERICA (Washington, 1828), p.28.

71. Charles Havens Hunt, LIFE OF EDWARD LIVINGSTON (1864), p.353.

72. Conkling, *supra,* note 10, p.170, fn.3.

73. Act of September 2, 1789, sec. 8, 1 STAT. 67.

74. Act of June 4, 1897, 30 STAT. 58.

75. Act of July 1, 1898, 30 STAT. 643.

76. Act of March 3, 1899, 30 STAT. 1116.

77. REPORT OF THE COMMISSION TO REVISE AND CODIFY THE CRIMINAL AND PENAL LAWS OF THE UNITED STATES. Senate. 57th Cong., 1st sess., doc. no. 68, Pt. 2, p.IV.

78. Act of January 15, 1897, sec. 1, 29 STAT. 487. This statute reduced several crimes, including piracy, from a capital offense.

79. REPORT, U.S. Attorney General 1900-01, p.404.

80. REPORT, U.S. Attorney General 1900-01, p.404.

81. Act of March 3, 1901, 31 STAT. 1181.

82. H.R. Rept. No. 2, Pt. 1, 60th Cong. 1st sess. p.2.

83. Act of March 4, 1909, 35 STAT. 1088.

84. H.R. Rept. No. 304, 80th Cong., 1st sess., p.3.

85. *Ibid,* p.4.

86. Act of November 8, 1966, P.L. 89-801, 80 STAT. 1516.

87. Act of October 12, 1984, P.L. 98-473, sec. 225(a), 98 STAT. 2017.

88. H. Snowden Marshall, "Federal Criminal Procedure," 1916 Md. Bar Assoc. Proc. 176, 177.

Chapter 14

CIVIL PROCEDURE
IN THE FEDERAL COURTS

In considering the procedure adopted and applied by the federal courts, the six general areas of jurisdiction — copyright, bankruptcy, admiralty, equity, criminal procedure and civil procedure — must be considered separately. Since the proceedings in copyright, bankruptcy and admiralty were federal questions, no difficulty was encountered in establishing uniformity in practice among the federal courts in these areas from the beginning by rules adopted by the Supreme Court. In civil cases, however, uniformity in practice in the federal courts was not possible. As one commentator has said, "the choice was between uniformity and diversity — or more accurately in this situation, between federal uniformity and federal conformity to state diversities."[1]

It is impossible to give the history of any particular procedure pursued in the federal courts, but an understanding of the sources from which these rules were derived contributes to an understanding of the complexity of federal practice. This history is divided into three periods. During the first period, the procedure used by the state courts at the time of their admission to the Union formed the basis of the procedure in the federal courts. In 1872, another period began when federal practice was required to conform to new developments in state practice, but so many exceptions were introduced by the courts that the procedure was difficult to understand or follow. Finally in 1934, the Supreme Court of the United States was authorized to adopt rules of civil practice to govern all federal courts. The rules have been considered as a model for all other jurisdictions since their introduction.

At its first session, Congress adopted statutes to establish the basis of federal law — rules of substantive law to be applied by the federal courts and the procedure which was to govern practice in federal courts. In both cases Congress adopted the contemporary state practice. The Rule of Decisions Act provided that the "laws of the several states, except where the constitution, treaties or statutes of the United States shall otherwise require or provide, shall be regarded as rules of decision in trials at common law."[2]

The Rule of Decisions Act passed by Congress was one of the most vexing questions in the federal jurisdiction over which a great amount of ink has been expended. The Act provided that the laws of the several states would be the rules for trials in common law courts throughout the states.[3] The federal courts applied this rule of decision inconsistently until the famous case of *Swift v. Tyson* in which Justice Joseph Story sought to give a definitive answer to this question.[4] As every student of constitutional law knows, this decision was reversed in the famous case of *Erie v. Tompkins*.[5] The debates that followed this reversal are based abstractly upon the teaching of the various decisions overlooking several factors not discussed in the reports which may have influenced the original doctrine and later led to its reversal.

The lack of uniform and regular reporting of the decisions of the federal trial courts during the Nineteenth Century made it impossible for a federal district court judge in one state to really follow the holdings of the circuit courts in another state. It should be stressed that until 1891, the Supreme Court was the exclusive appellate court, but the justices when they went out on circuit did hear limited appeals from the district court in the circuit court. The decisions of the Supreme Court were the only reports of federal courts that appeared on a regular basis. The position of reporter was established in 1817. The duties included preparing the volumes of the decisions with headnotes and other editorial matters generally found in a well edited series of reports. The decisions of the other federal courts appeared in a number of sources including magazines and in separate volumes. Most of these decisions were those of the justices of the Supreme Court on circuit, generally in cases on appeal from the district courts. An examination of these reports indicates that many of them were decisions of the courts in prize and admiralty cases. A federal district court judge would have the decision of his local state supreme court. It is questionable how many of them had at their disposal the decisions of the United States Supreme Court. Certainly these judges would have been aware of practice in their own states before their appointment to the bench and in all probability, except where the federal law was clear, would have applied that law. The establishment of the Circuit Courts of Appeals in 1891 gave emphasis to the establishment of two series, the famous FEDERAL REPORTER and the now forgotten UNITED STATES APPEALS. After that date, the federal judges had a series of reports from which they could determine what their colleagues were deciding in other parts of the country, and they would have been prone to follow those decisions.

Another factor which may help to explain the change in law concerning federal common law was the attitude of judges in the Nineteenth Century toward decisions. Justice Story and many of his colleagues both on the Supreme Court and the lower court adhered to the theory of Blackstone that decisions were only evidence of what the law is and not the law itself. Hence, the judges were free to make this discovery from all reported decisions. Today it would be truly an event if a judge admitted that decisions were not "law." Because they were free to make this discovery, it would have been a logical conclusion that only the positive law such as statutes of a state would be governing in the federal courts.

The decision in *Erie v. Tompkins* has not completely resolved the issues raised as to when state law governs the federal courts or settled the question of the applicable law in diversity cases. The introduction of the Federal Rules of Civil Procedure confused the issue somewhat and the trial courts were left to their own devices to resolve any questions.[6] The federal courts probably will be challenged to continue deciding this issue.

The other statute, known as the Process Act, provided that laws of the several states, "except where by this act or other statutes of the United States has otherwise provided, the form of writs and executions, except their style, and modes of process and rates of fees . . . in the circuit and district courts, in suits at common law, shall be the same in each state respectively as are now used or allowed in the supreme courts of the same." Upon adoption, this statute was only temporary and was continued until made permanent by the Act of 1792.[7]

These statutes applied to suits at common law rather than suits in equity or admiralty or other specialized proceedings then practiced and accepted. "Suits at common law" was a clearly defined area and fully understood at that time, but with the contemporary trend towards one form of action, this distinction has become obliterated. What Congress obviously intended was that the federal courts would follow both the substantive law and procedural laws of the state courts. Whether they were aware of the difficulties implied in such a concept was not recorded or preserved.

In 1792, the Process Act was reenacted permanently in practically the same words as the original act of 1789.[8] Minor changes in the later statute elaborated on fees payable to various officers and made other provisions concerning the payment of costs and how fees were to be recovered.

In considering the history of the Process Act, it is necessary to understand that practice and procedure at the end of the Nineteenth Century was considered in three segments: the original process which instituted the suit; the mesne process which was any proceeding between the commencement of the action and the final judgments including all motions; and the final processes which included the enforcement of the judgment. The impact of the Process Act was chiefly on the mesne processes.

The statute received its first construction in *Wayman et al. v. Southard et al.*[9] where Chief Justice Marshall held the Process Act of 1792 froze the federal practice as it existed in 1789. The federal courts, however, could modify state practice by "such alterations and additions as the said courts, respectively, shall, in their discretion, deem expedient, or [by] such regulations as the Supreme Court of the United States shall think proper, from time to time, by rule, to prescribe to any circuit or district court concerning the same."[10] The distinguished Chief Justice reasoned that this authorized the federal courts to make such improvement "in the forms and modes of proceedings, as their experience may suggest," or to adopt the state practice where there was an advantage to do so by court rule or by some other means. In furtherance of this argument, reliance was placed upon the authority of the federal courts "to make and establish all necessary rules for the orderly conducting of business in the said courts, provided such rules are not repugnant to the laws of the United States" which was a power given the federal courts in the First Judiciary Act.[11] Finally, the determining factor in Marshall's decision appeared to be that he could not accept the argument that the states could legislate for the federal courts. This principle of rejecting changes in state practice, made subsequent to the establishment of the federal courts, was earlier applied in the federal circuit court in New Jersey in 1803. Justice Bushrod Washington and Robert Morris, judge of the District Court for New Jersey, sitting jointly in the circuit court, refused to accept a subsequent change in a matter where state practice was changed after the local federal rules were adopted.[12]

It would presently be presumed that the adoption of any changes in state practice into the federal system had to be done by written rules, but it is easy to forget that such adoption could be done by simple continuance in practice. This is illustrated by the case arising in Ohio which adopted a statute requiring that all parties to a promissory note be joined in one suit. The Supreme Court stated that the Process Act of 1792 confined the adoption of the practice of the state courts in the federal system to those state procedures in existence on the day of the passage of the Process Act. Therefore, when the United States District Court was established in the state of Ohio in 1803, it had circuit court jurisdiction and could create a practice for its own guidance. This court adopted the established state practice "in the true spirit of the policy pursued by the United States." When the state was incorporated into a federal circuit in 1807, the justice of the Supreme Court who was the United States Circuit Court judge found that the practice of the Ohio courts had in fact been the practice of the circuit courts of the United States in that state. The state practice "by an uniform understanding, (had) been pursued by that court (the United States District Court) without having passed any positive rules upon the subject." Written rules obviously were "unquestionably to be preferred . . . but what want to certainty can there be, where a Court by long acquiescence has established it to be the law of that Court, that the state practice shall be their practice, as far as they have the means of carrying it into effect, or until deviated from by positive rules of their own making."[13]

It should be noted that the Process Act adopted the practice of the state courts of those states that existed at the time the Act was ratified and did not apply to states admitted subsequently. To remedy this defect, Congress passed an act in 1828 which in essence applied the Process Act to all states subsequently admitted and those that were to be admitted in the future. This statute has been viewed as reversing Marshall's decision in *Wayman v. Southal,* yet alternatively it has been viewed as sustaining his position.[14]

The Process Act of 1828 attempted to clear up application of the earlier statutes to the federal courts. The Act of 1789 had been construed to apply only to those states which were members of the Union at that date. The statute of 1828 made the "forms of mesne process, except the style, and the forms and modes of proceedings in suits in the courts of the United States" in suits at common law applicable to those states that were admitted after 1789.[15] Secondly, writs of execution and other final processes and the proceedings thereupon, again except as to their style, were to be those practices which were in use in the state. Both provisions were subject to the exception that any subsequent changes enacted by the state legislature could be incorporated into the federal practice by rules of the local federal courts. One commentator observed that "subsequent changes in the modes of proceedings in the state courts whether introduced by the legislature or by the courts themselves, are wholly inapplicable, per se, to the national courts."[16] In one sense, this statute does clear up Marshall's decision and in another sense expands and adopts his reasoning.

Again, the statute of 1828 was limited to those states admitted between 1789 and 1828. Congress again had to act. In 1842, the Process Act was made applicable to states admitted after 1828.[17] Through judicial interpretation, this act was extended to all states subsequently admitted to the union.[18]

It cannot be determined accurately from existing records the extent to which federal courts followed the rule that confined their practice to that followed by the state courts previously admitted to the union. Maybe this theoretical confusion was of little importance because the procedure in the state courts had not changed radically between the territorial period and statehood. It is known, for instance, that the federal court of Ohio, upon the establishment of the district court, adopted the then current state practice by rule of court, and hence, all changes in state procedure were reflected in the practice of the federal courts in that state.[19] Probably, this was done in other district and circuit courts.[20]

One contemporary commentator suggested that in order to determine a question of practice, one must determine:

> 1, whether it is specifically prescribed by any act of congress; and if not, 2, whether it is so by the rules of the court in which it arises; and if not, then finally, we are to inquire what was the practice upon the point in question in the supreme court of the state where the question arises, on the 29th of September, 1789, or if the question arises in one of the states since admitted to the Union, or if it concerns final process, what was the practice of the state court on the first of May, 1842. A careful and judicious application of these tests, though the process may in some instances require time and patience, cannot fail to lead to a correct decision.[21]

As can be ascertained from this discussion, it would be impossible to describe in accurate detail the procedure in the federal courts because of great variance in practice. The above commentator also remarked that it would be impossible to give a more explicit account of the procedure in the federal courts through the various stages of the case,

> with that degree of minuteness which is found in books treating of the practice of a single court, as of the king's bench in England, or of the supreme court of the State of New York, for example, so as to afford a perfect guide in regard to every particular, in every district of the Union, while it would be superfluous, would at the same time be impracticable.[22]

During the Nineteenth Century, the chief source of federal practice was that followed by the state courts in the locality in which the federal courts were located. This tends to overlook the important modifications made by Congress. In the Process Act itself, Congress made one significant change in the original process in that where a suitor had a choice of methods to pursue his action, and one of these choices included *capias ad satisfacendum,* he could begin his suit by this method rather than by meeting the requirements of the state practice. Under a *capias ad satisfacendum* in some jurisdictions, the defendant was taken into custody and his property seized. The practice that was becoming more acceptable and more widely used in the state courts to begin a lawsuit was the summons, and in some instances, upon the filing of the suit, only a nominal amount of the defendant's property could be seized.[23]

One of the most important rules of practice which was different in the federal courts than in the contemporary state courts was the requirement that the pleadings state the ground of jurisdiction for the courts. This was in recognition of the fact that the jurisdiction of these courts was limited and circumscribed by statute. A final area of federal practice governed solely by federal statutes was venue, or the forum in which the case must be tried. The federal statutes were rather explicit about this.

The lower federal courts played an important role in fashioning the method of procedure in the federal courts through their authority to adopt or modify contemporary state practice. The Supreme Court, however, was granted extensive authority which, like so many other missed opportunities in history, could have shaped federal procedure into a uniform system well before the modern Federal Rules of Civil Procedure which unified federal practice after 1934.

In 1842, the Supreme Court's authority to adopt rules to govern procedure was enlarged considerably. The statute of that year gave the Court the authority to alter the forms of writs and other processes, and a wide range of other forms were specifically mentioned such as filing "libels, bills, answers and other proceedings and pleadings, in suits at common law." Included was the authority to adopt "forms and modes of taking and obtaining evidence, and of obtaining discovery, and generally the forms and modes of proceeding to obtain relief, and the forms and modes of drawing up, entering and enrolling decrees." The most expanded grant of authority was "generally to regulate the whole practice of the said courts, so as to prevent delays, and to promote brevity and succinctness in all pleadings and proceedings therein, and to abolish all unnecessary costs and expenses in any suit therein."[24]

The reason for the passage of this statute is obscure. Why the Supreme Court did not act more aggressively by the authority to govern procedure through the rule-making process has not been determined. Perhaps the use of court rules was not thought to be an accepted practice in judicial administration.[25]

Another explanation for the failure of the Supreme Court to pursue the formal rule-making process may be found in the fact that in another century, institutions were not so formal in their organization or procedures. One justice of the Supreme Court suggested that the court could follow "a uniform mode of proceeding, for a series of years, and this forms the law of the court."[26] This being the situation, why the need for formal rules?

Apparently, the most commonly used method of conforming the federal practice to the state practice in matters of final processes was accomplished by the adoption of rules of court by the circuit courts incorporating the state practice. Obviously, these rules could not be in conflict with the Constitution or an act of Congress.[27]

A rule adopting or rejecting the state practice had to have the "concurrence of the circuit judge" and could not be adopted merely by the district court judge. Prior to 1869, each individual justice of the Supreme Court served as a circuit court judge, and hence, such rules needed his concurrence. In 1869, the office of circuit judge as separate from the office of United States Supreme Court Justice was created. Technically, such rules could have been made by him. In at least one decision, the Supreme Court rejected a rule of practice adopting the state law made by the district court judge alone.[28]

The precision of the local rule adopting the state practice varied considerably. The rule of the District Court for the Southern District of Florida adopted in 1858 was rather typical.

> The rules of practice, forms of pleading, and modes of proceeding in common law cases in this court, shall be the same as now prevail in the State courts, so far as they may be applicable and not inconsistent with the laws and constitution of the United States.[29]

The rules adopted for the Western and Eastern districts of Missouri in 1857 were more precise as to the source of the governing practice. These rules stated that the "forms of mesne process, except the style, and the forms of proceedings and practice, in suits at common law in this court, shall be the same as are prescribed in the Digest of the Laws of Missouri of 1835."[30]

In 1871, the court in the same jurisdiction adopted a more extensive rule. This rule cited the fact that Congress had intended to conform to the state practice and that the state had blended both equity and common law and that these areas were governed by the rules prescribed by the Supreme Court of the United States. In all other matters, "the court would be guided by Title XXXIV Practice in Civil Cases" of the Revised Statutes of Missouri of 1865 with certain exceptions which were specified.[31]

In some particular situations, the court would enter an order adopting a state practice for a specific type of suit. Again, Missouri in 1857 adopted an order stating that the district court practice in suits in ejectment involving land in the New Madrid District would conform to an act governing ejectment passed by the state of Missouri in 1845.[32] This specific rule was adopted along with other orders governing the ejectment proceedings and attachment.

The lack of the local court rules may have dictated an undesirable result. In a district court case, where the judgment could not be satisfied, the district court allowed an appeal, with ten additional days for the plaintiff to enter a request to the circuit court of appeals for a further stay accompanied by a statement that he found "a meritorious case". The judge found that in another district, by local rules, where there was an unsatisfied judgment, the plaintiff could request an order for the examination of the defendant and such witnesses as may be material. After this hearing, the court could enter an order for further discovery to satisfy the execution. This rule was a common practice in the equity courts which issued bills of discovery for this purpose.[33] Without such a rule, the district court judge felt that his only recourse was to allow an appeal.

How extensive the use of this rule-making authority in the federal trial courts in civil practice under these statutes is not clear. Unfortunately, the record is incomplete because the local federal court rules were published often in pamphlet form and have not survived. Very often, these rules were found in manuscript form in the clerk's office. Since the members of the bar practicing in the court were few, they were familiar with them and publication was not necessary.[34] The burden to prepare these rules was left to the local circuit court judge.

In 1872, Congress required the federal courts to follow the practice of the state courts in all matters. This statute became known as the Conformity Act.[35] The impact of this statute required that as the methods and procedures of practice were changed in the state, the federal courts were to follow those state practices within certain limits. Dicta in several decisions hint at the great diversity between the practice in the federal courts and in the state courts of the same territory. Justice Swayne stated that the difference between the federal and the state practices in the same locality were significant and had their origins in the enactment of codes by many of the states. Litigants in the federal tribunals adhered to the common law pleadings, forms and practice, while in the state courts of the same district the simpler forms of the local code prevailed.[36] The Justice goes on to state that "the inconvenience of such a state of things is obvious." The motive of Congress in adopting this statute was to require that the practice in the federal courts conformed to the practice that was followed in the state courts in the same locality "as near as may be." Another objective of the Conformity Act was "to relieve the legal profession from the burden of studying and of practising under two distinct different systems of the law of procedure in the same locality, one obtaining in the courts of the United States, the other in the courts of the State."[37]

The statute did not require absolute conformity to the local practice as there were a number of limitations upon the statute. The phrase requiring conformity "as near as may be" was not construed to mean "as near as may be possible or practicable." The Court explained that:

> it devolved upon the judges to be affected the duty of construing and deciding, and gave them the power to reject . . . any subordinate provision in such State statutes which, in their judgment, would unwisely encumber the administration of the law, or tend to defeat the ends of justice, in their tribunals.[38]

The distinction between equity and common law proceedings was continued, although many states had long since merged the two. Conformity could not fetter the judge in the personal discharge of his duties by encroaching upon the powers with which he was invested. Neither could the state practice be considered as binding on the federal courts where their purpose was to direct the officers in the performance of their duties.[39] In applying the statutes, the courts drew a distinction between those requirements of practice which were merely directory and those which were cautionary; and in either situation, failure to comply was not an error.

Although the objective of the Conformity Act was to have the practice of the federal courts uniform with the state courts in which they were located, many exceptions soon developed which gave the federal practice a greater complexity than the state practice. The instances in which Congress had enacted methods of practice obviously comprised the first exception. These tended to be very narrow, applying to specific types of suits such as forfeiture of bonds under the Revenue Act or under the Post Office Act. For example, a statute of 1791 provided that in suits brought by the United States against individuals, no claims or credit should be admitted at the trial unless it appeared that these claims had been presented to the accounting officers of the treasury and had been disallowed. If the party could prove that he had come into possession of vouchers and was prevented from exhibiting his claims to the treasury, then the party could be heard at the next succeeding term.[40] The federal statutes contain many such specific laws, as an examination of the

REVISED STATUTES (1874), where these specific practices are collected, will reveal.[41]

In administering the Conformity Act, the courts began to draft exceptions. Matters pertaining to the personal administration of the courts by the judges, such as how to charge the juries and other details of this nature, were not binding upon the federal courts. In such instances, the courts generally used such terms as "subordinate technical requirements" to describe items which were not binding and did not affect the federal courts. State practice affecting inherent authority of the court such as the discretion to set aside a verdict, modify the final judgment, or grant a motion for a new trial did not control the federal practice. Matters of practice decided by state courts and not involved in a state statute did not operate in the federal courts.[42] The federal courts continued to keep the distinction between proceedings in admiralty and equity, even though the latter had been abolished in a number of jurisdictions.

The appellate courts were often called upon to decide whether the federal courts could depart from the state practice. In one decision, Mr. Justice Pitney stated that, "whether, under the Conformity Act, . . . the trial court was required to adhere to the state practice governing the effect of the general verdict and the special findings may not be free from doubt" and proceeded to cite ten cases supporting that statement.[43] This is but one illustration of a small aspect of practice which the Supreme Court found not to be governed by the Conformity Act. However, such changes would come as a surprise to many district court judges who were trained in the practice of the state from which they were appointed and who would naturally follow this state practice.

Justice Blatchford found that the rules of the state courts "do not apply to proceedings in the Circuit Court taken for the purpose of reviewing (in the Supreme Court) a judgement of the Circuit Court, and that such rules and practice, embracing the preparation, perfecting, settling, and signing of a bill of exceptions, are not within the 'practice, pleadings, and forms and modes of proceeding' in the Circuit Court which are required" by the Conformity Act.[44] A few other areas in which the state practice did not control federal practice were those that required instructions to the jury to be reduced to writing or what papers could be taken by the jury when they retired, or the power of the circuit court to grant or refuse a new trial.

Without entering into further details, it is obvious that practice in the federal courts was rather confusing and that the Conformity Act fell far short of its objective of harmonizing the federal practice with the state practice. Evidence suggests that in some districts, the rules of the state practice were adhered to more strictly, ignoring some of the variations set up by decisions of the federal courts.[45]

Some of the more important areas in which the state practice was followed were in the following: form of action, except in equity practice;

set off or counter-claim; substitution of parties including form of process of notice; attachment; pleadings; joinder or severence of a cause of action; qualifications exempting a jury; order of trial issues; form in effect at verdict; judgments; and liens of judgment. The federal courts were controlled by federal rules in equity, service of process, amendments, evidence and depositions, production of books and papers, the mode of waiving trial by jury, execution of other proceedings after judgment, and appeal and error. Federal judges were not controlled by the state law in matters concerning instructions to the jury, although they were controlled by state practice in taking exceptions to the charge. The federal judge charged the jury orally, and he was permitted to comment on the evidence and give his views as to the weight of the evidence, provided he cautioned the jury that they were the final judges on questions of fact.[46] This was not the practice in many jurisdictions.

The federal government began to create new rights during the closing decades of the Nineteenth Century which brought additional cases into the federal courts and which in turn increased the number of lawyers practicing in this forum. To end the confusion in federal practice, a few leaders of the bar began a movement to give the Supreme Court of the United States the authority to prescribe procedure by rule of court rather than by legislation, as was the case in the majority of states at that period. As is so often the case, the argument became confused and instead of centering around the goal of accomplishing a simplification of the modes of procedure in the federal courts, the leaders argued about the existence of the court's inherent authority to govern rule-making procedure at all. This debate culminated in the statute of 1934 giving the Supreme Court of the United States such authority, again!

FOOTNOTES TO CHAPTER 14

1. Henry M. Hart and Herbert Wechsler, THE FEDERAL COURTS AND THE FEDERAL SYSTEM (1953), p.570.

2. Act of September 24, 1789, sec. 34, 1 STAT. 92.

3. Act of September 24, 1789, sec. 34, 1 STAT. 92.

4. Swift v. Tyson, 16 Pet. 1 (U.S. 1842).

5. Erie Railroad Company v. Tompkins, 304 U.S. 64 (1938).

6. Charles Alan Wright, HANDBOOK OF THE LAW OF FEDERAL COURTS (1963), p.209.

7. Act of September 29, 1789, 1 STAT. 93; Act of May 26, 1790, 1 STAT. 123; Act of May 8, 1792, 1 STAT. 275; Act of March 2, 1793, sec. 7, 1 STAT. 335.

8. Act of May 8, 1792, 1 STAT. 275.

9. Wayman v. Southard, 10 Wheat. 1 (U.S. 1825).

10. Wayman v. Southard, 10 Wheat. 1, 41 (U.S. 1825).

11. Act of September 24, 1789, sec. 17, 1 STAT. 83.

12. 1 Peter's C.C.R. 1 (D.C. 1792).

13. Fellerton et al. v. The Bank of the United States, 1 Pet. 604, 612-613 (U.S. 1828).

14. Ross and King v. Duval et al., 13 Pet. 45, 64 (U.S. 1839).

15. Act of May 19, 1828, 4 STAT. 278; Act of August 1, 1842, 5 STAT. 499.

16. Alfred Conkling, A TREATISE ON THE ORGANIZATION, JURISDICTION AND PRACTICE OF THE COURTS IN THE UNITED STATES (4th ed. 1864), p.302.

17. Act of August 1, 1842, 5 STAT. 499.

18. United States v. Council of Keokuk, 6 Wall. 514 (U.S. 1868); Smith v. Cockrill, 6 Wall. 756 (U.S. 1868).

19. Clark and Moore, "A New Federal Civil Procedure: The Background," 44 YALE L. J. 387, 401 (1935).

20. In Bennett v. Butterworth, 11 How. 667, 674 (U.S. 1850), Chief Justice Taney suggests that the United States District Court in Texas has adopted the state practice, but this adoption did not abolish the distinction between law and equity. Conkling, *supra,* note 16, p.314, gives an account of how the federal rules were conformed to the "radical reorganization" of the state courts and practice.

21. Conkling, *supra,* note 16, p.305.

22. *Ibid,* p.306.

23. *Ibid,* p.316.

24. Act of August 23, 1842, sec. 6, 5 STAT. 518.

25. This failure to prescribe rules in "proceedings at common law" is noted in Conkling, *supra,* note 16, p.302. Conkling's comment is more meaningful since he was a district court judge.

26. Duncan's Heirs v. United States, 7 Pet. 435, 451 (U.S. 1833).

27. Keary v. The Farmers' and Merchants' Bank of Memphis, 16 Pet. 89 (U.S. 1842).

28. Amis v. Smith, 16 Pet. 303 (U.S. 1842); Bronson v. Kinzie, 1 How. 311 (U.S. 1843), examines a local rule of the District Court of Illinois.

29. William Marvin, A TREATISE ON THE LAW OF WRECK AND SALVAGE (1858), Rule 18, p.306.

30. Rule 8, Rules of the Circuit and District Courts of the United States for the Missouri Districts (1958), p.80.

31. Rule 20, Rules of the Circuit and District Courts of the United States for the Missouri Districts and the Supreme Court of the United States (1871), p.98 [Pamphlet].

32. Rule 20, Rules of the Circuit and District Courts of the United States for the Missouri Districts (1858), p.41.

33. The Sagamore, 3 F.2d 689 (E.D. N.Y. 1924).

34. Rules of the Circuit and District Courts of the United States for the Southern District of Georgia (1897) shows an average of four to six lawyers admitted to the Bar of that court annually until 1860.

35. Act of June 1, 1872, sec. 5, 17 STAT. 196.

36. Nudd v. Burrows, 91 U.S. 426, 441 (1875).

37. Indianapolis & St. Louis R.R. Co. v. Horst, 93 U.S. 291, 300 (1876).

38. *Ibid,* p.301. For a general discussion of these and other problems, see Clark and Moore, "A New Federal Civil Procedure: The Background," 44 YALE L. J. 387, 402-409 (1935).

39. Bronson v. Kinzie, 1 How. 311 (U.S. 1843).

40. Act of March 3, 1797, sec. 3, 1 STAT. 514.

41. REVISED STATUTES (1874), p. 171 where there are collected 85 such sections.

42. Wall v. Chesapeake R.R. Co., 95 Fed. 398 (1899).

43. Spokane & I.E.R. Co. v. Campbell, 241 U.S. 497, 502, 688 (1915).

44. In the matter of Chateaugay Ore and Iron Co., 128 U.S. 544, 553 (1888).

45. James H. Wilkerson, "Federal Practice," 28 PROC. IND. BAR ASSOC. 84 (1924).

46. *Ibid,* p.103; Henry D. Clayton, "Uniform Federal Procedure," 84 CENT. L. J. 8 (1917).

Chapter 15

ADMIRALTY JURISDICTION

At the time of the American Revolution, the admiralty courts were well established in England with their own mode of procedure and a specialized bar consisting of proctors. The English admiralty courts had survived the attacks by the common law courts during the Seventeenth Century, although the limit of their jurisdiction was diminished and confined by the famous locality test of within "the ebb and flow of the tide" and below the first bridge.

England also established admiralty courts in the American colonies. These courts had become particularly unpopular because of their jurisdiction over cases involving the enforcement of the custom laws and the navigation acts — without a jury! At some time during the Revolutionary War, each state established an admiralty court. Some of these courts were actually organized.[1] The Articles of Confederation gave the Continental Congress appellate jurisdiction over cases of capture of prizes. At first, this jurisdiction was exercised by a committee, but by 1780, the Court of Appeals in Cases of Capture was established with regular judges. However, some of the decisions of this court were ignored by the state courts upon one technical ground or another, but chiefly because the local state admiralty judges did not recognize the legitimacy of the federal courts. It should be noted that the jurisdiction of this federal court was limited to questions of prize cases. Other aspects of admiralty jurisdiction were left to the jurisdiction of the state admiralty courts.

The Constitutional Convention delegated jurisdiction in admiralty causes of action to the courts of the federal government. This decision appears to have been accepted without controversy.[3] One writer observed that "the wisdom of the delegation of Admiralty jurisdiction to the tribunals of the United States has never been questioned, because so many of the questions arising in Admiralty Courts depend upon the Law of Nations, and affect the rights and interests of foreigners."[4]

The First Judiciary Act gave the district courts

exclusive original cognizance of all civil causes of admiralty and maritime jurisdiction, including all seizures under laws of impost, navigation or trade of the United States, where the seizures are made, on waters which are navigable from the sea by vessels of ten or more tons burthen, within their respective districts as well as upon the high seas; saving to suitors, in all cases, the right of a common law remedy where the common law is competent to give it.[5]

It should be noted that this statute has defined two different types of jurisdiction: first, the admiralty and maritime jurisdiction defined by the

Supreme Court as being limited to the ebb and flow of the tide; and second, seizures under the Revenue Acts of vessels of "ten tons or more" where the seizures are made on "waters navigable from the sea." Until the general admiralty jurisdiction was extended to encompass rivers and lakes beyond the ebb and flow of the tide, the geographical area of jurisdiction covered by revenue seizures was much broader than the admiralty jurisdiction. The issue was raised early whether the seizure cases came within the admiralty jurisdiction or the common-law jurisdiction of the district courts. The Supreme Court held that these cases were within the admiralty jurisdiction. It was suggested by one writer that "the reason of the legislature for putting seizures of this kind on the admiralty side of the court, was the great danger to the revenue if such causes should be left to the "caprice of juries."[6]

Pleadings and procedure in admiralty causes of action differed from procedure at common law in several significant aspects. Pleadings in admiralty practice did not require the same precision as pleadings in contemporary highly technical common-law pleading, but the cause of action had to be clearly set forth.[7] All admiralty actions were brought *in rem* against the ship and not *in personam* against individuals as at common-law. The pleading that initiated an admiralty suit was termed a libel. However, the most disturbing part of admiralty practice for the American lawyer was that issues were decided by the judge without a jury.

One of the most significant changes made in admiralty practice in this country was the introduction of "oral testimony and examination of witnesses in open court" by the First Judiciary Act.[8] The same statute made some other changes in traditional admiralty practices. Normally, all evidence was taken by depositions, but following the premise that all proceedings had to be in open court, the First Judiciary Act limited those who could give depositions to those persons about to go to sea or those who lived more than a hundred miles from the court or were "ancient and very infirm." The adverse party had to be notified so that he could attend the taking of the depositions. On appeal, depositions were limited to those which met the above criteria or were taken from witnesses since deceased. The First Judiciary Act did take great pains to introduce these new concepts in admiralty procedure which made possible the trend followed by the American courts to depart from admiralty procedure then practiced in England.

Traditionally, the admiralty court had jurisdiction of maritime contracts which included such contracts as charter-parties, contracts for maritime service in building, supplying and navigating ships, contracts between part-owners of ships, contracts and quasi-contracts respecting averages, contributions and jettisons.[9]

Prize and salvage problems make up one area which is of interest to the rights and interests of foreigners. Few prize cases come to the courts today because of the nature of naval warfare where ships built of iron or steel sink very easily. In the days of sailing vessels, it was customary for one nation to issue letters of marque and under that authority, ships would seize merchant ships of enemy states and if they were adjudged prizes under the rules of law, would be sold and the members of the crew, including captains and owners, would receive a definite portion of the proceeds arising from the sale of the ships and their cargoes. Such decisions, under traditional admiralty law, were considered as binding on all nations.[10]

Torts committed aboard ships on the high seas were triable in an admiralty court whether brought by passengers or crew members. Cases involving wages of seamen and problems of their care also were brought in admiralty court. In Massachusetts, the shares of seamen employed in whaling voyages were considered as wages since this was another mode of compensation.[11]

The location of a vessel has been the determinative factor as to whether a particular action could be tried in the admiralty courts or in the common law courts. The English courts had adopted the test of the ebb and flow of the tide. In other words, if a vessel was upon waters which were affected by the ebb and flow of the tide, admiralty courts had jurisdiction of actions against the ship or torts committed aboard. When this question first came before the American courts in 1825, the United States Supreme Court affirmed a decision which dismissed an action for a seaman's wage for lack of jurisdiction because the voyage took place on the Ohio and Missouri rivers above the ebb and flow of the tide. The Court concluded that the wages could not be considered as earned in maritime employment.[12] This was the first time that the Supreme Court had defined such a jurisdiction, although the issue may have been raised in the lower federal courts. It has been suggested that the reason for the Court's original ruling limiting admiralty jurisdiction to the ebb and flow of the tide in the *Thomas Jefferson* was in response to the anti-Court feelings in Congress at that period.[13]

Issues relating to shipping on the Great Lakes and the large navigable rivers in this country became a recurring problem for the courts, as the volume and importance of steamboat transportation increased. In 1837, a wage case involving a vessel which travelled between New Orleans and ports on the Mississippi River came before the Supreme Court. This action was brought as an admiralty case on the basis that the first port was below the ebb and flow of tide, and hence, within admiralty jurisdiction, but the court rejected this argument.[14] In 1845, Congress redefined the admiralty jurisdiction so as to include cases of contracts and torts

> arising in, upon, or concerning, steamboats and other vessels of twenty tons burden and upwards, . . . licensed for the coasting trade, and at the time employed in business of commerce and navigation between ports and places in different States and Territories upon the lakes and navigable waters connecting said

lakes, as is now possessed and exercised by the said courts in cases of the like steamboats and other vessels employed in navigation and commerce upon the high seas, or tide waters, within the admiralty and maritime jurisdiction of the United States.[15]

This statute was drafted by Justice Joseph Story and was approved by several of his colleagues.[16]

It was reported that the constitutionality of this statute was raised in a suit in the District Court for the Northern District of New York but not adjudicated at that time.[17] In fact, this court had exercised jurisdiction over a number of seizures under the Revenue Acts on the Great Lakes, and for that reason, had a fairly large number of suits on its admiralty docket. In 1851, in the famous case of *The Genesee Chief,* the Supreme Court, citing the statute of 1845, extended admiralty jurisdiction to a collision on Lake Ontario.[18] The chief issue presented to the Court was whether the statute was a constitutional exercise of federal power. This was answered in the affirmative. The Court reasoned that it was based upon the specific grant in the Constitution of admiralty jurisdiction to the federal courts rather than upon the regulation of commerce. The Court based its decision primarily upon the thesis that the tests of the English courts were not applicable to this country because of its geography. The Court stated that there was nothing "in the ebb and flow of the tide" that makes the waters peculiarly suitable for admiralty jurisdiction, nor anything in the absence of a tide that renders it unfit. If it is a public navigable water, on which commerce is carried on between different States or nations, the reasons for the jurisdiction is precisely the same.[19]

For a period following its decision in the *Genesee Chief* case, the Supreme Court denied federal jurisdiction over collisions on navigable rivers, holding that jurisdiction over the rivers was determined by the Judiciary Act of 1789.[20] However, in 1868, the jurisdiction of the federal courts was extended to include all navigable rivers in the famous case of *The Eagle.*[21] This case left open the definition of "public navigable waters" which was defined by the court in 1870 as those rivers which were normally used as highways for commerce and provided, by uniting with other rivers, "a continued highway over which commerce is or may be carried on with other States or foreign countries."[22] By 1870, the jurisdiction of the federal government over navigation on the rivers of this country was established. The significance of these decisions is that they extended the jurisdiction of federal courts to all crimes, and torts, committed on vessels on the "navigable waters" of the United States, and to contracts.

The extension of federal control over the regulation and inspection of all steam vessels preceded the extension of admiralty jurisdiction over the Great Lakes. It has been customary for centuries for ships to carry papers properly authenticated, generally by the customs service, to identify the ship and its home port, thus establishing its nationality. With the advent of the steam engine, Congress in 1838 provided that hulls and boilers of all steamboats should be inspected. This act applied to vessels that transported merchandise or passengers upon the "bays, lakes, rivers, or other navigable waters of the United States."[23] The Supreme Court construed this statute to include all vessels engaged in commerce on "navigable waters of the United States" as being subject to inspection, although a vessel may have been travelling between points in the same state.[24] The statute was found constitutional as an exercise of the commerce power of the federal government.

An area in which the extension of the jurisdiction in admiralty cases brought the federal courts into conflict with the state laws involved liens upon vessels for work done or for the supply of goods and services to the vessel. As the number of steamships increased, a number of states adopted statutes allowing liens to be placed against the vessels or their owners. Those liens on the ship itself were maritime liens and were enforceable in the district courts.[25] In 1819, the Supreme Court held that the federal courts in admiralty would enforce a state lien for supplies furnished at the home port, although no such lien was recognized by the admiralty law of this country or Great Britain. Justice Story, in writing the opinion, stated that "as to repairs and necessaries in the port or State to which the ship belongs, the case is governed altogether by the local law" of that state.[26] It was concluded by one author "that state courts or circuit courts of the United States may take cognizances of all maritime contracts and torts, if the relief sought is one which common law or chancery can give; but if the relief sought is peculiar to the court of admiralty, only the district courts of the United States can administer it."[27] If the remedy sought was *in personam,* the state courts had concurrent jurisdiction with the federal courts.

Another area in which the states had supplemented the admiralty jurisdiction was in the area of wrongful death actions. At common law, tort actions did not survive the death of either of the parties and the various states passed statutes providing a remedy in wrongful death actions. In one of the early cases before the Supreme Court, a suit was brought *in rem* for the deaths of a first officer in a collision on the territorial waters of Massachusetts. Both the states of Pennsylvania, the home port of the vessel, and Massachusetts gave an action for wrongful death provided it was brought within one year. In this suit, the Supreme Court recognized the remedy, but denied that it was applicable to the case because the suit was brought five years after the wrongful death.[28]

During this same period, it was difficult for the plaintiff in an employment injury case to be successful in a tort action because of the application of the fellow servant doctrine. Under this doctrine, an employee could not recover when the injury or accident was due to the negligence of a fellow employee. To simplify the recovery for industrial injuries, the various states adopted the Workmen's Compensation Acts.

When Congress extended the acts to cover injuries in the maritime industry, the Supreme Court held that the work of a longshoreman was maritime in nature and the extension of a workmen's compensation statute to cover such injuries was unconstitutional. Congress amended the Judicial Code in 1922 by reserving "to claimants the rights and remedies under workmen's compensation laws of any state".[29] This provision was struck down by the Supreme Court as being unconstitutional, but the Court hinted strongly that Congress could enact its own system of compensation.[30] Congress responded by enacting the Longshoreman's and Harbor Worker's Compensation Act of 1927.[31]

The preceding statute dealt with maritime workmen ashore, but what about the seaman injured in the course of his employment at sea? Traditionally, the seamen's recovery for work injuries was restricted to wages, maintenance and cure, except where the vessel was unseaworthy, in which event the seaman was entitled to indemnity. The Seaman's Act of 1916 abrogated the fellow servant doctrine for injuries occurring aboard the ship.[32] When the Supreme Court held this statute did not apply to longshoremen, Congress amended the statute by what has become known as the "Jones Act" which allows the seaman an election to sue for damages at law or under the action provided by the Railway Employer's Liability Act.[33]

Congress has extended the subject matter of admiralty jurisdiction by several statutes. The first of these statutes was the Limitation of Shipowner's Liability Act passed in 1851.[34] This statute was a reaction to the decision of the Supreme Court in *The Lexington* which held a shipowner fully liable for the value of a loss by fire of gold coins that were shipped on the vessel although the nature of the cargo was not declared in the bill of lading. The statute covers such problems as loss of property or personal injury in collision cases. A shipowner is held liable for losses caused by the "design or neglect of such owner." The owner's pecuniary liability to the third parties was limited to the value of the vessel at the conclusion of the voyage in instances where there was no causal neglect on the part of the owner. This statute has been modified in a number of ways, but in essence, the liability of the vessel owner for losses can be significantly limited in amount. The most controversial extension of the Limitation Statute has been to its coverage of pleasure craft.

The procedure in admiralty cases has been governed since 1844 by the rules prescribed by the Supreme Court of the United States. In 1792, the Supreme Court was given wide rule-making authority, especially in equity and admiralty.[35] This provision was repeated in the statute in 1842.[36] Pursuant to the statute, the Supreme Court adopted a set of admiralty rules in 1844. These rules were amended and completely revised in 1921. Before 1844, several local district courts drafted rules relating to admiralty cases. The two earliest sets were those adopted by the District Courts for the Southern and Northern Districts of New York. These rules were included in the two first texts published on American admiralty law, and for this reason, were probably copied widely.[37] Since there is no convenient collection of rules for the lower federal courts for the Nineteenth Century, it is impossible to determine how sophisticated admiralty practice was in these courts. Rules are the most fugitive of all legal materials, for if they were published, they were in pamphlets which have long since disappeared or were a part of some major work.

With the adoption of one form of action in the Federal Rules of Civil Procedure in 1940, the significance of admiralty practice and procedure for all practical purposes began to disappear. Within a few years (precise data cannot be determined), those federal district courts which had separate admiralty dockets discontinued them, and thereafter, all cases were filed on the civil docket. The Advisory Committee on Admiralty Rules recommended changes in 1964 unifying the admiralty and civil procedures.[38] The Committee provided specific exceptions in several civil rules to differentiate between the law and admiralty and provided supplementary rules for the special problems arising only in admiralty matters. The burden was placed upon the plaintiff to state if a claim was brought in admiralty or as a civil action.[39] Substantive maritime law is not affected by the merger. Distinctive admiralty remedies such as actions *in rem,* foreign attachment, and limitations of actions are all preserved. The special procedures associated with the admiralty practice have gradually disappeared until this special area of the law will be only of historical interest. The silver oar, which was the symbol of the Admiralty Court with its separate procedure, substantive law, officers and bar, has been retired.[40]

The admiralty law of the United States has been shaped by several outstanding judges. Several of the first federal court judges had experiences in admiralty courts before the Revolution or sat on the Court of Appeals in Cases of Capture or the local state admiralty court before the Constitution was adopted. William Paca of Maryland and Cyrus Griffin of Virginia had both served on the Court of Appeals in Cases of Capture under the Articles of Confederation. Thomas Bee, judge of the District Court of South Carolina, published a volume of admiralty decisions in 1810. Judge Albert Conkling of the District Court for the Northern District of New York wrote a text on the subject, first published in 1848, which went through several editions. Judge Samuel Rossiter Betts of the District Court for the Southern District of New York, who served on that court from 1826 to 1867, was well respected for his admiralty decisions, which were collected and first published in FEDERAL CASES. Justice Story should not be overlooked for his contributions. His decision in *DeLovio v. Boit*[41], in which the history of admiralty courts in England from which all subsequent writers have quoted, was recommended highly for study. He drafted the statute extending jurisdiction to the Great Lakes[42] and probably drafted the admiralty rules adopted by the Supreme

Court in 1844. Another indication of the importance of admiralty practice was the number of volumes of maritime decisions reported before the advent of the FEDERAL REPORTER.[43]

FOOTNOTES TO CHAPTER 15

1. Franklyn C. Setaro, "The Formative Era of American Admiralty Law," 5 N.Y. LAW FORUM 9 (1959); Harrington Putnam, "How the Federal Courts Were Given Admiralty Jurisdiction," 10 CORN. L. Q. 460 (1925).

2. Henry J. Bourguignon, THE FIRST FEDERAL COURT, THE FEDERAL APPELLATE PRIZE COURT OF THE AMERICAN REVOLUTION (1977), p.112.

3. Harrington Putnam, "How the Federal Courts Were Given Admiralty Jurisdiction," 10 CORN. L. Q. 460 (1925).

4. Andrew Dunlap, A TREATISE ON THE PRACTICE OF THE COURTS OF ADMIRALTY IN CIVIL CASES OF MARITIME JURISDICTION (2d ed. 1850), p.61.

5. Act of September 24, 1789, sec. 9, 1 STAT. 77.

6. Alfred Conkling, A TREATISE ON THE ORGANIZATION, JURISDICTION AND PRACTICE OF THE COURTS OF THE UNITED STATES (4th ed. 1864), p.231, quoting Justice Samuel Chase in United States v. The Betsy, 4 CRANCH. 443, 446 (U.S. 1808).

7. Jenks v. Lewis, Ware 51, 13 FED. CAS. 539; Brig. Sarah Ann, 2 Sum. 206, 21 FED. CAS. 432. The proceeding in admiralty praised in 2 WESTERN L. J. 566 (1845) and a case from Louisville (Ky.) Chancery Court applied the rule that if a collision happens without fault to either side, or if both are at fault, then each party bears one-half the cost. 2 WESTERN L. J. 480 (1845).

8. Act of September 24, 1789, sec. 30, 1 STAT. 88.

9. Dunlap, *supra,* note 4, p.60.

10. Williams v. Armroyd, 7 Cranch. 423 (U.S. 1813). In Glass et al v. The Sloop Betsey et al, 3 Dallas 6 (U.S. 1794), the question was raised whether Congress could give the district court jurisdiction in prize cases in peace time and this was answered in the affirmative.

11. Baxter v. Rodman, 20 Mass. (3 Pick.) 435, 439 (1825).

12. Steamboat Thomas Jefferson, 10 Wheat. 428 (U.S. 1825).

13. "Note, From Judicial Grant to Legislative Power: The Admiralty Clause in the Nineteenth Century," 67 HARV. L. REV. 1218 (1954). Although it is the general practice to ignore "student notes," this is certainly an exception, for it is thoroughly researched and raises many issues ignored by previous writers.

14. Steamboat Orleans, 11 Pet. 175 (U.S. 1837).

15. Act of February 26, 1845, 5 STAT. 726. Edgar H. Farrar, "The Extension of the Admiralty Jurisdiction by Judicial Interpretations," 33 ABA REPORTS 459 (1906), reviews the many decisions and argues that the courts have extended admiralty jurisdiction.

16. "The Limits of the Exclusive Jurisdiction of the Admiralty in the United States," 3 AMER. L. REV. 598 (1869).

17. Alfred Conkling, THE ADMIRALTY JURISDICTION, LAW AND PRACTICE (2d ed. 1857), v. 1, p.8. On page 12, Judge Conkling repeats the text of his first edition where he argues that the Statute of 1845, is based upon the power to regulate commerce.

18. The Propeller Genesse Chief v. Fitzhugh, et al., 12 How. 443 (U.S. 1851). *See* F. Dumont Smith, "Decisive Battles of the Constitutional Law, VIII, The Genesee Chief," 9 A.B.A. J. 527 (1923).

19. The Propeller Genesse Chief v. Fitzhugh, et al., 12 How. 443, 454 (U.S. 1851).

20. The Hine v. Trevor, 4 Wall. 555 (U.S. 1866).

21. The Eagle, 8 Wall. 15 (U.S. 1868).

22. The Daniel Ball, 10 Wall. 557, 563 (U.S. 1870).

23. Act of July 7, 1838, 5 STAT. 304.

24. Waring et al v. Clarke, 5 How. 441, 465 (U.S. 1847).

25. The Moses Taylor, 4 Wall. 411 (U.S. 1866).

26. The General Smith-Hollins, et al., 4 Wheat. 438 (U.S. 1819).

27. "History of Admiralty Jurisdiction," 5 AMER. L. REV. 618 (1871).

28. For a general discussion, *see* George C. Sprague, "The Extension of Admiralty Jurisdiction and the Growth of Substantive Maritime Law in the United States Since 1835," in LAW; A CENTURY OF PROGRESS 1835-1935 (1937), v. 3, p.307. The Harrisburg, 119 U.S. 199 (1886).

29. Act of June 10, 1922, 42 STAT. 634.

30. State of Washington v. W.C. Dawson and Co., 264 U.S. 219 (1924).

31. Act of March 4, 1927, 44 STAT. 1424.

32. Act of April 22, 1908, 35 STAT. 65.

33. Act of June 10, 1922, 42 STAT. 634.

34. Act of March 3, 1851, 9 STAT. 635.

35. Act of May 8, 1792, sec. 2, 1 STAT. 276.

36. Act of August 23, 1842, sec. 6, 5 STAT. 518.

37. Dunlap, *supra,* note 4; Conkling, *supra,* note 17.

38. REPORTS OF PROCEEDINGS OF THE JUDICIAL CONFERENCE OF THE UNITED STATES (1965), p.52.

39. Charles W. Joiner, "The New Civil Rules, A Substantial Improvement," 40 F.R.D. 359, 362 (1967). For a text of these rules with explanatory notes, *see* 39 F.R.D. 69, 146 (1966). The Special Committee Federal Rules of Procedure of the American Bar Association joined in the recommendation to merge the two procedures. 38 F.R.D. 95, 100 (1965).

40. Charles Merrill Hough, REPORTS OF CASES IN THE VICE ADMIRALTY OF THE PROVINCE OF NEW YORK (1925), p.xxviii.

41. 7 FED. CAS. 418 (C.C.D. Mass. 1815).

42. "The Project of Extending Admiralty Jurisdiction over the Lakes and Rivers of the United States," 2 WESTERN L. J. 563 (1845).

43. The reporters included, Peters, Bee, Sprague, Van Ness, Blatchford's Prize Cases, Fisher's Prize Cases, Newberry and Brown, a total of twelve volumes of admiralty decisions covering the period from 1792-1875.

Chapter 16

EQUITY JURISDICTION

Since equity as a separate system of law has disappeared, any interest in the subject is purely historical. From the beginning, the kings of England exercised the prerogative of interfering in legal cases where it was necessary to meet special needs. From this practice came the principle that "the jurisdiction of courts of equity is exercised either for the protection of rights which the common law does not recognize; or for the prevention or redress of wrongs for which the common law affords no adequate remedy."[1] Gradually, the chancellors began exercising the King's conscience to provide remedies where the law could not. Theoretically, precedents never had the binding force in the equity courts that they had in common law courts, but the tendency to follow the decisions of previous chancellors was very strong. By the Seventeenth Century or earlier, equity had developed into a system of law with its own rules, terminology and forms of procedure.[2] The underlying foundation of the system was the accepted principle that the Chancellor would not grant relief except in special circumstances and hence the maxim that where there was a remedy at law, there was none in equity.

Equity relief was extraordinary in the sense that it was granted at the discretion of the Chancellor and its decrees acted upon the individual rather than upon property which was within the jurisdiction of the common law courts. Equity could be used to prevent fraud or correct mistakes made by a party entering a contract. Its jurisdiction extended to enforcing rights of third parties in land and through its procedures, removing restrictions on the use of land, including termination of servitudes running with the property, could be removed. Equity could provide for specific performance of contracts. Another substantive area was the protection of intangible property rights including trade secrets. Suits by stockholders against the corporation to prevent fraud or to prevent the misuse of resources were brought in equity. Equity was used to protect the property rights of married women. It was in the Chancery Courts in England that the entire field of trust was developed.

A number of writs were exclusively used in equity. The chief weapon in the arsenal of equitable remedies was the injunction. If this was violated, the offender was punished by imprisonment for contempt. Through the bill of peace, equity could prevent the multiplicity of lawsuits against the single individual.

Pleading in equity was an entirely different system than in the common law courts. The case of *Jarndyce v. Jarndyce,* the fictional case reported in Dickens' BLEAK HOUSE, vividly describes the delays, the technicalities and the expense involved in a suit in chancery in England. This account was certainly overdrawn, but just how far is a matter of dispute. Unfortunately for many individuals, this fictional account is the extent of their understanding of equity and contributed to the system becoming unpopular. In the early days, the pleadings in the court were informal without any technical rules of pleadings. The suit in equity was initiated by a bill of the complainant followed by demurrer, or answer of the defendant, and the replication of the plaintiff. The trial was informal and often evidence was produced by written depositions. Many of the rules of evidence, such as the parol evidence rule, did not apply. The writ of *ne exeat* was one of the special writs which was issued to prevent the named party from leaving the country. The bill for discovery was a method to obtain evidence from the adverse party by production of books or papers or any other evidence in the possession of the other party. This practice had been taken over by the law side of the courts even before the two systems were merged. Equity could perpetuate testimony if there was a chance the evidence would be lost before the action was begun by the other party, a practice that has practically disappeared. All equitable remedies were discretionary. The equity court was opened to the parties at all times, whereas courts of law commonly observed terms.

In the American colonies, equity courts were established and administered by the Royal Governors, and for that reason, separate chancery courts were suspect. However, the biggest evil of these courts was that they proceeded without a jury.[3]

When the federal courts were established in 1789, equity was a well established system of law. Although there were few separate chancery courts in the American states, the best trained attorneys were well aware of equity and methods of procedure belonging exclusively to that system. When the federal courts were established, equitable powers were conferred upon the circuit court rather than the district court.

Probably as a result of the unfortunate colonial experiences, a number of limitations were imposed in the First Judiciary Act on the equity side of the courts. The First Judiciary Act stated that equity could not proceed where there was a plain, adequate and complete remedy at common law.[4] How strong this principle was in the contemporary English chancery practice is not clear, although by the end of the Nineteenth Century these courts had lost some of their power. Another provision gave all federal courts the authority after "due notice . . . to require the parties to produce books or writings in their possession . . . which contain evidence. . . ."[5]

Proceedings in Equity

The procedure in equity was entirely different from that followed in the common law side of the federal courts. Because the federal courts were free to completely regulate practice, it was uniform throughout the United States. All evidence tends to point to the fact that the technicalities of equity pleading as it was known at the end of the Eighteenth Century became completely obliviated by the beginning of the Twentieth Century.

The typical suit in equity was initiated by the filing of an information or a bill. Generally the information was used to protect the rights of those individuals who were wards of the court such as idiots, lunatics and infants. The information was required to state to the courts the rights which were claimed on the behalf of others. Any other suitor would have filed a bill which was in the nature of a petition to the court known as an English bill. This term arose because when pleadings in the common law were in law Latin or law French, these bills were written in the English language.[6]

Bills were divided into four classes: original bills, bills not original, bills in the nature of original bills, and bills in the nature of bills not original. Bills not original are those which relate to some matter previously litigated in the equity courts by identical parties and which are either in addition to or a continuance of an original bill or both. Bills in the nature of original bills are those which are brought before the court proceedings and decrees in a former suit, for the purpose of either obtaining their benefit, or procuring a reversal of the decree.[7] The original bills and the nature of bills not original included petitions to obtain perhaps a judicial construction of a previous decree[8] or to determine the rights of a claimant to funds in the hands of a federal marshal.[9]

The federal rules required that the bill should state in as "brief and succinct terms as it reasonably can" the facts, and it was to contain no unnecessary recitals, documents or any "scandalous matter not relevant to the suit."[10] Other strict rules included the fact that the bill should state the plaintiff's cause with sufficient certainty and should not be multifarious in joining two or more parties on unconnected grounds for equitable relief, each of which might be foundation for a separate bill.[11] These are but a few requirements of a bill.

At this point, the defendant was summoned to answer by a subpoena which again was different from the procedure in the common law courts. Many of the writs in the common law courts would require the arrest of the defendant who could then post a bond to answer. The subpoena merely summoned a defendant to appear and answer the bill. The mere filing of the bill was sufficient warrant for the clerk to issue a subpoena which had to be served by the marshal upon the defendant personally. If the defendant did not appear and was called three times on three different occasions, the plaintiff could move for a bill *pro confesso*.[12] With this, the court could proceed to a judgment. A second alternative was for the defendant to file a demurrer in which the defendant admitted the truth of the bill but claimed that he should be excused from answering for some particular reason, including a lack of jurisdiction. A demurrer admitted all facts well pleaded, but it did not admit to inferences or other arguments.[13]

The demurrer could be overruled, and in that event, the plaintiff was entitled to his costs up to that period. The defendant at this point could take his third alternative of filing an answer.

The answer to the bill was divided into several classes and again was surrounded with complicated rules. For example, a plea could only contain a single defense although it could state more than one fact, but it had to bring the matters in issue to a single point. Otherwise, the bill was open to the charge of duplicity and could be overruled.[14] Among the classes of pleas of answer were those to the jurisdiction of the court, to the persons involved, or to the pendency of another suit. The answer as contrasted to the demurrer allowed the plaintiff the benefits of discovery by oral examination of any party or persons involved in the case. The answer had to be responsive to all interrogatories.[15] An answer could be addressed only to one party. If there were several parties involved, the plaintiff had to file a cross bill.

The plaintiff could respond to the answer by filing a replication in which he put into issue the matters pleaded in the defendant's answer or plea. No replication could be filed to a demurrer. Again, there were several types of replications.[16]

There were other refinements of the practice process, such as bills of revivor, supplementary bills and other bills. The complexity of the extra pleading is obvious, and although it became greatly simplified and reformed in the federal courts, it was considered more complex in civil practice. For those familiar with the practice, the steps were considered logical and above all, required skill.

The most famous writ issued by the equity courts was the injunction. Generally, the plaintiff would file a bill in which he asked relief pending the suit. At one point, an injunction could be issued at the request of the plaintiff and without notice to the other party. The requirement of notice to the defendant gradually evolved. An injunction was issued to stay waste, and in this event, the plaintiff had to clearly state his title to the property and the nature of the waste which was sought to be enjoined.[17]

The above outline does not do justice to the intricacies of equity practice, but is intended to introduce the reader to its complexities. The classic guide to equity practice was prepared by Justice Joseph Story and first published in 1838 while he was a member of the Supreme Court and a professor at Harvard Law School. The tenth and last edition of this important work was published in 1892.[18]

Federal Equity Rules

Unlike cases at common law, the procedure in equity was governed by rules adopted by the Supreme Court, and in no way could it be changed by local state practice.[19] The chief interest in the history of equity in the federal system is not in the substantive rules which it enforced, but rather the rules adopted by the Supreme Court and how equity was kept as a separate system even in those states where equity was unknown or had been merged with common law.

Under the "Process Act" of 1789, the form of proceedings in equity and admiralty were to be according to the civil law.[20] Civil law, in this context, was understood to refer to both these systems which were based upon the Roman law. This act was later replaced by another which stated that the forms in equity would be according to the principles, rules and usages which belonged to a court of equity as distinguished from the courts of common law. This provision was construed as adopting the rules and usages of the Court of Chancery of England. The Supreme Court was given the authority to prescribe the rules to govern the equitable actions in the district courts.[21]

The Supreme Court first exercised its power to prescribe equity rules for the federal trial courts in 1822.[22] These rules were replaced twenty years later and continued in use with amendments until the next century.[23] Justice Joseph Story was the draftsman of the rules of 1842 and could have been responsible for the set adopted twenty years earlier.[24] Obviously, these rules were not a complete code of equity procedure nor a code of the substantive law on that subject. Where the equity rules prescribed by the Supreme Court did not apply,

> the practice of the Circuit Court shall be regulated by the present practice of the High Court of Chancery in England, so far as the same may reasonably be applied consistently with the local circumstances and local convenience of the district, where the court is held, not as positive rules, but as furnishing just analogies to regulate the practice.[25]

Justice Bradley referred to the first edition of Daniell, as well as the second edition SMITH'S PRACTICE, as being "the most authoritative work on English chancery practice in use in March 1842, when our equity rules were adopted."[26] The Justice cautioned that subsequent editions of Daniell were far removed from the standard adopted by the Supreme Court in 1842,

> but as they contain a view of the later decisions bearing upon so much of the old system as remains, they have, on that account, a value of their own, provided one is not misled by the new portions.[27]

A significant omission among Justice Bradley's recommendations are the two works by Justice Story, one of the substantive law of equity and the other on equitable procedure.[28] This oversight can only be explained by the fact that the volumes to which Bradley referred were directed towards English practice as dictated by the rules. American law's indebtedness to Justice Story for his contribution to the development of equity has not been fully evaluated.

To what extent the federal courts turned to English precedent is disputed. One authority concluded that, "It is fortunate that our courts have seldom had to go beyond their own rules and resort to the practice of the English court, because of the enormous difficulty of ascertaining what the practice of the English court was at any particular time."[29]

How effective the rules were is another matter of dispute. They were not followed strictly in all the federal courts, as practice in each varied greatly. One federal court judge, Eli S. Hammond of the District Court for the Western District of Tennessee, remarked on the equity rules that

> [e]xcept in a general way, very little attention has been paid to them, and I doubt if any case can be found in any of the courts where they have been scrupulously and exactly enforced, or where they have been even nearly followed. Besides, we mix our state and federal practice almost indistinguishably, and quite unconsciously.[30]

Another writer questioned whether a uniform system of equity could be established in the federal courts. Nathan Dane, in his famous ABRIDGEMENT, suggested that no separate equity system had been established in numerous states, "But in the constitution of the United States we have laid a solid foundation of such a system." He thought that the Supreme Court could formulate the practice, but that it would be impracticable to establish a uniform system in a subordinate federal court. However, he was optimistic that in the Supreme Court, equity would "slowly grow up to a high state of perfection. The judges of the court have, and probably always will have, the books, the abilities and the disposition to build it up."[31] But that was not to be!

During the Nineteenth Century, after the American equity rules were adopted, the English significantly modified their practice. Because of this, and the change in general attitude towards a more simplified practice, a need for a revision of the equity rules for the federal courts became obvious, and in 1912, the Supreme Court promulgated a new set. During the summer of 1911, Justice Horace H. Lurton (1844-1914) of the Supreme Court of the United States travelled to England and observed the operation and work of the English High Court of Chancery. Lurton had been chancellor in equity in Tennessee before going on to the supreme court of that state. In preparing the rules, the Supreme Court established a committee consisting of the Chief Justice, Edward D. White (1845-1921), and the two youngest members of the court, Lurton and Willis van Devanter (1859-1941). This committee was assisted by a group of lawyers in each circuit which gave suggestions to the court. This was the first time that the court had used this technique in preparing rules, a practice which later became a precedent for other rule-making projects. The rules went into force on February 1, 1913, but are referred to as the Equity Rules of 1912.[32]

These new Equity Rules made some noble departures in equitable practice in the federal courts. All technical forms of pleadings which were not prescribed or required by statute, were abolished, as were demurrers, pleas and replications. The rules spelled out the practice governing the issuance of injunctions which was fairly uniform, but not prescribed in the former rules.[33] The courts were given authority to vary the rules where necessary to prevent "substantial injustice" which liberalized the application of the rules.

It is important to note that until the abolition of equitable practice in 1938, the federal courts were governed completely by the federal rules, notwithstanding state statutes or state practice. In states like Louisiana, where no equity practice existed in the state courts, the federal courts had to administer a separate equity jurisdiction.[34] Chief Justice Taney made it very clear that the abolition of the distinction between the forms of actions in Texas did not apply in the federal courts of that state.[35] Several territories created after the Civil War had combined law and equitable procedures. In recognition of this, Congress enacted legislation stating that it would not be necessary for the courts in the territories to exercise separately "the common-law and chancery jurisdictions."[36] It is a strong possibility that when these territories were admitted as states, the federal courts did not separate the two systems. To put an end to this confusion, several writers suggested that equity be abolished and that federal practice follow state practice.[37]

State practices in some situations were more direct, but were not followed in the federal courts. For example, a married woman who could bring an action in the state courts had to proceed through a friend of the court in the federal courts. For this reason, the skillful advocate could reach different objectives in the federal court which could not be accomplished in the state courts.[38] Regardless of the improvements made by the Equity Rules, Congress felt it was necessary to make equitable defenses available in actions at law.[39] The abolition of equity had been advocated by some and was abolished as a separate system in several states in the Nineteenth Century. This was accomplished in the federal courts by the Rules of Civil Procedure in 1938.

Use of Masters in Equity

The labor of judges in chancery had been reduced by referring to masters the investigation of facts and the preparation of a report to the court. Certain other ministerial duties could be referred to a master, including examination of the pleadings to determine if they contained kin and creditors, and specialized duties arising from federal statutes, such as determination of infringement of copyright.[40] One of the most challenging of these duties was the examination of accounts and the superintendence of the performance of the receivers.

The circuit courts with the concurrence of both judges had the authority to appoint standing masters in chancery in their respective districts.[41] Otherwise, the masters were appointed by a decree or order of the court and their authority was generally limited by such a decree.

As soon as possible after a case was referred to him, the master was required to assign a time and place for the proceeding, and notice was given to the parties by service of warrants. Under the federal equity rules, the master had full authority to regulate the proceedings before him, and should he not act properly, the aggrieved party could apply to the judge for corrections in the proceedings.[42] The master had the power to examine the parties under oath and to examine all papers and other matters presented in the case. Witnesses were examined and were summoned by the subpoena which was served by the party who requested it. The findings were incorporated into a report which was presented to the judge, and if there were any errors, the solicitors, as attorneys who practiced in the chancery court were known, could file their objections. It is reasonable to expect that the federal judges referred many matters to masters for their consideration.

Receivers

When any property or other assets were involved, the court could appoint a receiver whose duty it was to gather and administer the assets. Most of the cases in the early part of the Nineteenth Century involved mortgages, but as corporations developed as a general form of business organization, it became necessary to appoint receivers to wind up the affairs of a company by taking charge and disposing of all property and distributing the funds among the creditors and owners. However, the federal courts departed from the English precedents by appointing receivers to manage railroads.[43] As corporations such as railroads and telegraph companies came to involve millions of dollars, the opportunity for charges of corruption grew.[44]

The appointment of receivers began to take on special significance in the area of railroads which were in financial difficulties. Traditionally, a receiver would be appointed to provide for the safety of property of a corporation pending litigation, but chiefly to obtain equitable assets for the foreclosure of a mortgage or dissolution in winding up affairs of partnerships or corporations. The receiver was charged with the responsibility of protecting the property and operating the business until the court had determined the issues.[45] Not only were receivers appointed for railroads, but they were also appointed for bankrupt cities such as in the famous case involving Memphis, Tennessee.[46] The use of the corporate structure was rapidly expanding at the end of the Nineteenth Century, and this rapidly increased the burden of the court. One justice noted that of the fifty or more railroads within his judicial circuit, "hardly half a dozen have escaped the hands of the receivers."[47] The justice observed that if the receivers had limited themselves to the traditional duties to "sell the roads, collect the means of the companies, and pay their debts, it might have been well enough. But this was hardly ever done." He indicated that the receivers who operated the railroads rarely paid the debts of the corporation, but more often added to them by "creating a new and superior lien on the property pledged to them."[48]

Federal judges were accused of appointing individuals as receivers who were not competent to run a business, and as one would expect, charges of favoritism were heard. In spite of the well known principle that courts of equity would not grant an extraordinary remedy like specific performance where the defendant would be caused a greater injury, yet the receivers were appointed upon flimsy allegations and often without notice to all parties.[49] Such appointments were very remunerative to the recipient, especially when appointed as a receiver of a large corporation such as a railroad or telegraph company. Lawyers had a questionable role in these transactions. A businessman who ran his own company without frequent legal advice would, upon appointment as a receiver, find that he could make no move without frequent advice from counsel. This summary of the abuses of the system is by a judge of the District Court of the Eastern District of Arkansas. This same author includes a quote from James Bryce to the effect that

> In the minds of certain New York judges, the old-fashioned distinction between a receiver of property in a court of equity and a receiver of stolen goods at common law, may be said to have been lost.[50]

What was said of receivers in New York could equally be said of those in the federal courts.[51] Often, the receivers came into conflict with the state officials who attempted to collect taxes or judgments. A constable in Missouri was cited for contempt in attempting to execute a judgment against a railroad in receivership.[52]

At different times, Congress would grant to different federal officials the right to appoint receivers for specific purposes. In 1876, the comptroller of the currency was allowed to appoint receivers to take over the assets of banks under his jurisdiction in the event of a failure.[53] Until the comptroller acted, the federal courts would appoint a receiver.

Abuse of the Injunction

The federal courts were viewed as having abused their equity power through issuing injunctions in two different situations which fueled the debate over the abolition of equity. During the first decades of the Twentieth Century, when the states were enacting regulatory statutes, the United States district courts were free in issuing injunctions against their enforcement based upon the argument that these statutes were unconstitutional.[54] Congress responded to this commonly held perception of abuse by enacting a statute requiring a three judge court to issue such an injunction on the theory that three judges would not be as quick to issue such injunctions.

During the decade following 1920, the federal judges used the injunction as a weapon to control the expansion of organized labor. In the Clayton Act, Congress attempted to prohibit the use of the injunction for organized labor activities such as participating in a labor dispute whether singly or in concert, becoming a member of the Union or paying strike benefits.[55] Nevertheless, the Supreme Court confined the interpretation of this act to the "immediate disputants," and the other members of the Union not standing in proximate relation as employer and employees could be enjoined.[56] This was certainly more restrictive than what Congress intended.

The federal judges apparently sought to outdo one another in making their injunctions as broad as possible. One injunction prohibited the union from publishing and distributing "directly or indirectly, in writing or verbally to any person, association of persons or corporations, any statement" which indicated that there was a strike at a certain mill or that the mill was unfair to organized labor or that the employers required all employees to subscribe to a "yellow dog" contract. This was an agreement that the employee would not join a union.[57] Injunctions in labor disputes as applied by the federal courts were described by one writer "by the expansion of a simple, judicial device to an enveloping code of prohibited conduct, absorbing, en masse, executive and police functions and affecting the livelihood and even lives of multitudes."[58] Another objection to these injunctions was the fact that any violation could be punished summarily often without the individuals knowing what conduct was being punished. In the view of one Congressional committee, this amounted to a federal judge unconstitutionally legislating and then punishing all offenders.[59] Obviously, some members of the Congress did not view the situation in this light and continued to insist that contracts signed by an employee upon employment agreeing not to join a union were valid.[60] Congress responded by passing the Anti-injunction Act.[61] A number of specific actions by organized labor could not be prohibited by injunctions. Further, the defendant could demand a jury trial in a contempt proceeding and ask that the judge who issued the injunction recuse himself from the trial. These were drastic limitations on the power of the federal courts to issue injunctions.

FOOTNOTES TO CHAPTER 16

1. Roger Foster, A TREATISE ON PLEADING AND PRACTICE IN EQUITY (1890), p.3.

2. *See* Henry L. McClintock, HANDBOOK ON EQUITY (1936), p.2; C.L. Bates, FEDERAL EQUITY PROCEDURE, A TREATISE ON THE PROCEDURE IN SUITS OF EQUITY IN THE CIRCUIT COURTS OF THE UNITED STATES (1901), v.1, p.21; H.D. Hazeltine, "Early History of English Equity," ESSAYS IN LEGAL HISTORY READ BEFORE THE CONGRESS OF HISTORICAL STUDIES (1913); Edward D. Re., SELECTED ESSAYS ON EQUITY (1955), pp.1-89.

3. Erwin C. Surrency, "The Courts in the American Colonies," 11 AMER. J. LEG. HIST. 271 (1967).

4. Act of September 24, 1789, sec. 16, 1 STAT. 82.

5. Act of September 24, 1789, sec. 15, 1 STAT. 82.

6. Joseph Story, COMMENTARIES ON EQUITY PLEADINGS AND THE INCIDENTS THEREOF (Boston, 1891), p.6, sec. 7. Tenth edition revised, corrected, and enlarged by John M. Gould.

7. Foster, *supra,* note 1, p.110.

8. Minnesota Co. v. St. Paul Co., 2 Wall. 609 (U.S. 1864).

9. Krippendorf v. Hyde, 110 U.S. 276 (1883); Freeman v. Howe, 24 How. 450 (U.S. 1860).

10. Federal Equity Rule 26 (1842) in Stephen D. Low, THE JURISDICTION AND POWERS OF THE UNITED STATES COURTS (1852).

11. Foster, *supra,* note 1, p.108.

12. Federal Equity Rule 18; O'Hara v. MacConnell, 93 U.S. 150, 152 (1876).

13. Foster, supra, note 1, p.170.

14. *Ibid,* p.180.

15. *Ibid,* p.217.

16. *Ibid,* p.230.

17. *Ibid,* p.332.

18. Story, *supra,* note 6.

19. Neves v. Scott, 9 How. 196 (U.S. 1850).

20. Act of September 29, 1789, 1 STAT. 93.

21. Act of May 8, 1792, sec. 2, 1 STAT. 276.

22. These rules are found in original editions of 7 Wheat. 5.

23. These rules are found in 7 Wheat 17, and 1 How. 41.

24. William W. Story, LIFE AND LETTERS OF JOSEPH STORY (1851), v. 1, p.405.

25. Rule 90 of 1842, 1 How. lxix. In rule 33 of the Equity Rules of 1822, 7 Wheat. 5, the word "present" was omitted and the limitation was not included. Stephen D. Law, THE JURISDICTION AND POWERS OF THE UNITED STATES COURTS. . . . (1852) The English rules and orders of the Chancery Court are included.

26. Edmund Robert Daniell, A TREATISE ON THE PRACTICE OF THE HIGH COURT OF CHANCERY: WITH SOME PRACTICAL OBSERVATIONS ON THE PLEADINGS IN THAT COURT (London, 1837); John Sidney Smith, A TREATISE ON THE PRACTICE OF THE COURT OF CHANCERY (London, 1834).

27. Thomson et al. v. Wooster, 114 U.S. 104, 112 (footnote)(1885).

28. COMMENTARIES ON EQUITY JURISPRUDENCE AS ADMINISTERED IN ENGLAND AND AMERICA (1836); COMMENTARIES ON EQUITY PLEADINGS (1838). The COMMENTARIES ON EQUITY JURISPRUDENCE went through fourteen American editions and three English editions; the last was published in 1920.

29. James Love Hopkins, THE NEW FEDERAL EQUITY RULES (4th ed. 1924), p.7.

30. Electrolibration Co. v. Jackson, 52 F. 773 (1892).

31. Nathan Dane, GENERAL ABRIDGMENT AND DIGEST OF AMERICAN LAW (1824), v.7, pp.516, 517.

32. The text of these rules is found in 226 U.S. 627.

33. Hopkins, *supra,* note 29, p.34.

34. Act of May 26, 1824, 4 STAT. 62, which confined the practice of the Federal Courts in Louisiana to rules of practices in the state courts, was construed not to include equity. Livingston v. Story, 9 Pet. 632 (U.S. 1835). This decision has been followed in other decisions. Arsons v. Bedford, 3 Pet. 433 (U.S. 1830), Gaines v. Chew, 2 How. 619 (1844).

35. Bennett v. Butterworth, 11 How. 673 (U.S. 1852).

36. Act of April 7, 1874, 18 STAT. 27.

37. Editorial 5 LAW NOTES 24 (1901).

38. Hopkins, *supra,* note 1, p.454.

39. Act of March 3, 1915, 38 STAT. 956.

40. Foster, *supra,* note 1, p.454.

41. Federal Equity Rules 82 (1842) in Stephen D. Low, THE JURISDICTION AND POWERS OF THE UNITED STATES COURTS (1852).

42. Federal Equity Rules 77 (1842) in Stephen D. Low, THE JURISDICTION AND POWERS OF THE UNITED STATES COURTS (1852).

43. Lawrence Godkin, "The Courts as Railroad Managers," 32 ALB. L.J. 45 (1885).

44. Note, 20 Amer. L. Rev. 749 (1886).

45. Foster, *supra,* note 1, p.343.

46. Meriwether v. Garrett, 102 U.S. 472 (1880).

47. Barton v. Barbour, 104 U.S. 126, 137-138 (1881).

48. *Ibid,* p.138.

49. Jacob Trieber, "The Abuses of Receiverships," 19 YALE L.J. 275 (1909); Seymour D. Thompson, "The Court Management of Railroads," 27 AMER. L. REV. 481 (1893).

50. Jacob Trieber, "The Abuses of Receiverships," 19 YALE L.J. 275, 279 (1909).

51. "Memorial of South Carolina to Congress," 28 AMER. L. REV. 283 (1894).

52. "Railway Receivership in the Federal Courts," 20 CENT. L.J. 42 (1885).

53. Act of June 30, 1876, 19 STAT. 63; An impressive list of national banks that had been in the hands of receivers from 1893 to 1908, *see* S.Doc. 296, 60th Cong., 1st sess. (1908).

54. *See* 13 VA. LAW REGISTER 417 (1907) where there is a discussion of this issue as applicable to the Virginia Corporation Commission.

55. Clayton Act, sec. 20, 38 STAT. 738 (1914).

56. Duplex Printing Press Co. v. Dearing, 254 U.S. 443 (1921).

57. S. Rept. No. 163, 72d Cong., 1st sess., p.17. This report cites other instances where these injunctions were drafted in very broad terms reaching conduct which could be considered outside the area of a labor dispute. These injunctions were rarely published in reports of decisions.

58. Felix Frankfurter, "Labor Injunctions and Federal Legislation," 42 HARV. L. REV. 766 (1929).

59. S. Rept. No. 163, 72d Cong., 1st sess., p.18.

60. For these views, *see* S. Rept. No. 163, 72d Cong., 1st sess., pt.2.

61. Act of March 23, 1932, 47 STAT. 70.

Chapter 17

CRIMINAL PROCEDURE
IN THE FEDERAL COURTS

It has been assumed that criminal procedure in the federal courts was more uniform, because of the requirements of the Bill of Rights and other federal statutes, than civil practice which was required to conform to those practices prevailing in the state courts. In 1916, one observer noted that "the administration of the criminal law throughout the United States is practically uniform."[1] This observation came from an individual who had served as a federal district attorney for a number of years in two different districts. Federal criminal procedure developed without the benefit of any appellate supervision, for it was not until 1879 that appeals in criminal cases were allowed.[2] The lack of reported cases tends to mask this state of confusion.

Federal criminal procedure was based upon the Bill of Rights, federal statutes and, more importantly, statutes adopting state practices. In numerous statutes, Congress adopted the prevailing practices of the states in criminal matters, and the judges turned to the state law for specific rules in criminal practice. In fact, the court became entangled with the question of whether the federal statutes adopted the state rules in effect at the time of their enactment or whether they included later changes in the state law.[3] At a later date, the courts refused to allow the "dead hand of the common-law rule of 1789" to prevent the defendant's witness from testifying because of a previous conviction of perjury.[4] Uniformity was not achieved until the adoption of the Federal Rules of Criminal Procedure. The selection of juries was not made uniform until 1948, and the restrictions on who could serve on the jury continued to be governed by state law until 1957.[5]

Before their independence, the states had developed an indigenous criminal procedure based upon the English common law. Chief among the changes were the appointment of a permanent prosecuting officer and the right of the accused to be represented by counsel. The states had retained the essentials of the English criminal procedure requiring an examination before a magistrate, an indictment, a trial by jury and a speedy execution of the punishment. It was quite common until this century for a defendant to be indicted during the first week of the term and tried during the second week, which was devoted to the criminal calendar. During the period following the American Revolution, significant changes were made in substantive criminal law, and the changes that were made in criminal procedure were confirmed.

The First Congress in 1789 took significant steps to prescribe criminal procedure by proposing the first ten amendments to the Constitution, which essentially are rules applying to criminal matters. Among the provisions of these amendments were that no person would be tried for a crime without first being indicted by a grand jury, that excessive bail was prohibited, and that the trial of the case must be held in the state where the crime was committed. Further, the accused was assured of an impartial jury and a speedy trial. He was to be informed of the nature of the accusation and was to have compulsory process for obtaining witnesses in his favor and assistance of counsel for his defense. The accused was prohibited from giving evidence against himself. The judges in the decades following stated that these provisions were adopted as a reaction to the criminal law as administered in England. This may be true as knowledge about the English practice becomes a faded memory based upon novels and conjectures from stray facts.

At the same time that these provisions were proposed to the states for adoption, some were included in the First Judiciary Act. For example, it was enacted that parties could plea and manage their own cases, and that in all cases, the accused could be admitted to bail except where the punishment was death.[6] These provisions were not contrary to the first ten amendments and were considered an expansion of them.

Later writers were to describe the criminal procedures in the federal courts as the "old practice at common law, except in so far as the same has been changed by federal statute."[7] Obviously, there is a problem as to what doctrines of common law were adopted or what period served as the point of reference. The need for a change in the criminal law as practiced in England was obvious, and the Americans on the state level had made significant changes by the time the federal courts were established. Pennsylvania had introduced degrees of murder and had reduced the number of capital crimes substantially by prescribing confinement in the newly established penitentiary system. However, the Supreme Court concluded that the common law and the rules of evidence as were used in the daily and familiar practice in the state courts in 1789 were to be followed in the federal courts. Great value was placed upon the trial by a jury, which was described as "a right of inestimable value, and the best and only security for life, liberty, and property."[8]

Another difficulty in understanding criminal procedure in the federal courts is the fact that for most of the Nineteenth Century there was no judicial review except upon a certification of opinion between the two judges holding the circuit court. These opinions are scarce, as are the reported decisions in the federal trial court. Students of criminal law practice at this particular time turned to the reports of trials in which many of these issues were discussed. The trial of Aaron Burr as reported in two volumes is the most often cited source for understanding the basic federal criminal procedure. This trial was conducted by Chief Justice Marshall in the United States Circuit Court for Virginia. During the course of this trial, Marshall had to rule on a wide range of procedural problems.[9]

The early texts on practice in the federal courts tend to ignore criminal procedure, and one of the best texts did not treat this subject until the edition of 1842. In another text published in 1909, criminal law was added only as a second thought as is indicated by the numbering of the sections in the book. [10]

What can be concluded is that for most of the Nineteenth Century, except for a few principles found in statutes and the Constitution, the precise criminal practice in each district varied. For example, the federal courts were divided on whether the presiding judge in a criminal trial could express his opinion on the evidence and whether the jury was bound by his explanation of the criminal law. One federal district court judge in writing his treatise on criminal practice examined this issue in some detail. [11] The author left no doubt that in the middle of the Nineteenth Century this issue had not been resolved.

Another factor impacting the criminal procedure was the growth in the federal government. The early statute placed much of the administrative aspects of the criminal procedure, such as issuing warrants and arresting individuals, on state officials. Whether Congress could constitutionally confer this authority was often questioned. It was argued that the judicial power was placed by the Constitution in the Supreme Court and such inferior courts as Congress should establish. Some courts held that the power to arrest and afterwards decide on probable cause seemed to be a judicial function rather than a ministerial one. One writer in the Northern District of New York testified that the power of state officials to arrest for federal crimes had been exercised and never "been disputed or complained of." [12] This dependence upon state officials was necessary because of the complete lack of administrative support in the federal system. By the close of the Eighteenth Century, there was an increase in the number of federal court judges, commissioners and locations where federal courts were held, which rendered the state officials' arrests less necessary. The United States commissioner, now the United States magistrate, assumed an important role in the issuing of warrants and conducting preliminary examinations as well as admitting individuals to bail.

One observes, in reviewing the history of criminal procedure, that its major principles have been in place for most of the existence of this government, but that the federal courts were responsible for filling in the gaps and modifying the procedure as circumstances dictated. Because so many of these guarantees in criminal procedure are so obvious, it is difficult to appreciate the new concepts introduced by the federal courts.

The first step in the criminal process is the issuance of a warrant by an officer designated in the common law as the "conservator of the peace." Before the Revolution, it was customary to issue such commissions to judges and the justices of the peace who, historically, were the first officials designated as conservators of the peace. The First Judiciary Act authorized the judges to issue warrants and allowed the justices of the peace or any magistrate of the state to issue warrants for federal offenses.[13] In 1793, commissioners appointed by the circuit court judges were authorized to issue warrants, and gradually they have become the federal officials responsible for this function. No question has been raised about this authority.

The warrant has a long lineage, having been used very early in English legal history as documentary evidence for the authority to perform a given act in the King's name. Gradually, through administrative practices and legal developments, a number of different warrants could be issued by any number of English officials. By the time of the Revolution, use of the warrant became associated in America with the authority for a criminal arrest, even though the term "warrant" was used to designate a document known as a land warrant to authorize an individual to settle a piece of public land. The term was used loosely by a few early writers, however, to include any order dealing with a prisoner, such as a warrant for confinement.[14]

Under English practice, which was probably followed in the American colonies, the justices of the peace could put a warrant in the hands of a private individual to serve and arrest the accused.[15] This was not the recommended practice by the end of the Eighteenth Century. The marshals and their deputies were the officials designated by federal law to execute the precepts including warrants issued by their respective courts. This function is now shared with a number of police organizations developed within the federal government during the Twentieth Century, which consequently has reduced this role of the federal marshals.

Many of the abuses arising from the issuing of warrants which this country at its inception sought to correct were due to over-zealous officials who lacked proper knowledge of these documents. The colonists felt that search warrants had been overused, and, for this reason, the Fourth Amendment required that warrants be issued only upon probable cause and be supported by an oath. This amendment appears to apply only to search warrants, but by interpretation has been extended to other types of warrants as well. The Fourth Amendment was designed not to introduce new principles but to guard against infringement of those rights which were already recognized.[16]

One of the early issues relating to a warrant was whether it was confined to the district in which it was issued or extended to the entire United States. Attorney General Roger B. Taney early held that a warrant arrest issued in the federal jurisdiction ran throughout the United States.[17] This rule was applied in several jurisdictions, but beginning in 1902, a series of decisions began to hold that a warrant did not run beyond the district in which it was issued. This meant that the issuing court had to send to the court of the district in which the accused was located a copy of the complaint, information or indictment, and the warrant.[18] The federal rules adopted in 1944 permit the forwarding of the original warrant to the district where the defendant is taken into custody.

The warrant could be issued prior to the indictment by a grand jury "upon probable cause." The required specificity of the warrant was a matter of great dispute in many cases beginning with a decision in 1806.[19]

Another method of bringing the defendant into court was by the use of the summons. This writ historically has been used to bring the accused before the court in summary matters. No less an authority than Blackstone, when he spoke of this procedure, stated that the common law would not permit any fact to be tried until the party concerned had been compelled to appear.[20] The rules surrounding this writ were not as elaborate as those governing the warrant or indictment. Its use in the early federal statutes was limited to notice to jurors, but about the time of the Civil War, the use of the summons was mentioned briefly in several statutes as a means of bringing the accused into court.[21] One function of the summons was its use in place of the warrant to bring corporations into court on criminal charges.[22] The Federal Rules of Criminal Procedure introduced the summons in lieu of the warrant at the discretion of the United States Attorney or the court. The practice had been in a great many districts to summon defendants in summary actions by letter or telephone to appear in the court at a specified time, without issuing a warrant.[23]

Normally, the warrant was returned to the issuing magistrate, but in the Burr trial, Chief Justice Marshall decided that one magistrate could lawfully commit on an affidavit made before another magistrate.[24] Marshall concluded that before the accused was put on his trial, all proceedings were *ex parte* and were done on the behalf of one party. In this event, the warrant should be acted upon very cautiously.

The warrant is usually returned to the issuing party, who is now generally the United States magistrate, for a preliminary hearing. At this time, the commissioner or magistrate must commit the accused for action by the grand jury, hold him for further action, or discharge him. If the accused is committed for further proceedings upon the preliminary examinations, the commitment must be for a short period.[25]

One of the first questions raised was whether the accused could put in a defense at the preliminary examination by producing witnesses at that time. The accused was given the right by statute in 1790 to offer evidence in his defense and to summon witnesses at government expense, which were rights not accorded to the defendant in a criminal case in England at that period.[26] The accused had the right to be represented by counsel at the preliminary hearing and to question witnesses but not to impeach them. It appears that the practice soon developed for the accused not to make a defense but merely to plead not guilty, for no statute or court decision seems to have dictated this course of action.

The admission of the accused to bail was a recognized practice in England for many centuries before the establishment of the federal government. Its use was limited to noncapital crimes which were very few in number under the English system. When admitted to bail, as one authority states, "in the Eye of the Law for many Purposes, [the accused is] esteemed to be as much in the Prison of the Court by which he is bailed, as if he were in the actual Custody of the proper Gaoler."[27] The purpose of bail is to assure the appearance of the prisoner before the court where he is charged. The Constitution does not require the prisoner to be admitted to bail, but it does prohibit excessive bail. What constitutes an excessive bail is certainly a matter which has occupied a great deal of judicial consideration, and no specific guidelines have ever been developed. The right to bail was reinforced by a statute which permitted bail even in capital cases, in which event the bail could only be granted by judges of the federal courts.[28] Otherwise, state officials could accept bail for many federal offenses. The federal courts usually followed local state practices in matters relating to the issuance of bail.

Witnesses could be required to give bail to assure their appearance at the proper time or could be committed to jail to be held for this purpose. To alleviate the condition of the witness, a statute was enacted requiring the marshals to pay those imprisoned "on account of inability to give security . . . for their attendance as witnesses on behalf of the United States" the same sum for each day of imprisonment as provided for by law for the witness actually attending court. This allowance was to be fixed and certified by the judge as in other cases.[29] This statute was later amplified when the district attorney was permitted to make an application to a judge showing that the testimony of a witness was necessary for a criminal cause, in which case such witness could be compelled to enter into recognizance, and, if he failed to do so, he could be committed to prison until brought before the court to testify or to take bail.[30] Later, a witness so committed could be entitled to a dollar a day in addition to subsistance.[31] Certainly, it seems unfair to lock up a witness or require bail without recompense.

The First Judiciary Act made the qualifications for forming juries the same as those in the laws of the state, but it made no distinction between grand juries and trial juries. Apparently, the intention was that the distinction would be determined by the law of the state. There is some evidence to support the assumption that the same individuals served on both juries. The federal courts were to direct from which part of the district the juries should be returned "as shall be most favourable to an impartial trial, and so as not to incur an unnecessary expense, or unduly to burthen the citizens of any part of the district with such services."[32] The writ *venire facias* was directed from the clerk's office to either the marshal or another "fit person as the court shall specifically appoint." If the jury panel was not sufficient, the marshal could return additional jurors by *detalibus circumstantibus* or, in other words, individuals available around the courthouse.

A number of interesting developments have taken place in the practice before the grand jury. In the Burr trial, Chief Justice Marshall held that the accused whose case was submitted to a grand jury had the same rights to challenge for cause before the jurors were sworn as he would before the petit jury. One writer, as late as 1864, stated that grounds for challenge were that the juror was either a prosecutor or a complainant upon the charge against the accused or that he was a witness on the part of the prosecution and had been subpoenaed. In 1862, one could challenge a grand or petit juror because he had taken up arms against the United States or given aid to the enemy. This same act provided that a juror had to take a loyalty oath to the United States and be impartial where the country was a party.[33]

Another rule that underwent changes in the Nineteenth Century was related to the type of evidence which could be presented before the grand jury. At the beginning, it seems that the grand jury could receive "probable evidence," but by the last part of the century, only "legal evidence" could be presented.[34] The modern day equivalent of this evidentiary rule allows broad latitude in discovering evidence but narrows the scope for determining admissibility.

There was an open question in 1790 as to whether a defendant could compel witnesses to attend the grand jury to testify on his behalf. John Marshall decided that Burr was entitled to this privilege, for "much delay and much inconvenience may be avoided by this construction; no mischief which is perceived can be produced by it."[35] However, Justice Bushrod Washington in 1807 ruled on circuit that witnesses for the accused are not examined at the preliminary hearing or sent before the grand jury.[36]

At that period, the grand jury was conceived as a body which called for the punishment of offenders from their own knowledge through a presentment. According to Blackstone, a presentment is "the notice taken by a grand jury of any offence from their own knowledge or observation . . . without any bill of indictment laid before them at the suit of the king" or by an individual.[37] In the American state courts, the term "presentment" was often used as an alternative for "indictment." It has been suggested that the use of the term in the Constitution was the same as that understood by Blackstone. The presentment fell into disuse in the federal courts because of the availability of the United States attorney and the decline of prosecution by private individuals.[38] Gradually, under the guidance of the United States attorney, the role of the grand jury has become to determine whether there is sufficient evidence to indict the accused. The rule developed that the defendant had no right to make a defense before the grand jury. How this decision was reached in each district court varied, and no specific history can be recited.

During the early days in many district and circuit courts, the need for a grand jury was strictly limited. One authority noted "the rarity of criminal prosecutions in the courts of the United States, where it often happened that the attendance of a grand jury was but an idle ceremony, owing to the limited criminal jurisdiction of these courts."[39] In 1846, Congress provided that no grand jury would be summoned to attend any circuit or district court unless the judge of such district court or one of the judges of the circuit court in his discretion notified the district attorney that such a jury would be necessary. The statute made clear that this did not provide for the imprisonment before indictment except as provided by law and did not curtail the accused's right to bail.[40]

One complicating factor was the existence of two trial courts with criminal jurisdiction. In 1846, Congress provided that should the grand jury in a district court indict a person for a crime which was properly within the jurisdiction of the circuit court, the district court could remit the case to the circuit court which would make an entry upon its minutes, and the case would proceed as if the case had been founded in that court. The circuit court could follow the same procedure if the grand jury found an indictment for a crime properly within the jurisdiction of the district court.[41]

The Bill of Rights gives the accused compulsory process for compelling witnesses to appear in his behalf and the assistance of counsel for defense. This provision was amplified in the Act of 1790 and has been construed as not being in conflict with the Constitutional requirement.[42] Alfred Conkling, a federal judge and author, raises interesting questions as to whether this statute and its amendment apply only to those crimes enacted in 1790, but concludes that this question has never been raised and that the provision has been extended to all crimes.

By the Fifth Amendment, "no person shall be held to answer for a capital or otherwise infamous crime unless on a presentment or indictment of a Grand Jury." During the colonial period, the colonial servants of the crown had used the process of filing information accusing someone of a crime as a method of bringing an individual to trial. The purpose of the Fifth Amendment was to limit the use of this process and to require an indictment for most criminal offenses. Certain types of penalties could be collected by the filing of information by the district attorney, but this was considered a civil rather than a criminal action.[43] In the present century when so many penalties have been imposed for violation of certain statutes, the filing of information has been the standard method of bringing such an action.

In various periods in English legal history, the filing of information was abused until a statute of William III prohibited certain English officials from filing information without express consent of the Court of King's Bench and required the prosecutor to give security to prosecute and pay costs to the defendant in case he was acquitted.[44] The British government had used this form of prosecution during the colonial period, and it is not clear whether the rule that it had to be sanctioned by a court was applied.

The early federal statutes seemed to have implied that the proper officials would bring a civil action in the federal courts for the recovery of penalties. The use of the information was introduced into federal practices by those courts located in states that allowed this procedure. The Federal Rules of Criminal Procedure extended the use of the information to all crimes where the defendant waived an indictment.[45] This was done so that if a defendant wanted to plead guilty to a charge without an indictment, he did not need to wait for a grand jury. This had been recommended by the judges and the attorney general.[46]

Apparently, the defendant was expected to pay the fees of all witnesses attending in his behalf. However, in 1846, Congress extended compulsory process to include those cases in which an indigent accused petitioned the court that there were certain witnesses within the district or within 100 miles of the place of the crime and that he did not have sufficient means to pay for the fees of such witnesses. The accused stated what he expected these witnesses to prove, and the court in vacation could order the witnesses to be subpoenaed and the cost paid as witnesses summoned on behalf of the government.[47]

After the indictment, if the defendant was not in custody or did not voluntarily appear, process had to be issued for the purpose of bringing him into court. The usual process was the writ of *capias,* or a bench warrant signed by the judge of the court. The customary practice was to have the bench warrant returned at the next session of the court, i.e., the next session after the arrest. In some courts, the district attorney was authorized by rule to get a *capias* under the seal of the court for the arrest of the person without waiting for the end of the term. This rule was necessary because under the English common law, the warrant could not be issued during the term of the court, as the term was considered to be one day and the prisoner had that period of time in which to voluntarily appear.

The abolition of the terms of court by the rules of criminal procedure had other implications as well. Not only could a bench warrant be served immediately upon indictment, but also other rights such as those governing motions for new trials had to be expressed in terms of the number of days after the verdict rather than terms of court.[48]

Another departure from the contemporary English criminal law was the requirement that the prisoner be furnished with a copy of the indictment and a list of the petit jurors summoned for the trial and the witnesses.[49] One cannot appreciate the significance of this requirement unless he realizes that at that time, in England, only those accused of treason were entitled to a copy of the indictment prior to the arraignment, including a list of jurors and witnesses.

The accused had the right to challenge members of the petit jury. The statute of 1790 embraced the English common law of the period, allowing any person indicted for treason to challenge more than thirty-five jurors and for other offenses to preemptorily challenge twenty members of the jury. When the question was raised whether the challenge extended to other crimes later defined, it was answered affirmatively. [50]

The guarantee of counsel was another important concession to the accused. As early as 1790, the federal statutes provided that any person accused of a crime was to be allowed to make his defense by counsel learned in the law and that the judge would assign such counsel not exceeding two, if the accused so desired. In contemporary English practice, the accused was allowed counsel in treason cases, but the role of the counsel was limited to advising the accused rather than presenting his case. The act of 1795 further directed that counsel have free access to the person indicted during all reasonable hours. Moreover, the accused was guaranteed the right to make a full defense by compelling witnesses to attend by the same process as used by the prosecution. [51]

Because there were no appeals in a criminal case in the federal courts except by a division of opinion among the judges, the courts were extremely liberal in granting new trials. Under the English law, no new trials were granted in cases of felonies or treason, and the only remedy available to a defendant convicted of any other crime was to apply for a pardon if the judge thought the conviction improper. The federal courts were reluctant at first to disregard these common law rules as is well illustrated by the reasoning of Judge Peters in 1799, who concluded that "the influence of public example, would not be impaired by the delay of a new trial." [52] When the question arose in 1834 whether a new trial could be granted upon the conviction of murder, the Circuit Court was divided. [53] Justice Story adopted the view that to retry a person would violate the double jeopardy provision of the Constitution, but the courts later accepted the argument that these guarantees were for the protection of the individual who may waive and relinguish this right. As a result, by the end of the century, a new trial became an accepted practice in criminal cases as the reasons for granting them grew.

Another controversial question related to the province and power of the jury. It was an accepted adage that the jury were judges of the law as well as of the fact. A study of the conduct of the juries in criminal cases in England in the Seventeenth Century indicates that the judges were willing to accept perverse judgments of the juries when the result was to exercise more humanity for those unfortunate individuals who were accused of crimes which were punishable by hanging. "Under such a code, it is no wonder that juries sometimes yielded to the claims of humanity rather than the demands of the law, and that judges were little disposed to interfere with their decisions." [54] For this reason, the maxim that no man shall be twice put in jeopardy of life or limb for the same offense became implanted in the American criminal law.

In an early federal case, the judge charged the jury about the law and then stated that "you will distinctly understand that you are the judges both of the law and fact in a criminal case, and are not bound by the opinion of the court; you may judge for yourselves, and if you should feel it your duty to differ from us, you must find your verdict accordingly."[55] The opinion of the court was unfavorable to the prisoner, and a verdict of guilty was brought in. When the codefendant was tried for the same offense, the attorney for the defendant appealed to the jury upon questions of law, and in the charge on that occasion, the same judge commented that the attorney had acted properly, but he repeated his earlier charges and added that the jury was not to lightly disregard previous decisions as expounded in the charge.

In another criminal case, the question of the constitutionality of the United States bank was raised, and the attorney argued the point to the jury. The judge charged that the constitutionality had been decided by the Supreme Court and was not a subject for their consideration.[56] Justice Story charged the jury in another case that they were not the judges of the law.[57] He argued it was the duty of the court to instruct the jury as to the law and was the duty of the jury to apply the facts to the law laid down by the court. This issue of the role of the judge in charging a jury was firmly decided in a long, exhausting opinion of the Supreme Court in 1894.[58] Justice John Marshall Harlan (1833-1911) examined a great many cases and decided that federal law did not permit juries to disregard evidence and principles of law received from the court. The Supreme Court in 1887 had given the federal judges the authority to comment on the evidence provided it was made clear to the jury that they were not bound by the judge's interpretation.[59]

Until 1957, the competency of a juror was determined by the state statute where the federal court was located. However, there was no fixed way for the federal courts to select prospective jurors. In some cases the clerks resorted to voter lists, while in others they used various directories. The most commonly used method of selection was designated the "key man system," which employed the list of names suggested by a citizen.[60] It was argued that this method of selection produced jurors that "possess as high a degree of intelligence, morality, integrity, and common sense as can be found."

This system may explain the concern of the Supreme Court in 1946 in ruling that an impartial jury assumes that it is "drawn from a cross section of the community."[61] Later cases expanded upon this, and a number of cases began to question various practices in the selection of the jury. Placing the names of white jurors on one color card and blacks on another was found to be discriminatory, and the habit of jury commissioners choosing only those people who they personally knew was declared unacceptable.[62] In 1966, the Judicial Conference of the United States recommended that the district adopt a system of random selection of jurors that would produce a fair cross section. This was followed by an act in 1968 which provided for jury selection and service in the federal courts.[63]

The only occasion when Congress provided for the jury to be selected from a specific location in the district was set out in 1789 in a statute which provided that for crimes punishable by death, the trial should be in the county where the offense was committed or where it could be held without great inconvenience. The twelve petit jurors were to be summoned from that county.[64] Later, the circuit courts could hold special sessions for the trial of criminal cases at a convenient place within the district nearest to the place where the offense was committed.[65] In the Burr trial, the crime was alleged to have been committed in Wood County, Virginia, one of the frontier counties of the state, but the trial was in the city of Richmond. Marshall directed that the petit jurors would be taken from Wood County unless waived by the accused and government.[66] One writer stated in 1843 that this was the practice in the federal courts.[67] The statute of 1789 was repealed in 1862, and the practice of jury selection from the entire district remained.[68] However, in actual practice, the jury was chosen from citizens from the immediate area around the location where the federal courts were held.

The question as to what rules would govern the admission of evidence in a criminal trial in the federal courts was never answered definitively by Congress. The federal courts applied the requirements of the Constitution and a few statutes enacted by Congress. Otherwise, the rules governing the introduction of evidence used in the states were applied. In 1851, the Supreme Court decided that the rules of evidence enforced in 1789 in the original states were to be applied by the federal courts.[69] However, although the Supreme Court stated that "some certain and established rule upon this subject was necessary to enable the courts to administer the criminal jurisprudence of the United States,"[70] it never decided what rules of evidence would be applied in those states admitted after 1789. Apparently, the current rules of evidence applied in the state courts governed similar proceedings in the federal courts.

Congress occasionally passed acts governing the admission of evidence. The statute in 1878 permitted the defendant to testify "at his own request."[71] In the REVISED STATUTES, the defendant was given an additional right to "be allowed . . . to make any proof that he can produce by lawful witnesses."[72] These statutes were few in number and had only limited impact. Since there was little legislation on the admission of evidence, it was left to the courts to decide such questions as whether corporate officials could refuse to produce books which would tend to incriminate the corporation or whether this was an individual right.[73]

Pleadings in criminal cases were rather technical. The defendant, according to Blackstone, could enter: "1. A plea to the jurisdiction; 2. A demurrer; 3. A plea in abatement; 4. A special plea in bar; or, 5. The general issue."[74] The federal courts spent considerable amounts of energy, in the Twentieth Century when more reported cases were available, determining whether the lack of legal qualifications of members of the grand jury was a plea in abatement or a motion to quash. Another enigma frequently addressed was whether a defect in the indictment or information other than failure to allege the offense could be raised by a motion to quash or a plea in abatement.[75] A few of these conflicts were resolved in federal courts by local rules. Many of the courts had by rule abolished the technical plea of misnomer which raised the issue of an incorrect name of the person accused in the indictment. Originally, a misnomer was grounds for a dismissal, but later the courts permitted the correction by amendment to the pleadings.[76] The federal courts were rescued from this quagmire they had created by the Federal Rules of Criminal Procedure, which abolished these various pleas and provided for raising them by a motion to dismiss or other appropriate relief.[77]

The Crimes Act of 1790 changed a number of punishments popular in the common law, e.g., attainder, which were prohibited by the Constitution.[78] Another was a procedure known as the benefit of clergy. Where the benefit was allowed, the defendant could claim the benefit after conviction in which event he was branded with a B generally in his right thumb to prevent his claiming the benefit again.[79] The federal law retained other punishments, such as fines, imprisonment, whipping and the pillory.

Another unusual punishment included in the Crimes Act was that the body of a person hung for murder may, in the discretion of the court, be delivered to a surgeon for dissection. The marshal was responsible for carrying out this part of the sentence. An attempt to rescue such a body was punishable by a fine not exceeding $100 and imprisonment for a term not exceeding twelve months.[80]

When the federal government was created, the penitentiary system had been introduced by such states as Pennsylvania and Virginia. In those states, when the criminal laws were reformed, many crimes which were formally punished by hanging were reduced to terms of imprisonment. The Crimes Act of 1790 provided for imprisonment, but retained the death penalty for a number of crimes including murder, treason, forgery and piracy.

No provision was made for federal penitentiaries or jails, and prisoners were held in the local jails, as is still done in many localities today. A number of jails were established, including those in the District of Columbia and Fort Smith, Arkansas. In each of the territories, penitentiaries were established which were controlled by the federal government until they passed into the hands of the newly established state governments.

By resolution on September 23, 1789, Congress urged the legislatures of the several states to pass laws making it expressly the duty of the keepers of all jails to receive all prisoners committed under the authority of the United States until they were discharged by due course of the law. The United States would pay for the upkeep of such prisoners at the rate of $50 per month for each prisoner.[81] Apparently, the states did not comply with this request of Congress, for two years later another resolution stated that should the states not comply with the request, the marshal in each district under the direction of the judge would hire a convenient place as a temporary jail and make necessary provisions for the safekeeping of prisoners until permanent provisions could be made for that purpose. The marshal was to be allowed reasonable expenses for this purpose.[82] Apparently, some states withdrew their consent, for a resolution passed in 1821 provided that any state "having complied with the *above* recommendation . . . shall have withdrawn, or shall hereafter withdraw, either in whole or in part, the use of their jails for prisoners committed under the authority of the United States."[83] Again, Congress in 1833 reiterated that the marshals were to find suitable accommodations for the housing of the prisoners under the direction of the judge of the United States District Court within the limits of the state.[84] The authority to contract for the housing of federal prisoners was transferred to the Department of Interior in 1864 and then to the Department of Justice in 1872.[85] The responsibility of the marshal ceased with the delivery of the prisoners to the keeper of the penitentiary, for the marshals no longer had custody.[86] Federal prisoners confined in a state penitentiary were subject to the same rules and same treatment as state prisoners.[87]

A number of the attorney generals of the United States commented on the need for a penitentiary for the confinement of prisoners. The attorney general was authorized to provide care and subsistence for the United States prisoners by making arrangements for their care and maintenance in the penitentiaries of the states. The department conducted periodic examinations of the state prisons, but had no control over federal prisoners. One attorney general reported that when these visits were made, the complaints which seemed meritorious were called to the attention of the prison authorities who seemed most anxious to comply. Prisons in which federal prisoners were confined were often degrading and the conditions inhumane. These prisoners were often sources of revenue for the wardens and sheriffs.[88] As of July 1, 1885, there were 975 United States prisoners confined in different penitentiaries throughout the United States. Each district and circuit court had designated a prison to which those convicted were sent. For example, prisoners from Alabama were sent to the Southern Illinois Prison in Menard, Illinois, and those from Florida and Georgia to the Albany County Penitentiary in Albany, New York.[89]

The Attorney General in 1887 reported the pressing need for jails to confine those awaiting trial in the federal courts. This demand was brought about by the increased number of new federal crimes defined in numerous statutes. It was not until 1891 that Congress acted upon these recommendations by providing for the establishment of a penal institution in Atlanta, Georgia, but no appropriations were provided for this purpose.[90] In 1895, the Department of Justice took over the military prison at Fort Leavenworth, Kansas. The next year Congress authorized the acquisition of 1,000 acres of the military reservation for the erection of the first federal penitentiary, which was completed on February 1, 1906.[91] The Atlanta Penitentiary was authorized in 1899 and completed in 1902. In 1929, a Congressional investigation revealed the shocking conditions of overcrowding in both the Atlanta and Leavenworth prisons and the need for parole and probation systems for federal offenders. Legislation providing for these changes and the establishment of the Federal Bureau of Prisons was adopted in 1930.[92] Since that time, the federal government has housed its own prisoners, except for those held for trial in the county or city jails.

There was considerable agitation after World War I to give the Supreme Court of the United States the rule-making authority for both civil and criminal matters. Up until that period, it had been a mixture of federal and state law which, as Justice Clifford described, "in legal effect amounts to no more than a direction to a judge sitting in such a criminal trial to conduct the same as well as he can, in view of the three systems of criminal jurisprudence."[93] Later, in 1931, speaking through Justice Butler, the Supreme Court held that "federal criminal procedure is governed not by state practice but by federal statutes and decisions of the federal courts."[94] The need for some uniformity was necessary.

In 1933, the Supreme Court was given the authority to make rules to govern all proceedings after the verdict in criminal cases.[95] The next year this authority was widened to include all proceedings after the verdict or a finding of guilty by the courts if a jury had been waived or a plea of guilty entered.[96] The Supreme Court promptly acted on this authority prescribing a set of rules known as the Criminal Appeals Rules. Probably the reason Congress did not give the Supreme Court greater authority was the concern that its rules would interfere with Constitutional guarantees.

In 1940, however, the Supreme Court's control over criminal procedure was expanded to include procedures authorized governing matters prior to and including the verdict or finding of guilty.[97] In 1941, the rule-making authority was extended to include the punishment for criminal contempt of court.[98] This was in response to a decision refusing to extend the rules of contempt. The Supreme Court appointed a distinguished group of practitioners and professors to draft these rules under the chairmanship of Arthur T. Vanderbilt, the dean of the New York University Law School and, later, chief justice of the Supreme Court of New Jersey. The rules were circulated in draft form to members of the bar and the judiciary for comment. The rules governing criminal procedure covering arrest through appeal were adopted in 1944.

The chief effect of these rules was to make the federal procedure in criminal matters as uniform as possible. The principal merit was to simplify procedure, omitting those rules which had become obsolete. In many courts, these rules reduced the indictment to "a plain, concise and definite restatement of essential facts constituting the charge."[99] A formal commencement and allegation of extraneous materials were to be omitted.[100] With the adoption of the Federal Rules of Criminal Procedure and the Jury Selection and Service Act, at last, criminal procedure became uniform in the federal courts.

FOOTNOTES TO CHAPTER 17

1. H. Snowden Marshall, "Federal Criminal Procedure," 1916 PROC. MD. BAR ASS. 176, 184.

2. Act of March 3, 1879, 20 STAT. 354.

3. United States v. Reid, 12 How. 361, 363 (U.S. 1851); United States v. Rundlett, 2 Curtis 41 (C.C. Mass. 1854).

4. Rosen v. United States, 245 U.S. 467, 471 (1917). The rule that a person convicted of perjury could not be a witness until pardon was removed by the Penal Code of 1909.

5. Act of September 9, 1957, 71 STAT. 638.

6. Act of September 24, 1789, sec. 33, 35, 1 STAT. 91, 92.

7. Roger Foster, A TREATISE ON FEDERAL PRACTICE, CIVIL AND CRIMINAL (1909), v.2, p.1343.

8. United States v. Reid, 12 How. 361, 364 (U.S. 1851).

9. *See* references in Alfred Conkling, A TREATISE ON THE ORGANIZATION, JURISDICTION AND PRACTICE OF THE COURTS OF THE UNITED STATES (4th ed. 1864), p.574; and in Foster, *supra,* note 7, p.1345.

10. Foster, *supra,* note 7, p.1343.

11. Conkling, *supra,* note 9, p.612.

12. *Ibid,* p.572.

13. Act of September 24, 1789, sec. 33, 1 STAT. 91.

14. Harry Toulmin and James Blair, A REVIEW OF THE CRIMINAL LAW OF THE COMMONWEALTH OF KENTUCKY (1806), v. 2, p. 142.

15. *See* Toulmin and Blair, supra, note 14, v.2, p.112. Much of this work is based on William Hawkins, A TREATISE OF THE PLEAS OF THE CROWN (1724), a well known book in America.

16. Conkling, *supra,* note 9, p.569, 3 Blackstone 291; 3 Story Comm. 748.

17. 2 Op. Att'y. Gen. U.S. 564 (1833).

18. *See* Alexander Holtzoff, "Reform of Federal Criminal Procedure," 12 GEO. WASH. L. REV. 119, 132, 133 (1944).

19. Ex parte Burford, 3 Cranch 448 (U.S. 1806).

20. Blackstone's COMMENTARIES Bk. 4, p.283.

21. Act of March 3, 1863, sec. 1, 12 STAT. 769; sec. 2 provides for penalties if person refuses or neglects to attend; Act of June 30, 1864, sec. 14, 13 STAT. 226, are two examples.

22. Foster, *supra,* note 7, v.3, p.2608.

23. Holtzoff, *supra,* note 18, p.119, 132, 133.

24. REPORTS OF THE TRIALS OF COLONEL AARON BURR, v.1, p.97 (1969).

25. United States v. Worms, 4 Blatch. 332, 28 FED. CAS. 773 (C.C. S.D. N.Y. 1859).

26. Act of April 30, 1790, sec. 29, 1 STAT. 118; Act of August 16, 1856, sec. 3, 11 STAT. 49.

27. Hawkins, *supra,* note 15, Bk. II, p.88.

28. Act of September 24, 1789, sec. 33, 1 STAT. 91.

29. Act of May 20, 1826, 4 STAT. 174.

30. Act of August 8, 1846, 9 STAT. 73, 74, REV. STAT. §878.

31. Act of February 26, 1853, 10 STAT. 167, REV. STAT. §881.

32. Act of September 24, 1789, sec. 29, 1 STAT. 88; Act of May 13, 1800, 2 STAT. 82 amended the above section by adding, "in each state or district." The reason for this amendment is not clear.

33. Act of June 17, 1862, 12 STAT. 430.

34. Conkling, *supra,* note 9, p.596, 597.

35. REPORTS OF THE TRIAL OF COLONEL AARON BURR, v.1, p.177 (1969).

36. United States v. White, 2 WASH. C.C. 29, 28 FED. CAS. 588 (C.C. Pa. 1807).

37. Blackstone's COMMENTARIES Bk. 4, p.301.

38. FED. R. CRIM. P., PRELIMINARY DRAFT (1943), p.32.

39. Conkling, *supra,* note 9, p.592.

40. Act of August 8, 1846, sec. 3, 9 STAT. 72, 73.

41. Act of August 8, 1846, sec. 2, 9 STAT. 72.

42. Conkling, *supra,* note 9, p.604.

43. Blackstone's COMMENTARIES Bk. 4, p.308.

44. *Ibid,* p.311.

45. FED. R. CRIM. P. 7(b).

46. FED. R. CRIM. P., PRELIMINARY DRAFT (1943), p. 31.

47. Act of August 8, 1846, sec. 11, 9 STAT. 74, 75.

48. Holtzoff, *supra,* note 18, p.119, 134.

49. Act of April 30, 1790, sec. 29. 1 STAT. 118.

50. United States v. Johns, 1 WASH. C.C. 363, 26 FED. CAS. 616 (C.C. Pa. 1806).

51. Act of April 30, 1790, sec. 29. 1 STAT. 118.

52. United States v. Fries, 3 Dall. 515, 519 (C.C. Pa. 1799).

53. United States v. Gibert, 2 Sumner 19, 25 FED. CAS. 1287 (C.C. Mass. 1834).

54. Conkling, *supra,* note 9, p.617.

55. United States v. Wilson, 1 Baldw. 78, 99, 28 FED. CAS. 699, 708 (C.C. E.D. Pa. 1830).

56. United States v. Shive, 1 Baldw. 510, 27 FED. CAS. 1065 (C.C. E.D. Pa. 1832).

57. United States v. Battiste, 2 Sumner 240, 243, 24 FED. CAS. 1042 (C.C. Mass. 1835).

58. Sparf v. United States, 156 U.S. 51 (1894).

59. Rucker v. Wheeler, 127 U.S. 85 (1887).

60. Arthur J. Stanley, Jr., "Federal Jury Selection and Service Before and after 1968," 66 F.R.D. 375 (1975).

61. Thiel v. Southern Pacific Co., 328 U.S. 217, 220 (1945).

62. Cassell v. Texas, 339 U.S. 282 (1949); Avery v. Georgia, 345 U.S. 559 (1952).

63. Jury Selection and Service Act, 82 STAT. 53 (1968). *See* "The Jury System in the Federal Courts," 26 F.R.D. 409 (1960).

64. Act of September 24, 1789, sec. 29, 1 STAT. 88.

65. Act of March 2, 1793, sec. 3, 1 STAT. 334.

66. REPORTS OF THE TRIALS OF COLONEL AARON BURR, v.1, p.353 (1969).

67. Conkling, *supra,* note 9, p.589.

68. Act of July 16, 1862, sec. 2, 12 STAT. 589.

69. United States v. Reid, 12 How. 361 (U.S. 1851).

70. United States v. Reid, 12 How. 361, 365 (U.S. 1851).

71. Act of March 3, 1875, 18 STAT. 479.

72. REV. STAT. §1034

73. Hale v. Henkel, 201 U.S. 43 (1905).

74. Blackstone's COMMENTARIES Bk. 4, p. 332.

75. *See* FED. R. CRIM. P., PRELIMINARY DRAFT (1943), p. 57, where these cases are arranged by type of plea.

76. *Ibid,* p.55. For the use of this plea, see Blackstone's COMMENTARIES Bk. 4, p.334.

77. *Ibid,* p.12.

78. U.S. Const. Art. III, sec. 3; Act of April 30, 1790, sec. 24, 1 STAT. 117.

79. Act of April 30, 1790, sec. 31, 1 STAT. 119.

80. Act of April 30, 1790, sec. 4 and 5, 1 STAT. 113.

81. Resolution of September 23, 1789, 1 STAT. 96.

82. Act of March 3, 1791, 1 STAT. 225.

83. Resolution of March 3, 1821, 3 STAT. 646, 647.

84. Act of March 2, 1833, sec. 6, 4 STAT. 634.

85. Act of May 12, 1864, 13 STAT. 74; Act of March 5, 1872, sec. 1, 17 STAT. 35.

86. Randolph v. Donaldson, 9 Cranch 76 (1815).

87. Act of June 30, 1834, 4 STAT. 739.

88. Homer Cummings and Carl McFarland, FEDERAL JUSTICE (1937), p.354.

89. *See* 1885 ATT'Y GEN. ANN. REPT. p.297.

90. Act of March 3, 1891, 26 STAT. 839.

91. Sanford Bates, PRISONS AND BEYOND (1938), p. 128; Act of June 10, 1896, 29 STAT. 380.

92. Act of May 14, 1930, 46 STAT. 325.

93. Tennessee v. Davis, 100 U.S. 257, 299 (1879).

94. United States v. Murdock, 284 U.S. 141, 150 (1931).

95. Act of February 24, 1933, 47 STAT. 904.

96. Act of March 8, 1934, 48 STAT. 399.

97. Act of June 29, 1940, 54 STAT. 688.

98. Act of November 21, 1941, 55 STAT. 779.

99. FED. R. CRIM. P. 7(C)(1).

Chapter 18

THE FEDERAL RULES OF CIVIL AND CRIMINAL PROCEDURE

Courts have exercised the right to promulgate rules to govern the details of their business ranging from the hours the clerk's office is open to other details of administration. However, the authority to adopt rules governing procedure was limited by reluctance of the courts to enter this field without a clear mandate from Congress, which did not come until the decades of the Twentieth Century. Until then, the trial courts in the federal system used the procedure of the local state courts except for equity and admiralty.

The adaptation of the local state practice in common law cases presented many problems. The local practice could not be fully implemented because of the nature of some matters coming into the federal jurisdiction and the peculiar requirements of federal practice resulting from the decisions of the Supreme Court. Obviously, no uniformity of practice was possible in the federal district and circuit courts. This was not a problem until the closing decades of the Nineteenth Century when it became more common for lawyers to litigate matters for the same clients in different judicial districts. The railroads, banks and the telegraph companies contributed to this process of nationalizing the federal courts. This led to a growing demand for a uniform practice in all federal courts. This non-uniformity limited the ability of federal judges to go into another judicial district in another state to conduct trials.

The state courts began independence with the common law forms of action with its writs and technicalities in pleading. This system was developed over a long period of time in England and involved the use of different writs for given types of actions. In medieval England, no individual could begin a suit without a writ issued by the King through his chancellor. These writs were the authority of the judge in the English courts to adjudicate certain issues and none other. Over time, these writs became standardized, allowing for no deviations. This form of procedure was confined to the common law courts — the King's Bench, Exchequer and Common Pleas — but not in chancery or admiralty.

The most famous of these writs was that of trespass which was used to collect monetary damages for the unlawful entry upon land, but others have disappeared from the legal vocabulary. This writ of trespass was later extended to include trespass upon one's person resulting in some type of injury known as *trespass vi et armis*. These different writs initiated the law suits in different ways. Upon the service of a writ of debt, the defendant was taken into custody and could be released upon the posting of a bond which the sheriff could accept. Upon the service of detinue, the sheriff seized the property. In some situations, the suit could be dismissed if the wrong writ had been used. How technical the practice was varied from state to state.[1] In time, this system became awkward and antiquated, although frequent changes were made by legislative action.

Immediately following the Revolution, Georgia and several other states introduced a simpler practice, but in states like New York, where common law pleading was followed, any changes awaited the introduction of the system known as code pleading in 1848.[2] David Dudley Field, a proponent of codification, secured the passage of a code of procedure which was widely adopted in other states. Generally, the forms of action were abolished although some of the titles of the writs were kept. In its day, code pleading was considered much simpler and a great improvement over the common law pleading. Under both systems, the legislatures had a significant role in changing local practice. The contribution of the courts to these systems was limited to interpreting the application of the statutes.

The next revolution in procedure was the assignment to the highest court the authority to govern procedure in all courts by the use of rules adopted by the court. This was slow in coming to reality, but the experiment in the federal courts was so successful in simplifying procedure that it was admired and copied in a few states. Allowing the Supreme Court to prescribe rules governing procedure was not new in the federal courts.

The Court was given the authority to prescribe rules of procedure in admiralty and in equity from its establishment. The Act of 1792 provided that the procedures in those areas would be "according to the principles, rules and usages which belonged to Courts of Equity and to courts of admiralty" except where altered by statute or by "such regulations as the supreme court of the United States shall think proper from time to time by rules to prescribe to any circuit or district courts."[3] This rule-making authority was further recognized in 1793 by a statute which gave the court the authority to make rules and orders to govern the

> returning of writs and processes, the filing of declarations and other pleadings, the making of rules, the entering and making up judgments by default, and other matters in vacation and otherwise in a manner not repugnant to the laws of the United States, to regulate the practice of the said courts respectively, as shall be fit and necessary for the advancement of justice. . . .[4]

This statute limited the rule-making authority to definite areas and did not extend over all areas embraced by procedure.

The general rule-making power given earlier to the Supreme Court was reaffirmed in 1842 when the Supreme Court was given

> full power and authority, from time to time to prescribe and regulate and alter, the forms of writs and other process to be used in the district and circuit courts of the United States, and the forms

and modes of framing and filing bills and libels, answers and other proceedings of pleadings in suits at common law, or in admiralty and equity pleadings.[5]

Several other statutes, including the statute creating appeals in a criminal case, recognized the limited authority of the Court to prescribe rules.[6] None of these statutes gave the Supreme Court the power to prescribe rules governing procedure.

The Court acted on the power to adopt rules governing equity and admiralty proceedings by adopting equity rules in 1822 and admiralty rules in 1842. Since the Court never did act in this area of the common law where it had statutory authority, this led to the withdrawal of the rule-making authority in 1872 by the adoption of the Conformity Act.[7]

The reluctance of the Supreme Court of the United States not to promulgate any extensive set of rules is illustrated by its failure to adopt a comprehensive set of rules governing its own practice until 1884. Many state supreme courts had adopted extensive rules to regulate admissions to their bar and time limits for filing writs. The Court did issue individual rules beginning at its first term providing for the appointment of John Tucker as clerk of the court and directing him to keep his office at the seat of the national government. At each term of court, additional rules were adopted.

However, agitation for the Supreme Court to act on a larger scale never ceased. As early as 1833, Mr. Justice Story mentioned in a decision that

> Congress may adopt state laws affecting the operation of the process or proceedings in the National Courts directly, by a substantial enactment or they may confide the authority to adopt them to the courts of the United States.[8]

However, at no other time did the Supreme Court endorse the views of Justice Story or urge Congress to give the courts this authority. The Court has commented and upheld its authority to make certain rules such as the rule allowing any justice, or judge in the appropriate circuit, to grant bail after a writ of error had been requested.[9]

As early as 1883, the American Bar Association had established a Committee on Judicial Administration and Remedial Procedure primarily to discuss the structure of the federal courts. The Committee began early to consider proposals to modify the practice of the federal courts. One of the earliest recommendations was to urge Congress to consider a bill to prepare a federal code of procedure to regulate both the civil and criminal matters. It is clear that the members had great reservations about the utility of a code of procedure because of the experience in New York. One speaker termed the proposition an "insidious suggestion."[10] Two years later, the current code of procedure of New York adopted in 1880 was described as the "most unhealthy and abnormal development."[11] During these debates, the practice in admiralty and equity, which was regulated by rules adopted by the Supreme Court, received compliments for their definitiveness and directness. From these debates on matters of federal procedure emerged the policy giving authority to the Supreme Court of the United States to prescribe the rules for the federal trial courts.[12]

The model adopted by the English government was often cited as an example of how well the practice of granting the rule-making authority to the courts functioned. In 1872, the Lord Chancellor and the Lord Chief Justice with other judges were authorized to make rules governing practice, pleading and procedure in the English courts.[13] This group acted through "orders" — which by common consent reduced the complexity of practice. The chief virtue of this method was the argument that details could be finely adjusted as they became apparent rather than the cumbersome process of calling this to the attention of the legislative body and goading them to act. If local bar associations urged their legislative bodies to give the courts in their state this authority, such efforts have not received wide attention.

By 1912, some forty-two state bar associations supported the program of the American Bar Association to make the practice in the federal courts uniform.[14] The issue of whether the Supreme Court had this authority independent of a legislative mandate was widely discussed. In 1912, the American Bar Association established a Committee on Uniform Judicial Procedure under the chairmanship of Thomas W. Shelton for the purpose of securing a bill through Congress to implement this program. Another member of this Committee was William Howard Taft, long an advocate of judicial reform. A bill granting the Supreme Court the necessary authority was introduced into the Congress in 1913, and members of the Committee were led to believe that the bill had been enacted.

However, upon arriving in Washington to witness the signing of the bill, it was discovered that the wrong measure had passed.[15] The bill was introduced into succeeding Congresses, but failed to pass because of the opposition of Senator Thomas J. Walsh of Montana (1859-1933), the chairman of the Senate Judiciary Committee. Senator Walsh opposed this measure because he argued the federal courts followed the local state procedure and a uniform method of procedure for all the federal courts would require the practitioner to learn two systems. Since Walsh was a popular speaker before bar groups, he expressed his misgivings many times about granting to the Supreme Court this authority. He thought the Court could not do this work as it was "overwhelmed with the labors now before it."[16] American lawyers have always argued that a statute is ineffective until the Supreme Court has interpreted it. The senator argued that there would be "miscarriages of justice" until the courts had had a chance to construe the particular rule. The stock cry of the Twentieth Century American lawyer that such a grant of authority was "unconstitutional" was not overlooked.

Shelton worked industriously to secure the passage of this bill but died in 1930 having failed in this objective. The new chairman of the Committee expressed the opinion that uniformity in federal actions was not a desirable goal.[17] In 1933, the American Bar Association terminated the existence of its Committee on Uniform Judicial Procedure,[18] and the impetus for this change began to come from sources other than the organized bar.

In 1933, Senator Walsh was designated as Attorney General in the first Roosevelt Cabinet, but he died before assuming this office. He was succeeded by Homer S. Cummings who took up the sponsorship of the bill to grant the Supreme Court the power to make the rules.[19] He recommended that law and equity be combined into one form of action. This suggestion had been made first by Chief Justice Taft in a speech before the American Bar Association in 1922.[20] A bill granting the Supreme Court of the United States the authority to prescribe rules of procedure in civil cases was introduced and passed with little or no opposition in 1934.[21] In a sense, this statute increased the authority that the Supreme Court once had but did not exercise.[22]

Chief Justice Hughes announced the intention of the Supreme Court to make effective use of the power granted to the Court. On June 3, 1935, nearly a year after the bill was signed, the Court issued an order appointing a committee chaired by William D. Mitchell of New York to prepare a draft of the proposed rules.[23] The committee was responsible directly to the Supreme Court and functioned under guidelines prepared by the Court. The chairman had served as solicitor general under President Calvin Coolidge, and upon the unusual recommendation of the justices of the Supreme Court, as attorney general under President Hoover.[24] Mitchell enjoyed the confidence of the justices and had interest in such reforms of the federal courts.

During the year between the enactment of the rule-making statute and the appointment of the committee, each judicial circuit had a conference to make suggestions on new rules for the consideration of the committee.[25] The committee held its first meeting in Chicago on June 20, 1935, and appointed a reporter, Dean Charles E. Clark of Yale, to prepare a tentative draft of the rules.[26]

The committee had few American precedents to draw upon in preparing such a dramatic change in the procedure in the federal district courts. The rules prepared by the English courts were useful and were referenced in the notes under the appropriate rule. The Federal Rules of Equity adopted in 1912 by the Supreme Court provided the organizational framework and frequent references are made in the notes to these rules.[27] Among the members of the committee were professors and others who had knowledge of procedures and practices in the American states who prepared drafts for the consideration of the committee.

The work of the committee was followed through the pages of professional journals with great interest by members of the bar. The committee prepared three drafts which were extensively reviewed by the judiciary and the bar. The final draft of the Rules of Civil Procedure were submitted first to the Supreme Court, which incorporated some amendments of its own. A final draft was submitted to Congress as required by the statute and became effective 60 days after the termination of the session of Congress, which was September 16, 1938. At last, a uniform system of pleading and practice for the federal courts had come into existence. These rules received close scrutiny at institutes held in different cities which various members of the drafting committee attended. [28]

The rules for civil procedure have been widely acclaimed for their simplicity and innovativeness. The chief accomplishment was to deemphasize pleadings as the controlling element in the decision but to use procedure as an aid to understanding the case rather than restrict the parties. [29] The rules introduced notice-pleading which restricts the pleadings to giving notice of the general claims and leaves to the discovery process the development of the dispute. The weakness of pleadings as a means of developing the facts was the lack of basis to test the allegations and denials. Law and equity procedures were merged and steps were taken to make the rules of procedure uniform in other areas such as copyright, patents and admiralty. The rules introduced some new procedures such as discovery, pretrial conferences and summary judgments. Discovery had long been advocated by writers as a means for the parties to be fully prepared for trial, but this innovation was greeted with some reservations. The rule establishing pre-trial deposition-discovery mechanisms was "one of the most significant innovations of the federal rules." [30] In due course, discovery was abused. [31] The pre-trial conference was conceived as a means of narrowing the issues and to get an agreement on certain issues that were not in dispute. However, some judges have used this as a means to force settlements, a practice not fully appreciated by all members of the bar. Like all innovations, neither discovery nor pre-trial conferences have accomplished all that their advocates had hoped.

Another innovation was the summary judgment which permitted the judge to enter a judgment without proceeding to the full conclusion of the trial when it became apparent that no case had been presented. The chief contribution of the rules was to enforce uniformity of practice in all the federal courts throughout the United States. One unforeseen result of the rules was the introduction of more judicial management of cases through the discovery process and the pre-trial conferences.

Surprisingly, these rules have not been amended as frequently as it would have been thought necessary in view of the dramatic changes brought into the federal district courts. The first amendment was rather minor in that the rules were extended to apply to proceedings under the Longshoremen's and Harbor Workers' Compensation Act. [32] An extended review was undertaken by the Advisory Committee at the request of the Supreme Court which resulted in the adoption of rather extensive amendments by the Supreme Court in 1946.[33] The adoption of the Judicial Code of 1948 dictated some changes which were made and came into effect in 1949.[34] A further amendment was made in 1951 governing condemnation proceedings and this was the final amendment proposed by the Advisory Committee.[35]

On October 1, 1956, the Supreme Court terminated the Advisory Committee which had proposed the original rules and had proposed several minor amendments. After that date, no machinery existed to aid the Court in its rule-making function. Chief Justice Earl Warren recognized this deficiency and urged that this function be given to the Judicial Conference of the United States.[36] The Conference in 1958 was authorized to make a continuous study of the rules and recommend changes to the Supreme Court.[37] In 1959, a committee under the chairmanship of Judge Albert Maris was appointed to review all rules including admiralty.[38] The rules were revised and original rules for admiralty, bankruptcy and copyright were integrated where possible. Since this period, the Judicial Conference has amended the rules rather frequently. When transmitting amendments to Congress, Justices Douglas and Black dissented to the adoption of certain amendments, proposing instead that the Supreme Court be removed from the rule-making function and vest this duty in the Judicial Conference which originally proposed these rules.[39] Their views have not prevailed.

The most controversial set of rules proposed by the Supreme Court through the Maris Committee was that covering admission of evidence, which was submitted in November 20, 1972 to Congress. Immediately, the objection was raised that the Court did not have the authority since evidentiary rules were not included in its general rule-making authority. Immediately, various members of the Senate, including the influential chairman of the Senate Committee on the Judiciary, John L. McClellan, objected to the proposed rules and secured the passage of legislation to defer their implementation until Congress had sufficient time to study them.[40] No one doubted the wisdom of attempting to make the rules uniform for the federal courts, but different individuals found fault with individual rules. As a result, Congress enacted a set of rules and gave the Supreme Court the authority to modify these rules.[41]

The original proposal of the American Bar Association granting rule-making authority to the Supreme Court (apparently by its broad terms) included rules governing criminal procedure. The resolution would have granted to the Supreme Court the authority to prescribe "by rules the forms for the entire pleading, practice, and procedure to be used in all actions, motions, and proceedings at law."[42] However, the Supreme Court was given the authority to prepare the rules of criminal procedure in a piece-meal fashion.

In 1933, Congress gave the Supreme Court authority to prescribe rules to govern procedure and practice in criminal cases after verdict, including appeals.[43] This statute predates the one giving authority to prescribe rules of civil procedure. The two statutes differ in that the civil procedural rules were required to be submitted to Congress for possible veto, but under the statute authorizing criminal rules, they became effective at the time promulgated. The Supreme Court drafted a set of rules immediately which took effect May 7, 1934.[44] These rules were referred to as the Criminal Appeals Rules. The reason most often given for the failure to extend this rule making to include the entire criminal trial was the fear of circumscribing the constitutional guarantees. The authority of the Court was extended to prescribe rules to regulate practice and procedure before the commissioners for the trial of petty crimes.[45] In the meanwhile, efforts were being made to persuade Congress to grant a more extended rule-making authority to the Supreme Court.

In 1938, Attorney General Cummings suggested that the Court be given authority to prescribe criminal rules prior to and including verdict.[46] The authority to prescribe rules governing procedure before verdict was given to the Supreme Court in 1940.[47] This grant generated very little opposition.[48] In doing this, Congress required the Court to submit the rules to Congress for possible veto as was required with the Rules of Civil Procedure.

Acting under these statutes, the Supreme Court appointed an advisory committee under the chairmanship of Arthur T. Vanderbilt in 1941.[49] The committee prepared a number of drafts and circulated its "Secondary Preliminary Draft" for comment among the bar and the judges. These rules received wide attention in professional literature as did the Rules of Civil Procedure.[50] The rules were prepared during the war years and were submitted to Congress in December 1945[51] and became effective March 21, 1946,[52] when the nation's attention was directed to international affairs and the problems of the demobilization of the armed forces.[53] Many lawyers were returning to their practices.

These rules were derived from a number of sources including the Rules of Civil Procedure, federal statutes, the rules after verdict drafted by the Supreme Court, decisions of the federal courts, and the criminal procedure of the several states. The Rules of Criminal Procedure made no startling innovations in criminal procedure. The values the rules sought to implement are stated in Rule 2 as consisting of a "just determination of every criminal proceeding." The rules were to be construed "to secure simplicity in procedure, fairness in administration and the elimination of unjustifiable expense and delay."[54] The rules clarified and brought together into one source all the diverse rulings found in statutes, the Constitution and the glosses of the federal courts on these sources through their decisions. This was an accomplishment, as the number of criminal cases in the federal courts began to rapidly increase.

The rules of civil and criminal procedure have been widely acclaimed for their simplicity and innovativeness. After their adoption, very little opposition developed, a fate ascribed by one authority to the support of the American Bar Association and other local bar associations. In drafting the rules, the committee widely consulted organized groups which may have been a measure to diffuse political opposition.[55] The adoption of the rules caused some states to follow the example of the federal courts. Three states — Arizona, Colorado and New Mexico — initially adopted the federal rules in full, whereas in Pennsylvania, the court completely rewrote their own rules.[56] In other states, portions of the federal rules were adopted either by statute or by action of the courts. However, the reform of procedure has seemed to have lost its urgency by the closing decades of the Twentieth Century. In time, this method of preparing rules of procedure may become obsolete.

Local Court Rules

Under the Federal Rules of Civil Procedure, the local courts are free to adopt supplementary rules as long as they do not conflict with a federal statute or the general rules.[57] The district and circuit courts had early adopted rules governing the administration of their courts and the rules which clarified practice. The comprehensiveness and the extent of these local rules varied extensively, as did the nature of the rules.

Some courts were confused as to whether an administrative appointment, such as the appointment of the clerk, was a rule and should be included. A clear demarcation between a rule which had some general applicability and was designed as a guide for future conduct, from an order, which made some type of appointment or ruling in a given case, was slow in evolving. These rules were generally entered into the minutes of the court and were known to the limited bar of that period. If published, the rules were encompassed in a small pamphlet of a few pages. Other local rules were published with collections of the rules for the local state courts. However, a study of a limited number of these rules reveals some interesting facets of the history of the federal courts.

The first such local rules appear to have been published in 1812 to govern the circuit courts in the First Circuit which was then presided over by Justice Joseph Story.[58] The author of these rules is not known. Since these rules were applicable to the circuit courts in the First Circuit, one may presume that Joseph Story was responsible. Story had shown his interest in rules by the preparation of the equity rules adopted by the Supreme Court. The first several rules governed the admission of attorneys and others outlined the necessary steps in attaching costs and defining duties of the clerks and marshals. The clerk was required to enter the judgments of the court, and other rules indicated the days in advance that certain processes would be issued. This is the only set of rules adopted to govern procedure in all the circuit courts within a given circuit.

The burden to prepare these rules was left to the local district court judge with the approval of the circuit judge who was the justice of the Supreme Court. It would be interesting to determine those courts in which the rules developed by accretion, as the courts issued individual orders as the need arose, and those where the rules were completely rewritten after much thought. The rules of the District Court for the Northern District of New York were revised in 1831, five years after Albert Conkling became judge in that court and about the same time he wrote a book on federal practice.[59] One may assume that this revision was at the instigation of Judge Conkling.

Traditionally, the District Court for the Southern District of New York has been the forum of admiralty litigation, and for this reason, it is not surprising that this court had developed a set of rules governing proceedings in prize cases very early.[60] A more elaborate set of rules extending more generally to admiralty was adopted in this court in 1828. William P. Van Ness was judge of the District Court for New York and later for the District Court of the Southern District from 1812 to 1826. Judge Van Ness was noted for his decisions in the admiralty area and many of them were collected and published in FEDERAL CASES. A new set of admiralty rules was adopted in 1828, approximately two years after Samuel R. Betts became judge of that court. Betts was likewise known for his interest in admiralty.[61] The Supreme Court did not adopt admiralty rules for the district courts, as it was authorized to do by statute, until 1842. Perhaps the experience in New York influenced the Supreme Court.

The admiralty rules of the Southern District of New York were well known as they were included in a number of books on this subject and in one general practice book. Because of their general availability, it may be presumed that these New York admiralty rules influenced local practice in other federal judicial districts.[62]

Without a doubt, the rules adopted by the judge of one district were copied in other districts. A hand-written note in a text containing the rules of the Circuit Court for the Northern District of New York informed the reader that the rules governing appeals from the district to the circuit court of New York were adopted in Michigan in 1848.[63] It would be of great interest to have some explanation of the reason for this adoption and the extent of borrowing in other districts, if there was any!

These local rules often reflected the local problems. The rules of the Southern District of Florida prescribe the licensing procedure for "wreckers," or in more normal admiralty practice — salvagers! In fact, the only other important provision is the adoption of Florida practice as a guide to practice in that court.[64]

A set of one hundred rules adopted for the Circuit Court of Georgia in 1823, although not published until 1846, may serve as a model to indicate the matters generally covered.[65] The first group of rules governed the mode of initiating a law suit in that court which was by "petition and process" as practiced in the superior courts of the state of Georgia. The clerk was given extensive authority to rule on different matters on the first Monday of the month, and no rule on a process could be taken in open court when the clerk could have issued it. The next group of rules governed the issuance of the judgment and prescribed how a judgment could be taken and the method of service by the marshals and his returns to the court. The method by which a docket was to be kept and which types of cases would be given priority formed another group of rules. Other rules governed the selection of juries, marshal's sales, fines and forfeitures, and special commissions. The one subject found in other rules but not included in this set is the process by which attorneys were admitted to the bar of the court. From a review of these rules which were signed by Justice William Johnson and J. Cuyler, the district court judge, it becomes evident that great effort was put into drafting these rules. A few had been earlier adopted individually and are found in the minutes of the court.

This survey gives some appreciation to the extent of the rule-making practices of the federal trial courts prior to the enactment of the Conformity Act of 1872. To what extent other federal district and circuit courts adopted rules as extensive as these during this period is not clear. One fact that is clear is that these rules aided in the work of the court, and that some federal judges sought to promote the aims of justice by their patience in drafting rules for the guidance of the bar. How these rules were adopted and the names of the judges responsible for them is an unknown chapter in the history of the federal courts.

After 1872, it appears that few rules were adopted by the local federal courts until the adoption of the Rules of Civil Procedure. Since then, the courts have freely used the rule-making function to clarify their practices to promote a better administration of justice. As more judges preside in the same court, and the number of litigants increase, rule-making provides a means of establishing a desirable amount of uniformity.

FOOTNOTES TO CHAPTER 18

1. A good survey of the sources of state practice is bound in the report of the Committee on Uniformity of Procedure and Comparative Law, 19 ABA REPT. 424 (1896).

2. Robert Wyness Millar, CIVIL PROCEDURE OF THE TRIAL COURT IN HISTORICAL PERSPECTIVE (1952), p.53, 79. The Code of 1848 was revised in 1876 and 1880. This revisor was the target of much criticism.

3. Act of May 8, 1792, sec. 2, 1 STAT. 276.

4. Act of March 2, 1793, sec. 7, 1 STAT. 335.

5. Act of August 23, 1842, sec. 6, 5 STAT. 518.

6. Act of February 6, 1889, sec. 6, 25 STAT. 656.

7. Charles E. Clark and James William Moore, "A New Federal Civil Procedure," 44 YALE L. J. 392 (1935); Editorial, 24 A.B.A. J. 546 (1938).

8. Beers v. Haughton, 9 Pet. 359 (U.S. 1833).

9. Hudson v. Parker, 156 U.S. 277 (1894).

10. 19 ABA REPT. 44 (1896). The activity of the American Bar Association in this area is recounted in "Supreme Court Adopts Rules for Civil Procedure in Federal District Courts," 24 A.B.A. J. 97 (1938).

11. 21 ABA REPT. 455 (1898).

12. Thomas Wall Shelton, "Uniform Judicial Procedure - Let Congress set the Supreme Court Free," 73 CENT. L. J. 319 (1911).

13. Millar, *supra,* note 2, p.43.

14. Report of the Committee, 1 A.B.A. J. 386 (1915).

15. Report of the Committee, 3 A.B.A. J. 521 (1917).

16. 1926 PROC. ARK. BAR ASSOC. 82, 87.

17. 57 ABA REPT. 117-119, 575 (1932). The chairman was Judge George W. McClintic of the United States District Court for the Southern District of West Virginia.

18. 58 ABA REPT. 108-110 (1933).

19. Homer C. Cummings, "A Rounded System of Judicial Rule-Making," 24 A.B.A. J. 513 (1938); Homer S. Cummings, "Modernizing Federal Procedure," 24 A.B.A. J. 625 (1938).

20. William Howard Taft, "Possible and Needed Reforms in the Administration of Justice in Federal Courts," 8 A.B.A. J. 601 (1922), 47 ABA REPT. 250.

21. Act of June 19, 1934, 48 STAT. 1064.

22. The AMERICAN BAR JOURNAL took the editorial position that the Act of 1934 returned to the Court the authority it had before removal by the Conformity Act. 24 A.B.A. J. 546 (1938).

23. 295 U.S. 774 (1934).

24. The best biographical sketch of Mitchell is found in DICTIONARY OF AMERICAN BIOGRAPHY, Supp. 5.

25. 21 A.B.A. J. 69 (1935).

26. "Advisory Committee on Federal Procedure Meets in Washington," 21 A.B.A. J. 762 (1935).

27. Charles C. Montgomery, "Changes in the Federal Practice Resulting From the New Federal Rules of Civil Procedure," 1 F.R.D. 337 (1941).

28. RULES OF CIVIL PROCEDURE FOR THE DISTRICT COURTS OF THE UNITED STATES WITH NOTES . . . AND PROCEEDINGS OF THE INSTITUTE ON FEDERAL RULES, CLEVELAND, OHIO, JULY 21, 22, 23, 1938. (1938).

29. Charles E. Clark, "The Influence of Federal Procedure Reform," 13 L. & CONT. PROB. 154 (1948). The author has used Judge Clark's appraisal for he served on the drafting committee.

30. Hickman v. Taylor, 329 U.S. 495, 500 (1947).

31. Milton Pollack, "Discovery — Its abuses and Correction," 80 FRD 219 (1979).

32. This amendment submitted to Congress in 1940, 308 U.S. 642 (1940).

33. The members of the Advisory Committee were asked to continue by order of the Court January 5, 1942, 314 U.S. 720 (1942), 329 U.S. 839 (1946).

34. 335 U.S. 919 (1948).

35. 341 U.S. 962 (1951).

36. "Rule Making Function," 21 F.R.D. 117, 139.

37. Act of July 11, 1958, 72 STAT. 356. *See* S. Rept. 1744, 85th Cong., 2d sess.

38. 1958 Annual Rept. Judicial Conf. U.S. p. 6; Earl Warren, "Address," 25 F.R.D. 213, 215 (1960).

39. 374 U.S. 865, 869 (1963).

40. Act of March 30, 1973, 87 STAT. 9.

41. Act of January 2, 1975, 88 STAT. 1949.

42. 1 A.B.A. J. 386, 392 (1915).

43. Act of February 24, 1933, 47 STAT. 904; Amended Act of March 8, 1934.

44. 292 U.S. 661 (1934).

45. Act of October 9, 1940, sec. 2, 54 STAT. 1058. Rules found in 311 U.S. 733 (1941).

46. Alexander Holtzoff, "Codification of the Federal Criminal Procedure," F.R.D. 275 (1946).

47. Act of June 29, 1940, 54 STAT. 688.

48. S. Rept. 1934, 76th Cong. 3d sess. (1940); H. Rept. 2492, 76th Cong. 3d sess. (1940).

49. The Appointment of the Advisory Committee is given in 312 U.S. 714 (1941).

50. A complete bibliography is presented in Lester B. Orfield, "The Federal Rules of Criminal Procedure," 26 NEB. L. REV. 572, note 6 (1947).

51. 323 U.S. 821 (1944).

52. Rules found in 327 U.S. 825 (1947).

53. This was recognized by Arthur T. Vanderbilt. *See* George H. Derson, "The New Federal Rules of Criminal Procedure," 55 Yale L.J. 699, fn.19 (1946).

54. FEDERAL RULES OF CRIMINAL PROCEDURE WITH NOTES . . . AND PROCEEDINGS OF THE INSTITUTE CONDUCTED BY NEW YORK UNIVERSITY SCHOOL OF LAW (1946), p.1, and discussion, p.120.

55. Clark, *supra,* note 29, p.144, 159.

56. *Ibid,* p.161.

57. Fed. Rules Civ. Proc. 83; Fed. Rules Crim. Proc. 57.

58. Rules of the Circuit Court of the United States for the First Circuit. (1812), 15 p.

59. Alfred Conkling, A TREATISE ON THE ORGANIZATION, JURISDICTION AND PRACTICE OF THE COURTS IN THE UNITED STATES (1831), p. 315.

60. Rules of the District Court of the United States for the District of New York, in Prize Cases (1812), 16 p.

61. Conkling, *supra,* note 59, p.435. A pamphlet containing these rules published in 1838 states after the title "by Samuel R. Betts."

62. Andrew Dunlap, A TREATISE ON THE PRACTICE OF COURTS OF ADMIRALTY IN CIVIL CAUSES OF MARITIME JURISDICTION (2d ed. 1850), p. 327; Alfred Conkling, THE ADMIRALTY JURISDICTION, LAW AND PRACTICE OF THE COURTS OF THE UNITED STATES (2d ed. 1857), v. 2, p.467. This copy of Conkling is in the University of Georgia Law Library.

63. Conkling, *supra,* note 62, v.2, p.465.

64. William Marvin, A TREATISE ON THE LAW OF WRECK AND SALVAGE (1858), p.300. These rules do not contain any mention of requirements for admission to the bar.

65. Rules of the Sixth Circuit of the United States for the District of Georgia Adopted December Term, 1823 (1846), 24 p.

Chapter 19

DEVELOPMENT OF APPELLATE REVIEW

Under the First Judiciary Act, the Supreme Court was the principal appellate court in the federal system, with a limited judicial review vested in the circuit court. Since the district courts had exclusive jurisdiction in admiralty, the appropriate method of review was by an appeal to the next circuit when the value exceeded $300. In all civil actions brought in the district courts, where the sum exceeded $50, a writ of error could be taken to the circuit court.[1] The only method of review by the Supreme Court of decisions from the circuit courts was by the writ of error. The appeal and writ of error involved two different procedural methods, but this distinction between these two writs eroded during the subsequent decades as the technical points of the practice became less distinct. A factor which led to this decline was that the stenographic records became more common during the succeeding decades, rendering the question of what documents were properly a part of the record less important.

The writ of appeal by the provision of the First Judiciary Act was used to bring a maritime case from the district to the circuit court. A number of technical practices made the writ of appeal differed from the writ of error. The distinction between the two writs becomes apparent from their history, for the writ of error was used in the common law courts (Court of King's Bench, Court of Common Pleas and Exchequer Court) and the writ of appeal was used in the courts based upon the civil law (the admiralty and chancery courts). No single court to which all appeals were taken existed in England at the close of the Eighteenth Century. Each group of English courts was supreme in its own sphere. Each system had its own procedural method of proceedings, for in the common law courts, the testimony was presented orally and no record was made except for documents presented to the court, whether they were pleadings or documents properly introduced into evidence. In admiralty and chancery, the evidence was recorded in depositions. The First Judiciary Act adopted the procedure of the common law court by mandating that "the mode of proof by oral testimony and examination of witnesses in open court shall be the same in all courts of the United States, as well *as* in the trial of causes in equity and of admiralty and maritime jurisdiction".[2] This method of trial procedure caused more difficulty in keeping the distinction between the two writs, as was done in the English courts. However, efforts were made continually to separate the two.

A writ of error at the beginning of the Nineteenth Century was used to consider some error of law in matters of substance which were apparent upon the face of the record or verified by issuing a writ of certiorari for the purposes of amending the papers to be brought before the court upon an allegation of diminution, or as the practice developed, presented in a Bill of Exceptions.[3] Because the record was limited, a lawyer had to use various procedural means of getting the material into the record during the trial. A demurrer to the evidence incorporated only the evidence produced, not the rulings of the court; therefore only evidence could be reviewed on a writ of error.

The technical distinction between the two writs involved the extent of the record brought up to the reviewing court, but there were other procedural differences which may explain some variations in practices in American courts. In those cases in which the writ of appeal was the proper remedy, the motion for the court to grant the writ had to be made in open court, whereas the writ of error could be sought from the judge in chambers within a prescribed period of time. Since in those cases where the writ of appeal was the proper remedy, all evidence before the trial court was in writing and the review was much wider ranging, for as the previous writers have taught, the reviewing court reviewed both the facts and the law. Justice Moody in 1906 stated that the "appeal brings up questions of fact as well as of law, but upon a writ of error only questions of law apparent on the record can be considered, and there can be no inquiry whether there was error in dealing with questions of fact."[4] Although this statement is essentially correct, it leaves many differences unexplained. For the writ of error, only those documents presented to the court, such as pleadings and other written documents introduced during the course of the trial and properly admitted as evidence, constituted the record. Many other matters such as rulings by the court during the trial had to be preserved in a Bill of Exceptions. For this reason, the writ of error was known as confining the examination of the reviewing court to the rulings and hence to the law involved in the case. Questions such as the consideration of evidence to determine its competency as a point of law as tending to prove the fact could be reviewed by a writ of error, but whether the jury drew the correct inferences could not be examined. The writ of error could not be used to consider matters addressed to the discretion of the lower courts such as denial of a new trial.[5] Even where the parties agreed to have the court answer questions not raised in the record, such cases could not be reviewed by the writ of error.[6]

The Bill of Exceptions was the most common method of incorporating matters in the lower court into the record so that these matters could be reviewed by a writ of error. The Bill of Exceptions was created in the trial court by appropriate objections to evidence presented; this evidence, the grounds for the objections and the court rulings were recorded and signed by the judge.

The Bill of Exceptions was not mentioned in any of the early statutes governing the jurisdiction of the federal courts, but it was a well recognized writ in the practice of the English common-law courts. As early as the reign of Edward I, a party could write out any exception to the court's rulings on evidence and pray that the justices put their seals to the Bill.[7] Originally, this was not a matter of right as it later became in American practice. Since the Bill was a question of practice, it was shaped by a number of court decisions. The Bill of Exceptions first covered questions of law which arose in the admission or exclusion of evidence and on charges of law given by the court; the Bill was not applicable in admiralty or equity suits.[8] An exception had to be drawn up and signed by the judge although his seal was not necessary, and an agreement of the parties as to the facts could not dispense with the Bill of Exceptions. The Bill was usually drawn up during the term of court and signed at that time or as soon as practicable thereafter. A mere clerical mistake could be corrected by certificate of the court, but generally all defects in the record were corrected by certiorari.[9] The Supreme Court adopted a rule in 1832 that the Bill should contain only as much of the testimony as might be necessary to explain distinctly the ruling upon the issues involved,[10] not the entire testimony.[11] The judges of the circuit and district courts were not to allow any Bill that contained the complete charge of the court to the jury upon a general exception to the whole charge. The matters the courts could allow in a Bill of Exceptions were those that were matters of law to which the party took exception.[12]

It is not clear when the Bill of Exceptions was dropped from the practice of the federal courts, but during the Nineteenth Century, the use of stenographers in the courts became a common practice. By using the transcript of the entire proceedings, the material in the Bill was fuller and without a doubt, verbose. The rules of the Supreme Court adopted in 1928 provided that only the evidence necessary to present clearly the questions involved could be incorporated into the Bill in a narrative form.[13] Since all statutes and decisions referred to the "record", the transition to the complete elimination of the Bill of Exceptions was gradual. All references to the Bill of Exceptions were dropped in the rules of the United States Supreme Court in 1954, although the use of the Bill had been discontinued much earlier. This transition was opposed by some courts of appeal. The objection of these judges was to the full stenographic record, although signed by the trial judge as a Bill of Exceptions.[14] One judge remarked, "giving it the requisite name does not make it a lawful thing."[15]

The first use of the term "transcript" was in the Act of 1802 allowing a review of appeals in admiralty and equity to the circuit courts and from there, to the Supreme Court.[16] "Transcript" was carried forward into the REVISED STATUTES (1874) where the term "transcript of the record" was used in relation to admiralty and equity appeals.[17] In 1911, this term described the record on an appeal to the Circuit Courts of Appeals and then to the Supreme Court.[18] From all this, we may surmise that the practice of using the transcript of a stenographer gradually replaced the Bill of Exceptions.

A minor distinction between the writs of error and appeal was the title given to the parties. The moving party for a writ of appeal was known as the appellant, whereas the moving party for a writ of error was known as the plaintiff in error, regardless of whether the moving party was the plaintiff or defendant in the lower court.

A number of matters could not be reached by a writ of error, although the amount involved was within the required jurisdictional amount. A judgment for nonsuit or other matters within the discretion of the trial judge or refusing a new trial could not be reviewed by a writ of error.[19] Basically, the writ of error could review any problem arising during the course of the trial that was properly preserved in the record. However, it generally did not include motions after the trial. For this reason, a motion for a new trial did not waive the right to a writ of error unless specifically waived by the parties.[20] Any attempt other than to show that there were matters which could not be reviewed under the writ of error would require a full practice book of the period.

The district courts had jurisdiction over admiralty and maritime causes. Cases arising in these areas could be taken to the circuit courts by "appeal". However, when judicial review was sought on an appeal made to the circuit court, it was decided that the method of bringing the case to the higher court was by the writ of error.[21] The Supreme Court decided that these terms were used in their technical sense, and hence, nothing but the proceedings, together with a sentence or decree, would be open for review.[22] The Court stated that the methods by which cases were brought before it were conferred by Congress and they were not free to change or modify them.[23] This technical defect was changed by statute which provided that on an appeal in such cases, all documents should be transmitted to the Supreme Court which could receive new evidence if necessary.[24] This gave the Court the jurisdiction to examine fully any maritime or equity case brought to it by the writ of appeal. However, this led to a distinction between review of maritime or equity and civil cases removed from the district court to the circuit court.

Originally, the circuit courts were given jurisdiction to review by the writ of error all civil actions from the district courts where the matter exceeded the value of $50. Where a case was removed by the writ of error from the district court to the circuit court, the decision of the circuit court was final as between the parties.[25] Such a case could not be reviewed by the Supreme Court on a writ of error. This rule was changed by a statute in 1840, and the Court was directed to consider all cases which originally were brought to the circuit court by a writ of appeal as fully as any other cases.[26]

One very significant departure from contemporary practice was the requirement that the writ of error or appeal could be brought only after final judgment.[27] The judge of the circuit court could not by mandamus nor any similar procedural writ direct the district court to allow amendments to pleadings or other parts of the record.

The First Judiciary Act does not use the term "writ of appeal" but mentions an appeal in admiralty and equitable cases. It was not long before the question was raised whether the Judiciary Act of 1789 confused the terms. However, it was determined that the term should be understood by its technical meaning. [28]

The writ of appeal was prescribed as a method of review in other types of cases. In an act providing the procedure for settling land disputes in Missouri and Arkansas, the federal courts were mandated to proceed as a court of equity. [29] For this reason, such questions were reviewed by the Supreme Court by writ of appeal. The statute authorized the attorney of the United States in the district in which the case arose to transmit to the attorney general of the United States a statement concerning the facts of the case, and the points of law on which it was decided. If the attorney general decided that the decision of the district court was erroneous, the district attorney was to direct an appeal to the Supreme Court. [30] The time limit in such a case required an appeal within one year of the final judgment. An appeal had to be moved in open court and could not, as in a writ of error, be issued by the clerk of the court. [31] As the decisions of the Supreme Court are examined for the closing decades of the Nineteenth Century, one may recognize, without tangible proof, that the many technical distinctions between the writ of error and appeal were gradually losing any significance.

One practice in the appellate courts which is distinctly unique is the possibility of proceeding to consider a case when one of the other parties does not appear. In the trial court, an attorney of record can not withdraw from the case without the consent of the court and there were numerous reasons for creating this rule. [32] As early as 1801, the Court adopted a rule which provided that where the defendant in error failed to appear, the plaintiff could proceed *ex parte*. [33] A few years later, the rules were slightly changed. [34] The plaintiff in error was entitled to prosecute his appeal if the defendant did not appear and to receive "judgment according to the right of the cause." It was slightly more serious for the plaintiff in error not to appear for then the defendant could move "to dismiss the writ of error or open the record and ask for an affirmance." These provisions were dropped in 1954 apparently because they had lost their significance.

Historically, the writ of appeal had been used in the chancery and admiralty courts where the review extended to both the facts as well as to the law. Since evidence was taken in these courts by depositions rather than the evidence being presented before a jury, as is customary in the common law courts, the court was in the position to review the facts of the case. The Judiciary Act of 1789 required the judges of the circuit court to have the facts clearly appear in the pleadings or decree in equity and admiralty cases. [35] The First Judiciary Act limited the taking of depositions in admiralty cases to the taking of testimony of a person who lived more than a hundred miles from the place of trial, one who was about to leave the United States or the district, or one who was an infirm person.[36] Otherwise, all proceedings including admiralty were required to be presented orally. If the parties made clear to the judge in the district court in an admiralty case that they would be unable to produce the witness on an appeal, then the clerk of the court would take down the testimony.

Admiralty and equity cases from the circuit courts could only be reviewed by the Supreme Court through a writ of error, the effect of which was to make the decision of the circuit court final.[37] This practice was changed in 1803 when Congress passed a statute authorizing review in any cases of equity, admiralty and prize from the circuit courts, or the district courts acting as a circuit court where the matter in dispute, exclusive of cost, exceeded the sum of $2,000. In hearing such an appeal, the Supreme Court could not hear new evidence except in admiralty and prize cases; these appeals were to be governed by the rules prescribed in writs of error.[38] The history of appellate review since 1790 has seen the obliteration of these technical distinctions to the arrival at our present practice of reviewing any error regardless of its merit or whether the disputed proposition was raised in the court below under the claim of con-stitutionality.

In all cases of review at the beginning of the Nineteenth Century, the first criteria was the amount in controversy. A writ of error could be taken to the Supreme Court where the matter in dispute exceeded the sum of $2,000. Where the demand was not for money and its value was not found in the declaration, the value could be proved by evidence.[39] However, it soon became apparent that in certain types of cases, this amount should be modified. In 1844, final judgments from the circuit court in any civil action brought by the government for the enforcement of the Revenue Laws or for the collection of duties on imported goods could be examined in the Supreme Court by writ of error without regard to the amount involved.[40] The other cases in which the amount in dispute was not germane to the jurisdiction of the court were appeals from the highest state courts. In 1864, appeals from prize cases had a monetary limit of $2,000, but the judge of the district court could certify that "the adjudication involves the question of difficulty and general importance" regardless of the amount involved.[41] Upon the establishment of the Circuit Courts of Appeals in 1891, all monetary limits on the amount involved were repealed, and as the Supreme Court stated, this act created "a new and complete scheme of appellate jurisdiction, depending upon the nature of the different cases, rather than upon the pecuniary amount involved."[42]

For those accustomed to the time limits placed on appeal in present appellate practice, the fact that the writ of error could be brought within five years of the final judgment seems extraordinary. An infant, *feme covert,* or a person *non corpus mentis,* or imprisoned, would have the period of his disability plus five years to petition for a writ of error.[43] This period was reduced to two years in 1872.[44] When the Circuit Courts of Appeals were established in 1891, a number of different time periods were introduced. The period for appeals was reduced to six months "after the entry of the order, judgment or decree sought to be reviewed" by the appellate court.[45] However, the same act provided for an appeal within thirty days from a district court or a circuit court where an injunction had been granted or continued, or on a final decree in equity. Writs of error or appeal taken to the Supreme Court from the Circuit Courts of Appeals had to be taken within one year.[46] Congress passed a number of statutes establishing varying time periods for reviewing appeals from different courts and administrative bodies.[47] A federal judge writing in 1926 could state:

> In nearly all cases there are statutory limits upon the time in which appeals may be taken. They have been fixed by different acts, passed at different times, and drawn by different men, who, for the most part, apparently cared nothing about the uniformity.[48]

The same author attempts to list all of these variations grouped by time periods.

The courts at the beginning of the Nineteenth Century were concerned that the appellate review process should not be used as a method of delay. By statute, the Supreme Court used its discretion to award single or double costs to the respondent in error for damages when the review was brought to delay the execution of the judgment.[49] In some jurisdictions at this time, the attorney had to make an oath that the purpose of the appeal was not for the purpose of delay. The rules of the Supreme Court as late as 1928 provided for a rate of ten percent penalty in addition to the rate of interest applied by the court in the state where the judgment was rendered when the proceeding "appears to have been sued out merely for delay."[50]

It is not clear in the early part of the Nineteenth Century whether the writ had to be applied for in writing or whether an oral motion in term was sufficient. However, it can clearly be stated that as late as the middle part of the century, no petition setting forth the cause for the writ was required, although the judge had to be satisfied that such a writ should be allowed. Many judges would conscientiously exercise this discretion, but others would grant the writ for very little cause.

The form of the writ is interesting as it alleges that "a manifest error hath happened, to the great damage" of the complainant, in the judgment rendered in the captioned case. The writ continues:

> We being willing that error, if any hath been, should be duly corrected, and full and speedy justice done to the parties aforesaid in this behalf, do command you, if judgment be therein given, that then under your seal, distinctly and openly, you send the record and proceedings aforesaid, with all things concerning the same, to

the Supreme Court of the United States, together with this writ, so that you have the same at Washington, on the Monday of next, in said supreme court to be then and there held; that the record and proceedings aforesaid being inspected, the said supreme court may cause further to be done therein to correct that error, what of right, and according to the laws and custom of the United States, should be done.

The writ was in the name of the chief justice of the Supreme Court, but was allowed by a circuit court judge who generally was the local district court judge.[51]

Logically, the writ should be allowed to come from the clerk's office of the appellate court to which it was returned, whether it was the Supreme Court or the circuit court. However, it became obvious that great inconveniences would result from having the writ issued by the clerk of the Supreme Court if the writ was returnable to that court. In 1792, Congress directed justices of the Supreme Court to formulate a writ of error and transmit this form to the clerks of the circuit courts so that the writ could be issued from their offices.[52] When the Circuit Courts of Appeals were established, no authority was granted to the clerks of those courts to issue the writ until 1912.[53] The writ is always returnable to the clerk's office of the appellate court.

The opposing party was entitled to thirty days notice by the serving of a citation and did not need to enter his appearance until the expiration of this period.[54] The plaintiff in error was required to deposit a copy of the original writ of error, the citation and the bond with the clerk of the court where the original judgment was rendered. The clerk would then make a true copy of the record without references *aliunde* and all the papers, exhibits, depositions and other proceedings were authenticated by the seal of the court. Here it appears that the custom varied in different parts of the country during the first part of the Nineteenth Century and that either the attorney for the plaintiff in error or the clerk of the lower court forwarded the papers to the clerk of the Supreme Court.

A writ of error directed to the state court under Section 25 of the First Judiciary Act was issued by one of the circuit court judges, and after 1792 issued from the office of the clerk of the circuit court. The citation would be signed by the chief justice of a state supreme court or by a justice of the United States Supreme Court. Here the practice differed from the application for a writ of error from the circuit court to the Supreme Court in that a petition had to be drawn and signed by the party, addressed to the judge to whom application was made, and had to show that a case existed and the reason for such a writ. The petitioner had to declare what question was raised and decided adversely to the right he claimed. The issuing of the citation varied because the citation had to be lodged in the clerk's office where the record was located within ten days after the entry of the judgment or decree, and for this reason the five year period did not apply.

The plaintiff in error had to follow the other formality of giving bond to cover the entire amount of damages, entries and costs involved in the writ.[55]

The appeal in an admiralty case could involve the reviewing court taking additional evidence which certainly was not the practice in a civil case removed by the writ of error. In equity cases, the Supreme Court was not permitted to receive new evidence. Hence, in admiralty and prize cases, the full evidence could be examined by the Supreme Court, and if necessary, new evidence could be obtained. This practice continued until 1875 when the review of admiralty cases was limited to questions of law.[56] All evidence upon which the decision was rendered had to be incorporated into a Bill of Exceptions as was the practice when the writ of error was used. This placed the review of an admiralty case on the same basis as any other question brought to the Supreme Court.

The writ of error was taken as a matter of right, and on numerous occasions the Supreme Court issued a writ of mandamus to the appropriate judge ordering him to sign the writ of error.[57] This case rule became applicable to an appeal.

The federal courts soon after their establishment adopted a liberal rule in permitting the amendment of any of the necessary papers filed with the writ of error or writ of appeal. One writer announced that "there are always two contending forces on this subject: those who desire to discourage laxity and produce accuracy of proceedings; and the other are those who make allowances for laxity, and perhaps some degree of carelessness, and pass it over, if possible".[58] The Act of 1872 liberalized any rules which the court had adopted concerning amending a defect in the pleadings.[59]

By the end of the Nineteenth Century the distinction between a writ of error or appeal was becoming blurred, although some cases were being denied review by the Supreme Court because the wrong writ was used.[60] This blurring of the distinction between the two writs evolved gradually with the passing of time. The decisions of the Supreme Court did not show any conscious efforts to abolish this distinction. As early as 1876, where a party had brought a writ of error and an appeal, the court denied the motion to dismiss stating "he has but one cause; and, when we come to examine it, we will determine whether it is properly here by appeal or by writ of error and will proceed accordingly."[61] A text writer on appellate procedure stated in 1911 that "it is sometimes hard to determine which form of proceeding to employ. When the moving party is uncertain as to the nature of his remedy he may, out of abundant caution to guard against the possible chance of dismissal, take the case to the appellate court in two ways. This is frequently done".[62]

In 1916, Congress directed that the mistakes in bringing the wrong writ should be disregarded.[63] Finally, in 1928, the writ of error in all cases was abolished and all relief sought by that writ could be obtained by an appeal.[64] This statute made a significant change in that no allowance of an appeal would be required except for reviewing judgments of state courts.

The writ of error did not act as a supersedas to stay the execution of a judgment unless the writ was served within ten days after the judgment was rendered or the decree complained of was entered. The justice signing the citation on a writ of error was required to take the security to assure that the plaintiff in error would prosecute his writ and be answerable for all damages and costs.[65]

An illustration of how the practices of procedure on judicial review were changed without a new rule or acknowledgement of a change can be seen in the situation where one of several parties in a suit desired to seek a judicial review and the others refused to join in. The original rule was that all parties had to join in the writ of error, and their interests could not be separated. The reason for this was obvious, for the court may have needed to decide the same issue a second or third time and the prevailing party would be greatly inconvenienced in enforcing the judgment. After 1842, a party moving for a writ of error could join the other party by summons, and if the other refused to become a part of the judicial review, then their interests could be severed.[66] Technically, this procedure was known as summons and severance. By 1870, the Supreme Court was insisting that the record show that the other parties were notified in writing and then the review could address itself solely to the interest of the appealing parties.[67]

The Act of 1891 establishing the Circuit Courts of Appeals introduced a third method of review by the Supreme Court, the writ of certiorari.[68] But the use of this writ has been confined to the practice in that court with few exceptions, whereas appellate procedure in the court of appeals has continued the development from the writs of appeals and error.

Upon the establishment of the Circuit Courts of Appeals, the rules relating to appellate review developed by the Supreme Court during the preceding century became applicable to judicial review in these new appellate courts. In fact, the rules of the Supreme Court became the basis of procedure in the courts of appeals.

The statute itself was silent about a number of questions concerning the powers of the Circuit Courts of Appeals, including whether the courts could issue mandamus in furtherance of their appellate jurisdiction and the writ of certiorari. This question was generally answered in the negative, but it was finally determined that the courts of appeals had such authority.

No major changes were made in appellate practice in the Twentieth Century, but minor differences did arise among the circuits in the procedures following. Although the amount of time for argument was generally the same in all circuits, some did allow a lesser amount for certain types of arguments — arguments on motions rather than the merits is one example. The original practice was to request permission of the court to petition for reargument, but in some circuits a petition for rehearing could be filed within the time specified by the rules. At the urging of the Judicial Conference, the Supreme Court was given statutory authorization to prescribe uniform rules of appellate practice.[69] Here again, no significant changes were made and as each circuit has the authority to supplement these rules, local variations continue to exist, which should be expected.

Changes in appellate review were not dramatic and came about very slowly whereby all the technical rules of the writ of error and the writ of appeal were gradually abolished and the process became more comprehensive. Some writers praise this transition from emphasis on procedures to consideration of substantive law, but viewing the results, it may be questioned if the lack of procedure has accomplished any great improvements in the administration of justice. Perhaps the reason that appellate review has not received attention from scholars is that it is a lawyer-made law and a procedure involving only the legal profession. Filing fees in the appellate courts generally are not raised to reflect the value of money, but remain low in comparison to the economics. Lowering this barrier has made an appeal more affordable. For all these reasons, judicial review has become a separate form of procedure more commonly used in the closing decades of the Twentieth Century.

FOOTNOTES TO CHAPTER 19

1. Act of September 24, 1789, sec. 22, 1 STAT. 84.
2. Act of September 24, 1789, sec. 30, 1 STAT. 88.
3. Alfred Conkling, A TREATISE ON THE ORGANIZATION AND PRACTICE OF THE COURTS IN THE UNITED STATES (1864), p.625.
4. Behn, Meyer & Co. v. Campbell & GoTauco, 205 U.S. 403, 407 (1907).
5. Conkling, *supra* note 3, p.629, and Suydam v. Williamson, 20 How. 427 (U.S. 1857) where Justice Clifford writes a very good exposition of the writ of error.
6. Bradstreet v. Potter, 16 Pet. 317 (1842).
7. Statute of Westminster II, 15 Ed.1 c.31.
8. The S.C. Tryon, 105 U.S. 267 (1881). A statute of February 16, 1875 provided for use of a jury in a limited circumstance and made this a part of the Bill of Exception. However, the Supreme Court limited the application of this statute.
9. A very good account of the practice relating to the Bill of Exceptions is found in P. Phillips, THE STATUTORY JURISDICTION AND PRACTICE OF THE SUPREME COURT OF THE UNITED STATES (1872), p.119. Later treatises on practice before the Supreme Court do not give much prominence to the subject.
10. 6 Pet. iv (U.S. 1832).
11. Hickman v. Jones, 9 Wall. 197 (U.S. 1869); Springfield F. & M. Ins., Co. v. Sea, 21 Wall. 158 (U.S. 1874) are but two decisions to that effect.
12. U.S. Supreme Court Rule 4, Rule 1844, 210 U.S. 471. This rule was adopted in 1873 and dropped from the rules in 1954.
13. Rule 8, 275 U.S. 600 (1928).
14. Linn v. United States, 251 Fed. 476 (C.A.2d 1918); Spencer v. Commonwealth, 250 Ky. 370, 63 S.W.2d 288 (1933).
15. Fraina v. United States, 255 Fed. 28, 30 (C.A.2d 1918).
16. Act of March 3, 1803, sec. 2, 2 STAT. 244.
17. REV. STAT. (1874) §698.
18. Act of February 13, 1911, § 1, 2, 36 STAT. 901.
19. Barr v. Gratz's Heirs, 4 Wheat. 213, 220 (U.S. 1819); Blunt's Lessee v. Smith, 7 Wheat, 248 (U.S. 1822); Columbian Insurance Co. v. Wheelright, 7 Wheat. 534 (U.S. 1822).
20. United States v. Hodge, 6 How. 279 (U.S. 1848).
21. Act of September 24, 1789, sec. 30, 1 STAT. 83.
22. The San Pedro, 2 Wheat. 132, 140 (U.S. 1817). In Minor et al. v. Tillotson, 2 How. 392 (U.S. 1844), the Court held to this distinction between the writs in a civil case.
23. United States v. Curry, 6 How. 106, 113 (U.S. 1848).
24. Act of March 3, 1803, 2 STAT. 244.
25. United States v. Goodwin, 7 Cranch. 108 (U.S. 1812); Sarchet v. United States, 12 Pet. 143 (U.S. 1838).
26. Act of July 4, 1840, 5 STAT. 393; Stephen D. Law, THE JURISDICTION AND POWERS OF THE UNITED STATES SUPREME COURT... (1852), p.106.
27. Smith v. Jackson, 1 Paine 453, 22 Fed. Cas. 576 (Cir. Ct. N.D.N.Y., 1825).
28. Wiscart v. Dauchy, 3 Dall. 321, 327 (U.S. 1798).
29. Act of May 26, 1824, sec. 2, 4 STAT. 53.
30. Act of May 26, 1824, sec. 9, 4 STAT. 55.
31. Villabolor v. The United States, 6 How. 81 (U.S. 1848).
32. United States v. Yates and McIntyre, 6 How. 605 (U.S. 1848).
33. Sup. Ct. Rule XV (1801).
34. Sup. Ct. Rule XIX (1806).
35. Act of September 24, 1789, sec. 19, 1 STAT. 83.
36. Act of September 24, 1789, sec. 30, 1 STAT. 88.

37. Blaine v. Ship Charles Carter, 4 Dall. 22 (U.S. 1800).

38. Act of March 3, 1803, 2 STAT. 244.

39. Ex parte Bradstreet, 7 Pet. 634, 649 (U.S. 1833). .

40. Act of May 31, 1844, 5 STAT. 658.

41. Act of June 30, 1864, sec. 13, 12 STAT. 760; 13 STAT. 319.

42. The Paquetee Habana, 175 U.S. 677, 681 (1899).

43. Act of September 24, 1789, sec. 22, 1 STAT. 85.

44. Act of June 1, 1872, 17 STAT. 196.

45. Act of March 2, 1891, sec. 11, 26 STAT. 829.

46. Act of March 2, 1891, sec. 6, 7, 26 STAT. 828.

47. Act of March 3, 1863, sec. 5, 12 STAT. 766, established a ninety-day period. This appears to be the first statutory departure from the standard practice.

48. John C. Rose, JURISDICTION AND PROCEDURE OF THE FEDERAL COURTS (3d ed. 1926), p.579.

49. Act of September 24, 1789, sec. 23, 1 STAT. 85.

50. Rule 30(2), U.S. Supreme Court, 275 U.S. 617 (1927).

51. B.R. Curtis, DIGEST OF THE DECISIONS OF THE SUPREME COURT OF THE UNITED STATES (1856), p.599.

52. Act of May 8, 1792, §9, 1 STAT. 278.

53. In re Issuing Writs of Error, 199 Fed. 115 (C.C.A. 6th, 1912).

54. Rule 16, U.S. Supreme Court; First adopted in 1803, Walsh v. Mandeville, 5 Cranch 321 (1809).

55. Curtis, *supra,* note 48, p.596.

56. Act of February 16, 1875, 18 STAT. 315.

57. Ex parte The South and North Alabama Railroad Co., 95 U.S. 221 (1877); Davidson v. Lanier, 4 Wall. 447 (U.S. 1866).

58. George Ticknor Curtis, JURISDICTION, PRACTICE AND PECULIAR JURISDICTION OF THE COURTS OF THE UNITED STATES (1880), p.87.

59. Act of June 1, 1872, sec. 3, 17 STAT. 197.

60. *See* Goodwin v. United States, 295 F. 856 (C.C.A. 6th, 1924).

61. Hurst v. Hollingsworth, 94 U.S. 111 (1876).

62. Frank O. Loveland, THE APPELLATE JURISDICTION OF THE FEDERAL COURTS (1911), p.49.

63. Act of September 6, 1916, 39 STAT. 727.

64. Act of January 31, 1928, 45 STAT. 54; Act of April 26, 1928, 45 STAT. 466.

65. Act of September 24, 1789, sec. 22, 1 STAT. 85. Amended, Act of December 12, 1794, 1 STAT. 404.

66. Todd v. Daniel, 16 Pet. 521 (U.S. 1842).

67. Masterson v. Howard, 10 Wall. 416 (U.S. 1870).

68. Act of March 2, 1891, sec. 6, 26 STAT. 828.

69. Act of November 6, 1966, 80 STAT. 1323.

Chapter 20

APPEALS IN FEDERAL CRIMINAL CASES

To those accustomed to the controversy over the holdings on appeal of the Supreme Court of the United States in criminal cases, it comes as a rather mild surprise that this jurisdiction is only slightly more than a century old. Congress did not provide for appeals in criminal cases in 1789 when it established the federal courts, for appellate review did not exist in the then contemporary English practice. As originally envisioned, the criminal proceeding was very different than it is today. The absence of appeal in criminal procedure was not due entirely to the indifference of the bar or the public, but may be explained in part by the judicial organization of the period.

Criminal law to an Eighteenth Century English barrister was as foreign as Roman law is to the current American lawyer. Criminals in England generally were not allowed representation by counsel until the Nineteenth Century. Criminal trials were held in a separate court system from those in civil cases. Some of the same judges who sat on the Court of Kings or Queens Bench presided on Assizes and in the special criminal courts in London. During the colonial period, in Virginia and Pennsylvania for example, the judges of the colonial Supreme Courts held separate Courts of Oyer and Terminer for the trial of capital criminal offences, which included almost all crimes. The post-colonial American contribution to review of criminal cases was that of frequent new trials. In certain jurisdictions such as Pennsylvania, the Supreme Court would use the writ of certiorari to remove criminal cases from the lower trial courts, known as the Court of Quarter Sessions presided over by the justices of the peace, for trial before that Court or for trial in another court selected by it.

Another reason for the lack of appellate review may be explained by the American public's great faith in the findings of juries. These bodies were considered to be a safeguard against arbitrary government action and often found individuals accused of unpopular crimes, such as the violation of the customs laws enforced by the English government, not guilty. There can be little doubt that Americans, at the beginning of the Nineteenth Century, held the jury in great awe as a means of protection for those charged with a crime.

Congress took the first step in the direction of allowing review of criminal cases in 1802 by passing a law which authorized the judges of the circuit court to certify questions to the Supreme Court of the United States when the judges could not agree.[1] The need and application of this statute becomes apparent from an examination of the federal circuit court organization at that time. The circuit courts were essentially trial courts which had jurisdiction in most of the criminal cases. According to the 1802 statute, these courts were held by a justice of the Supreme Court and a district court judge. This same statute authorized the district court judge to hold court in the absence of the justice of the Supreme Court. As a result, the attendance of the justice of the Supreme Court at these sessions became less frequent toward the middle decades of the century. Also, in some states, the only federal court was the district court, held by a district court judge, which exercised the sole federal jurisdiction for the area. A further limitation was the fact that a district court judge was disqualified from sitting on the circuit court where a case came to that court by a writ of error from his court.[2] Thus certification could only be used in cases from the circuit courts. One authority concluded that the practice was "satisfactory" and "very often used".[3] Thus, it is apparent that this statute regarding certification of questions to the Supreme Court of the United States was of limited use, and only a few criminal cases came to the court under this procedure. The Supreme Court, in construing this statute, laid down the rule that the Court was confined to those questions certified to it and was not free to raise or examine any other issues.[4]

The Supreme Court itself confused the issue of whether a writ of error could be used to bring a criminal case before it in the first decade of the Nineteenth Century by taking jurisdiction in one case and denying the writ in another. Jurisdiction by a writ of error in *United States v. Simms* was based on the argument that the Supreme Court had been given the authority to issue certain writs under Section 14 of the First Judiciary Act of 1789, and it was thought that this would include a writ of error or a writ of appeal in a criminal case.[5] In *United States v. More,* the Supreme Court obtained jurisdiction by writ of error by petition of the United States from the Circuit Court for the District of Columbia, but overruled the *More* case, arguing that the question of jurisdiction had been passed over *sub silentio.* Hence, the Supreme Court did not consider itself bound by the previous case.[6] The chief justice, in writing the opinion for the court, indicated that Congress had the power to create inferior courts and to prescribe when writs of error or writs of appeal could be taken. In this instance, however, the Court reasoned that Congress had provided for appellate jurisdiction on a writ of error in the District of Columbia in civil cases only. After this decision, it was settled that criminal cases could not be brought from a circuit court of the United States to the Supreme Court by a writ of error, but only by a certificate of division of opinion and only upon a specific question of law.[7]

The only other method by which a criminal case could be reviewed after the verdict was by the writ of habeas corpus.[8] This writ, however, was not issued by the federal courts prior to 1867 except to prisoners held under the authority of the federal law. The few cases that came before the Supreme Court by use of this writ generally did not reach substantive questions of criminal law.

Other attempts were made to circumvent this lack of jurisdiction. Under Section 25 of the First Judiciary Act, the Supreme Court was authorized to review the decision of the highest court of the state by a writ of error where the decision was adverse to the validity of a federal statute or the Constitution. One defendant in 1868 sought to invoke this jurisdiction by claiming that his rights under the Fifth and Sixth Amendments of the United States Constitution had been violated in his criminal trial. The Supreme Court, in examining this claim, held that this question was not essential to the decision of the criminal case, and hence, was not sufficient to give the Court jurisdiction by a writ of error under this section.[9] The Court later laid down the doctrine that the Fifth and Sixth Amendments to the Constitution did not apply to the states. This doctrine effectively blocked this avenue of appeal. The theory, however, has eroded, and the provisions of the Bill of Rights in the federal Constitution are now generally applicable to all criminal cases in the state courts under the Fourteenth Amendment.

The frustration that the lack of appeal caused is illustrated by a case where the defendant had been found guilty of piracy and was sentenced to death by hanging. The defendant asked that his case be certified to the Supreme Court on a division of an opinion, but his request was denied because the circuit court was not divided in its opinion. He then asked the Supreme Court for a writ of prohibition and a writ of certiorari, but the court denied the motion. The Court stated that the only time it could express an opinion in a criminal case was in the event of a division of opinion. The defendant had no right to ask for such a certificate, and the judges could not grant it if they agreed in the application of the law. The Supreme Court could not order a ministerial officer to refrain from performing his duty which the circuit court had a lawful right to command. Thus, a writ of prohibition could not be allowed. The Court stated that no appellate power in criminal cases was given it by law.[10] This case and probably others as well caused Congress to enact a statute in 1869 declaring that in any criminal case in which the defendant was sentenced to death, the writ of error or appeal would act as a stay of execution.[11] Why Congress felt that this statute was necessary when no judicial review of a criminal case was provided is unclear.

In 1872, Congress enacted the "Split of Opinion" statute to provide that either party, upon entry of final judgment, could secure a Certificate of Division of opinion for removal of the case to the Supreme Court. This statute, however, was repealed two years later.[12]

It was not until 1879, nearly a century after the First Judiciary Act, that Congress provided for any appeal in criminal cases. The appeal was by writ of error from the district courts to the circuit courts in all criminal cases where the sentence was imprisonment, or fine and imprisonment, or where the fine exceeded $3,000.[13] The circuit courts interpreted this statute as empowering them to reduce excessive sentences.[14] Judge Crummund states that:

the object of the statute was to give to the circuit court authority, not only over the rulings of the district court during the trial, but also over the degree of punishment imposed upon the party, if, upon the whole record before the circuit court, it should appear in the judgment of the court that the penalty was not in conformity with law; as where a fine was imposed when the statute authorized imprisonment only, or imprisonment where it authorized a fine only, or otherwise was lawful, or where it was too lenient or too severe.[15]

With this limited exception for review, the defendant had no avenue of appeal of his conviction by any other court.[16] It should be noted that by this date, the presiding judge in both the circuit court and the district court, was often the same individual. Where two judges were present, the crowded dockets often mandated that they hold court separately to dispose of the maximum number of cases. For this reason, it has been assumed by some writers that the defendant was in the position of appealing from one court to another court which was presided over by the same district judge.[17] However, this assumption overlooks the fact that there was a circuit court judge in each circuit who could be called upon to handle this type of appeal. Unfortunately, for defendants, there was little possibility of obtaining the opinion of the Supreme Court through certification.[18]

The first criminal appeals act was not a general act applying to all federal courts, but was limited to appeals from the Supreme Court of the Territory of Utah where a defendant was sentenced to capital punishment or was convicted of bigamy or polygamy.[19] This statute was enacted in 1874 and was a reaction to the controversy over the Morman practice of polygamy.

The Supreme Court later confused the issue by exercising jurisdiction by a writ of error in two criminal cases under a general act passed in 1885 regulating appeals from the supreme courts of the territories. This statute provided that no appeal or writ of error should be allowed from the supreme court of a territory unless the matter in dispute exceeded $5,000. This amount did not apply to any case in which the question concerned the validity of a treaty or statute made under the authority of the Constitution of the United States.

In all such cases, an appeal or writ of error may have been brought without regard to the sum or value in dispute.[20] In 1885, the Court, under the Act of 1874 and without objection by either party, decided the merits of a case brought to it by a writ of error from the Supreme Court of the Territory of Utah by a defendant convicted of the crime of cohabitation with two different women. During the same term, however, after argument upon its jurisdiction of a similar writ of error, the Court dismissed both writs of error, and in answering the objection that it had taken jurisdiction of the first writ and therefore should take jurisdiction in the second case, said:

> The question of jurisdiction was not considered in fact in that case,
> nor alluded to in the decision, nor presented to the court by the
> counsel for the United States, nor referred to by either party at the
> argument or in the briefs. Probably both parties desired a decision
> on the merits. The question was overlooked by all the members of
> the court. But . . . the want of jurisdiction . . . is clear. [21]

The question whether the provision of the Act extended to other criminal
cases was then left open until 1888, when it was decided in the negative. [22]
Up to that date, the decision of the federal court in a criminal case was
final. This was changed by a statute in 1889.

It is difficult to determine the precise factors that gave impetus to the
passage of the statute in 1889 which gave a right of appeal to the Supreme
Court in a criminal case where the defendant had been sentenced to
death. [23] The public attitude was changing, but certainly Isaac Parker,
judge of the United States District Court for the Western District of
Arkansas, was one of the contributing factors. The District Court for the
Western District of Arkansas had jurisdiction of cases arising within that
state as well as the area of the present state of Oklahoma, which was
known as the Indian Territory where only the Indian courts existed. The
jurisdiction of these courts was confined to the members of the various
Indian tribes. During Parker's twenty years (1875-1895) on the district
court, approximately 173 individuals were found guilty of capital crimes
and sentenced to be hanged, 83 of whom were executed. It is no wonder
that Parker's reputation as a "hanging judge" spread beyond the limits of
his court. Some of his rulings seem capricious to those persons outside the
jurisdiction, whose knowledge of the character of any of the famous
Western outlaws was limited to their reading of the newspaper and the
"dime novels". For these and other reasons, Congress, in 1889, authorized
the defendant to take a writ of error to the Supreme Court in all capital
cases. [24] This appellate jurisdiction was inadvertently extended by the
addition of the phrase "and other infamous crimes" in the statute creating
the Circuit Courts of Appeals two years later. [25]

On February 2, 1891, on writ of error from Parker's court, the
Supreme Court reached its first of two opinions under the Act of 1889. In
one case the judgment was reversed, and in the other case the judgment
was affirmed. In the following five years, 50 written opinions were
delivered by the Supreme Court in criminal cases which had been appealed
from Parker's court. Many of Parker's decisions were reversed after the
right of appeal was given. The reversals were often based on Parker's
failure to follow procedural law. Justice Harlan, in reversing Parker
stated:

> Neither sound reason nor public policy justified any departure
> from settled principles applicable in criminal prosecutions for
> infamous crimes. Even if there were a wide divergence among

authorities upon this subject, safety lies in adhering to established modes of procedure devised for the security of life and liberty.[26]

The "departure from settled principles" committed by Judge Parker was the failure of the record to clearly show that the defendant was formerly arraigned. Parker has been a favorite subject for writers of Western fiction.[27]

In providing for an appeal in a crime carrying the death penalty, the writ was to be issued as a matter of right "under such rules and regulations as the said court may describe". The defendant did not have to post bond for the cost of the prosecution of the case or for the court costs. Further, the issuing of the writ was to operate as a stay of proceedings, and such an appeal would require it to be "advanced to the speedy hearing on motion of either party". Immediately after the enactment of this statute, a number of defendants from Parker's court exercised this right.

Another statute which further weakened Judge Parker's jurisdiction was the establishment in 1889 of the United States Court in the Indian Territory with jurisdiction over minor offenses, but not over those punishable by death or imprisonment at hard labor.[28] The law removed a part of the criminal jurisdiction of Parker's United States District Court for the Western District of Arkansas. Six years later, on September 1, 1896 this territorial court was given jurisdiction of all offenses committed in the Indian Territory.[29] Parker's unique jurisdiction came to an end with the passage of the Act, and he died soon thereafter.[30]

The appellate process is such an integral part of the American law in the present century that it is difficult to determine whether the lack of review of a criminal case by higher authority for over a century in the federal law worked a grave injustice. Any evaluation is purely subjective. Certainly, the issue in the Nineteenth Century was whether the defendant was guilty of the crime charged rather than the emphasis of the present century on observing proper procedure from arrest to the imposition of the sentence. A justice of the Supreme Court observed that:

> It may be said to the credit of the district and circuit court that, in the Ninety years in which their judgments were made final criminal cases, I know no case in which it was charged that their power was oppresively exercised and that a writ of error was finally allowed more from a conviction that a criminal ought not to be deprived of any remedy allowed to parties in civil cases, than from any belief that this power had been abused in practice.[31]

When the Circuit Courts of Appeals were created in 1891, for the purpose of relieving the Supreme Court, the drafters of the act gave these courts limited jurisdiction to review criminal cases but left appeals of capital and other "infamous crimes" to be taken directly to the Supreme Court. The drafters of the Act of 1891 overlooked the fact that the Supreme Court had defined the term "infamous crimes" to include any offense where the defendant was sentenced to the penitentiary.[32] The effect of this statute was to leave the bulk of criminal cases to be reviewed as a matter of right by the Supreme Court.[33] Later, direct review by the Supreme Court was limited to capital offenses. All other criminal cases were taken to the Circuit Courts of Appeals.[34] This direct appeal was abolished in 1911, and thereafter, all criminal appeals, including capital crimes, were taken first to the Circuit Court of Appeals and could be reviewed by the Supreme Court only by the writ of certiorari.[35]

Appeal as of right to the Supreme Court in criminal cases arising in federal courts was not available to a defendant after 1911 unless the decision of the Circuit Court of Appeals was one where the affirmance of the conviction in the Circuit Court of Appeals was based upon holding a state statute unconstitutional.[36] Similarly today, cases in the courts of appeals may be reviewed by the Supreme Court on appeal only when a party is relying on a state statute held by a court of appeals to be invalid as repugnant to the Constitution, treaties or laws of the United States.[37]

Under common law, the state could not appeal a criminal case, and hence, the government was powerless to correct errors made by the trial courts. This was forcefully brought to the attention of Congress by the attorney general of the United States, who pointed out that a single district court judge by quashing an indictment could defeat criminal prosecution instituted by the government and in effect annul a criminal statute. No method to remedy this defect was available to the government. The question raised by the attorney general did not cause any concern in Congress until 1906, when Judge J. Otis Humphrey, sitting in the Circuit Court of the Northern District of Illinois, quashed the indictment of the individuals involved in the so-called Beef Trust.[38] This decision caused the administration of President Theodore Roosevelt concern that a single judge could defeat his program of trust-busting. The President directed the attention of Congress to this matter in his annual message, and Congress enacted the Criminal Appeals Act of 1907, allowing the government to appeal criminal cases within rather narrow limits.[39]

Under this statute, an appeal could be taken by the government from a decision in the district court, dismissing an indictment which is based upon the validity or construction of a statute or from a decision arresting judgment of conviction for the same reason or for sustaining a motion in bar where the defendant is not put in double jeopardy. It was argued that this kind of appeal did not violate the accused's constitutional protection against double jeopardy because at that point in the proceedings, a jury had not been sworn or empaneled and therefore the accused had not yet been put in jeopardy. However, the troubles of the government before federal judges unsympathetic of certain federal criminal statutes were not over. The Supreme Court held that the government could not obtain a review of a decision in the court of appeals by certiorari where the ruling of the district court was upheld.[40] This was explicitly granted by statute in 1911.[41]

Though the Act of 1907 has undergone modification since its enactment, it has retained its remedial purpose —

> to avert the danger of frequent conflicts, real or apparent, in decisions of various district or circuit courts, and the unfortunate results thereof, and to eliminate the 'impossibility of the obtaining of final and uniform rulings by the United States by recourse to a higher court'. [42]

Even when there was no appeal as of right from the lower federal courts, the old circuit courts could certify questions to the Supreme Court and similar authority was given to the Circuit Courts of Appeals upon their creation. [43] The power to certify was declared in 1896 to belong to the Circuit Courts of Appeals, and it has been said to be improper for the parties to move for certification. [44] Originally, the circuit court certified a case when the two judges before whom it was heard were divided in opinion, and frequently the judges would disagree deliberately in order to bring a question to the Supreme Court. Later, however, the court of appeals recognized that certificates should be granted only when they were in fact in doubt on a question. [45] Today the Supreme Court may review decisions of the courts of appeal by certification of any question in a civil or criminal case as to which instructions are desired, and upon such certification, the Supreme Court may give binding instructions or require the entire record to be brought up for decision of the matter in controversy. [46] However, the use of certification by the courts of appeals has fallen into disuse.

In the Judiciary Act of 1891, the Supreme Court, for the first time, relied upon its own discretion in review of certain cases. [47] The Supreme Court could issue a writ of certiorari to a circuit court of appeals or to the highest court of a state, provided an adequate federal question was present and property preserved. [48] In 1896, the Court, when speaking of the Act of 1891, said that "the generality of this provision was not a mere matter of accident. It expressed the thought of Congress distinctly and clearly, and was intended to vest in this Court a comprehensive and unlimited power". [49] In 1906, the Court could issue a writ to a court of appeals regardless of the subject matter of the case, the citizenship of the parties, or the amount in controversy. [50] Like most of its other business, criminal appeals are now principally heard by the Supreme Court on certiorari rather than by certification or appeal.

The writ of habeas corpus was used historically to test the legality of a confinement. The colonists had contended and the British government had denied that the famous Habeas Corpus Act extended to the New World. Because of this constitutional dispute, the framers of the Constitution guaranteed that this writ of habeas corpus would not be suspended. [51] During the nearly two centuries of federal law, the writ of habeas corpus has developed from a method of testing whether the original court had jurisdiction of the prisoner to a method of review of the criminal procedure.

When the federal courts were established, those lawyers who were familiar with their Blackstone COMMENTARIES were aware that there were several different writs of habeas corpus.[52] The Americans claimed the English Habeas Corpus statute enacted by Parliament in 1679 as a part of their legal heritage and included it in many of the compilations of laws published during the early decades of the Nineteenth Century.[53] The writers of the Constitution provided that the writ would not be suspended except "in case of rebellion or invasion, as the public safety may require it".[54]

The writ to which the Constitution referred was known as *habeas corpus ad subjiciendum* at the common law. This writ was directed to the individual having custody of the prisoner ordering him to produce the prisoner at a time and place prescribed in the writ and to show sufficient cause for the prisoner's detention. The purpose of the writ was not to determine the prisoner's guilt or innocence but to release him from unlawful imprisonment on the issue of whether the accused was being deprived of his liberty without due process. This writ was described by Blackstone as "the most celebrated writ in the English law" and as "the great and efficacious writ, in all manner of illegal confinement".[55] The only other writ found used in the federal courts was *habeas corpus ad textificandum* which was issued to bring into court a person whose testimony was required but who was in lawful custody. Immediately upon testifying, the prisoner was returned to custody.[56]

The First Judiciary Act provided that the "courts of the United States shall have power to issue the writ of *scire facies,* habeas corpus, and all other writs not specifically provided for by statute which may be necessary for the exercise of their respective jurisdictions and agreeable to the principles and usage of law".[57] In a very early case, Chief Justice Marshall had occasion to searchingly examine the authority of the Court to issue this writ. Since the Supreme Court's original jurisdiction could not be extended by an act of Congress, the Court concluded that the writ was appellate in nature since it was a revision of a decision of the inferior court.[58] Hence, it was within the Court's jurisdiction. In another case, it was decided that habeas corpus was not "a proper remedy in a civil case".[59] A case in the circuit at a later date, before Chief Justice Marshall and Judge Barbour of the district court, raised the jurisdictional question again, and the court concluded that the writ did extend to prisoners on civil process. This conclusion seems never to have been doubted.

The Supreme Court earlier stated that the writ of habeas corpus was a part of its appellate function, but at the same time, has proclaimed in numerous decisions that the writ was not a substitution for a writ of error or a writ of appeal. "Mere error in the judgment or proceedings, under and by virtue of which a party is imprisoned, constitutes no ground for the issue of the writ."[60] The Court did allow one exception where the error was apparent in the imprisonment, and in this event, the Court, in its discretion, could then give immediate relief and thus save the parties the delay of taking out a writ of error. Under the modern expansion of the concept of constitutionalism, it could be argued that the writ of habeas corpus has been used as a substitute for other methods of review. The history of the writ in the federal courts has been an interesting evolution.

Under the Judiciary Act of 1789, the use of the writ was limited to those in custody of federal authorities.[61] During the period of the Nullification Act in South Carolina, Congress extended the use of the writ of habeas corpus to prisoners in confinement for acts done or alleged to have been done in pursuance of a law of the United States whether held by federal or state authorities.[62] A special act was passed in 1842 extending the use of the writ to foreign extradition proceedings.[63] This statute was passed as a consequence of a prosecution of McLeod in the courts of New York for his participation in the burning of the "Caroline", which caused some public indignation at the time.[64]

During the Civil War years, the use of habeas corpus was affected by several acts. One act authorized the President of the United States to suspend the writ in various parts of the country and provided for procedures to terminate the imprisonment of those arrested by the authority of the President. In those areas where the writ was not suspended, if a grand jury had not indicted the individuals, then the judge sitting on the circuit court had the authority to terminate their imprisonment by the writ of habeas corpus upon the prisoner taking an oath to support the government.[65] The most significant extension of the writ was in 1867 when the court was authorized to grant the writ "in all cases where any person may be restrained of his or her liberty in violation of the Constitution, or of any treaty or law of the United States".[66] One significant change allowed the petitioner to deny the facts set forth in return and the judge to proceed in a summary way by hearing testimony and arguments of the party as to the legitimacy of the confinement. Formerly, the court was confined to considering the matters contained in the writ to determine the legality of the confinement. Under the new federal statutes, the court could go beyond the original record to determine the facts in a summary procedure.

The objective in passing the Act of 1867 was to protect the newly freed slaves and prevent any state court from interfering. One of the first questions presented under the act was whether the state prisoner must exhaust his local remedies before applying for a writ of habeas corpus in the federal courts. Within eight years, the courts were holding that state prisoners did not have to exhaust the state appellate procedures before winning release if they could prove the unconstitutionality of their conviction.[67] The federal courts did not adhere to this principle with consistency.

This act significantly changed appellate procedure as it was then understood, and made possible collateral attacks upon all criminal convictions. Under appellate practice, no appeal could be brought unless timely objection was made and only questions raised at the trial level could be considered. Under the act of 1867, though, the accused could raise a constitutional objection after his trial in a petition for the writ, which had to be reviewed in a summary way by the circuit court. The court was not confined to considering the facts on the record as was required before 1867; new evidence and contentions could be introduced. There were no appeals by the state in the event the circuit court decided that a state statute was unconstitutional. Another change the act made was by extending the coverage of the writ. The early conception was that the writ was available only where the convicting court was without jurisdiction of the person or the subject matter at the inception of the trial.

Very shortly after extending the writ to state prisoners, the power to review the grants of the writ of habeas corpus by the federal trial court was withdrawn from the Supreme Court and was not reinstated until 1885.[68] During this interval, the circuit courts would consider petitions for habeas corpus by state prisoners, but these decisions would not be reviewed by the Supreme Court, and hence, were final.

The development which gave impetus to a wider application of the writ of habeas corpus by state prisoners was the application of the first ten amendments to govern state criminal procedure by the Supreme Court in the period after 1950. This caused an increase in the number of habeas corpus applications filed in the federal district courts by state prisoners. The number jumped from 127 in 1941 to 9,063 in 1970.[69] Although 95 percent of these applications had no merit, the total number of applications imposed a heavy and unnecessary burden upon the federal courts.[70] Again, the review of the decisions of state courts by a federal district court engendered controversy and difficult feelings between the two judicial systems.[71] There was agitation that abolished this type of review. The Judicial Conference of the United States sought legislation which was enacted in 1966 which gave finality to the finding on the writ. An exception was made where the court was satisfied that newly discovered evidence was not deliberately withheld by the state prisoners.[72] Applications by state prisoners for writs of habeas corpus continued to come before the federal courts.

The idea of an appeal by the defendant from a sentence has been suggested by numerous writers. In the Organized Crime Control Act of 1970, the United States was granted the right, "under specified conditions, to appeal the sentence imposed upon a 'dangerous special offender'". Obviously, the new Act was attacked as subjecting the defendant to double jeopardy.[73] The Court, nevertheless, upheld the right to appeal since the Act did not subject the defendant to a second trial but only to a review of the sentence.

Review of inferior courts, however, is only one aspect of the problem of appeal as of right to the Supreme Court. The Court may also review a criminal case arising in the state courts. Up to 1925, defendants could take an appeal as of right to the Supreme Court from the decision of the highest state courts in a considerable number of cases.[74] Today, however, appeal as of right from the highest state courts exists only in two classes of cases: when the validity of a state statute under the federal Constitution is challenged and sustained, or when a federal statute or treaty is involved and its validity denied.[75]

In 1983, the Supreme Court was given jurisdiction to review decisions of the United States Court of Military Appeals by writ of certiorari. Some writers viewed this as an extension of constitutional guarantees to a group of citizens to whom it was assumed such rights were denied, the members of the military forces.[76] It is doubtful whether such an extension of the court's jurisdiction was necessary for the reasons given at a period of time when the court was complaining the loudest about its crowded docket.

In 1889 when Congress at last granted an appeal in a criminal case, no particular form of procedure was prescribed except that review should be by writ of error. Certain procedures were already associated with this writ on the civil side, which the federal courts began to apply to criminal cases. The first step was an application to the court to issue a writ of error, an act within the court's discretion. The next step was to have the court put its seal on a Bill of Exceptions which contained the objections made in the trial court and the evidence presented at that point. It was customary by this late date in major cities of the country to have complete stenographic records of the decision. The text of the record was incorporated into the Bill of Exceptions. Finally, the writ and the Bill of Exceptions or other papers were deposited with the clerk of the appellate court. The Constitution of the United States limits review of facts found by the jury by prohibiting such facts to be "re-examined in any Court of the United States and according to the rules of the common law".[77] Strictly speaking, the writ of error only considered the questions of law made during the course of a trial at common law. This clause is held to mean that the appellate courts could not review the finding of facts of a jury that had to grant the writ of *venire facies de novo* when a new trial was necessary.[78] This seems to indicate that the precise procedure followed in getting a review of the district court to the Circuit Court of Appeals varied considerably.

In 1933, the Supreme Court was given the authority to make rules with respect to all proceedings after the verdict in a criminal case. In the next year it was amended to include cases where there is a finding of guilt by the court on waiver of a jury.[79] The rules promulgated under these acts abolished petition for allowing an appeal. These rules envisioned the trial judge as giving the United States attorney and the attorney of the appellant appropriate directions in respect to the preparation of the record on appeal, including the transcript of testimony in proceedings. The appellant was to file a statement of errors with the clerk. The appellant was required by these rules to file with the clerk of the court a Bill of Exceptions setting forth the proceedings upon which the appellant wished to rely in addition to those shown by the clerk's record.[80] Under the rules adopted in 1944, the Bills of Exceptions were abolished in criminal cases and the record was prepared as in any civil case. At last the transcript of the case was officially recognized as the record.[81]

FOOTNOTES TO CHAPTER 20

1. Act of April 29, 1802, 2 STAT. 156, 159.

2. United States v. Lancaster, 5 Wheat. 434 (U.S. 1820).

3. Benjamin Robbins Curtis, JURISDICTION, PRACTICE AND PECULIAR JURISDICTION OF THE COURTS OF THE UNITED STATES (1880), p.82-83.

4. United States v. Briggs, 5 How. 208, 209 (1847).

5. United States v. Simms, 1 Cranch 252 (U.S. 1803).

6. United States v. More, 3 Cranch 159 (U.S. 1805).

7. *Ibid,* p.172.

8. Act of September 24, 1789, sec. 14, 1 STAT. 81; Act of February 5, 1867, sec. 1, 14 STAT. 385, which extended the federal courts jurisdiction to issue the writ of habeas corpus when a person is restrained of their liberty in violation of the Constitution or laws of the United States. The history of this writ in the federal courts is reviewed in Fay v. Noia, 372 U.S. 391 (1963).

9. Twitchell v. United States, 7 Wall. 321 (U.S. 1868).

10. Ex parte Gordon, 1 Black. 503 (U.S. 1861).

11. Act of March 3, 1869, 15 STAT. 338.

12. Act of June 1, 1872, 17 STAT. 196.

13. Act of March 3, 1879, 20 STAT. 354. In 1928, the writ of error was abolished and the term "appeal" was substituted to designate all appeals as of right. Act of January 31, 1928, 45 STAT. 54.

14. Bates v. United States, 10 Fed. 92 (CC Ill. 1881) and United States v. Wynn, 11 Fed. 57 (CC Mo. 1882).

15. United States v. Bates, 10 Fed. 92, 96 (CC Ill. 1881).

16. United States v. More, 3 Cranch 159 (1805); Ex parte Kearney, 7 Wheat. 38 (1822). *See* sketch of history of criminal procedure in United States v. Sanges, 144 U.S. 310, 319 (1892).

17. Orfield, "Federal Criminal Appeals", 45 Yale L.J. 1224 (1936).

18. McCrary, "Needs of the Federal Judiciary", 13 Central L. J. 167, 168 (1881).

19. Act of June 23, 1874, sec. 3, 18 STAT. 254.

20. Act of March 3, 1885, 23 STAT. 443.

21. Cannon v. United States, 116 U.S. 55 (1885) and 118 U.S. 355 (1886); Snow v. United States, 118 U.S. 346, 354 (1886).

22. Farnsworth v. Montana, 129 U.S. 104 (1889).

23. Act of January 25, 1889, sec. 6, 25 STAT. 1889.

24. Act of February 6, 1889, sec. 6, 25 STAT. 656; J. Gladston Emery, COURT OF THE DAMNED, p.174.

25. Act of March 2, 1891, sec. 5, 26 STAT. 827.

26. Crain v. United States, 162 U.S. 625, 644 (1896).

27. Numerous fictionalized biographies have been written about Judge Parker. A recent such work is Mack Stanley, HANGING JUDGE AND HIS DESPERADOES (1983).

28. Act of March 1, 1889, 25 STAT. 783.

29. Act of March 1, 1895, 28 STAT 693.

30. Malone, "Isaac C. Parker", DICTIONARY OF AMERICAN BIOGRAPHY.

31. Henry B. Brown, "The New Federal Judicial Code", 73 Cent. L. J. 275, 277 (1911).

32. Act of March 3, 1891, sec. 5, 26 STAT. 828; In re Claasen, 140 U.S. 200 (1891).

33. *See* statements by Chief Justice Fuller, and Attorney-General Harmon in 23 CONG. REC. 3285 (1892); Sen. Rep. No. 265, 54th Cong., 1st sess. Ser. No. 3362 (1895).

34. Act of January 20, 1897, 29 STAT. 492.

35. Act of March 3, 1911, sec. 128, 240, 36 STAT. 1133, 1157.

36. Act of March 3, 1911, sec. 240, 36 STAT. 1157.

37. 28 U.S.C.A. 1254 (1966).

38. United States v. Armour & Co., 142 Fed. 808 (N.D. Ill., 1906). *See* also Felix Frankfurter and James M. Landis, THE BUSINESS OF THE SUPREME COURT (1928), p.113-119. It should be noted that as early as 1892, the Supreme Court recognized that the Act creating the Circuit Courts of Appeals, passed in 1891, had left the United States without any right of review in criminal cases, even where the defendant had not been put in jeopardy. United States v. Sanges, 144 U.S. 310 (1892).

39. Act of March 2, 1907, 34 STAT. 1246. Act held constitutional in United States v. Bitty, 208 U.S. 393 (1908); United States v. Heinze, 218 U.S. 532 (1910). For a complete history of this statute, *see* Kurland, "The Mersky Case and the Criminal Appeals Act: A Suggestion for Amendment of the Statute", 28 U. CHI. L. Rev. 446-455 (1961).

40. Act of March 2, 1907, Chap. 2564, 34 STAT. 1246. Appeal did not lie after a verdict of not guilty, even for the purpose of ascertaining the law for future cases. United States v. Evans, 213 U.S. 297 (1909).

41. Act of March 3, 1911, sec. 240, 36 STAT. 1157.

42. United States v. Mersky, 361 U.S. 431 (1960). *See, Note,* "The Proposed Right of Appeal by the Government in Criminal Cases", 20 HARV. L. REV. 219 (1906).

43. Act of March 3, 1891, §6, 26 STAT. 826, 828.

44. Louisville, N.A. & C. Ry. v. Pope, 74 Fed. 1, 9 (7th Cir. 1896); Cella v. Brown, 144 Fed. 742, 765 (8th Cir. 1906).

45. *See,* Williams v. Order of Commercial Travelers of America, 41 F.2d 745, cert. denied 282 U.S. 876 (1930) in which the Sixth Circuit Court of Appeals held "We do not certify a question of law unless it seems to us so difficult or doubtful that we feel the necessity of a Supreme Court decision..."

46. Supreme Court Rules (1980) Rule 24 as codified in 28 U.S.C. 1254(3) (1980).

47. Act of March 3, 1891, 26 STAT. 826, 828 §6.

48. Act of March 3, 1891, 26 STAT. 826, 828.

49. Forsyth v. City of Hammond, 166 U.S. 506, 513 (1896).

50. United States v. Dalcour, 203 U.S. 408, 420-421 (1906).

51. U.S. Const. Art. I §9.Cl.2.

52. Blackstone, COMMENTARIES Bk. III, p. 129.

53. This statute was included in many of the compilations of American laws. *See* Prince, DIGEST OF GEORGIA LAWS (1837), as an example.

54. U. S. Const. Art. I, §9.

55. Blackstone, COMMENTARIES Bk. III, p. 129, 131.

56. Mr. Justice Field in Ex parte Cuddy, 40 Fed. Cas. 62; In re Hamilton, 11 Fed. Cas. 319.

57. Act of September 24, 1789, §14, 1 STAT. 81.

58. Bollman & Swartwout, 4 Cranch. 75 (U.S. 1807).

59. Ex parte Wilson, 6 Cranch 51 (U.S. 1810).

60. Ex parte Siebold, 100 U.S. 371, 375 (1879). Ex parte Clarke, 100 U.S. 399 (1879). *See* Hannis Taylor, JURISDICTION AND PROCEDURE OF THE SUPREME COURT OF THE UNITED STATES (1905), p.475.

61. Judiciary Act of 1789, 1 STAT. 85.

62. Act of March 2, 1833, 4 STAT. 632.

63. Act of August 29, 1842, 5 STAT. 539.

64. Fay v. Noia, 372 U.S. 391, 401 fn.9 (1963).

65. Act of March 3, 1863, 12 STAT. 755.

66. Act of February 5, 1867, 14 STAT. 385.

67. Ex parte Bridges, 2 Woods 428 (C.C. Ga. 1875); 4 Fed. Cas. 98. *See* Fay v. Noia, 372 U.S. 391 (1963). After several decades of inconsistent holdings, the Supreme Court ended the controversy by allowing Noia's release before all state appellate avenues had been used.

68. Act of March 27, 1868, 15 STAT. 44; Act of March 3, 1885, 23 STAT. 437. See REV. STAT. 1874, sec. 763, 764.

69. The number of such applications taken from the statistics of the Administrative Office of the Courts:

    1941 = 127
    1945 = 536
    1950 = 560
    1955 = 660
    1960 = 872
    1965 = 4,664
    1970 = 9,063
    1975 = 7,843
    1980 = 7,031

70. S. Rept. No. 1797, 89th Cong. 2d sess., p.2.

71. Report of the Special Committee on Habeas Corpus to the Conference of the Chief Justice, June 1953, reprinted in H.R. Rept. 548, 86th Cong., 1st sess.

72. Act of November 2, 1866, 80 STAT. 1105.

73. United States v. DiFrancesco, 449 U.S. 117 (1980).

74. *See,* § 25 of the Judiciary Act of 1789, 1 STAT. 73, 85, as interpreted in United States v. More, 3 Cranch 159 (1805); Fox v. Ohio, 5 How. 434 (1847); Twitchell v. Commonwealth, 7 Wall. 321 (1868).

75. Act of June 25, 1948, 62 STAT. 929.

76. Act of December 6, 1983, 97 STAT. 1406, P.L. 98-209.

77. U.S. Const. Amend. 7th.

78. Capital Traction Co. v. Hof, 174 U.S. 1 (1898).

79. Act of February 24, 1933, 47 STAT. 904; Act of March 8, 1934, 48 STAT. 399. *See* H. Rept. 858, 73 Cong. 2d sess.; S. Rept. 257, 73d Cong., 2d sess.

80. Rules VII, VIII, IX, 292 U.S. 661 (1933).

81. FEDERAL RULES OF CRIMINAL PROCEDURE, SECOND PRELIMINARY DRAFT (February 1944), Rule 39, Notes, p.136.

Chapter 21

JURISDICTION OF THE SUPREME COURT

The history of the jurisdiction of the Supreme Court of the United States illustrates the subtle changes in the role of the Court, but efforts to illuminate these changes are beset with some difficulties at the outset. The jurisdiction of the Court has been defined in several general statutes, but these statutes are much like an iceberg — the great bulk is not seen. Hidden in other statutes, most of which are concerned with a wide range of matters other than the judiciary, are found sections governing the appeals to this Court in limited areas. These statutes are so varied and are of such limited application that they are mainly of interest in indicating the diversified work of the Court. On occasion, Congress has taken away the jurisdiction of the Court to prevent it from dealing with an unpopular political case as it did in the *Ex parte McCardle* case.[1] Determining how these statutes are treated in practice however is not an easy task.

Another difficulty in understanding the changes in the nature of the Court is the fact that only rarely does the Court not, in some way, speak of its jurisdiction. But, behind all the statutes and decisions, are the unwritten practices and traditions that have greatly influenced the growth of the Court's jurisdiction. The Supreme Court has reminded us that it is not necessary for the Court to change or establish its practice by the adoption of written rules, for this can be accomplished by a uniform mode of procedure over a course of years.[2] This established practice forms the law of the Court. Through these changes in jurisdiction and practices, the nature of the work of the Supreme Court has changed, and the Court has evolved into an institution which the founding justices did not foresee.

The Constitution states that "the Supreme Court shall have appellate jurisdiction, both as to Law and Fact, with such Exceptions, and under such Regulations as the Congress shall make." From this Constitutional provision, the Court early concluded that its jurisdiction was controlled by statute and that it had no inherent right to expand it.[3] During the Nineteenth Century, the Court frequently stated that its authority was derived from statutes and that it had no inherent jurisdiction since it was not a court whose jurisdiction and powers were defined in terms of one of the existing English courts. Recently, such acknowledgements have become increasingly rare.

The history of the Court's jurisdiction may conveniently be divided into three periods: 1. the period from 1789 to Evart's Act of 1891 which created the Circuit Courts of Appeals; 2. the period from this statute to the Judges' Act of 1925; and 3. the period since then. During the first period, Congress passed several general acts and many special acts dealing with the court's jurisdiction. The Court, however, became so overburdened with cases that relief was sought by the creation of the Circuit Court of Appeals to which appeals in most cases would first be brought from the district courts. The creation of these new appellate courts brought some relief, but again the number of cases began to mount. The pressure was relieved by granting the Court authority in 1925 to choose the cases it would hear. It is well known that in the last decades of the Twentieth Century the caseload of the Court has, in the opinion of the Court, grown unmanageably large. Congress has sought to relieve this burden by limiting the cases where appeals to the Court are brought as a matter of right. Other proposals have been made to relieve the Court, including the creation of another court to which some cases could be referred or the establishment of a court that would decide what cases the Supreme Court would hear.

Original Jurisdiction

Under the Constitution, the Supreme Court was given both original and appellate jurisdiction.[4] Its original jurisdiction extended to suits affecting ambassadors and other public ministers and suits in which a state was a party. The Court began its career with several suits by individuals against states. Cases in this area of litigation promised to increase so rapidly that the Court would have been overwhelmed by cases at *nisi prius*.

The Judiciary Act of 1789 added the requirement that all trials be by jury. The first jury was empanelled to hear the suit of the *State of Georgia v. Brailsford* at the February Term, 1794. The final jury was empanelled at the August Term, 1797.[5] The Eleventh Amendment, which took away the Court's jurisdiction in suits against states by citizens of other states, was adopted by the requisite number of states in 1795, but it was not proclaimed by the President until January, 1798. With the promulgation of this amendment, the need for a jury in the Supreme Court was ended.

Since the abolishment of the Court's jurisdiction over suits by citizens of different states against a state, primary original jurisdiction left in the Court is mainly over suits brought by one state against another. Strenuous objections were lodged against this type of jurisdiction on a number of grounds, both political and legal. In the early cases, the states protested that Congress had prescribed insufficient rules of procedure and that the Court possessed no adequate means of enforcing its judgment.[6] These objections were rejected. In a suit brought in equity to ascertain the boundaries of the states of Rhode Island and Massachsuetts, jurisdiction was contested on the ground that the nature of the controversy pertaining to the rights of sovereignty of the respective parties was not a matter for judicial resolution. However, the Court examined this issue and sustained the jurisdiction.[7] In exercising this jurisdiction, the state must be a party in fact and not in name only.

The Supreme Court has not had the occasion to speak often of its proceedings in exercising its original jurisdiction. As late as 1894, the Supreme Court said it would frame its proceedings according to those which had been adopted prior to 1791 in the English courts and to analogous cases, although it declared that it was not bound to follow the practice where it would be embarrassed by technicalities or where it would defeat justice.[8]

The Court generally does not hear suits brought under its original jurisdiction, but rather as was common in equity practice, refers matters to masters to hold hearings and prepare their findings. The Court generally ratifies the findings of the master.

The type of cases brought by the states as parties generally involves boundary disputes, but other matters may be brought to the Court as well. Proceedings in these cases are in the nature of equitable proceedings. However, since the merger of law and equity in the federal courts, the Federal Rules of Civil Procedure are applicable to these proceedings. The Court does not have any means of guaranteeing the appearance of a state or of enforcing its decrees in these suits.

Although the Constitution gave the Supreme Court original jurisdiction in suits affecting ambassadors and other public ministers, the Judiciary Act of 1789 made this jurisdiction concurrent with the circuit courts, which were the trial courts in the federal system. The question was raised early whether Congress could in fact confer concurrent jurisdiction on these lower federal courts. Acting as circuit court judge, Justice Wilson expressed the opinion that Congress could do this.[9] Later, the Supreme Court asserted in its decision in another case, where the suit was brought originally in the Supreme Court, that it could have been instituted in the circuit court as well.[10] The court's jurisdiction over ambassadors and other public ministers was never fully implemented and has been left to the lower federal courts.

The question whether Congress can take away any of this original jurisdiction has never been answered, although it was raised in at least one decision.[11] The converse of this question, whether Congress could add to the original jurisdiction of the Court, was raised in the famous case of *Marbury v. Madison*[12] and answered in the negative. In the Act of 1789, Congress had attempted to give the Supreme Court the power to issue writs of mandamus in cases other than those coming under its original jurisdiction. The Court has adhered to the decision that Congress cannot enlarge the Court's original jurisdiction. The Supreme Court was destined never to become a trial court, as happened to several state supreme courts, and since it establishment, its chief function has been to review appeals from the lower courts.

Another important limitation on the Supreme Court's authority to review was the amount in every controversy which was defined in the First

Judiciary Act as exceeding $2,000.[13] Because of this provision, the Court did not have jurisdiction to review decisions of the lower federal courts where the matter in dispute was the custody of a child or the freedom of a petitioner.[14] In the application of this section, the Supreme Court earlier held that the matter in controversy must have an ascertainable pecuniary value of this amount. For example, if the value of a piece of property in question claimed by the plaintiff exceeded $2,000 and the judgment was for the defendant, a writ of error would not lie in that case because of insufficient evidence of the sum in dispute which would enable the Court to entertain jurisdiction.[15] In any action where the judgment of the Court was less than $2,000 for the plaintiff, the defendant could not bring a writ of error, but the plaintiff could.[16] Questions whether certain factual situations fell within the jurisdictional amount were raised in a number of cases.

The First Judiciary Act created, in addition to the circuit courts, the district courts which had jurisdiction chiefly in admiralty and revenue matters. Review of the decisions and findings of the district courts was made by the circuit courts in cases where the amount involved exceeded $50. Where no circuit court had been organized, which was the situation in some states, and where the district court was the only federal court, the Supreme Court could review the decisions of these courts under the same regulations as decisions from the circuit courts.

The Supreme Court kept the distinction between the writ of error and writ of appeal in reviewing decisions from these two courts. Where a decision of the district court was first reviewed by circuit courts on a writ of error, the Supreme Court decided early that the decision of the circuit court was final. This rule did not apply to those cases taken from the district courts to the circuit courts by a writ of appeal. However, this distinction was abolished by statute in 1830.[17] After this act, appeals by writ of error could be taken from the circuit courts to the Supreme Court in cases that had been taken originally to the circuit courts from the district courts.

Section 25

The most controversial aspect of the Supreme Court's jurisdiction was the famous Section 25 of the First Judiciary Act. This section authorized appeals from the highest state courts where a decision drew into question

> the validity of a treaty or statute, of, or an authority exercised under the United States and the decision is against their validity; or where is drawn in question the validity of a statute of, or an authority exercised under any State, on the ground of their being repugnant to the Constitution, treaties, or laws of the United States, and the decision is in favor of their validity, or where is

drawn in question the construction of any clause of the Constitution, or of a treaty, or statute of, or commission held under the United States and the decision is against their validity.[18]

Jurisdiction under this section was determined by subject matter rather than the amount involved which was the determinate factor in all other cases.

The Court has invoked this jurisdictional review of decisions of state courts on a number of occasions since 1797, but its constitutionality was not questioned until the famous case of *Martin v. Hunter's Lessee.*[19] The Court, through an opinion prepared by Justice Story, upheld Section 25. This aspect of the Court's jurisdiction has been vindicated in a great many cases since *Martin.* However, the Court's upholding the constitutionality of this section has not ended the controversy; many bills have been introduced into Congress since 1816 to repeal it.[20] In 1831, a concerted effort was made to repeal this section and life tenure for judges.[21] The struggle over Section 25's repeal involved the question of the political relation between the states and federal government.

The jurisdiction of the Court in such appeals must appear on the record strictly considered, and therefore the certificate of the clerk of the state court attached to the record showing that documents were read and relied upon at the trial could not influence the determination of the jurisdiction of the Court.[22]

This section did not authorize the Supreme Court to review cases where a state court upheld a claimed federal right; it could review cases only where such rights were denied. On occasion, bills were introduced into Congress to grant the Supreme Court this authority, but all failed to pass. In the revision of Section 25 in 1867, the provision which limited appeals under this section to federal questions was omitted.[23] Counsel in *Murdock v. Memphis*[24] urged that this omission authorized the Court to hear appeals in all questions found in the record, including those not of federal concern. That position was rejected by the Court, and consequently, its docket did not become burdened with this type of appeal.

One decision however, that caused a change in the judicial attitude was *Ives v. South Buffalo Railway Co.*[25] The New York Court of Appeals unanimously held the Workmen's Compensation Act unconstitutional under the federal Constitution and because the state court had upheld a claimed constitutional right, an appeal could not be taken to the Supreme Court. The *Ives* decision aroused great criticism from Congressmen and other notable Americans, including Theodore Roosevelt. Thus, a committee of the American Bar Association urged that Congress pass a statute allowing review of cases where the highest state court upheld as well as denied federal rights. Such a bill was enacted in 1914.[26] This was the last bill enlarging the appellate jurisdiction of the Supreme Court.[27]

Supervisory Power

Text writers on procedure of the Supreme Court during the early part of the Nineteenth Century spoke of the "supervisory powers" of the Supreme Court. This was taken from the concept of the Court of King's Bench, which could and did issue extraordinary writs to the lower courts and acted as an overseer of their functions. This type of power was exercised through such writs as that of prohibition, mandamus, certiorari, habeas corpus, scire facias and others which have since lost their vitality. During this period, the Supreme Court did not exercise the power that such writs had given it. For example, the Court had jurisdiction to issue writs of prohibition to "the District Courts, when proceeding as courts of admiralty and maritime jurisdiction." This writ rarely has been used and has only been used on one occasion to prohibit the Court from proceeding in a case which was not considered to be within its jurisdiction.[28]

The Supreme Court was authorized by statute to issue the writ of mandamus "in cases warranted by the principles and usages of the law, to any court appointed, or persons holding office, under the authority of the United States."[29] This writ was made famous in the case of *Marbury v. Madison*. The Supreme Court decided that the expansion of its original jurisdiction was not warranted by the Constitution, but such writs could be used only in furtherance of its appellate jurisdiction. Through this decision and a series of decisions that followed, the use of the writ was very narrowly limited. The Court had decided that the writ would not be used to direct a subordinate judicial officer to decide and issue any particular writ, or to fill in blanks in judgments or any other matters within the discretion of the judge.[30] The Court held that in all cases the only remedy was through the writ of error after the final judgment.

The supervisory power of the Supreme Court was further extended when the Court was given the power to "issue writ of scire facias, habeas corpus, and all other writs not specially provided for by statute, which may be necessary for the exercise of their respected jurisdiction and agreeable to the principles and usages of law."[31] The use of the habeas corpus was limited in this first statute, but of all these extraordinary writs this writ has been used continuously and must be examined separately. As far as can be determined, the Court did not make use of the other writs found in the arsenal of the Court of King's Bench. By its failure to take advantage of these writs, the Court had limited itself and its authority to govern the judicial department of the government, in the same manner the Court of King's Bench, through the writ of certiorari, could supervise minor judicial officers in the performance of their duties. The failure to accept the writ of mandamus as part of the original jurisdiction of the court was a determining factor in forming the practice of a review of a decision after final judgment, and in establishing the trend where federal trial courts became independent subject only to this narrow review of legal decisions.

Of all the extraordinary writs, the writ of habeas corpus has been the most widely used by the Court. Authority to issue the writ was given by the First Judiciary Act of 1789, but only in cases to inquire into causes of commitment of prisoners held in custody or under the authority of the United States.[32] The first reported case in which the writ was issued was in 1795.[33] The defendant was accused of committing treason, and the Court admitted him to bail but without any extended discussion of the writ. The first consideration given to the extent of the power of the Court to issue the writ was before Chief Justice Marshall in the case of *Bollman & Stwartwout*.[34] The question raised was whether the restricted words "which may be necessary for the exercise of their respective jurisdictions" limited the power of the Court to issue such writs in those cases where it was necessary to enable the courts to exercise their respective jurisdictions. Chief Justice Marshall decided that the Court had such authority and that the point had been settled by an earlier case. The Court had another obstacle to overcome and that was its decision in *Marbury v. Madison* where it held that the Supreme Court could not exercise original jurisdiction except that which was given by the Constitution. Again, the Court decided that this was the exercise of the writ in furtherance of its appellate jurisdiction.

Organization

The First Judiciary Act required that the Supreme Court meet on the first Monday of February and August at the seat of government. Chief Justice John Jay and two associate justices, William Cushing and James Wilson, gathered on February 1, 1790 to open the Court. Since there was no quorum, the Court adjourned until the next day when Associate Justice John Blair joined the group.[35]

These founding justices did not leave any evidence of what their thoughts were as to the nature of the court they were organizing, nor its jurisdiction and powers beyond what was specified in the statute. Obviously, the justices were required to ride the circuit where they probably assumed the bulk of their work would be done. The first item of business recorded in the minutes was a letter from James Duane, district court judge for the District of New York, requesting that a special term of the circuit court be held for the speedy trial of certain individuals charged with the violation of custom laws. The Court ordered that special sessions be held in New York and that a special session of the circuit court be held in the City of Philadelphia. In the first case recorded in the minutes, *Nicholas and Jacob Vanstaphorst v. Maryland*, the Court set the precedent of serving the process on the governor and the attorney general of the state where a state was a party. Other practices were established through these decisions. Events would soon prove that the First Judiciary Act did not provide for all matters coming before the Court such as appeals from the territorial courts.

Appeals from Territorial Supreme Courts

Appellate jurisdiction over the circuit courts had been given to the Supreme Court under the First Judiciary Act, but when the question was raised whether an appeal from the courts established by Congress in the territories could be perfected, the Court decided it could not because such jurisdiction had not been granted by statute.[36] These courts exercised the powers granted to both the circuit and district courts "in all cases in which the United States are concerned." Appeals were authorized to the Supreme Court under the same regulations as those taken from the district court in Kentucky two years later.[37] In practice, this meant that a writ of error could be brought from a territorial supreme court to the Supreme Court of the United States where the amount involved exceeded $2,000, but Congress did vary this jurisdictional amount for some of the territories. Because of this monetary limitation, many issues from these courts could not be brought to the Supreme Court, and in these areas, the territorial supreme court decisions were final.

Later, appeals were specifically provided for in the organic acts which created the territories. Generally, the amount involved had to exceed $1,000, but this amount varied. In cases from the Supreme Court of the Territory of Washington the amount had to exceed $2,000.[38] In 1885, the jurisdictional amount was raised to $5,000 for all appeals from the territorial supreme courts, thus making the amount uniform.[39] Appeals in all federal question cases were governed by the appropriate statutes, and appeals in patent, trademarks, copyright cases, and where the validity of a federal law or authority exercised under the authority of United States was in question could be taken from the territorial supreme courts to the Supreme Court without regard to amount in controversy. When the Circuit Courts of Appeals were created in 1891, appeals from the then existing territorial supreme courts were taken to these new appellate courts. The Supreme Court was given authority under this statute to assign the territories to a particular circuit for purposes of appeal. The Supreme Court could then review these decisions on the same basis as other appeals from the Circuit Courts of Appeals.[40]

Certification

The structure of the circuit courts which was presided over by two judges gave rise to an equal division of opinion. To remedy this condition, Congress, in 1802, authorized the judges of the circuit courts, when they disagreed, to certify the point of disagreement to the Supreme Court.[41] To understand the necessity of this practice, it is necessary to understand the structure of that court. The original Judiciary Act of 1789 provided for a circuit court to be held by two justices from the Supreme Court and the district court judge, thus creating a court of three judges. The justices of the Supreme Court were required to divide the circuits up among themselves. A few years later the number of justices required to hold a circuit court was reduced by one, thus producing a court consisting of two judges. Since the justices rotated the circuit courts among themselves, the same justice would not necessarily hold the next term of the circuit court in any particular locality; and hence, any of the two attending judges could express their opinions. At the next term of the court, the other justice would resolve any dispute.[42] In 1802, the practice of the justices of the Supreme Court holding the circuit court was modified by grouping the states into circuits with one justice assigned to each circuit. After this modification, the same justice along with the district court judge would preside at the terms of the circuit court.[43] Because the bench then consisted of two judges, a division of opinion could arise. To prevent this deadlock, in 1802, Congress provided that should any question arise before the circuit court where the opinions of the judges were opposed, the judges could certify the question under seal of the court to the Supreme Court upon the motion by the parties. Counsel appeared to argue the certified points before the Supreme Court. The decision would be remitted to the circuit court and entered on the record. The case could continue at trial if, in the trial court's opinion, further proceedings would not be prejudiced; in practice, it appears that in the majority of cases certification suspended the case until the instructions of the Court were received. The possibility of certifying a question was not limited to civil cases, but could include criminal cases as well. The sentence of the trial court was suspended until the questions certified were answered by the Supreme Court. Justice Story described this process as a "novel mode of obtaining the decision of the appellate court."[44] Since the Court had no precedent from English practice to govern this type of procedure, it had to develop its own practice.

A number of cases came to the Court by certification, from which certain practices developed. For example, the certification did not bring up the whole case but only the precise point that was in disagreement.[45] The original case continued in the control of the circuit court and not all types of questions could be certified. Questions that depended on the discretion of the Court could not be certified on a division of opinion.[46] The statute required that this disagreement happened "during the same term" and could not be a matter pertaining to a ruling out of term nor a collateral issue. Although counsel could move that the point be certified, this was within the discretion of the judges to do so. The Supreme Court discouraged the practice of certifying a question when no real division of opinion occurred.[47]

On one occasion, Congress tried to expand this novel practice of review. In 1864, Congress authorized the transfer by certification of any prize case where the amount was less than $2,000 and where the trial court could certify that a question of general importance was involved.[48] This provision was held unconstitutional on the ground that it required the

Supreme Court to exercise original jurisdiction that it did not possess under the Constitution.[49]

In 1872, Congress modified the practice of certification by providing that in the circuit court the opinion of the presiding justice or judge would prevail and "be considered the opinion of the court."[50] This statute was passed in recognition of the perceived defect that certifying a question often prevented a case from coming to a final judgment. After final judgment, the judges could certify their difference of opinion to the Supreme Court. This did not affect the right of either party to remove the judgment by writ of error or appeal, subject to the laws governing the use of these writs.

In 1891, Congress again modified the structure of the federal courts by establishing the Circuit Courts of Appeals which required a change in the certification practice. These courts consisted of the existing two circuit court judges, a justice of the Supreme Court, and in the event of the need for a third judge, a district court judge could be invited to sit. The statute did not require a panel of three judges because it stated that two judges were a quorum. However, "the circuit court of appeals at any time may certify to the Supreme Court of the United States any questions or propositions of law concerning which it desires instruction of the court for its proper decision."[51] From the terms of this statute, it appears that an equal division of the Court's opinion was no longer a prerequisite for certifying a question for instruction, which was the original concept of the process. Whether this statute was a recognition of an existing practice of the Supreme Court or a change cannot be determined. There were no provisions for the judges in the district courts or the circuit courts to certify questions to the new Circuit Courts of Appeals.

There was little change in the practice of certifying questions to the Supreme Court until 1907; the courts decided that a case could not be certified when the judgments or decrees of the Circuit Courts of Appeals were final and otherwise not reviewable. This view was rejected by the Judicial Code of 1911.[52] In 1925, the right to certify a case to the Supreme Court was given to the Court of Claims and to the United States Court of Appeals for the District of Columbia.

Because of this increase in the amount of work, the practice of certifying questions was discouraged. A study showed that the number of certifications for the period 1927-1936 was 85 and for the next ten year period of 1937-1946 only 20.[53] From 1946 to 1974, only three cases were certified.[54] During the consideration of the Judicial Code of 1948, the Congressional committees considered removing this provision from the statutes. The judges of the Supreme Court, however, favored keeping it in.[55] Since then, the use of certification has considerably declined to a point of nonexistence.

The Decades before the Civil War

During the period between 1789 to 1860, no dramatic changes were made in the Supreme Court's jurisdiction. During the half century preceding the Civil War, the size of the country expanded in both area and population, and with this growth came an increase in the number of federal courts. It is a demonstrated fact that the growth in the number of trial courts causes an increase in the workload of the appellate courts. During this period, the Supreme Court was the only appellate court in the federal system. The circuit courts exercised limited judicial review over the district courts. The workload of the Supreme Court increased naturally without any statutes adding jurisdiction. Few statutes impacting the general public were passed during this period that would increase the burdens of the federal courts. The statutes disposing of the public lands were an exception. During this first half century, Congress established a trend to grant judicial review in a number of areas without regard to the amount involved. A second line of statutes which significantly affected the Supreme Court's caseload was the expansion of the removal statutes, whereby actions filed in state courts against federal officers could be removed into federal courts.

It was an accepted principle that the federal courts did not have jurisdiction over a matter unless it was specifically granted by statute. For example, it took the Act of 1819 to confer jurisdiction on the federal courts to enforce the rights given under the patent and copyright laws originally passed some thirty years earlier. This statute granted the courts authority to issue injunctions to prevent the violation of the privileges granted under these acts, and individuals could bring suits for their violation in equity or at common law.[56] This statute was later amplified and the jurisdiction of the Supreme Court clarified in that a writ of error or appeal, as the case may require, would lie under any law granting or confirming to inventors the exclusive rights to their inventions or discoveries.[57]

On a few occasions, the Supreme Court was mandated to hear certain appeals. One example was under the Charter of the Second Bank of the United States where the President, if he believed that the Charter had been violated, could apply for a writ of *scire facias* in the Circuit Court for the District of Pennsylvania where every issue of fact between the government and the bank was to be tried by a jury. The final judgment of the court "shall be examinable in the Supreme Court . . . by writ of error" where the decree could be reversed or affirmed according to the law.[58] Similar examples of mandatory jurisdiction of the Supreme Court are often buried in statutes and only become known when an appeal is taken.

Another area in which the jurisdiction of the Supreme Court was never general but depended upon a specific statute was an appeal involving land claims in the public domain. For example, in the Act of

1824, where the decision to a claim in Missouri went against the United States and more than 1,000 acres were involved, the district attorney transmitted to the attorney general a statement containing the facts of the case and the points of law in which the same was cited. The attorney general decided whether the decision of the district court was erroneous and was then authorized to direct an appeal to the Supreme Court.[59] In another section of the same statute, if the decision was against the claimant, he apparently had a right to appeal to the Supreme Court regardless of the amount of land involved. This act was also made applicable to the Arkansas territory. If the judgment was against the United States and involved 500 acres or more, the district attorney could follow the same procedure of transmitting to the attorney general the necessary facts and points of law to determine if an appeal should be taken. When this statute was applied to the state of Florida, an appeal could be taken by the government where the claim exceeded one square league.[60] Congress never made uniform these appeals until after the Civil War.

The earliest act granting appellate jurisdiction to the Supreme Court without regard to the amount involved was enacted in 1844 when an appeal could be taken by the government in any action involving the enforcement of the revenue acts.[61] This act was later extended by the court to include those cases where the Postmaster General sought to recover revenues or settle the accounts of the postmasters throughout the United States.[62] Another significant statute which provided a number of appeals was the Civil Rights Act of 1866 and 1871 that authorized appeals to the Supreme Court without regard to the amount involved.[63] Many similar statutes allowing appeals without regard to the amount in controversy were enacted in later years.

The post-Civil War period produced some interesting legislation touching the jurisdiction of the Supreme Court. In the famous case of *Ex parte McCardle*, which questioned the constitutionality of the Reconstruction Act, Congress removed jurisdiction from the Supreme Court and the Court could not decide the case.[64] A similar instance of less notoriety was an act of 1870 which declared the policy of the government that an individual prove his loyalty irrespective of any executive proclamation, pardon, or grant of amnesty in certain claims. The Supreme Court was directed on appeal to dismiss cases for want of jurisdiction "in all cases where judgment shall have been heretofore rendered in the court of claims in favor of any claims on any other proof of loyalty than such as is above required or provided."[65]

Congress attempted to extend the Court's appellate jurisdiction in maritime appeals. An act of 1864 allowed an appeal in a prize case without regard to the amount involved where the judge certified that the case "involved a question of general importance." The same act authorized the transfer to the Supreme Court of any prize case where the amount involved exceeded $2,000 or if the court certified that a question of general importance was involved, regardless of the amount involved.[66] This provision was held unconstitutional on the ground that this required the Court to exercise original jurisdiction that it did not possess under the Constitution.[67]

These are a few examples of a trend to make special provisions for appeals in matters which at the time of their consideration by Congress appeared to merit exceptional judicial consideration.

Criminal Appeals

Congress did not authorize appeals from criminal cases in any form until 1889. Prior to this date, criminal cases could only be reviewed by the Supreme Court when the circuit court certified that a division of opinion existed among the judges[68] or when brought up by the writ of habeas corpus. The latter method was rather limited in its scope and the former method was rarely used as the circuit courts came to be held by a single judge. The first criminal appeals act was not a general act applying to all federal courts, but was limited to appeals from the Supreme Court of the Territory of Utah where a defendant was sentenced to be hung or was convicted for bigamy or polygamy.[69]

The need for review of criminal cases was brought to the attention of Congress and the public by the decisions in the District Court for the Western District of Arkansas where approximately 173 individuals had been found guilty of capital crimes and sentenced to hang. It came as a surprise to many that these cases could not be reviewed by a higher court. In 1889, Congress authorized the defendant to take a writ of error to the Supreme Court in all capital cases.[70] Immediately, a number of these individuals exercised this right.

When the Circuit Courts of Appeals were created, appeals to these courts in criminal cases were authorized, but cases would be taken directly to the Supreme Court for capital and other "infamous crimes." Earlier, the Supreme Court had defined this term to include any offense where the defendant was sentenced to the penitentiary.[71] The effect of this statute was to enlarge significantly the right of review in criminal cases and to add to the burdens of the Supreme Court. Later, direct review by the Supreme Court was limited to capital offenses while all others had to be taken to the Circuit Courts of Appeals.[72] In 1911, all criminal appeals were first taken to the Circuit Courts of Appeals and could then be reviewed by the Supreme Court by the writ of certiorari.[73]

Relief for the Court

It became apparent in the last part of the Nineteenth Century that some relief for the Supreme Court was imperative, which has been a constant refrain ever since. The Court began its term in 1870 with 630 cases and its 1880 term with 1,212 case on its docket.[74] The Court was getting further behind each term with its caseload. Often it took three years after a case was docketed before it was heard by the Court. The number of cases continued to mount, and it became obvious to the legal profession and to Congress that some relief was necessary.[75] The form of this relief varied from increasing jurisdictional amounts to narrowing time limits for appeals, and finally, establishing intermediate appellate courts. But it was not a consistent policy of Congress to limit the Court's jurisdiction, for other statutes were enacted which expanded upon it.

One of the interesting developments during this period was the Congressional assignment of precedent to cases on the docket of the courts. In 1866, in the statute reducing internal taxation, Congress extended the review of the Supreme Court over criminal cases from the state courts for the same reason prescribed under Section 25 of the First Judicial Act, namely, in those cases where the validity of a treaty or statute was drawn into question and the decision was against their validity.[76] This statute further provided that such cases would be given precedent on the docket of the Supreme Court over all cases "to which the government of the United States is not a party excepting only such cases as the court, at their discretion, may decide to be of public importance."[77] Apparently, no criminal cases were brought to the Supreme Court under this section. This may be explained by several factors. This section authorizing such appeals was a single section in a long revenue act. How it came to be inserted in the Act is not clear from any existing sources. Also, within seven months, Congress restated Section 25 without making any material changes in the statute.[78] For these reasons, this section was overlooked.

In 1879, all federal courts were required to give priority to suits where a state was a party or where the revenue laws of the states were stayed by judicial process over all private suits.[79] In an appropriation act, the Secretary of the Treasury was given the authority to withhold all disputed payments to any railroad company. The company could bring an action against the government in the Court of Claims "and either party to such suit may appeal to the Supreme Court." What makes this statute of interest is the requirement that the courts give "precedence over all other business" to these cases.[80] Congress continued to give priority to certain types of cases until the priority system became a morass that rationally could not be administered or followed. In 1984, Congress proposed to remove all these priorities but was without success.[81]

The Court took steps in the Nineteenth Century to streamline its procedures. Traditionally in appellate practice, counsel was allowed to argue as long as he wished. The first limitation on arguments was enforced by the Supreme Court in 1812 when a rule was adopted limiting the number of counsel for each side to two.[82] In the famous case of *McCullough v. Maryland*, however, this rule was dispensed with because of the great public importance of the constitutional question. The Court, speaking through Justice Story on February 1, 1844, asked counsel to curtail their arguments in view of the congestion of the Court's docket.[83] In 1848, another rule limited the time of argument to two hours for each counsel. This meant that in some cases, the argument could extend over an eight hour period by allowing two representatives for each side to speak for two hours each. A modifying rule was adopted in 1872 limiting counsel to two hours for each side.[84] The time for argument has been restricted further until presently the allotment is one half hour for each side unless extended by order of the Court. Traditionally, Chief Justice Hughes, who served as chief justice from 1930-1941, was very strict about the time limit and was known to stop counsel in the middle of an argument.[85]

The Supreme Court could do little to reduce its caseload so the Court sought relief through Congress. The first congressional attempt to relieve the burden of the Supreme Court was a statute raising the jurisdictional amount to $5,000 in 1875.[86] This increase, however, did not affect those statutes conferring jurisdiction in well-defined areas without regard to the amount involved in each case. Attempts to relieve the appellate court's backlog by raising jurisdictional amounts have generally been unsuccessful. This is not because lawyers would merely raise their stated claims, but rather such failure is better explained by the economic growth in this country. As an example, in 1875, a corporate capitalization of one million dollars was considered astronomical; now, a century later, it is not.

Certiorari

The only structural change made by Congress to relieve the Supreme Court docket was the establishment of the Circuit Courts of Appeals in 1891.[87] Congress had been urged by such individuals as Senator David Davis, a former associate justice of the Supreme Court of the United States and then a member of the Senate, and the Attorney General A.H. Garland, who had served in the Senate as a member of the Judiciary Committee over several previous decades, to establish an intermediate appellate court. The proposals differed in detail as to how this task was to be accomplished. However, some type of an intermediate appellate court was envisioned. Congress responded by taking the existing geographical circuits and organizing in each, a Circuit Court of Appeals, consisting of the circuit judge who was authorized in 1869 and increasing their number by one in each of the circuits, bringing the total number of circuit judges to two. The third judge on the court was the justice of the Supreme Court but when he was unable to do so, then a district court judge could be assigned this task. It is interesting to note that upon organizing, all the Circuit Courts of Appeals adopted rules governing the assignment of district court judges. Congress had managed to preserve the existing judicial machinery by assigning the circuit judge along with the associate justice of the

Supreme Court, who was normally expected to function as a circuit judge, to this new court.

The statute of 1891, known as the Evarts Act after William M. Evarts, a Senator from New York, provided that most appeals would be taken from the existing district courts or the circuit courts to the new Circuit Courts of Appeals. However, some members of Congress felt that certain important issues should be taken directly from the trial courts to the Supreme Court.[88] At that time, appeals could be taken directly from the district courts or the circuit courts to the Supreme Court in the following cases: where jurisdiction was questioned, for final decrees in prize cases, where construction of the Constitution of the United States was at issue, where the constitutionality of any law or validity of any treaty was questioned, or for the conviction of capital or other infamous crimes. The addition of the last phrase "other infamous crimes" made possible an appeal in practically all criminal cases. The previous practice of taking appeals from the highest state courts was continued.[89]

The decisions of the Circuit Courts of Appeals were made "final" in diversity, equity, criminal, admiralty cases and in suits under the revenue and patent laws. The term "final" had been used to indicate that no further review was possible. All questions of law, however, could be certified to the Supreme Court, or those cases which were final could be reviewed by the Supreme Court by a writ of certiorari. The writ of certiorari was introduced for the first time as a means of bringing a case up for judicial review, a departure from previous practice.[90] The writ of certiorari had been previously used sparingly by the Court to bring up the record on appeal or to expand the record, but never to bring the case itself up for review. In early English practice, the writ was used to bring a case before the Court of King's Bench for disposition at whatever stage the case had reached at the time the writ was issued.[91] The circumstances under which the writ could be issued were not defined by statute, so the Court had to formulate the applicable rules. On the first occasion when this question was presented, the Court concluded that the writ could only be issued where "questions of gravity and importance" were presented.[92]

One of the most frequent objections to the creation of separate Circuit Courts of Appeals was that these courts would reach different conclusions on the same issue. It is for that reason that the Supreme Court was authorized to issue the writ of certiorari to bring cases up for review.

The use of the writ of certiorari presented several questions of practice. The Court recognized that a power so

> broad and comprehensive, if carelessly exercised, might defeat the very thought and purpose for the Act in creating the court of appeals. So exercised it might burden the docket of this court with cases which it was the intent of Congress to terminate in the court of appeals and which [if] brought here, would simply prevent

promptness of the decision which in all judicial actions is one of the elements of justice.[93]

When the question arose at which stage of the proceedings in the Circuit Courts of Appeals the writ of certiorari would be granted, the Supreme Court held that the statute did not alter the established rule that an appeal would lie only from a final judgment. The Court reasoned that the omission of the word "final" in the statute could not have been intended to make such a fundamental change in the practice of the Court.[94]

A proposal was advanced several times in Congress to require the Supreme Court to take jurisdiction of cases where there was a conflict in the decisions of the Circuit Courts of Appeals. Such proposals were never seriously considered, but the Court gradually developed principles to govern the granting of certiorari to the Circuit Court of Appeals. In its rules adopted in 1925, the Supreme Court stated that review on the writ of certiorari was a matter of "sound judicial discretion" and would be granted "where a circuit court of appeals has rendered a decision in conflict with the decision of another circuit court of appeals on the same matter."[95] This principle was restated in the rules adopted in 1954.[96] The extent of conflict among the circuits is a matter of considerable dispute.[97] The same data has been examined by different writers who have reached diametrically opposing conclusions whether a conflict exists, or whether the difference cannot be distinguished.[98] Whenever any alteration in the jurisdiction of the Supreme Court or a change in the geographical arrangements of the circuits is professionally discussed, this phantasm of conflict is raised. The unifying factor which contributes to limiting any conflict is the publication of the opinions of the courts of appeals in one series of reports rather than the publication of these decisions by circuit. This method of reporting contributes to lessening any conflict by making opinions readily available as if all originated in one court.

Several inconsistencies soon became apparent in the relationship of the territorial courts to the Circuit Courts of Appeals. The Appellate Court was given jurisdiction of an appeal from any final judgment of the Territorial Supreme Court in which the judgments of the Circuit Court of Appeals were made final as specified in the Act of 1891. Where an appeal did not fall within one of these headings, it was found that appeals to the Supreme Court of the United States were governed by previous acts which had not been repealed.[99] Thus the situation arose where judicial review by the Supreme Court of the final judgment of a court of last resort in the territories was broader than an appeal to the same court from the district or circuit courts of the United States. This situation was found to exist in the District of Columbia as well.

In 1885, Congress made the judgment of a Supreme Court of the territory final in all amounts under $5,000. Previously, the jurisdictional amount varied slightly. This did not apply to patents, copyrights or cases where the validity of a treaty or statute was raised or the authority was

exercised under the laws of the United States.[100] It should be noted that
the decisions of the Territorial Supreme Courts were final in amounts
under the jurisdictional limit and there were certain matters in which no
amount was possible to establish jurisdiction, such as in divorce cases.
Under this statute, a divorce case could not be appealed to the Supreme
Court of the United States from the territorial court of Arizona.[101]

Another major accomplishment of the Evarts Act of 1891 was the
constricting of the interlude between the final judgment and the time when
the writ of error or the writ of appeal could be brought. Under the
Judiciary Act of 1798, an appeal could be taken from the circuit court or
the district court to the Supreme Court within five years of the final
judgment.[102] This period of limitation was calculated from the date of
filing of the writ rather than its issuance by the trial court.[103] In 1872, the
period was limited to two years and this provision was carried over into
the REVISED STATUTES.[104] This section was considered obsolete and
repealed in 1933.[105] Congress made the change because the Judiciary Act
of 1891 provided that these writs be taken to the court of appeals within
six months with the exception that equity cases be brought up within
thirty days. Appeals or writs of error had to be taken to the Supreme
Court within one year of final judgment.[106] Congress continued to
prescribe the period of time in which a writ of error or appeal had to be
taken to the Supreme Court in specific types of cases. In 1903, an appeal in
an anti-trust case had to be taken within sixty days.[107] These time periods
became confusing and varied according to the type of cases and in time
became redundant as the rules of court came to prescribe these periods.

No time limits were prescribed by the statute governing the period
between final judgment and the application for the writ of certiorari. The
statute provided that all writs of error and appeals from the Circuit Courts
of Appeals be taken within one year after the entry of the judgment sought
to be reviewed.[108] When the Supreme Court considered the omission from
the statute of a period of time for the application of the writ of certiorari,
the one year rule was applied.[109]

Appeals from the District of Columbia

The Act of 1891 failed to change the power of review of the Supreme
Court over the courts in the District of Columbia. Up until that date,
appeals from the Supreme Court of the District of Columbia were the
same as that from the Circuit Courts of the United States. When the Act of
1891 curtailed the appeals from the district courts and the circuit courts to
the Supreme Court, the courts in the District of Columbia were inadvertently omitted. The result was that a wider appeal was available from
the District of Columbia than from any other federal court.[110] This left the
right of judicial review from the Supreme Court of the District of
Columbia to be governed by statutes which the Act of 1891 had
repealed.[111]

This was not the first time that the courts in the District of Columbia were governed by statutes which were repealed. The first court created in the District of Columbia was the circuit court, and its jurisdiction was defined by the ill-fated Judiciary Act of 1801.[112] Appeals from this court and its successor, the Supreme Court of the District of Columbia, were taken to the Supreme Court in the same manner as appeals from a circuit court.[113] During the period of time after 1891, the number of cases appealed from the District of Columbia to the Supreme Court grew to approximately ten percent of the total number of cases handled in the Supreme Court of the United States. As one justice commented, this was one out of every ten cases on the court's docket.[114]

In 1893, Congress created a Court of Appeals in the District of Columbia to take over the appellate work of the Supreme Court of the District of Columbia as well as appeals from the patent office.[115] Surprisingly, the act did nothing to narrow the appeals from this court to the Supreme Court of the United States. Congress was not unaware of this anomaly, for the Attorney General, in his annual report from 1906 until 1910, urged that appeals from this court in the District of Columbia be governed by the same laws governing appeals from the Circuit Courts of Appeals in other parts of the country.[116]

This was not accomplished until the Judiciary Act of 1911 which limited appeals from the District of Columbia to those cases arising under the federal Constitution, laws and treaties, and "the construction of any laws of the United States".[117] Since all the laws in the District of Columbia were enacted by Congress, they could in a sense be considered federal laws. However, the Supreme Court did not adopt that interpretation; rather it construed the statute to place the court on the same basis as the other Circuit Courts of Appeals.[118] The Court of Appeals for the District of Columbia was given the same status as the other courts of the same title in the federal system in 1925.[119]

Three Judge Court

In 1910, Congress adopted the Three-Judge Court Act which addressed the irresponsible conduct of some federal district court judges who issued interlocutory injunctions against the enforcement of state regulatory statutes, which were unpopular in many circles.[120] In 1908, the Supreme Court had held that district court judges could issue an injunction to prevent the enforcement of unconstitutional state statutes.[121] Acting on this theory, a number of unpopular temporary injunctions were issued. Two justifications of the Act were that the three judges would be less likely to imprudently issue an injunction and that the states would be relieved of the fear that their regulatory programs would be enjoined by the federal courts. The original act prohibited federal district court judges from issuing interlocutory injunctions against allegedly unconstitutional state statutes and required that such cases be heard by a three-judge court. This statute applied to interlocutory injunctions, but an amendment in 1925 made the statute applicable to permanent injunctions as well.[122] Congress extended the concept of a three-judge court to other areas. In 1913, a three-judge court was required to issue an interlocutory injunction suspending or restraining the enforcement of an order of the Interstate Commerce Commission.[123] In 1937, as one of the court reform proposals, the three-judge court was extended to review cases seeking injunctions against acts of Congress which were claimed to be unconstitutional.[124] The statute further provided for a direct appeal to the Supreme Court which added to that court's docket. The number of such cases in the federal courts increased dramatically between 1963 and 1973 when their number nearly doubled. In the October 1969 term of the Supreme Court, 22% of the cases considered by the court were appeals from three-judge courts.

The rules concerning appellate review of the opinions of such courts were in hopeless confusion. If the district judge refused to convene a three-judge court, a mandamus could be sought from the Supreme Court or an appeal went to the Circuit Court of Appeals. Some of these courts would reverse the district judge because the attack on the state statute was substantial as required by the law governing the issuance of an injunction, and the question whether the statute was constitutional was not considered. Was the proper order to reverse the district court on the merits or to order a three-judge court convened?[125] As a result of the confusion, judges and scholars joined the movement to repeal the three-judge court.

The members of the Supreme Court both individually and in opinions spoke out against the use of the three-judge district court characterizing it as a "drain upon the federal judicial manpower" especially "in regions where, despite modern facilities, distance still plays an important part in the effective administration of justice."[126]

In 1976, the use of a three-judge court was limited to actions challenging the constitutionality of apportionment of congressional districts or the apportionment of any state-wide legislative body or "when otherwise required by Act of Congress." This act further allowed the state to intervene even though not a party; this was a privilege previously denied them.[127]

Direct Appeals

During the period from the establishment of the Circuit Courts of Appeals in 1891 until the passage of the Judges' Act of 1925, a number of statutes were passed affecting the types of cases that could be taken to the Supreme Court without going through the intermediate appellate courts. The term "infamous" crime, as used in the criminal appeals statute allowing appeals from the circuit court in capital cases and other infamous crimes, was construed to include any offense where the defendant was sentenced to the penitentiary.[128] The establishment of the bulk of criminal cases came directly to the Supreme Court from the circuit courts until

1897, when appeals were limited to capital cases.[129] Appeals in capital cases continued to go to the Supreme Court directly until 1911, when this jurisdiction was given to the Circuit Court of Appeals.[130]

Other cases which began to crowd the docket of the Supreme Court of the United States were those arising under the Federal Employer's Liability Act of 1908.[131] The first cases arising under this statute were those which challenged the constitutionality of the statute and were heard by the Supreme Court on a direct appeal from the district court.[132] The other cases came to the Court for review by the writ of error or appeal as the judgment of the Circuit Court of Appeals was not final in these cases. The central question in most of these cases under the Federal Employer's Liability Act was whether the employee was engaged in interstate commerce at the time of the injury. One can imagine the fine lines which the courts were forced to draw in these cases, resulting in applied standards which were imprecise and difficult in application.[133] Relief was sought from Congress which responded by an act making the decisions of the Circuit Court of Appeals "final" in these decisions, except where the Supreme Court chose to grant a review by the writ of certiorari. At the same time, Congress narrowed the consideration of cases from the Supreme Court of the Phillipine Islands to review by certiorari.[134]

The Judges' Bill

The problem of the caseload before the Supreme Court was still far from solved, for an excess of 500 cases remained on its docket at the end of the October term of 1914, 1915 and 1916.[135] The acts of 1915 and 1916 had reduced this load somewhat, but these reductions were offset by new federal statutes. The federal legislation passed during World War I had a tremendous effect on the dockets of the federal courts, and this in turn increased the number of cases taken to the Supreme Court for review. Beginning in 1920, the number of undisposed cases remaining on the docket at the end of a term began to show an increase. At the end of the October term 1924, 533 cases were undecided.

William Howard Taft, long an advocate of judicial reform, became Chief Justice of the United States in 1921. At his instigation, a committee of the justices under Justice Van Devanter, prepared a bill to restate and limit the jurisdiction of the Supreme Court. This bill, known as the Judges' Bill, was signed into law in 1925.[136].

Under this statute, the Supreme Court continued to review directly decisions of an interlocutory or final judgment under the antitrust and the interstate commerce acts, appeals by the United States in criminal cases, appeals of suits to enjoin orders of the Interstate Commerce Commission and appeals from three-judge district courts. The historic review by an appeal from the highest state court where the decision was against the validity of the constitutionality of a federal or state statute was preserved.

The certification of questions by the Court of Appeals and the Court of Claims was not affected by this new statute, but its use was declining. The significant feature of this bill was the extension of the writ of certiorari to many more areas where the appeals were once mandatory. Appeals from the Court of Claims were abolished and certiorari was substituted.

This extension of the use of the writ of certiorari allowed the Court to decide what cases it would hear, and thus control the cases placed on its docket, but limitations on this power existed. The Court of Appeals for the District of Columbia was elevated to the same status as the other Circuit Courts of Appeals, which reduced the types of cases the Supreme Court could review from that court. The Judges' Act was widely acclaimed and hailed as a piece of legislation long overdue.[137]

With the Judges' Act, a new era in the jurisdiction of the court was introduced. Between 1891 and the enactment of the Judges' Bill, unless the decision of the Circuit Court of Appeals was made "final", any interpretation of the federal statutes or enforcement of federal rights could be taken to the Supreme Court on a writ of appeal or error. Although the technical distinctions of these two writs had lost their meaning by this date, within three years, all distinctions remaining were abolished. The review by appeal was nearly mandatory. The Court could issue certiorari to bring up any decision in areas which the decision of the Circuit Courts of Appeals was final and from the supreme courts of the territories. Certain statutes authorized an appeal to the Supreme Court directly from the district courts. After 1925, except for areas where Congress mandated an appeal to the Supreme Court, the Circuit Court of Appeals became the final appellate court unless the Supreme Court decided in its discretion to issue certiorari to review a case.

This bill established the Supreme Court as a court to determine policy questions of national concern. Following this premise, the only occasions when attempts have been made to restrict its jurisdiction are in those areas where the Supreme Court's decisions have caused great controversy. No further adjustments of the Court's jurisdiction has since been made by Congress, although numerous proposals have been considered.

Appeals from the Specialized Courts

One last significant area of the Supreme Court's appellate jurisdiction has been in appeals from the various specialized courts. The statutes governing these appeals were neither uniform nor consistent, and for this reason, the reviewing power of the Court varied, depending upon the specialized court or territorial court from which the case was appealed. The Court of Claims, the first specialized court, was created in 1855, but appeals to the Supreme Court from its decisions were not authorized until 1863.[138] However, in the first appeal brought under this act, the Supreme

Court denied that it could take jurisdiction because the decisions of the Court of Claims could be reviewed and revised by the Secretary of the Treasury.[139] This defect was abolished in 1866.[140] Appeals could be taken from the Court of Claims to the Supreme Court where the amount in controversy exceeded $3,000. The Supreme Court had previously held that an appeal from the Court of Claims in cases involving $3,000 or more was a matter of right.[141] The statute of 1866 authorized an appeal by the government without regard to amount when the presiding judge certified that the decree furnished a precedent for future action by the executive department in the adjustment of similar claims.[142] A later statute authorized an appeal by the government without regard to amount which made the above provision obsolete. One unforeseen result of this appeal was that the government had an unfair advantage because it would apply for a new trial before the Court of Claims while at the same time prosecuting an appeal in the Supreme Court.[143]

The Supreme Court considered several interesting problems in relation to its jurisdiction over these appeals. One such question involved the problem of whether the Supreme Court could hear appeals from cases arising under the Abandoned and Captured Property Act of 1863. This act assigned these claims to the Court of Claims for adjudication, but did not specially provide for appeals. The Supreme Court held that an appeal could be taken under the general appellate power found in the statute creating the court.[144]

In 1925, the review of the Supreme Court by writ of error of the decisions of the Court of Claims in matters exceeding $3,000 was abolished. Decisions of the court could be reviewed by the Supreme Court only by the writ of certiorari or the Court could certify "any definite and distinct questions of law concerning which instructions are desired for the proper disposition of the cause".[145]

Appeals could be taken from the Court of Private Land Claims to the Supreme Court within six months without regard to the amount involved. In appeals from the Court of Private Land Claims, the Supreme Court was granted additional powers not generally accorded an appellate court. The Court could amend the record and retry issues of facts. A review of the United States Reports indicate that these powers were not utilized.[146].

The conditions under which an appeal could be taken to the Supreme Court from the Commerce Court were governed, as the statute establishing the court stated, under the same regulations as those governing appeals from the Circuit Courts of Appeals. However, certain limitations were placed upon this process. The appeal did not stay the decisions of the Commerce Court unless the justice of the Supreme Court so directed. Decisions of the Commerce Court granting or continuing an injunction restraining the enforcement of an order of the Interstate Commerce Commission could be appealed to the Supreme Court if done within thirty days. These appeals had priority over all cases on the docket of the

Supreme Court except for criminal appeals.[147] The Commerce Court was born amid controversy and died after a very short life.

The Court of Custom Appeals was established in 1909. Congress provided that the decisions of this court were to be final on appeals from the Board of General Appraisers.[148] However, in 1914, Congress authorized an appeal to the Supreme Court from the Court of Custom Appeals in cases where the decision drew into question the construction of the Constitution or a treaty or statute. The Attorney General could certify that the case was of such importance as to render expedient its review by the Supreme Court "either by writ of certiorari or otherwise."[149]. In 1930, the requirement that the Attorney General certify "that the cases of such importance to render expedient its review by the Supreme Court" was repealed, making it possible for the Supreme Court to review the decisions of the Court of Customs and Patent Appeals by certiorari provided the petition was filed within sixty days.[150] This statute provided that the writ of certiorari should be treated "with the same power and authority in the case as if it had been carried by appeal to the Supreme Court." No evidence exists to suggest that the Supreme Court has treated a case from the Court of Customs and Patent Appeals any differently than a case from any other court brought up for review.

Proposals for Limiting Jurisdiction Since 1945

During the period between the enactment of the Judges' Bill and the end of World War II there was literally no change in the jurisdiction of the Supreme Court. Following the war, Congress enacted some sweeping legislation including the Civil Rights Act and many other pieces of legislation which introduced federal rights where none had existed before. Beginning with the Judicial Code of 1948, the number of federal judgeships was increased on several occasions. Then, too, the Supreme Court itself extended its concept of constitutionalism, especially governing petitions for prisoners alleging violations of their constitutional rights by the use of the writ of habeas corpus. The number of such petitions increased dramatically. All these factors impinged upon the docket of the Supreme Court.

Chief Justice Warren Burger was the first to raise a call for relief of the Supreme Court in 1970 and various proposals were advanced to accomplish this purpose. The old proposal of eliminating diversity cases from the federal courts was seriously considered but never adopted.[151] In 1974, two small measures were adopted which impacted the docket of the Supreme Court. The curtailment of the use of the three-judge district court with a direct appeal to the Supreme Court removed a number of appeals. Further, the change in the Expediting Act of 1903 eliminated direct appeals from the district courts to the Supreme Court in certain antitrust cases.[152]

Very soon after becoming Chief Justice, Warren Burger urged the Federal Judicial Center to undertake a study of the caseload of the Supreme Court. The report is often known as the Freund Report after Professor Paul A. Freund who chaired the committee. This was the first study of the docket of the Supreme Court, and this group made the first proposal for a National Court of Appeals to relieve the Supreme Court. The purpose of this court was to screen cases and determine which ones the Supreme Court should hear. The judges would be selected from the Courts of Appeals and assigned on a rotating basis.[153]

In 1972, again at the urging of Chief Justice Burger, a Commission on Revision of the Federal Court Appellate System was established to study the present division of the United States into judicial circuits and to study the structure of internal procedures of the federal courts of appeals.[154] The most controversial proposal of this Commission was the establishment of a National Court of Appeals.[155] This court was first proposed by the Freund Commission, but this suggestion for a new court was not well received by the majority of the federal judges and the members of the legal profession. To overcome some of these objections, under the Commission on Revision of the Federal Court Appellate System's proposal, the court would consist of seven judges appointed by the president holding office during good behavior and would sit *en banc* in Washington, D.C. The court would have jurisdiction of cases referred to it by the Supreme Court or would have jurisdiction transferred to it by the Courts of Appeals. Under the proposal of the Freund Commission, this court would screen cases for the Supreme Court to decide. The arguments for and against this type of court were discussed extensively in literature mostly on hypothetical facts. It is the nature of legal arguments to put forth the worst possible scenario, raising issues including the decline of justice and invoking the memory of the founding fathers.

In 1977, Congressional committees began to study a proposal to permit the Supreme Court to take cases only on the writ of certiorari and to abolish all mandatory jurisdiction which embraced all cases taken to the Court by an appeal. Several times the proposal was dropped because attempts to add less popular provisions to the measure were made on the floor of Congress.[156] Since such changes apparently require a long incubation period, this statute has not been adopted. The reformers urged freeing the Supreme Court to decide cases involving principles, "the application of which are of wide public importance or governmental interest, and which should be authoritatively declared by the final court."[157] The dimension of this concept has never been defined and will probably be determined by the popular fads in constitutional law at that time.

FOOTNOTES TO CHAPTER 21

1. Ex parte McCardle, 7 Wall. 506 (U.S. 1868).
2. Abner L. Duncan's Heirs and Representatives v. United States, 7 Pet. 435, 451 (U.S. 1833).
3. U.S. Const. Art. III, sec. 2; Wiscart v. Dauchy, 3 Dall. 321 (U.S. 1796).
4. U.S. Const. Art. III, sec. 2(2). The jurisdiction of the Supreme Court is discussed in detail in "The Original Jurisdiction of the United States Supreme Court," 11 STAN. L. REV. 665 (1959). A list of cases arising under this original jurisdiction is included.
5. Erwin C. Surrency, ed., "Minutes of the Supreme Court of the United States," 5 AMER. J. LEG. HIST. 188 (1961); 7 AMER. J. LEG. HIST. 253, 254 (1963).
6. Alfred Conkling, A TREATISE ON THE ORGANIZATION, JURISDICTION AND PRACTICE OF THE COURTS OF THE UNITED STATES (1864), p.15.
7. Rhode Island v. Massachusetts, 12 Pet. 657 (U.S. 1838).
8. California v. Southern Pacific Co., 157 U.S. 229, 249 (1894).
9. United States v. Ravara, 2 Dall. 297 (Cir. Ct. Pa. 1794); Commonwealth v. Kosloff, 5 Serge. & Rawle 545 (Pa. 1816), where an indictment against a Consul General was quashed because the state court did not have jurisdiction.
10. State of Pennsylvania v. The Wheeling and Belmont Bridge Co., 13 How. 518 (U.S. 1851).
11. United States v. Ortega, 11 Wheat. 467 (U.S. 1826).
12. Marbury v. Madison, 1 Cranch 137 (U.S. 1803).
13. Act of September 24, 1789, sec. 22, 1 STAT. 84.
14. Barry v. Mercein, 5 How. 103 (U.S. 1847); Lee v. Lee, 8 Pet. 44 (U.S. 1834).
15. Cooke v. Woodruff, 5 Cranch. 13 (U.S. 1809).
16. Wise & Lynn v. The Columbia Turnpike Co., 7 Cranch. 276 (U.S. 1812); Gordon et al., v. Ogden, 3 Pet. 33 (U.S. 1830); Smith v. Honey, 3 Pet. 469 (U.S. 1830).
17. Act of July 4, 1840, c. 43, sec. 3, 5 STAT. 393. United States v. Goodwin, 7 Cranch 108 (U.S. 1812); United States v. Barker, 2 Wheat. 395 (U.S. 1817); Sarchet v. United States, 12 Pet. 143 (U.S. 1838).
18. Armstrong v. The Treasurer of Athens County, 16 Pet. 281 (U.S. 1842); John F. Dillon, REMOVAL OF CASES FROM STATE COURTS TO FEDERAL COURTS (1881).
19. Martin v. Hunter's Lessee, 1 Wheat. 304 (1816); *see* Charles Warren, THE SUPREME COURT IN UNITED STATES HISTORY (1922), v.1, p.443-453; *see* Charles Warren, "Legislative and Judicial Attacks on the Supreme Court of the United States", 47 AMER. L. REV. 1 (1913).
20. Robert G. McCloskey, THE AMERICAN SUPREME COURT (1960) p.64; Charles Warren, "Legislative and Judicial Attacks on the Supreme Court of the United States — A History of the Twenty-Fifth Section of the Judiciary Act", 47 AMER. L. REV. 1, 161 (1913).
21. William S. Carpenter, JUDICIAL TENURE IN THE UNITED STATES (1918), p.166.
22. Fisher v. Cockerell, 5 Pet. 248 (U.S. 1831); Lessee of Reed v. Marsh, 13 Pet. 153 (U.S. 1839); Craig et al v. The State of Missouri, 4 Pet. 410 (U.S. 1830).
23. Act of February 5, 1867, sec. 2, 14 STAT. 385.
24. Murdock v. Memphis, 20 Wall. 590 (U.S. 1874).
25. Ives v. South Buffalo Railroad Co., 201 N.Y. 271 (1911).
26. Act of December 23, 1914, 38 STAT. 790.
27. Felix Frankfurter and James M. Landis, THE BUSINESS OF THE SUPREME COURT (1928), p.198. The history of the passage of this act is reviewed on pages 189-198.
28. Ex parte Christy, 3 How. 292 (U.S. 1845); The United States v. Peters, 3 DALL. 121 (U.S. 1795).

29. Act of September 24, 1789, sec. 13, 1 STAT. 80.

30. Conkling, *supra,* note 6, p.49-50, where these decisions are listed.

31. Act of September 24, 1789, sec. 13, 1 STAT. 80.

32. Act of September 24, 1781, sec. 14, 1 STAT. 81.

33. United States v. Hamilton, 3 Dall. 17 (U.S. 1795).

34. Bollman & Swartwout, 4 Cranch 75 (U.S. 1807).

35. "Minutes of the Supreme Court of the United States", 5 AMER. J. LEG. HIST. 69 (1961).

36. Clarke v. Bazadone, 1 Cranch 212 (U.S. 1803).

37. Act of March 3, 1805, 2 STAT. 338.

38. Act of March 2, 1853, sec. 9, 10 STAT. 175.

39. Act of March 3, 1885, 23 STAT. 443.

40. Act of March 3, 1891, sec. 15, 26 STAT. 830.

41. Act of April 29, 1802, 2 STAT. 152.

42. This is the procedure that is prescribed in Act of March 2, 1893, sec. 2, 1 STAT. 334.

43. This history is recited by Chief Justice Marshall in United States v. Daniel, 6 Wheat. 542 (U.S. 1821).

44. Veazie v. Wadleigh, 11 Pet. 55, 60 (U.S. 1837).

45. White v. Turk, 12 Pet. 238 (U.S. 1838).

46. Parker v. Nixon, 10 Pet. 408 (U.S. 1836).

47. The best discussion of the practice of certification is found in William M. McKinney, THE ENCYCLOPEDIA OF PLEADING AND PRACTICE (1895), v. 3, pp.918-956.

48. Act of June 30, 1864, sec. 3, 13 STAT. 310.

49. The Alicia, 7 Wall. 571 (U.S. 1868).

50. Act of June 1, 1872, 17 STAT. 196.

51. Act of March 3, 1891, sec. 6, 26 STAT. 826.

52. James William Moore and Allan D. Vestal, "Present and Potential Role of Certification in Federal Appellate Procedure", 35 VA. L. REV. 1, 18 (1949).

53. *Ibid,* p.26.

54. Robert L. Stern and Eugene Gressman, SUPREME COURT PRACTICE (5th ed., 1978), p.592.

55. Moore and Vestal, *supra,* note 52, p.7.

56. Act of February 15, 1819, 3 STAT. 481.

57. Act of July 4, 1836, sec. 17, 5 STAT. 125.

58. Act of April 10, 1816, sec. 23, 3 STAT. 276.

59. Act of May 26, 1824, sec. 9, 4 STAT. 53.

60. Act of May 23, 1828, sec. 6, 4 STAT. 284.

61. Act of May 31, 1844, 5 STAT. 658.

62. United States v. Bromley, 12 How. 88 (U.S. 1851).

63. Act of April 9, 1866, sec. 10, 14 STAT. 29; Act of April 20, 1871, 17 STAT. 13.

64. Ex parte McCardle, 7 Wall. 506 (U.S. 1868).

65. Act of July 12, 1870, 16 STAT. 235. This statute was in response to the decision of the Supreme Court in the United States v. Anderson, 76 U.S. 56 (1869) and United States v. Padelford, 76 U.S. 531 (1869).

66. Act of June 30, 1864, sec. 3, 13 STAT. 310.

67. The Alicia, 7 Wall. 571 (U.S. 1868).

68. Act of April 29, 1802, sec. 6, 2 STAT. 159.

69. Act of June 23, 1874, sec. 3, 18 STAT. 254.

70. Act of February 6, 1889, sec. 6, 26 STAT. 659; J. Gladston Emery, COURT OF THE DAMNED, p.174.

71. Act of March 3, 1891, sec. 5, 26 STAT. 828; In re Claasen, 140 U.S. 200 (1891).

72. Act of January 20, 1897, 29 STAT. 492.

73. Act of March 3, 1911, sec. 128, 238, 240, 36 STAT. 1133, 1157. Capital offenses were omitted in sec. 238.

74. Frankfurter and Landis, *supra,* note 27, p.60.

75. *Ibid,* p.96, Footnote 177 gives a bibliography of articles urging some relief for the Supreme Court. *See also,* "Relief of the Supreme Court of the United States," 23 AMER. L. REV. 427 (1889).

76. Act of July 13, 1866, sec. 69, 14 STAT. 172.

77. Act of July 13, 1866, sec. 69, 14 STAT. 172.

78. Act of February 5, 1867, sec. 2, 14 STAT. 385.

79. Act of June 30, 1870, 16 STAT. 176 required the federal courts to give priority to suits where states are a party, or where revenue laws of a state are stayed by judicial process over private civil suits.

80. Act of March 3, 1873, sec. 2, 17 STAT. 508.

81. U.S. Cong. House Rept. 97-824; House Committee on the Judiciary. Sub-committee on Courts, Civil Liberties, and the Administration of Justice. Hearings, Mandatory Appellate Jurisdiction of the Supreme Court Abolition of Civil Rights. Serial 65.

82. Stephen D. Law, THE JURISDICTION AND POWERS OF THE UNITED STATES COURTS (1852), p.380. Some lawyer had the effrontery to inquire if this rule was intended to prevent division of the cause into distinct points and hearings of two counsellors on each point. The court considered the rule inflexible "whatever may be the number of points". 7 Cranch. 1 (U.S. 1812).

83. Carl B. Swisher, HISTORY OF THE SUPREME COURT: THE TANEY YEARS 1836-64 (1974), p.278.

84. U.S. Supreme Court rules, 14 Wall. xi (U.S. 1872). This rule was promulgated November 16, 1872 to take effect January 1, 1873.

85. Edwin McElwain, "The Business of the Supreme Court as Conducted by Chief Justice Hughes", 63 HARV. L. REV. 5, 17 (1949). Some doubt existed in some courts whether the time for argument could be limited. *See* A.G. McKean, "Limiting the Time of Argument of Counsel," 14 CENT. L. J. 45 (1882).

86. Act of February 16, 1875, sec. 3, 18 STAT. 315.

87. Act of March 3, 1891, 26 STAT. 826.

88. *See* the list of areas where a review in the Supreme Court was a matter of right prepared by Chief Justice Taft in Frankfurter and Landis, *supra,* note 27, p.261.

89. Act of March 2, 1891, sec. 5, 26 STAT. 827.

90. Hannis Taylor, JURISDICTION AND PROCEDURE OF THE SUPREME COURT OF THE UNITED STATES (1905), p.556-559.

91. Courts of Appeals, 1 LAW NOTES 33 (1897). Erwin C. Surrency, "The Development of the Appellate Function: The Pennsylvania Experience," 20 AMER. J. LEG. HIST. 176 (1976). Some of this history is reviewed in Hartranft v. Mullowny, 247 U.S. 295 (1917).

92. Ex parte Lau Ow Bew, 141 U.S. 583, 587 (1891); the practice of the Court is reviewed at some length in Forsyth v. City of Hammond, 166 U.S. 506 (1896); "Certiorari to the United States Circuit Courts of Appeals", 1 LAW NOTES 33 (1897).

93. Forsyth v. City of Hammond, 166 U.S. 506, 513 (1896).

94. McLish v. Roff, 141 U.S. 661 (1891). This rule was first established in Lorgay v. Conrad, 6 How. 201, 204 (1848).

95. Rules 35(5)(a), 266 U.S. 681.

96. Rule 19, Rule 1954, 346 U.S. 945.

97. Commission on Revision of the Federal Court Appellate System, 67 F.R.D. 195, 221, 298.

98. Robert Stern, "Denial of Certiorari Despite a Conflict", 66 HARV. L. REV. 465 (1953) and Edward and Sheila Roehner, "Certiorari — What is a Conflict Between Circuits", 20 U. CHIC. L. REV. 656 (1953), 67 F.R.D. 222, 298 (1975).

99. Shute v.Keyser, 149 U.S. 649 (1892).

100. Act of March 3, 1885, 23 STAT. 443.

101. Simms v. Simms, 175 U.S. 162 (1899).

102. Act of September 24, 1789, sec. 22, 1 STAT. 84.

103. Brooks v. Norris, 11 How. 204 (1850).

104. Act of June 1, 1872, sec. 2, 17 STAT. 196, REV. STAT. (1874), sec. 1008.

105. Act of March 3, 1933, 47 STAT. 1428.

106. Act of March 3, 1891, sec. 6, 7, 11, 26 STAT. 828, 829.

107. Act of February 11, 1903, 32 STAT. 823.

108. Act of March 2, 1891, sec. 6, 26 STAT. 828.

109. The Conqueror, 166 U.S. 114 (1896).

110. *See* Order of Clerk, Supreme Court of the United States, 210 U.S. 503. It is understood that the document appeared in a printed form of two pages for distribution. *See* Furness, Withy, & Co. v. Yang-Tsze, 242 U.S. 430, 434 (1916).

111. In re Heath, 144 U.S. 92 (1891).

112. Judiciary Act of 1801, Act of February 13, 1801, sec. 10, 11, 2 STAT. 92; repealed by Act of March 2, 1802, 2 STAT. 132. Circuit Court in the District of Columbia established by Act of February 27, 1801, sec. 3, 2 STAT. 103.

113. D.C. REV. STAT. (1874), sec. 846.

114. Henry H. Brown, "The New Federal Judiciary Code", 73 CENT. L. J. 275, 278 (1911). Frankfurter and Landis, *supra,* note 27, p.121.

115. Act of February 9, 1893, sec. 8, 27 STAT. 434, 436.

116. 1910 ANNUAL REPORT U.S. ATTY. GENERAL 81; 1925 ANNUAL REPORT U.S. ATTY. GENERAL 5.

117. Act of March 3, 1911, sec. 250, 36 STAT. 1159.

118. American Security & Trust Co. v. District of Columbia, 224 U.S. 491 (1912).

119. Act of February 13, 1925, sec. 6(b), 43 STAT. 940.

120. Act of June 18, 1910, sec. 17, 36 STAT. 577.

121. Ex parte Young, 209 U.S. 123 (1908)

122. Act of February 13. 1925, sec. 6, 13, 43 STAT. 940, 942.

123. Act of October 7, 1913, 38 STAT. 220.

124. Act of August 24, 1937, sec. 3, 50 STAT. 752.

125. Testimony of Henry J. Friendly, Judge, Court of Appeals for the Second Circuit, quoted in Senate Report 94-204, p.6.

126. Quoted in Bennett Borkey and Eugene Gressman, "Recent Reforms in the Federal Judicial Structure — Three-Judge District Courts and Appellate Review", 67 F.R.D. 135, 140 (1976).

127. Act of August 12, 1976, 90 STAT. 1119.

128. In re Claasen, 140 U.S. 200 (1891).

129. Act of January 20, 1897, 29 STAT. 492.

130. THE JUDICIAL CODE OF THE UNITED STATES (Washington, 1913), in a note to section 238 made it clear that this change was made.

131. Act of April 22, 1908, 35 STAT. 65.

132. Howard v. Illinois Central Railroad Co., 207 U.S. 463 (1907).

133. Frankfurter and Landis, *supra,* note 27, p.207 has an extensive list of these cases.

134. Act of September 6, 1916, 39 STAT. 726. Mr. Justice McReynolds argued that this statute "may greatly increase" the number of petitions for certiorari. Furness, Withy & Co. v. Yanz-Tsze Insurance Co., 242 U.S. 430, 434 (1916).

135. 1916 ANNUAL REPORT U.S. ATTY. GENERAL 74; 1925 ANNUAL REPT.

U.S. ATTY. GENERAL 8. The following tables show the number of cases pending at the end of the term:

1914	524
1915	522
1916	532
1917	495
1918	408
1919	386
1920	343
1921	417
1922	368
1923	438
1924	533

136. Act of February 13, 1925, 43 STAT. 939.

137. William Howard Taft, "The Jurisdiction of the Supreme Court Under the Act of February 13, 1925", 35 YALE L. REV. 1 (1925).

138. Act of February 24, 1855, 10 STAT. 612; Act of March 3, 1863, sec. 5, 12 STAT. 766.

139. Gordon v. United States, 2 Wall. 561 (U.S. 1864).

140. Act of March 17, 1866, 14 STAT. 9.

141. United States v. Adam, 6 Wall. 101 (U.S. 1867).

142. Act of March 3, 1863, sec. 5, 12 STAT. 766.

143. Act of June 25, 1868, sec. 1, 2, 15 STAT. 75, United States v. Ayres, 9 Wall. 608 (U.S. 1869).

144. In re Zellner, 9 Wall. 245 (U.S. 1869).

145. Act of February 13, 1925, sec. 3, 43 STAT. 939.

146. Act of March 3, 1891, sec. 9, 26 STAT. 858.

147. Act of June 18, 1910, sec. 2, 36 STAT. 11.

148. Act of August 5, 1909, sec. 29, 36 STAT. 11.

149. Act of August 22, 1914, 38 STAT. 703.

150. Act of June 30, 1930, 48 STAT. 762.

151. Speech, Warren E. Burger, 1973 PROC. A.L.I. 25.

152. Act of December 21, 1974, 88 STAT. 1706; January 2, 1975, 88 STAT. 1917.

153. Report of the Study Group on the Caseload of the Supreme Court, 57 F.R.D. 573 (1973).

154. Act of October 13, 1972, PL 92-489, 86 STAT. 807; 1972 U.S. CODE CONG. & ADM. NEWS. 3602.

155. The Report of the Commission entitled, "Structure and Internal Procedure: Recommendations for Change", 67 F.R.D. 195, 236 (1976).

156. House Committee on the Judiciary. Subcommittee on Courts, Civil Liberties and the Administration of Justice. Hearings. Mandatory Appellate Jurisdiction of the Supreme Court Abolition of Civil Priorities, p.33.

160. *Ibid.,* p.22.

Chapter 22

PROCEDURE BEFORE THE UNITED STATES SUPREME COURT

The mechanics of initiating a suit before a court is not the kind of material that thrills historians or lawyers, yet this knowledge is essential during all periods in history, for these monotonous details occupy so much of the daily legal activity. In establishing the Supreme Court, the First Judiciary Act gave some details on seeking judicial review by the writ of appeal, the writ of error and certain original writs.[1] It would be inaccurate to use the term appeal, for this term had a technical meaning. The writs of appeal and error were known to colonial lawyers, especially in the decades preceding the Revolution, but the practice surrounding them was not well established in the American courts. Thus, when the Supreme Court was established, there was very little or no American precedent to follow, except that provided by English practice.

For guidance, the Supreme Court turned to the English legal literature. This will help to explain why the Supreme Court, at its August term in 1791, stated that the practice in the Court of King's Bench and of Chancery afforded "outlines for the practice of this court".[2] This rule made English books such as William Tidd's PRACTICE OF THE COURTS OF KING'S BENCH AND COMMON PLEAS, which incidentally was first published in 1790, an essential book for an American lawyer, in that it served as a guide to the legal niceties involved in each step.[3] The Court did not see the need to drop this rule until the revision of its rules in 1939, although it had previously been slightly changed to limit this guidance to "matters not covered by its rules or decisions, or the laws of Congress."[4]

It would be extremely tedious for a reader if changes in the steps necessary to get a case before the Supreme Court were presented in a chronological manner, for to follow this trend would require constant returning to the details that had been earlier discussed. Instead, the procedural steps that were required by practice during the first several decades of the Nineteenth Century were outlined without incumbering them with all the legal principles as would be found in a practice book. Changes were made in slow, incremental ways, and only after several decades or longer can these alterations be detected. In several situations, these steps were clarified or changed by statute.

The practice before any court is never precisely stated in the statute, but must be supplemented by rules or decisions. Important as these sources are, the bench with the help of that versatile court official — the clerk — is a repository of all the fine procedural points.[5] The Supreme Court's reliance on its clerk is evidenced by its directions to him on a number of matters including the preparation of procedures governing the issuance of the writ of certiorari. On occasion, the Court has sought his opinion regarding the practice governing a given set of circumstances. On one occasion, the clerk declared what the practice had been, but the Court failed to follow his directions.[6]

The First Judiciary Act gave the Supreme Court jurisdiction to review cases from the circuit courts by the writ of error.[7] A number of steps in the review process are specified which shaped appellate practice for decades. The attachments to the writ of error included "an authenticated transcript of the record, an assignment of errors, and prayer for reversal, with a citation to the adverse party," who must have had at least twenty days' notice.[8] For a case to be reviewed by the Court, the value in dispute must have exceeded $2,000, exclusive of costs. The judge signing the writ of error was required to take "good and sufficient security, that the plaintiff in error shall prosecute his writ to effect, and answer all damages and costs if he fails to make his plea good".

Further, the Supreme Court was limited in reversing a decision in several significant aspects. The first of these was that it could not issue a reversal for any error in fact, nor for any error in ruling on any plea in abatement, other than a plea to the jurisdiction of the Court or a plea to a petition or a bill in equity in the nature of a demurrer. The significance of this clause has been lost, since the petition to dismiss with its broader application has been substituted. Essentially, these were matters addressed to the discretion of the trial judge. The Court was authorized to render a judgment such as the district court should have rendered, but if they reversed a decision in favor of the original plaintiff, the case was to be remanded to the original court for a final decision. The procedure here was to issue a writ of *venire facias de novo* which directed the lower court to hold a new trial if the winning party was willing.[9] Also, the Supreme Court could not order an execution.

When a judgment was entered, the dissatisfied party's first step was to find a responsible person who would provide his "security". Security was defined a few years later as an amount sufficient to answer for all costs.[10] The writ of error, when issued in contrast to the writ of appeal, did not act as a supersedeas of the judgment. To alleviate this procedural flaw, the appellant could post a penalty bond in a sufficient amount to cover all damages recovered in the court below, "should the decision be affirmed within ten days after the judgment of the trial court was rendered."[11]

Obviously, many questions were raised in the courts about the sufficiency of the penalty bond and any other argument which the opposing party could raise. The Court provided no particular form for the bond, but through the use of formbooks, this soon became standardized. The bond was absolutely essential for the Court to hear the case, but this requirement gradually lost its impact.

It should be noted that this bond or security was not meant to cover any costs arising in the Supreme Court. The first step taken by the Court in requiring a bond to cover court costs of the appellant was in 1807, when security for costs was required of "all parties in this court, not being residents of the United States."[12] It was not until 1831 that the Court required that the clerk take a bond to respond to costs in the amount of $200 from the appellant.[13] This practice has continued until the present time.

The next step was to obtain a writ of error from the clerk of the circuit court and to prepare a citation to be served on the opposing party. In the first case in which a case was brought to the Supreme Court by a writ of error, the writ was issued from the office of the clerk of the Circuit Court for Rhode Island. It was objected that the writ had to be issued by the clerk of the Supreme Court, and in this argument the Court agreed.[14] This must have raised some questions in the minds of lawyers, for Congress in the following year provided by statute that the clerk of the Supreme Court would draft a form for the writ of error, which was to be approved by any two of the justices and transmitted to the clerk of the circuit courts, who would issue these writs under the seal of that court, returnable to the Supreme Court.[15]

To secure the writ of error to remove a case from the highest state court to the Supreme Court, it was necessary to prepare a petition setting forth the facts which would permit the review, and praying for the allowance of the writs and a citation from a federal judge or the judge of the state court from which the appeal was taken. If the judge was convinced of the sufficiency of the bond, he would endorse the writ. The bond had to be filed with the clerk of the court, along with the writ of error, in all cases. It should be noted that from the earliest decades, the writ was granted as a matter of right rather than at the discretion of the judge.

The next step in this process was to serve the citation upon the adverse party and attach an affidavit to the original, showing that this service was performed. After this was filed, the clerk of the court transmitted to the clerk of the Supreme Court a transcript of the record and copies of any other document necessary for the Court to understand correctly the questions in controversy. If the error complained of was clear on the face of the official documents, nothing else was necessary. However, if there was some question of the introduction of evidence, competency of witnesses, the overruling of a challenge, or the refusal of a demurrer to evidence, it was necessary to have a Bill of Exceptions. The Bill of Exceptions has passed into oblivion, and the legal rules governing its use have been all but forgotten.

All of these documents were described collectively as the return, and this had to be received by the Supreme Court during its following term or the cause would be dismissed on motion by the opposing party.[16]

However, the Court adopted a rule in 1803 that should the writ of error be issued within thirty days before the meeting of the Court, the defendant could enter his appearance or otherwise the case would be continued.[17] Later, the rule provided that the return had to be filed and placed upon the calendar by the sixth day.[18]

Once the case was on the docket of the Supreme Court, the moving attorney had another responsibility of ascertaining whether the return was complete and if not, of requesting a writ of certiorari to the court below to supply the deficiency. Either of the parties to suit could suggest such a defect in the record, which was technically known as a diminution. At first, it was customary to make the motion orally. A rule adopted in 1824 declared that certiorari would not be granted in the future unless a motion was made in writing and the facts on which it was founded, if not admitted by the other party, were verified by affidavit.[19] This motion had to be made at the first term of the entry of the cause or the writ of certiorari would not be granted unless the moving party satisfactorily accounted for the delay. All omissions from the record could not be supplied in fashion unless the judge before whom the case was tried certified that the matter was excepted at the trial.[20] This practice was dropped in the 1954 rules[21], but surely the need for a suggestion that the record was incomplete had ceased years before.

A wide range of matters could be raised on oral argument on motion day. The most frequent motions were those moving that the suit be dismissed for any number of technical reasons, such as the lack of a seal[22] or that the records did not agree with the names of the parties in the suit below.

Apparently, the Court continued to have difficulty in that attorneys failed to furnish a complete record. In 1823, the Court stated that it would not hear a case "until a complete record shall be filed, containing in itself, without references aliunde, all the papers, . . . necessary to the hearing in this court."[23] The term "by proof aliunde" meant that any deficiency in the record could not be supplied orally.

Apparently, the question of what constituted a record was not one that demanded much attention from the Court. The return, as the record was called in the Nineteenth Century practice, included all documents presented to the Court and entered as a matter of evidence. The citations were not a part of the record, for it formed "no part of the proceedings of the court below."[24] The Court held that whether there was a citation could "be proved aliunde." The marshal's return of death of the party to an execution did not make the fact of the death a matter of record.[25]

Another frequent question before the courts during the founding decades was the extent to which a writ of error could be amended. The First Judiciary Act clearly stated that "no summons, writ, declaration, return, process, judgment, or other proceedings in civil cases in any of the courts of the United States, shall be abated, arrested, quashed or reversed, for any defect or want of form".[26] In English practice, such amendments generally were not allowed, although allowed under a limited circumstance by an act of Parliament from the reign of George I. The Supreme Court decided that the writ of error was not amendable.[27] If the citation at the trial level was defective, the appearance of the opposing party on appeal constituted a waiver of any objection to irregular citation if no objection was made below.[28] Other questions such as insufficient jurisdiction were raised, but the Court held that the writ could not be dismissed because of a contested claim of the jurisdiction of the court below. Obviously, the purpose of the writ was to test that jurisdiction.[29] In 1838, the Supreme Court adopted a rule that all motions had to be in writing with a brief statement of the facts, and the object of the motion.[30] The Court continued having a motion day well into the Twentieth Century, but when it was officially discontinued is not clear.

One of the essentials of the writ was an assignment of errors and a prayer for reversal. This was to be annexed to the writ of error and returned with the transcript of the record, and it should be apparent that this had to be done by filing the assignment with the clerk of the trial court.[31] Apparently, this statutory requirement fell into disuse, for an early rule of the Court provided that the errors should be assigned as soon as the record was filed with the clerk "if errors shall not have been assigned in the court below".[32]

Since appellate procedure was in its infancy at the time the federal courts were established, one concern was whether an appeal was brought merely for the matter of delay. The First Judiciary Act gave the Supreme Court the authority to "adjudge or decree to the respondent in error just damages for his delay, and single or double cost at their discretion."[33] In 1803, the Court adopted a rule providing that if the writ of error was for the purpose of delay, "damages shall be awarded, at the rate of ten per centum per annum on the amount of the judgment".[34] The application of this rule was later limited to calculating the damages to the day of the judgment of the Supreme Court.[35] The normal rate of interest allowed was six per cent. The awarding of the interest for delay was a matter within the discretion of the Supreme Court, and it could not be awarded by the court below.[36] In 1876, a rule was amended to provide that should a writ of error to a state court be "so frivolous as not to need further argument," a motion to affirm in addition to the motion to dismiss could be requested.[37] This rule was later extended to encompass either writ.[38] It is unfortunate that some method of control of frivolous appeals is not similarly applied in modern appellate practice.

The practice of establishing a jurisdictional amount was slightly confusing. It was the responsibility of the moving party to show "to the satisfaction of this court, that the matter in dispute exceeds the sum or value of two thousand dollars exclusive of costs".[39] It should be noted that this was an order issued in a specific case, but it was not included in the compilations of the rules. It appears that the Court had become dependent upon the amount in controversy appearing in the pleadings or evidence in the record, and where in some cases such value was not clearly ascertainable, an affidavit could be produced.[40] This dependence upon amounts involved as a basis for jurisdiction was abolished with the establishment of the writ of certiorari, but continued to apply in cases where a direct appeal was permitted from the circuit and district courts.

Appeals in admiralty to the Supreme Court were always treated slightly differently throughout the Nineteenth Century than were those in other areas. In all admiralty cases, the Supreme Court could issue a commission to take new evidence upon interrogatories filed by the parties applying for the commission.[41] The issuance of an order for purposes of taking depositions was not a matter of course. Such commissions were awarded where the evidence was contradictory and ambiguous.[42] The practice was to hear the appeal and then decide if additional evidence was necessary.[43] In all cases except admiralty, interest was awarded on the judgment from the date of the judgment below until it was paid.[44]

The next step that altered the procedure before the Supreme Court was the establishment of the Circuit Courts of Appeals in 1891.[45] Although this statute provided for certain matters which could be reviewed by the newly created courts, still a greater number of cases remained totally within the realm of the Supreme Court's jurisdiction on either appeal or writ of error. The review of cases by using the two historic writs was to be displaced, for nothing changed the procedural practices of the courts as greatly as did the provision authorizing the Supreme Court "by certiorari or otherwise" to review those matters which were made final in the Circuit Courts of Appeal. Although the writ of certiorari was as old as the writs of error and appeal, it did provide a simpler method of procedure. The drafters of this statute apparently knew the implication of this writ and how it had been used to bring cases before the reviewing courts at its discretion regardless of the stage reached in the litigation process.[46]

The writ of certiorari was not initially introduced in 1891, for it had been used in the previous century, chiefly to supply imperfections in the records of cases already before the courts.[47] The writ was first used in 1797 for the purpose of supplying notice of a defect in the record or technically to supply a dimunition of the record.[48] This practice was abolished by the rules adopted in 1954, although it may be concluded that the practice had been discontinued much earlier.[49]

Historically, the writ was used in some state courts as well as in English courts to bring a case before the court issuing the writ in whatever stage the litigation had reached at the time the writ was issued for final disposition. In other words, a writ could have been used to bring up a case for trial. It was never used for that purpose by the Supreme Court, although on one occasion the Supreme Court noted that when a case was brought up by a writ of certiorari, the Court had complete jurisdiction to decide all issues. An interesting illustration of this procedure was in a case where a defendant had been cited for contempt because he insisted on bringing suit against a bank in the hands of a receiver instead of its former officers. He had acquired a judgment from a state court that directed the receiver to turn over certain funds to the lower court. The Supreme Court held on the writ of certiorari that it could decide whether the defendant had a right to use the name of the bank in suing out a writ of error and to decide all those questions exclusively within its control.[50]

It would be reasonable to assume since certiorari would become the predominant method of the Court reviewing a case, the justices would be interested in what changes this would cause in their practice. But, if such concerns existed, it is not apparent from action in drafting new rules or from dicta in opinions. Speculation would lead to the conclusion that such a matter was discussed informally. At that point in time, the Court was more concerned in clearing its calendar of cases which belonged in the Circuit Court of Appeals, for the declared purpose of the statute "was to facilitate the prompt disposition of cases in the Supreme Court, and to relieve it of the enormous overburden of suits and cases resulting from the rapid growth of the country and the steady increase of its litigations."[51] The court wasted no time in implementing this aspect of the statute.

The justices may not have perceived the changes that the writ of certiorari would bring. The Supreme Court, immediately upon the passage of the statute of 1891, issued rules governing the assignment of error when a case was brought up from the district or the circuit courts.[52] A rule governing certification of questions by the Circuit Court of Appeals was promulgated, but in these four new rules, the writ of certiorari was not mentioned. However, the clerk, probably at the direction of the Court, issued a circular which prescribed in detail the procedure for filing for the writ of certiorari and what such a petition had to contain.[53] All motions for the granting of the writ of certiorari were made on Monday, the motion day for the court, in open court without argument.

Between 1891 and 1925, the practice of issuing a writ of certiorari was developed by the Supreme Court, as the statute of 1891 did not spell out any standards. One explanation for the 34 year lapse is that few petitions for certiorari were presented to the Court. In the October term of 1915, the Court received fifty-four petitions for certiorari, but an increase in that number was foreseen when the Circuit Courts of Appeal received part of the Supreme Court's former jurisdiction.[54] Six terms later, 420 petitions were filed.[55]

In many decisions during this period, the Supreme Court stressed the necessity of uniformity among the Circuit Courts of Appeal. The Court decided that it did not need to wait until a final determination was made by a Circuit Court of Appeals before issuing a writ. The Court emphatically announced that its power to issue a writ of certiorari "extends to every case pending in the circuit court of appeals and may be exercised at any time during such pendency, provided the case is one which but for this provision of the statute, would be finally determined in that court."[56]

The importance of a forceful argument in the petition for certiorari was emphasized by the outline of the steps taken by the Court in considering their disposition of the request. Every petition went to each of the justices who examined them and each case was separately considered in conference. The Court was not aided by oral arguments and had to rely upon the petition and supporting briefs. "Unless these are carefully prepared, contain *appropriate* references to the record, and present with *studied accuracy, brevity and clearness* whatever is essential to ready and adequate understanding of points requiring our attention," the petition would probably be denied.[57] [Italics added by the Court.]

If the writ were granted, the brief in support of the writ became the basis for consideration by the Court. For some time after 1891, the practice followed was that the clerk of the Supreme Court would issue a writ of certiorari to the lower court commanding it to send up a certified transcript of the record. If the transcript had been filed with the writ of certiorari, the lower court would return the writ with a stipulation that the record was already on file. Since the case had already been filed and placed upon the docket, the only further steps needed were for the petitioner to file a complete and new brief or a supplement to the brief filed in support of the petition.[58] The case would be called in order as filed on the docket.

A factor which made the consideration of practice surrounding the writ of certiorari a necessity in 1925 was the adoption of the Judges Bill which further limited the cases in which the Supreme Court would review by writ of error or appeal.[59] With the anticipated increase in the number of petitions for the writ of certiorari, the Court used the rules as an opportunity to "indicate the character of reasons which will be considered" in granting the writ.[60] These reasons had been suggested in previous decisions, but it was the first time they were stated in the form of a rule. These rules also made a change in the method by which the application would be considered, in that after a period of two to three weeks after the first motion day, the clerk would submit the record and brief to the Court for its consideration. Hence, the practice of moving for a writ of certiorari on motion day was abolished.

As the number of appeals to the Supreme Court were limited in other statutes between 1925 and the present, the practice surrounding the granting of the writ has solidified. Presently, a petition for a writ of certiorari is presented to the Court, and if the request is granted, the case is placed upon the calendar and the parties present briefs. Finally, when the case is reached by the Court, the attorneys may appear to present an oral argument. This is certainly a more direct procedure than those under the original writs of error or appeal. Later rules have prescribed the size of the printed documents, the color of the covers, time limits for oral arguments, and similar details, but in essence, the basic steps are settled. Whereas the procedure before the Court has become less complex, the rules surrounding the administration of the review have become more complex.

The Court has commented upon the use of the writ of certiorari, arguing generally that its use to review cases was broader than the use in the English common law courts. The Court stated on several occasions that the writ had not been used as freely as by the Court of King's Bench in England.[61] It was never used to bring up an issue from any inferior court, although the First Judiciary Act would seem to have sanctioned its use as fully as at common law.[62] The Court very early established the principle that certiorari would not be used to bring a case merely because of a defect of jurisdiction, and some of the justices implied that it would not be used in federal courts to change venue in the case when a fair trial was possible.[63] Whether the use of the writ of certiorari to bring cases up from the Circuit Courts of Appeal was broader or narrower than the English practice is a matter beyond resolution. The purpose of this writ

> was intended to vest in this court a comprehensive and unlimited power. The power thus given is not affected by the condition of the case as it exists in the Court of Appeals. It may be exercised before or after any decision by that court and irrespective of any ruling or determination therein.[64]

Oral argument in the American appellate courts today is limited in time, but this has not always been the situation. For most of the first century of the Court's existence, no time limit on the oral argument was imposed. During the same period, attorneys would appear to make various motions and to argue them as well. It was a grand occasion when such legal giants as Daniel Webster, William Pinkney, William Wirt and many others argued cases and the public attended to hear these oral arguments.[65] The case of *Rose v. Himely* was argued for nine days by a total of ten lawyers.[66] The legal arguments recorded in the reports do not capture the eloquence of the speakers or the prose of the arguments.

The first time limitation on arguments was imposed by the Supreme Court in 1812 when a rule was adopted limiting the number of counsel for each side to two.[67] In the famous case of *McCullough v. Maryland*, this rule was dispensed with because of the great public importance of the constitutional question. The Court, speaking through Justice Story on February 1, 1844, asked counsel to curtail their argument in view of the congestion of the Court's docket.[68] In 1848, the time of argument was limited to two hours for each counsel to a case. This meant that in some cases the argument could extend over an eight hour period by allowing two representatives from each side to speak for two hours each. A modification of this was adopted in 1872 when counsel was limited to two hours for each side.[69] Two hours of argument were continued until 1911 when the court made a more elaborate rule concerning time. Normally, the time limit was one and a half hours except for certain cases, such as those certified from the circuit court or those involving the question of the jurisdiction of the court below where argument was limited to forty-five minutes per party.[70] Time was again limited in 1954 to thirty minutes for the summary docket and one hour for all other cases and in 1970, a thirty minute period was imposed on all arguments.[71] Traditionally, Chief Justice Hughes, who served as chief justice from 1930 to 1941, was very strict about the time limit and was known to stop counsel in the middle of an argument.[72]

Another unique area of appellate jurisdiction was a provision conferred upon the Supreme Court by Section 25 of the First Judiciary Act. This review was established to provide for a review of federal constitutional claims raised in the state courts, as few of these questions could initially be brought in the federal courts due to their limited jurisdiction. This provision provided for a review by a writ of error from a final judgment or a decree in the highest court of the state where the question of the validity of a treaty, statute or state constitution was declared repugnant to the Constitution of the United States. There were several differences in appellate procedure under this provision. No mention was made of a monetary amount in this section, but jurisdiction was based upon the questions set forth in the statute.[73] Further, this jurisdiction extended to civil and criminal cases.[74] Finally, the citation had to be signed by the justices of the Supreme Court of the United States who were judges of the circuit courts or by the judge of the highest court in the state. The writ of error to a state court was not a matter of right, but was based upon a determination of whether those questions prescribed by statute were raised in the state court and were evidenced upon the face of the record.[75]

Judicial review in this area was governed by the same technical rules of what constituted a record as applied in the practice governing the writ of error. When the question of whether the report of the decision of the judge who tried the case should be a part of the record was raised, it was decided that it should. A written decision, although required by state law or custom, was not a special verdict or an agreed statement of fact submitted for the judgment of the Court. Such a decision was described as *in pais* which meant that it was made without legal proceedings.[76] The decisions defining what constitutes the record are numerous, and in 1836 Justice Story attempted to address this issue without success.[77]

Another trend adopted by the Supreme Court in governing such an appeal was the question of whether the pleadings should state the precise section of the Constitution which the petitioner felt was being violated. The Court decided that judicial notice could be taken of anything in the Constitution and that neither the defendant nor the plaintiff had to make a precise reference to the Constitution in the pleadings.[78] Interestingly enough, the jurisdiction of the Supreme Court did not extend to the same issues raised in a territory.[79]

In 1867, Congress restated the jurisdiction of the Supreme Court over appeals from the state courts. This statute brought about two important changes. Under the Act of 1789, after a judgment, the Supreme Court had to remand the case to the appropriate state court. If the state court did not follow the directions of the Supreme Court, it could then be brought up on writ of error and the Supreme Court could proceed to a final decision and award execution. The Act of 1867 made it possible for the Supreme Court to exercise its discretion and to render a final judgment and award an execution in the first instance. Secondly, under the Act of 1789, the Supreme Court was confined to matters appearing on the record as understood at common law, but this restriction was removed by the Act of 1864.[80] This statute was amended again in 1875 without significant change.[81]

Briefs

The documents most closely associated with the appellate process are known as the records and briefs or the points and briefs. The formal contents of these documents as they are now prescribed by rules were not known when the Supreme Court was organized. In tracing this development, the distinction must be maintained during the earlier decades of the Nineteenth Century between the record and a statement of the points to be argued. The brief was a later development.

The first step in this evolution was taken on February 4, 1795, when the Supreme Court gave notice "to the gentlemen of the bar" that they expected to be furnished with a statement of the material points of the case from each counsel.[82] A distinction had to be made between the statutory requirements of the assignment of errors and the points to be argued, for these were two separate documents.

It would be interesting to know how prevalent this rule was in the contemporary state courts. The Supreme Court of Pennsylvania, as early as 1786, required the parties to prepare in writing the points in controversy and deliver two copies to the court.[83] In 1807, the Superior Court of Connecticut adopted a similar rule,[84] and such requirements were common in the early decades of the Nineteenth Century in other courts.

The record gives some hints that on occasions, during this early period, counsel failed to provide the points to be argued. On one occasion, Chief Justice Marshall called for a written statement from the defendant in error, but the defendant expressed his belief that the rule applied only to the plaintiff in error. The Court corrected this erroneous assumption by stating that such a statement was expected from all parties. A note states that no statements were prepared for this argument. The Chief Justice then informed the gentlemen of the bar that "unless statements of the case are furnished according to the rule, the causes must either be dismissed or continued."[85] At least one case was dismissed by the court for failure of counsel to furnish such a statement.[86]

The first time that the term "brief" was used by the Supreme Court was in 1821 in an order or rule. The brief had to be printed and had to contain "the substance of all the material pleadings, facts, and documents on which the parties relied and the points of law and the facts intended to be presented at the argument."[87] This was the first time that it was required that the briefs be printed and that the facts be included. Through this rule, the Court had taken a first step towards adopting the modern concept of a brief.

In 1833, the Court made possible the submission of cases without the need of oral argument by the use of the "printed argument". The Supreme Court stated that it would "accommodate counsel and save expenses to the party, to submit cases upon printed arguments". It was up to the counsel on both sides to choose whether to submit a case on brief only. Either side could decide to rely upon the printed brief and these cases were treated the same as other materials.[88] This established a precedent for later considering applications for the writ of certiorari on printed briefs without oral argument.

This practice of submitting a case for consideration without oral argument was reinforced by a 1837 rule, which provided that when a printed argument was filed, the case stood on the same basis as if counsel appeared.[89] This rule was later modified to permit one of the parties to submit its case by argument.[90] It was envisioned by these rules that the printed argument was in substitution for the oral argument.

The popularity of this practice has varied. By 1881, the practice of considering some cases on submission of briefs and dispensing with oral arguments had become prevalent, for the Attorney General noted in his annual report that the Supreme Court in the October term of 1880, considered 93 cases submitted on printed arguments.[91]

This practice fell into disfavor, but was retained in the rules until 1954. In the revision of the rules that year, the Court stated that it looked with disfavor on any submission without oral argument.[92] Rarely are cases presented to the Supreme Court without arguments, although this has become a frequent practice in the state courts and in many of the United States Courts of Appeals.

The rules of 1884 made some significant changes in the required contents of the brief. The contents of the briefs were specified as containing a concise abstract of the "questions involved and the amount in which they are raised" in addition to a specification of the errors relied upon.[93] For the first time, the argument was specified to be a part of the brief, where it was required that a clear statement of the points of law with references to the pages of the record and authorities relied upon to support each one, was to be a part of the brief. If a statute of a state was essential to the argument, the text of such statutes was to be included.

The defendants in error were required to file their briefs at least three days before the case was called for argument, but they could omit specifications of errors and a statement of the case unless the statement in the brief of the opposition was controverted. The rules of 1884 required counsel for plaintiff in error to file twenty-five copies of a printed brief with the court at least six days before argument. Interestingly, the opposing counsel was to be furnished a copy upon "application".[94] With each revision of the rules, the contents of the brief were specified in greater detail. This change is apparent when the rules of 1884 are compared to those of 1954.

Rarely has such a mundane document presented to any court created such a sensation as did the Brandeis Brief. In the case of *Muller v. Oregon*, Louis Brandeis appeared as the counsel for the State of Oregon and in his brief introduced a sociological analysis of the effect of labor upon women as a possible solution to the constitutional issue presented.[95] The brief includes two pages of legal argument and over one hundred pages of evidence from reports of commissions and inspectors of factories supporting the thesis that long hours were dangerous to the health of women. Brandeis strongly supported the need for this type of evidence, stating,

A judge rarely performs his functions adequately unless the case before him is adequately presented. Thus were the blind led by the blind. It is not surprising that under such conditions the laws as administered failed to meet contemporary economic and social demands.[96]

The influence of this type of brief on the court has been questioned. Language will be found in the *Muller* decision which justifies the conclusion that the eight-hour law for women would have been sustained even without the support of such evidence.[97] Courts have long stated that judicial notice is taken of all matters of general knowledge. The Brandeis Brief is believed to be the first brief containing this type of evidence, which was not specifically used in the trial court.

The early documents speak of the clerk of a district or circuit court sending "up the record" to the Supreme Court. It is doubtful that this meant literally that the original documents from the trial court were forwarded to the Supreme Court, as was done in some jurisdictions where the reviewing court met in the same building as the trial court. This was definitely clarified in 1797 by a statement that the clerk of the court to which any writ of error was directed would transmit a copy, not the original, of the record and all proceedings in the case.[98] Later rules specified the time in which the record had to be filed. However, the original papers could be sent up when "in the opinion of the presiding judge in any circuit, or district court" the original papers should be inspected by the Supreme Court. The presiding judge would make such rules for the safekeeping, transportation and return of the original paper as he saw proper. However, this did not replace the transcript of the proceedings.[99] Apparently, there is some question as to whether the record could be supplemented orally, and this was clarified in 1823, when the Court stated that no cause would be heard unless a complete record "without reference *aliunde*" was supplied.[100] In the early days of the Court, the printed record consisted of all the pleadings and other papers filed in the court below. Rarely was a separate document such as the Bill of Exceptions filed, but it was included in the record. The only change that has taken place is the inclusion of the transcript of testimony given in the trial court which has become a part of the record, and the precise date that this took place is not ascertainable. Because the printing of the record was supervised by the clerk, the size of the document tended to be uniform. The rules of 1954 were the first to specify the size of both briefs and records.[101]

From the founding of the courts, it was the responsibility of the clerk to oversee the preparation of the record. Thus in 1831, when the Court first required the records to be printed, the clerk was directed to have fifteen copies of the record printed for the Court. Plaintiff was required to deposit a sum of $200 to cover the costs, and the clerk was to deliver a copy to both parties and tax both parties for the cost of the copy.[102] Justice Baldwin dissented from the adoption of these rules in which he traced the history of awarding costs and argued that the Court did not have the authority to tax costs unless authorized by some statute.[103] In the January term of 1831, the Attorney General of the United States applied to the Court to take the original papers and have them printed. He stated that he understood that it was a habit of the clerk to charge only half fees. However, Chief Justice Marshall stated that the clerk was entitled to certain fees for a manuscript copy. In rules adopted in 1882, the clerk's responsibility was to supervise the printing and to index the printed copy for one half the fees.[104] The devious custom of charging both parties for a manuscript, although none was made, enriched many court clerks.

One of the new components added to the brief in 1928 was the requirement for a jurisdictional statement in cases brought up on appeals. One of those erroneous impressions which was generally believed in the legal profession was that review was obligatory and that an appeal was a matter "as of right". Because of this erroneous assumption, the entry on many cases brought up by a writ of error from state courts was "dismissed for want of jurisdiction." The rule adopted in 1928 required a written statement disclosing the basis for the jurisdiction. Since oral motions were becoming the exception rather than the general rule, the written statement was expected to explain why the court had the jurisdiction.[105]

Reference has been made to the decline of the classic motion day, which was a procedural feature of every court. It is not clear whether the Supreme Court had established such a practice before 1824. It ordered that on Saturdays, when the Court was sitting, motions which were not required to be put upon the docket would be received. The moving party had to make his motion before the Court began hearing the assigned cases. If it seemed strange that the Court would be sitting on Saturdays, this is understandable as the justices came to Washington for the purpose of holding sessions of the Supreme Court and immediately after the conclusion of the term returned to their homes. The Court was anxious to accomplish as much work as possible in a short period of time. [106] In 1858, the motion day was changed to Friday, and in 1884 to Monday. [107] This remained the practice until 1954 when it was declared that "no motion shall be presented in open court other than a motion for admission to the bar, except when the proceedings to which it refers is being argued". [108] By 1962, one authority could write that "motions do not play an important part in Supreme Court practice". This author states that "few motions are necessary . . . and most of these are concerned with matters of procedure or form which do not go to the merits or substance of a case and are often uncontested". [109]

Supreme Court Rules

Although it is the current custom to look to the rules of a particular court for guidance to its practice, the Supreme Court of the United States managed for several decades without preparing a comprehensive set of rules. During this period, the Court was content to issue individual orders or rules which were entered into a special record. If the first justices saw the need for a body of rules as a guide to its practice, no mention was made in the available documents. Until 1954, the practice before the Court was never fully reflected by the rules.

However, the members of the Court became acutely aware of the need to provide for administrative functions through some type of official action. At the Court's second meeting on February 3, 1790, its first order required the clerk to keep his office at the seat of government and not practice as an attorney in the Court while he continued as clerk. [110] This became the first rule and the text remained essentially unchanged for over a century.

The authority of the Court to issue rules was recognized by statute and has never been seriously challenged. The First Judiciary Act authorized the Supreme Court and all other federal courts, "to make and establish all necessary rules for the orderly conducting [of] business". [111] The only limitation upon this power was that the rules could not violate the laws of the United States. The Court recognized as another limitation that it could not by rule enlarge or restrict its own jurisdiction or those of other courts of the United States. [112]

In addition to the authority under the statute of 1789, Congress directed the Court to prepare rules to govern procedure of cases coming to it for special circumstances. For example, the statute that created the

Court of Claims stated that an appeal from the court could be made under such rules and regulations as established by the Supreme Court.[113] In response to the extension of the federal jurisdiction by habeas corpus, the Court issued rules governing the holding of prisoners and other details.

What prompted the issuance of a particular order or rule can not be readily determined from any existing documents. In interpreting the rule which provided that the Bill of Exceptions could not contain the charge of the Court at large unless there was an exception to the whole charge, Chief Justice Waite stated that this rule was promulgated for the purpose of giving "substantial effect" to a long line of decisions.[114] Some of the earlier rules were promulgated by the Court from the bench without drafting or meaningful consideration and often in response to a particular practice arising on that occasion.

Some confusion arose as to what constituted a rule of the Court. The first eighteen rules issued before 1803 all began with the statement "It is ordered" and generally with the additional phrase "by this Court". It is understandable why confusion should exist over what was properly a rule when the Court used terms such as "General Rule" as a title for a decision.[115] The fact that many rules began with "It is ordered" will explain why Rule 24 containing the allotment of justices to the circuits in 1812, is the only occasion when this assignment was included as a rule. Later collections of the rules would generally substitute or add a footnote as to the current assignments of the justices.

It should not come as a surprise, considering the nature of its decision-making, that the Court has never expressed an opinion on the role of the rules in controlling its practice. However, justices have dissented over the adoption of a particular rule as did Justice Baldwin when Rule 37 was adopted in 1831. His was the first such dissent. This rule provided that the moving party would pay for one copy of the record, and in the event of dismissal of the suit, each party would be charged one half the costs. Justice Baldwin felt that the Court did not have the authority to adopt a rule of this nature since costs were penal in nature and should be based upon statutory authorization.[116] Several justices since have followed Baldwin's example.

Although the right of the Court to prescribe rules was recognized, the Court was slow in taking action. It occasionally issued an order or rule to clarify procedural matters, and these rules were published individually in the official reports. Each reporter of the decision would collect the rules and publish them in the first volume of his series.[117] In addition, the rules of the Supreme Court were often published with the rules of other federal courts or local courts and in practice books.

The rules were first numbered in the collection made in 1803 by William Cranch, the reporter. The practice of numbering the rules sequentially was not immediately established until 1810 with Rule 23. Although the same number was generally designated to the same rule until

1858, this does not imply that the numbering system was precise or that the numbers corresponded with the same rules in the compilations made by each of the reporters. Two of the rules were omitted from the compilations made by Wheaton and Peters because they had not been entered with the other rules by the clerk of the Court at the time of their adoption.[118] Because of these inconsistencies, it is apparent that confusion arose as to what rules were included. However, one should not conclude that these rules were of so little importance, for the texts were included in many books on federal practice at that time and in collections of local rules.[119]

To end this confusion, the Court, on February 4, 1859, directed its clerk, W. T. Carroll, to collect "all the rules adopted by this Court" and specified that those rules that were in force be arranged under appropriate headings.[120] A later chief justice stated that Chief Justice Taney was responsible for initiating this step.[121] Since the rules are merely reorganized and put under headings, there was little significant change. The rules of 1859 clarified some practices and introduced some minor procedural changes.[122]

One may express disappointment that the opportunity to extensively revise the rules and make them more explicit was neglected, but such a total revision had to wait for nearly a century. It is arguable that court rules at this time did not reflect the practice before any court, for the number of lawyers involved was limited and this small group would have been familiar with the outlines of practices and the wishes of the Court. Besides, it was an old legal adage: "ask the clerk!" who was the repertoire of all practice.

The next revision after 1859 by the Court of its rules was in 1884.[123] During the previous thirty year period, a number of amendments had been adopted, but other factors were slowly precipitating major changes which would significantly modify the practice of the Court. The increase in the number of cases coming before the Court was such a factor. Another was the statutory authority to prescribe fees for the clerk.[124] This was the first time the fees that the clerk could charge were incorporated into the rules. The chief innovation of these rules was the establishment of the contents for a brief.[125] Other than these two examples, this compilation of the rules accomplished little more than incorporating amendments. The rules have the same numbers as were assigned in 1858, and new matters were incorporated as additional rules were added at the end.

The rules were slightly modified again in 1911, but events were slowly causing further changes.[126] In 1925, the Judges Act was adopted and since this statute limited significantly the number of cases coming to the Supreme Court by an appeal, changes in the rules became a necessity.[127] Such matters as certification of the questions by the Court of Claims and review of decisions of the Supreme Court of the Philippine Islands by certiorari had to be accommodated.

The most significant changes in the rules for 1925 were in the matter of admission to practice before the courts, new requirements concerning the size and contents of the printed brief, and the new rules governing certiorari. [128] The time limit on oral argument was established according to the purpose of the presentation. [129] This was the first time the summary docket was mentioned. [130] The sequence of other rules was changed. Obviously, these rules were adapted from previous rules and practices and some changes were made necessary by new statutes.

The most consequential addition to the rules was number 35, entitled "Review on writ of certiorari of decisions of state courts, circuit courts and Court of Appeals of the District of Columbia." This was the first rule that the Court adopted which specifically addressed the practice of review by the writ which has become the chief means of getting a case heard by the Court. An unusual feature was the reference to decisions in the rule concerning the practice governing the issuance of the petition for the writ. No particular form was prescribed for this application, but a statement of the facts involved and reasons relied on for the allowance of the writ were essential. The understatement in the rule was "A supporting brief may be included in the petition." The most interesting part was the summary of reasons for the Court to grant the writ which has remained a part of the rules ever since. A special provision governing the issuance of the writ from the Court of Appeals of the District of Columbia was necessary until that court was recognized as the equivalent of any other Court of Appeals in the federal system.

Three years later, the statute abolishing the distinction between the writ of error and the writ of appeal made necessary changes in the rules. [131] The wording of the rules had to reflect the abolition of any vestiges of much difference.

The most complete and thorough revision of the Supreme Court rules was made in 1954. [132] This thorough revision may be explained by the success of the Federal Rules of Civil and Criminal Procedure—an entirely new concept in American jurisprudence whereby practice was prescribed by rules prepared and, when necessary, amended by the highest court. After several decades of Congress refusing to act, the Supreme Court was finally given authority to prescribe rules of civil and criminal procedure to govern the practice in the district courts. To prepare these rules, the Court had appointed an advisory committee. In revising its own rules, the Supreme Court acted on that precedent by establishing a similar committee consisting of justices, lawyers and academics. The objective of the committee was to have the rules reflect more accurately the practice before the Court.

The Court took the opportunity to drop obsolete materials such as the rule stating that the practice of the Court of King's Bench would afford "outlines for the practice of this court in matters not covered by rules or decisions or the Laws of Congress" and many similar obsolete rules. [133]

The rules were again revised in 1967 at which time the period for perfecting a writ of certiorari was reduced by eliminating the period of 60 days between final judgment and notice of applying for the writ. Other modifications were made in the mechanics of the filing of the record and other aspects of the procedure. In recognition of newer technology in reproducing the printed documents, the rules accepted these newer forms of reproduction in substitution for printing. [134]

The rules of the Supreme Court were again modified in 1970 to reflect changes in practice relating to the number of copies to be filed, the elimination of the requirement of filing the record from the court below with the application for review, and the adoption of a noon recess. The time allowed for argument of each case was reduced to thirty minutes unless extended upon a timely request to the Court, which was probably the most important change. [135]

Again, in 1980, the Court adopted a new set of rules which most importantly dictated the colored code for the various types of documents presented to the Court. In addition, there was a significant increase in the fees charged by the clerk. [136] None of the rules since 1954 have changed materially the practice before the Court, but rather have added more details to many matters. Administrative matters had to be accommodated by rules such as those prohibiting law clerks from practicing before the Court for a period of time. Now that the Court has become accustomed to legislating by rules, future developments will address more administrative matters and add refinements to the practice.

FOOTNOTES TO CHAPTER 22

1. Act of September 24, 1789, sec. 13, 1 STAT. 80.

2. Sup. Ct. Rule 7, August 8, 1791; This was the third term of the court. *See* Erwin C. Surrency, "Minutes of the Supreme Court of the United States," 5 AMER. J. LEG. HIST. 67, 79 (1961).

3. *See* Argument of Counsel in Mussina v. Cavazos, 6 Wall. 355 (U.S. 1867).

4. Sup. Ct. Rule 4, 1925, 266 U.S. 655.

5. Winchester v. Jackson et al., 3 Cranch 515 (U.S. 1806);

6. Ex parte Bradstreet, 4 Pet. 102 (U.S. 1830).

7. Act of September 24, 1789, sec. 22, 1 STAT. 84.

8. Act of September 24, 1789, sec. 22, 1 STAT. 84.

9. Alfred Conkling, A TREATISE ON THE ORGANIZATION AND PRACTICE OF THE COURTS OF THE UNITED STATES (1864), 4th ed., p.674; M'Lanahan v. Universal Insurance Co., 1 Pet. 165, 192 (U.S. 1828).

10. Act of December 12, 1794, 1 STAT. 404.

11. Cartlet v. Brodie, 9 Wheat. 553 (U.S. 1824).

12. Sup. Ct. Rule 21, February Term, 1807, 4 Cranch 561 (U.S. 1807).

13. Sup. Ct. Rule 37, January Term, 1831, 5 Pet. 724 (U.S. 1831).

14. West v. Barnes, 2 Dall. 401 (U.S. 1791).

15. Act of May 8, 1782, sec. 9, 1 STAT. 278.

16. The Steamer Virginia v. West, 19 How. 182 (U.S. 1856); Bacon et al v. Hart, 1 Black. 38 (U.S. 1861); Mesa v. The United States, 2 Black. 721 (U.S. 1862).

17. Sup. Ct. Rule 16, February Term, 1803.

18. Sup. Ct. Rule 19, 3 Cranch 240 (U.S. 1806).

19. Sup. Ct. Rule 32, 9 Wheat 13 (U.S. 1824).

20. Stimpson v. West Chester Railroad Co., 3 How. 553 (U.S. 1845).

21. Sup. Ct. Rule 32, 346 U.S. 981. In Hannis Taylor, JURISDICTION AND PROCEDURE OF THE SUPREME COURT OF THE UNITED STATES (1905), p.567, these three steps from the informal suggestion, and then the formal petition to the petition for leave to file.

22. Mussina v. Cavazos, 6 Wall. 355, 363 (U.S. 1867).

23. Sup. Ct. Rule 31, 8 Wheat. 17 (U.S. 1823).

24. Innerarity v. Byrne, 5 How. 295 (U.S. 1847).

25. Walden's Lessee v. Craig's Heirs, 14 Pet. 147, 152 (U.S. 1840).

26. Act of September 24, 1789, sec. 32, 1 STAT. 91.

27. Hodge v. Williams, 22 How. 87 (U.S. 1859); 5 Geo. I, c.13.

28. Chaffee v. Hayward, 20 How. 208 (U.S. 1851).

29. The Steamer Brigadier-General R.H. Stokes, 22 How. 48 (U.S. 1859).

30. Sup. Ct. Rule 51, 12 Pet. 4 (U.S. 1838).

31. Act of September 24, 1789, sec. 22, 1 STAT. 84.

32. Conkling, *supra*, note 9, p.663. *See* Mussina v. Carazos, 6 Wall. 355, 359 (U.S. 1867), where Justice Miller acknowledges that the general practice had been not to assign errors or ask for reversal with the record. Sup. Ct. Rule 19 (1806).

33. Act of September 24, 1789, sec. 23, 1 STAT. 85.

34. Sup. Ct. Rule 17, February Term, 1803.

35. Sup. Ct. Rule 20, February Term, 1808. This rule was incorporated into the Rules of 1858 (Rule 23), and 1884 (Rule 23).

36. Boyce's Executors v. Grundy, 9 Pet. 275, 289-90 (U.S. 1835).

37. Sup. Ct. Rule 6, 91 U.S. 4 (1876).

38. Sup. Ct. Rule 6, 108 U.S. 576 (1884).

39. Sup. Ct. Rule 13 (1800).

40. Richmond v. City of Milwaukee, 21 How. 391 (1858); Red River Cattle Co. v. Needham, 137 U.S. 632, 635 (1890).

41. Sup. Ct. Rule 27, February Term, 1817.

42. The Samuel, 1 Wheat. 9, 16 (U.S. 1816).

43. The London Packet, 2 Wheat. 371 (U.S. 1817).

44. Sup. Ct. Rule LXIII, 16 How. v (U.S. 1853); Hemmenway v. Fisher, 20 How. 255 (U.S. 1857).

45. Act of March 2, 1891, 26 STAT. 826.

46. Erwin C. Surrency, "The Development of the Appellate Function: The Pennsylvania Experience," 20 AMER. J. LEG. HIST. 173, 176 (1976).

47. Conkling, *supra,* note 9, p.652.

48. Fenemore v. United States, 3 Dall. 357 (U.S. 1797).

49. Supreme Court Rule 32, 396 U.S. 981.

50. Ex parte Chetwood, 165 U.S. 443 (1896).

51. McLish v. Roff, 141 U.S. 661, 666 (1891). *See also* Hannis Taylor, JURISDICTION AND PROCEDURE OF THE SUPREME COURT OF THE UNITED STATES (1905), p.154.

52. 139 U.S. 705 (1891).

53. 210 U.S. 503, 514 (1917).

54. Furness, Withy & Co. v. Yang Zsze Insurance Assn., 242 U.S. 430, 434 (1916). The Court was correct in this assumption as the following table indicates:

The Supreme Court of the United States

	Appeals Docketed	Petitions for Cert. Applied for
1910	394	113
1911	373	145
1912	405	130
1913	408	104
1914	424	101
1915	402	130
1916	421	129
1917	443	208
1918	356	233
1919	320	269
1920	317	256
1921	325	230
1922	390	279
1923	406	305
1924	425	300
1925	503	350
1926	326	520
1927	260	589
1928	257	596
1929	224	644
1930	279	690

55. Southern Power Co. v. North Carolina Public Service Co., 263 U.S. 508 (1922).

56. Forsyth v. Hammond, 166 U.S. 506 (1896).

57. Furness, Withy & Co. v. Yang Zsze Insurance Assn., 242 U.S. 430, 434 (1916). The annotations with this case in 61 L.Ed. 410 is a collection of cases on the practice involving the writ of certiorari.

58. Reynolds Robertson, APPELLATE PRACTICE AND PROCEDURE IN THE SUPREME COURT OF THE UNITED STATES (1928), p.72.

59. Act of February 13, 1925, 43 STAT. 936.

60. Sup. Ct. Rule 35(5), 266 U.S. 681 (1925).

61. American Construction Company v. Jacksonville, Tampa, Key West R.R. Co., 148 U.S. 372, 380 (1892).

62. Act of September 24, 1789, sec. 14, 1 STAT. 81.

63. Fowler et al. v. Lindsey, 3 Dall. 411 (U.S. 1799).

64. Forsyth v. Hammond, 166 U.S. 506, 513 (1896).

65. Charles Warren, THE SUPREME COURT IN UNITED STATES HISTORY (Rev. ed.) v.1, p.482.

66. Rose v. Himely, 4 Cranch 241 (U.S. 1808).

67. Stephen D. Law, THE JURISDICTION AND POWERS OF THE UNITED STATES COURTS (1852), p.380. Some lawyers had the effrontery to inquire if this rule was intended to prevent division of the cause into distinct points and hearings of two counsellors on each point. The court considered the rule inflexible "whatever may be the number of points". 7 Cranch 1 (U.S. 1812).

68. Carl B. Swisher, HISTORY OF THE SUPREME COURT: THE TANEY YEARS 1836-64 (1974), p.278.

69. U.S. Supreme Court Rules, 14 Wall. xi (U.S. 1872). This rule was promulgated November 16, 1872 to take effect January 1, 1873.

70. Sup. Ct. Rule 22 (1911), 222 U.S. App. 28.

71. Sup. Ct. Rule 44 (1954), 346 U.S. 995 (1970), 398 U.S. 1058.

72. Edwin McElwain, "The Business of the Supreme Court as Conducted by Chief Justice Hughes", 63 HARV. L. REV. 5, 17 (1949). Some doubt existed in some courts whether the time for argument could be limited. *See* A.G. McKean, "Limiting the Time of Argument of Counsel," 14 CENT. L. J. 45 (1882).

73. Buell v. Van Nes, 8 Wheat. 312 (U.S. 1823).

74. Twitchell v. Commonwealth, 7 Wall. 321 (U.S. 1868).

75. Twitchell v. Commonwealth, 7 Wall. 321 (U.S. 1868); Gleason v. Florida, 9 Wall. 779 (U.S. 1869).

76. Inglee v. Coolidge, 2 Wheat. 363 (U.S. 1817); Rector v. Ashley, 6 Wall. 142 (U.S. 1867); Gibson v. Chouteau, 8 Wall. 314 (1868).

77. Crowell v. Randall, 10 Pet. 368 (U.S. 1836); Armstrong et al. v. Treasurer, 16 Pet. 281 (U.S. 1842).

78. Messenger v. Mason, 10 Wall. 507 (U.S. 1870).

79. Bethel v. Demaret, 10 Wall. 537 (U.S. 1870).

80. *See* discussion of this in Taylor, *supra,* note 21, p.323.

81. Act of February 18, 1875, 18 STAT. 329.

82. Sup. Ct. Rule 8, February 4, 1795.

83. Pennsylvania Supreme Court Appearance Docket, January 13, 1786.

84. 3 Day 29 (Conn.). This rule was adopted May 26, 1807, twelve years after the United States Supreme Court Rule.

85. Peyton v. Brooke, 3 Cranch 91 (U.S. 1808).

86. Schooner Catherine v. The United States, 7 Cranch 92 (U.S. 1812).

87. Sup. Ct. Rule 30, 6 Wheat xiii (U.S. 1821).

88. Sup. Ct. Rule 40, 7 Pet. iv (U.S. 1833).

89. Sup. Ct. Rule 44, 11 Pet. vii (U.S. 1837).

90. Sup. Ct. Rule 58, 8 How. vi (U.S. 1850).

91. ANN. REPT. ATT'Y. GEN. U.S. 1881, p.5.

92. Sup. Ct. Rule 15, 346 U.S. 960 (1954).

93. Sup. Ct. Rule 21(2), 210 U.S. 487 (1907).

94. Sup. Ct. Rule 21(1), 108 U.S. 584 (1884).

95. Oregon v. Muller, 208 U.S. 412 (1908). Brandeis joined Felix Frankfurter in preparing similar extensive briefs in Bunting v. Oregon, 243 U.S. 426 (1917). Justice Brewer in Oregon v. Muller acknowledged the benefits the Court derived from these judicial sources. 208 U.S. at 419.

96. Brandeis, "The Living Law", 10 ILL. L. Rev. 461, 470 (1916) quoted in Alpheus Thomas Mason, BRANDEIS: LAWYER AND JUDGE IN THE MODERN STATE (1933), p.107. *See* also, Roscoe Pound, "Legislation as a Social Function," 7 Pub. Am. Soc. Co. 148 (1913).

97. Alpheus Thomas Mason, BRANDEIS: LAWYER AND JUDGE IN THE MODERN STATE (1933), p.114. *See* Charles Warren, "The Progressiveness of the United States Supreme Court," 13 COL. L. REV. 294 (1913), and Louis M. Greeley, "The Changing Attitudes of the Courts Towards Social Legislation," 15 ILL. L. REV. 222 (1910). Frankfurter supported this brief. *See* Felix Frankfurter, "Hours of Labor and Realism," 29 HARV. L. REV. 351 (1916). He cited other cases where a similar brief was presented to the court.

98. Sup. Ct. Rule 11, 3 Dall. 356 (U.S. 1797).

99. Sup. Ct. Rule 26, 2 Wheat. 7 (1817).

100. Sup. Ct. Rule 31, 6 Wheat. 5 (1821).

101. Sup. Ct. Rule 39, 346 U.S. 989 (1954).

102. Sup. Ct. Rule 37, 5 Pet. 724 (U.S. 1831).

103. Sup. Ct. Rule 37, 5 Pet. 724 (U.S. 1831).

104. Amendments to Rules 1 and 10, 108 U.S. 1 (1882).

105. Sup. Ct. Rule 12, 275 U.S. 603 (1928); Harold B. Willey, "Jurisdictional Statements on Appeals to U.S. Supreme Court," 31 A.B.A. J. 239 (1945).

106. Sup. Ct. Rule 34, 1 How. xxxii (1824).

107. Sup. Ct. Rule 27, 21 How. xv (1858); Sup. Ct. Rule 6(6), 108 U.S. 575 (1884).

108. Sup. Ct. Rule 35(3), 346 U.S. 985 (1954).

109. Robert L. Stern and Eugene Gressman, SUPREME COURT PRACTICE (3d ed. 1962), p.391.

110. Erwin C. Surrency, ed., "The Minutes of the Supreme Court of the United States," 5 AMER. J. LEG. HIST. 70, 71 (1961).

111. Act of September 24, 1789, sec. 17, 1 STAT. 83.

112. Hudson v. Parker, 156 U.S. 277, 284 (1894).

113. 3 Wall. vii (U.S. 1866).

114. Relfe v. Wilson, 102 U.S. clxxxix.

115. For one example, see 7 Cranch 1 (1812).

116. Sup. Ct. Rule 37, 5 Pet. 724 (U.S. 1831).

117. The first collection was published in 1 Cranch xvi (U.S. 1803). It appears that thereafter each reporter, as he began his series of the reports, included a collection of these rules. 1 Wheat. xiii (U.S. 1816); 1 Pet. v (U.S. 1828); 1 How. xxiii (U.S. 1843).

118. 3 Pet. xvii.

119. The rules are found in Law, *supra,* note 67, p.368, with notes as to sources and interpretations. The rules are published in Conkling, supra, note 9, p.411.

120. Quoted in Frederick B. Wiener, "The Supreme Court's New Rules," 68 HARV. L. REV. 34 (1954).

121. *See* comment in Osborn v. United States, 23 L.Ed. 871, 872 (1876). This decision is not reported in the official reports.

122. 1 Cranch xv (U.S. 1803); 1 Wheat. xiii (U.S. 1816). The Rules of the Supreme Court were often published in various books, but just when the rules were first issued as a separate pamphlet has not been definitely ascertained. However, a pamphlet containing the rules was printed by J. & G. S. Gideon in 1845. The original rules and all amendments through 1858 and the collection of rules adopted that year are found in William Whitwell Dewhurst, THE RULES OF PRACTICE OF THE UNITED STATES COURTS ANNOTATED (1907). The rules of 1911 are published in the second edition of this work published in 1914.

123. 222 U.S. 7.

124. Act of March 3, 1883, 22 STAT. 631.

125. Sup. Ct. Rule 21, 26(7), 210 U.S. 492.

126. 222 U.S. App. 1-40.

127. 266 U.S. 645 (1925).

128. Sup. Ct. Rules 2, 24, 266 U.S. 653, 671 (1925).

129. Sup. Ct. Rule 26, 266 U.S. 673 (1925).

130. Sup. Ct. Rule 18, 266 U.S. 667 (1925).

131. Sup. Ct. Rules of 1928, 275 U.S. 595; Sup. Ct. Rules of 1939, 306 U.S. 685.

132. Frederick Bernays Wiener, "The Supreme Court's New Rules," 68 HARV. L. REV. 20 (1954).

133. Sup. Ct. Rule 4, 266 U.S. 655 (1925).

134. 275 U.S. 577 (1928); 306 U.S. 671 (1939); 346 U.S. 951 (1954); 388 U.S. 929 (1967); Bennett Boskey and Eugene Gressman, "The 1967 Changes in the Supreme Court's Rules," 42 F.R.D. 139 (1968).

135. *See* Bennett Boskey and Eugene Gressman, "The 1970 Changes in the Supreme Court's Rules," 90 S.Ct. 2337, 49 F.R.D. 679 (1970).

136. Bennett Boskey and Eugene Gressman, "The Supreme Court's New Rules for the Eighties," 85 F.R.D. 487 (1980).

Chapter 23

APPOINTMENT OF FEDERAL JUDGES

The office of judge is a very ancient position, with four or more centuries of history in England before the establishment of the federal courts. When the federal government was established, the function of the judge was fairly understood with all of its powers and traditions which had become attached to the office.

Just what was expected from this official? The Magna Carta described the judge as an individual who knew the laws and would "be well inclined to observe them".[1] Francis Bacon wrote an extensive essay on the duty of judges which has been commented upon and accepted by later writers.[2] James Wilson, an associate justice of the United States Supreme Court, draws very heavily on Bacon's essay in his lectures and stresses that a judge "should bear a great regard to the sentiments and decisions of those, who have thought and decided before him."[3]

Only in the Massachusetts Constitution of 1780 is it declared that "it is the right of every citizen to be tried by judges as free, impartial, and independent as a lot of humanity will admit".[4] In the oath for judges prescribed in the First Judiciary Act, the incumbent promises that he "will administer justice without respect to persons, and do equal right to the poor and to the rich, and . . . will faithfully and impartially discharge and perform all the duties incumbent on me".[5] The duties of a judge are truly awesome and require great humility. The rules governing the conduct of those holding judicial office are generally found in tradition rather than in statutes. For the American judge of the Nineteenth Century, much of this tradition was molded by Biblical teachings. The Old Testament contains many verses expounding the proper conduct for a judge. The high ethical standards in the teachings of the Bible made it unnecessary for the founders of this nation to spell out the conduct expected of a judge.

Whether the judge makes law or merely enforces the law has been a question which has plagued writers in the field of jurisprudence. Blackstone in his COMMENTARIES stated that judges were "the depositaries of the laws; the living oracles, who must decide in all cases of doubt, and who are bound by an oath to decide according to the law of the land." He stressed that the duty of the judge is to follow precedent, and there is no doubt that he was not to "pronounce a new law, but to maintain and expound on the old one."[6] Blackstone conceded that a judge was to correct precedent when the law was misapplied, although judges should not "pretend to make a new law but to vindicate the old one from misrepresentation". James Wilson stressed that a judge should "bear a great regard to the sentiments and decisions of those, who have thought and decided before him."[7] Wilson argues that the judge must pay attention to the authorities, for "judicial decisions are the principal and most authentic evidence, which can be given, of the existence of such a custom as is entitled to form a part of the common law."

The teaching of Chief Justice John Marshall is instructive:

Judicial power, as contradistinguished from the power of the laws, has no existence. Courts are the mere instruments of the law, and can will nothing. When they are said to exercise a discretion, it is a mere legal discretion, a discretion to be exercised in discerning the course prescribed by law; and, when that is discerned, it is the duty of the court to follow it. Judicial power is never exercised for the purpose of giving effect to the will of the judge; always for the purpose of giving effect to the will of the legislature; or, in other words, to the will of the law. [8]

It is certainly open to question if these principles have not been eroded or disregarded by the judges of later generations!

Under the Constitution, the federal judges were given life tenure following the tradition established in England by statute in 1700 and as the result of constitutional arguments with the Mother Country. [9] During the colonial period, the judges were appointed "during our pleasure and his residence in our said province". [10] In the Declaration of Independence, George III was accused of making the "Judges dependent on his Will alone, for the tenure of their offices, and the amount and payment of their salaries." Life tenure during good behavior for federal judges was an accepted political doctrine, for the topic received limited debate in the Constitutional Convention. But life tenure has had an important impact on the federal bench. Chancellor Kent gave two reasons why "we may anticipate the still increasing influence of the federal government": the "tenure of the office of the judges, and the liberal and stable provision for their support." [11]

Although the Constitution gave federal judges life tenure, a proposal which has withstood attempted changes at various periods in the history of the federal courts, the importance accorded to this provision by the Founding Fathers has lost its significance. [12] The writers of the FEDER-ALIST devoted a considerable amount of space to justifying life tenure in the Constitution. [13] The attempt to influence judges by the monarchs of England, especially James II, and the strong feeling engendered by controversies over tenure for the colonial judges were vivid memories at the time the Constitution was written. Later writers, such as Kent and Story, extensively defended the concept of life tenure. [14]

The Appointment Process

The First Judiciary Act prescribed no qualifications for a federal judge, for it has never been stated by statute that appointees must be members of the bar or have practiced before the federal courts. No individual who lacked membership in the legal profession has ever been appointed to the federal bench. Perhaps this custom has established a constitutional precedent.

It is understandable that with the establishment of the federal courts, appointees could not have had any previous practical experience before the courts. Two of the original district court judges, James Duane of New York and Richard Law of Connecticut, had served on the only federal court established under the Articles of Confederation, the Court of Appeals in Prize Cases. James Wilson and Samuel Chase, both of whom were appointed to the Supreme Court, served on this court. Although no statistical study has been made, it would not be surprising to find that few of the individuals appointed to the bench in the Nineteenth Century had practiced extensively before the federal courts.

President Washington, in considering appointments, conscientiously selected those individuals whom he knew and thought to be well-qualified, and perhaps his selections were outstanding.[15] By the end of the Nineteenth Century, the only qualification was loyalty to the party in power.[16] Beginning with Theodore Roosevelt, the trend in the Senate has been to give more consideration to the candidates' qualifications.[17] This trend parallels the movement of the introduction of the Civil Service reforms. This does not imply that party membership was not a requirement for nomination, but on the whole, partisan politics has played a lesser role in the selection and confirmation of federal judges since that date.[18]

The method of selecting candidates for positions of judges has changed. Since about 1840, the federal district judges normally have been recommended by the senators from the state, provided they are from the same party as the president.[19] This was not the exclusive method of applying for a judicial appointment. One candidate wrote President Lincoln seeking the appointment of district court judge in Indiana, stating that he was told that "no one could get an office from you without personally seeing you". David McDonald did not go to see Lincoln on that occasion, but when the same position became open several years later, he visited the President and received the appointment.[20] It is not surprising that the senators will consult local political leaders for additional suggestions, but presidents and senators have continued to clash over these appointments. Sometime in the Twentieth Century, the Attorney General assumed the responsibility of making the selection in consultation with the senators. President Carter recognized this practice of selection made by the Attorney General in consultation with senators when he issued an Executive Order directing the Attorney General to recommend to the President "persons to be considered for appointment who are qualified to be district judges".[21] Objections have been raised to this method because the Constitution provides for appointment by the President, although technically he continues to make the appointments recommended to him.

Of the thousands of federal district court judges, present and past, it is difficult to characterize them as all good or all bad. President Hoover, however, has been given high marks for raising the standards of these appointments with the expectation of reducing the influence of partisan considerations. His Attorney General publicly made the announcement that the administration would appoint judges of high qualifications without regard to reward for political activity.[22]

After a name had been proposed to the President for appointment, President Eisenhower and other Presidents have asked a committee of the American Bar Association to pass upon the candidate's qualifications.[23] This committee adopted a system of ratings including the category of "not qualified". Rarely did this have any impact on the appointment, for the candidates were usually confirmed. A rating of not qualified would not necessarily block the confirmation. These ratings were decided after the nomination and for this reason would have little impact on the decision about the qualifications of the individual. President Carter promised to change this, and with the consent of the Judiciary Committee of the Senate, created commissions in each circuit to pass upon the qualifications for candidates appointed to the courts of appeals, but not to consider appointments to the district court judgeships.[24] A few senators in their own states created such commissions for this purpose on their own initiative.[25] The commission would propose three to five names for each position on the court of appeals. Often district court judges who were desirous of going up to the appellate bench would apply, but they would not have had this opportunity except by the commission system. President Reagan discontinued the commission system.

The appointment of justices to the Supreme Court has demanded wider attention than appointments to the lower courts. One study indicated that nearly one-fifth of the nominations for the Supreme Court sent to the Senate have been rejected.[26] Roger Taney and Stanley Matthews were both rejected because of lack of qualifications, and several very outstanding individuals, who had established records as judges on other counts, were rejected for other reasons.[27] In the Twentieth Century, both Congress and the President have agreed upon the need to appoint qualified individuals to the Supreme Court.

Increase in Number of Judges

The Judiciary Act of 1789 provided for a single district court judge in each state, a total of thirteen district judges. With the six justices of the Supreme Court, the total number of federal judges in 1789 was twenty-one. When Rhode Island and North Carolina adhered to the Constitution, these states were likewise organized into single districts with a judge in each district. The new states admitted to the Union were organized into single districts with a single judge without any regard to the size of the district. Only once was a state, Oklahoma, organized into two judicial districts at the time of its admission. Each district contained one judge.[28]

This departure from previously established practice in this instance may be explained by the fact that two separate territories were incorporated into one state. Looking back, one can only conclude that Congress was completely unaware of the geographical extent of the federal judicial district to which one judge was assigned, for otherwise, how can one account for the organization of Texas into a single district?[29] The District Court in Texas was held in Galveston until 1857 when sessions were directed to be held in Austin and, at the discretion of the judge, in Brownsville and Tyler.[30] From the establishment of the federal courts, district court judges had to travel between cities where sessions of court were held.[31] The court officials, including the clerk, marshal and attorney, all had to travel to attend these sessions. Additional clerks, deputy clerks and other officers were provided, but not necessarily additional judges.

As the need for additional judges became apparent, the solution frequently adopted in the Nineteenth Century was to divide the district. The creation of a second district within a state did not invariably indicate the appointment of an additional judge, for some states were subdivided to provide additional locations for holding the federal courts.[32] Alabama was divided into two districts in 1824 and into a third district in 1839.[33] No additional judge was authorized for the state until 1886, when a judge was authorized in the Southern District, and the incumbent judge presided in the Northern and Middle Districts.[34] In 1911, the same judge presided in all districts of four states.[35] South Carolina, for example, had only one judge in both districts until 1911, when a second judge was authorized, one for each district.[36]

Congress experimented with several alternatives to increase the number of permanent judges in a district. One innovation was the appointment of an additional judge to preside in two or more districts, commonly referred to as a "roving judge". During the Nineteenth Century, Congress had appointed such a judge who presided in two separate districts and who was the only judge in those districts. Again, Alabama provides an example. In 1886, there was one judge for both the Northern and Middle Districts. In 1936, Congress provided additional manpower by appointing a single judge for the two districts in Iowa, Kentucky, Missouri, and West Virginia and in the three districts of Oklahoma.[37] Similar judgeships have been established in other states. Another form of supplying judicial manpower was by appointing temporary judges. In 1910, an additional judge was authorized in the district of Maryland but with the proviso that the next vacancy would not to be filled.[38] This was the first appointment of a temporary judge. This type of appointment was used in 1922 when twenty-three temporary judgeships were created.[39] But one by one, in separate acts, these positions created in the 1922 Omnibus Judgeship Act were made permanent. In 1948, only nine temporary judgeships existed in the federal judicial system.[40] Five additional temporary judges were authorized in 1954, but all of these positions have since been made permanent.[41] The temporary judgeship was found not to violate the Constitution since all the individuals appointed have life tenure and the districts have the services of another judge for an indefinite period. The temporary judgeships created in the 1978 statute provided that these positions would not be filled until after the expiration of a five-year period. In other words, this section envisioned that should the permanent position or the temporary position become vacant during the period of five years from the effective date of the statute, either or both of the positions would be filled. These temporary positions are not generally included in the UNITED STATES CODE where the number of judges are tabulated.[42]

In providing for temporary judgeships, some special circumstances were required for their creation. The temporary judgeships created in the Eastern District of Kentucky and the Southern District of West Virginia were brought about by the increase in the black lung cases in those courts.[43]

The business of the federal courts grew during the last decades of the Nineteenth Century, and additional cities in which the court was required to meet were needed for the convenience of the parties. A certain amount of civic pride was involved in providing new sites for the meetings of the courts. This increased travel burden weighed heavily on existing district court judges in a number of districts. Congress was wedded to the idea that only a single judge was desirable in each district, for if two judges were appointed, one judge would invariably be subordinate to the other, which was contrary to the concept of judicial independence.[44] It was only hesitatingly that an additional judge was added to the same court. During the Twentieth Century, this practice became more prevalent and acceptable as a means of providing additional judicial manpower.

The only experiment of two judges in a single district during the Nineteenth Century was made in New York in 1812.[45] A second judge was appointed and the senior judge was required to sit on the circuit court with the justice of the Supreme Court. In his absence, the junior judge could sit. This experiment continued for two years at which time New York was divided into two districts with a single judge in each district.[46]

The first time Congress authorized second judges for the same district other than the New York experiment was in 1903,[47] when an additional judge was authorized for the state of Minnesota, and for the Southern District of New York. These acts directed that the senior circuit judge would make all necessary orders for the division of the business and the assignment of cases for trial within these courts. Since 1903, Congress has frequently passed acts increasing the number of judges in individual districts, until 1922, when Congress passed an Omnibus Act authorizing additional judges in several districts.[48] Since 1949, the practice of Congress is to authorize additional judges by omnibus bills.[49] The number of federal judges has continued to increase, often in large increments.[50] In 1941, the number of permanent federal district court judges was 197, and by 1984, this number stood at 561. The largest increase occurred when the Omnibus Judgeship Bill of 1978 created 113 district judgeships and 35 circuit judgeships. Increasingly, the federal courts reported backlogs in their caseloads which could only be handled by additional judges. Congress concluded that adding judges was not the answer to increased caseloads, but rather, improvements were needed in the administration of justice.[51] During the decades following World War II, various federal courts have experimented with a number of means to streamline the administrative procedures of the courts. The business of the federal courts has continued to expand, and it has been found that additional judges were needed in spite of improvements in the methods of conducting the business of the courts.

The manpower needs of the federal judiciary until the middle of the Twentieth Century have been met through the influence of individual Congressmen, although little consideration was given to the entire judicial system. Since the creation of the Judicial Conference in 1922,[52] the judges have increasingly participated in formulating recommendations for the improvement of the courts including sponsoring and supporting legislation for the creation of additional judicial positions.[53] Since 1964, the Judicial Conference has conducted quadrennial surveys of the needs for additional judges. Congress has acted upon these recommendations, although somewhat belatedly.[54] These recommendations are based upon the studies of the Administrative Office of the number of filings of cases in the federal courts and other statistical data. Such information had been used in the Nineteenth Century for this same purpose. All these facts are set forth in the hearings and reports of the Congressional Committees in considering the legislation creating new judges.

During the middle decades of the Twentieth Century, the failure to appoint judges to existing vacancies has contributed to the failure to reduce the backlog of cases pending in the federal courts. Observations are made that the Congress moves very slowly on authorizing additional judges and that the President moves very slowly in filling these new positions. With resignations and deaths among the federal judges, it is difficult to keep all the positions filled. Another compelling reason to seek alternatives to the appointment of new judges is the cost of each new judicial position. It is estimated that in 1977, the cost to establish each new federal judgeship was $298,000, with the support cost totalling $245,000 annually.[55]

The courts have used other personnel to take over some of the judicial functions. During the time when equity was a separate practice, the judges could appoint masters who would make a finding of fact and a recommendation to the court. The equity rules of 1842 imply that the references shall be confined to accounts, but by adopting the English rules, a much broader range of topics could be referred for the masters' finding.[56]

The rules adopted in 1913 stated that references to a master should be "the exception, not the rule, and shall be made only upon a showing that some exceptional condition required it."[57] The extent to which the various district courts referred matters to masters probably varied greatly.[58]

Another official who relieved the federal judges of some judicial functions was the commissioner, who later became known as the magistrate. The cases referred to commissioners for hearing were mostly the misdemeanor offenses.

Judicial Conduct

Judicial conduct is presently governed by adopted standards, but such standards have not always been necessary. The members of the judiciary during the early period felt governed by Christian ethics as expressed in the Bible. However, certain misconduct was proscribed by statute.

Several of the early prohibitions applicable to judges were criminal statutes, but other statutes were directed toward the conduct of judges with no penalties attached. In 1790, Congress made it a crime to attempt to bribe a judge, but no penalty was prescribed for accepting a bribe.[59] This omission may be explained in part by the fact that it never occurred to them that a judge would be guilty of such an offense. In 1792, Congress did provide that a district court judge who had an interest in the case or was involved as counsel for either party should disqualify himself and certify the case to the next circuit court in his state. The circuit court was to proceed in the case as if it had been originally filed there.[60] In 1821, the statute was amended to add kinship as a disqualification and authorized the transfer to a circuit court in an adjacent state.[61] Surely, some incident took place somewhere in these United States to cause Congress to adopt this amendment, and it is unfortunate that the historic reason for this statute has been lost.

Since 1812, it has been a requirement that the district and territorial judges live in the district in which they are appointed. At a later date, the statute was amended to add penalties for the failure to live in the district. This statute likewise prohibited federal judges from practicing law in any court.[62] All of these statutes have remained a part of the current law and have been modernized, but rarely have these issues been litigated.

One of the perceived needs in the closing decades of the Twentieth Century was the need for canons of ethics to explain why a judge should refrain from doing a particular act. Some writers have raised the question of whether certain judges of the Nineteenth Century were not acting unethically by sitting when distant members of their family had an interest in the case. The probable answer would have been that the particular judge felt that he was impartial and would judge any case on its merits alone "without respect to persons" as required by his oath. A more fundamental reason for this lack of a code was the strong tradition established by the

Old Testament of the Bible where there are so many ethical teachings pertaining to judges.[63] This created a perception that such a code of judicial ethics was unnecessary.

As a part of the movement to raise the standards of the legal profession, which began at the close of the Nineteenth Century, efforts were made to adopt the Canons of Judicial Ethics to parallel those of the legal ethics. The proposal was first made in 1909, but it was not until 1922 that a committee of the American Bar Association was appointed to draft such canons.[64] On the committee were two leaders in the efforts to improve the judiciary, William H. Taft, later to become chief justice, and George Sutherland, who later joined the Supreme Court. The Canons were finally approved in 1924 by the American Bar Association.[65] The impetus for the adoption of the Canons was the discovery that a federal district court judge was supplementing his $7,500 a year salary with $42,500 a year for legal services rendered to the national commissioner of the baseball association. Since there were no statutes or standards which prohibited such conduct, the only thing that could be accomplished was a resolution of censure against that particular judge.[66]

There were various reasons to oppose the adoption of the Canons. Many members of the profession thought that the real issue was one of competency of those appointed to the bench, while others believed that it was not the role of the bar to impose standards on the judiciary.[67] Georgia was the first state to adopt the Canons at the annual meeting of the Georgia Bar Association in 1925.[68] California next adopted the Canons in 1928, but the supreme court of that state declared that these canons had no effect since the Bar Association had no jurisdiction over the conduct of the judiciary.[69] In the aftermath of World War II, renewed interest in the Canons was evidenced when several of the highest state appellate courts adopted them. There was a feeling, however, that the Canons needed revising, and in 1972 the American Bar Association adopted the Code of Judicial Conduct. Although the Code of Judicial Conduct has never been adopted officially to govern the judges of the federal courts, it has provided an informed basis for measuring judicial conduct. In 1978 Congress enacted a financial disclosure act, which has frequently been amended, with far reaching ethical considerations.

Removal of Judges

The Constitution provides that judges can be removed by impeachment upon "Conviction of, Treason, Bribery, or other high Crimes and Misdemeanors."[70] The law governing impeachment has never been clarified, and much of the precedent is derived from earlier English practice. Can Congress define certain acts as "high Crimes and Misdemeanors"? The statute of 1812 prohibited judges from exercising "the profession or employment of counsel or attorney" or from engaging in the practice of law, and declared that such person who offended against this prohibition would be "deemed guilty of a high misdemeanor."[71] Was this an attempt to declare such conduct as sufficient grounds for impeachment?

The first impeachment of a federal judge was brought against John Pickering, judge for the United States District Court of New Hampshire, on charges of tyrannous conduct. Judge Pickering was senile, but the offer on his behalf to resign was rejected. He was successfully impeached and removed by the Senate in 1804. At the same time, impeachment proceedings were brought against Justice Samuel Chase of the United States Supreme Court.[72] The charges grew out of his intemperate conduct and his strong comments in charges before two juries in support of the Alien and Sedition laws. This proceeding is often construed as an attack on the federal courts as an attempt to subordinate the judges to the Congress by the impeachment process. It is accepted wisdom that if Chase had been removed, charges would have been brought against John Marshall. Up to 1970, Congress had investigated some 55 federal judges, eight of whom were impeached and removed from office.[73] It has been fairly conceded that the impeachment process is both costly and difficult.

Other methods of removing federal judges for lesser offenses, including misconduct, have been studied, but their constitutionality has generally been questioned, chiefly on the grounds that the Constitution provides for only one method of removal — impeachment! Congress has often considered legislation introduced in part to remove unqualified judges which would have required a Constitutional amendment, but all these proposals have been rejected.[74] This is unfortunate, for at least one federal judge, Harry E. Claiborne, was found guilty in 1984 of federal income tax evasion and refused, both after the indictment and after his sentencing, to resign from the bench.[75] Where possible, Congress has provided for the removal of judges of legislative courts by some judicial body. The judges of the United States Claims Court can only be removed for "incompetency, misconduct, neglect of duty, engaging in the practice of law, or physical or mental disability" by the judges of the Court of Appeals for the Federal Circuit.[76] The judges of the Claims Court are not appointed under Article III, and their conduct can be regulated in other ways than by impeachment.

The removal of judges for reasons of physical disability has been a recurring problem that has not been adequately resolved. When a federal judge becomes senile, the question is often debated whether an age should be set at which time the judge must step down. Senility was not a serious problem when federal judges were given life tenure in the Constitution, but since 1787, federal judges tend to live longer and their mental abilities have become impaired although they remain on the bench.

Solutions have been suggested and debated. In 1809, a proposed Constitutional amendment would have prohibited federal judges from continuing in office after reaching sixty-five years of age.[77] Another attempt was made in 1826, to raise the proposed age limit to seventy years.

In 1835, a motion was made to inquire "at what age judges should be rendered incompetent to serve", but the proposal was never adopted. A third attempt was made in 1869 when a proposed Constitutional amendment would have mandated retirement at seventy years of age or after a term of twenty years on the bench. Part of this proposal was accomplished through an act of the same year, which provided that after a federal judge had served ten years and reached the age of seventy, he could resign and receive his salary for the balance of his natural life.[78] In the debates on this statute, the example of Justice McLean was cited, for it was well known at that time that his friends relieved him of all labor in preparation of opinions and that he would sleep on the bench during arguments. Justice Grier was forced to resign for the same reason in 1870. To meet the exigencies of an immediate problem, Congress has provided for special pensions for justices. In 1910, Congress provided a special pension for Justice Moody who had not reached seventy or served a full ten years.[79]

The problem of how to encourage judges to retire has never been resolved, although suggestions have been offered. Attorney General James Clark McReynolds in 1913 realized that this had become a problem and proposed that where a federal judge does not retire voluntarily at the age of seventy after ten years of service, the President should appoint another judge who would preside over the court and have precedent over the older judge. This proposal was incorporated into a bill, but was never passed.[80] This is certainly similar to the famous court-packing plan of President Roosevelt, and it is a matter for speculation if Justice James Clark McReynolds saw this relation.

No proposal affecting the federal courts ever caused as much public controversy as did President Franklin D. Roosevelt's proposal to appoint additional federal judges to all federal benches, including the Supreme Court, when the judge or justice reached seventy years of age and had ten years of service and did not retire. This proposal was perceived as being directed chiefly at the Supreme Court, which had declared unconstitutional a number of economic proposals of that administration. One of the arguments advanced in support of this proposal was the crowded status of the dockets which was ascribed in part to the impaired capacity of the elderly judges. The American Bar Association and other groups came to the defense of the courts, and the issue was widely debated in the public press. Many expressed their indignation over such a dastardly attack upon the justices! Probably no other proposal since the repeal of the Judiciary Act of 1801 called forth such public outcry.[81]

The President has had authority since 1919 to appoint a second judge to any circuit or district where a disabled judge sat if he found "that any judge is unable to discharge efficiently all the duties of his office by reason of mental or physical disability of permanent character, . . . when necessary for the efficient dispatch of business."[82] In 1957, the circuit judicial councils were given the responsibility of determining if judges were unable to discharge efficiently their duties because of mental or other disabilities. The council then would make a recommendation to the President who would make a new appointment.[83] As far as can be determined, this provision has not been applied, but the threat of its application has had the desired affect.[84]

Since the establishment of the Circuit Conferences in 1939, these bodies have increasingly acted on accusations of judicial misconduct.[85] No particular procedure has evolved from these informal approaches, and it has generally been felt that any statutory authority other than impeachment would be unconstitutional as well as undesirable from the perspective of the independence of the judiciary.[86] The Judicial Council of the Circuit has statutory authority to "make all necessary orders for effective and expeditious administration of the business of the courts within its circuit",[87] and from that statutory duty follows some responsibility over the conduct of federal judges. Generally, the chief judge of the circuit, upon advice from the Judicial Council, has moved informally by suggesting to judges certain changes in their conduct which have usually been followed.[88] In the event that the informal procedure does not work, the Council may take a more formal approach by issuing a rule in the nature of a request to take action directed at the offending judge.[89] Retirement can only be brought about by informal pressures on the part of the chief judge of the circuit. A most notable case of this type of action by the Judicial Conference was against Judge Stephen Chandler of the Western District of Oklahoma. In December of 1965, the Council of the Tenth Circuit issued an order prohibiting Judge Chandler from acting in any cases. The Supreme Court decided that the council was nothing more than an "administrative body functioning in a very limited area in a narrow sense as a 'board of directors' for the circuit." The Court held that it had no appellate jurisdiction over this administrative matter.[90]

Within a decade of the establishment of the federal courts, the question arose whether federal judges could be legislated out of office. Upon the establishment of the circuit courts under the Judiciary Act of 1801, a number of district court judges had accepted appointments from President Adams to these newly created courts. During the debates over the repeal of this statute, Congress heatedly argued the issue of removing judges from office. Congressmen ridiculed the arguments claiming that the office of judge belonged to the people and that when the court was abolished, the position was abolished.[91] Justice Story commented: "How this can be reconciled with the terms or the intent of the constitution, is more than any ingenuity of argument has ever, as yet, been able to demonstrate."[92] When the Commerce Court was abolished, the judges were distributed among the existing Circuit Courts of Appeals, but the vote in Congress on retention was very close.[93]

Visiting Judges

The authors of the First Judiciary Act recognized the fact that the judge may be absent from the prescribed term of court and made provisions for this. If a judge was not able to attend the district court, he could issue a written order to the marshal to adjourn the court until the time appointed in his written order. Further, in the case of the death of the judge, "all process, pleadings and proceedings of what nature soever" were to be continued until the next stated session after the appointment of his successor.[94]

Congress made one attempt during the antebellum period to provide for situations where the district court judge was absent or suffered under some disability. Such a statute was vetoed by James Madison in 1812. The bill imposed upon the justices of the Supreme Court the duty of holding the sessions of the district court when the district court judge was absent or disabled. Madison objected to this proposal on several grounds, including its incompatability with the original office of justice of the Supreme Court and its creation of an appeal from a judge sitting in one court to that same judge sitting in the circuit court. Further, the absent district court judge could sit in the circuit court on an appeal and render a decision in a case which he should have heard in the beginning. President Madison pointed out that these additional services would require the justices to travel greater distances, and no reimbursement would be made for the additional expenses. Further, the President of the United States, as Madison noted, was in no position to decide whether a district court judge was disabled to perform his duties as required by the bill.[95]

No regular provision was made for a district court judge to perform judicial services outside of his district until 1850. In 1826, by a special statute, the judge in the Western District of Virginia was authorized and given full authority to go into the Western District of Pennsylvania and try those cases where District Court Judge William Wilkins had been of counsel before going on the bench.[96] Before 1850, it is not clear whether the justice of the Supreme Court going on circuit would try the cases on the docket of the district court in the absence of a district court judge or whether the cases were just continued as envisioned under the First Judiciary Act. In 1850, nevertheless, the clerk of the district court was required by statute to certify to the circuit judge that the district court judge was absent because of illness, and the circuit judge would in turn designate another district judge within the circuit to hold the term of the district court with the full authority the absent judge would have exercised. In the event that no circuit judge was resident within the circuit, the clerk could certify this matter to the chief justice, who could appoint a substitute from the circuit or from an adjoining circuit.[97] This statute was amended to authorize the clerk to notify the chief justice or the circuit judge when there was such an accumulation of judicial business that an additional judge was needed. In this event, both judges could hold separately a district or circuit court and "discharge all the judicial duties of a District Judge therein".[98] In 1907, the Chief Justice of the United States could assign a judge from a foreign circuit other than an adjacent one to aid a disabled district court judge when a certificate was issued by the circuit judge of the receiving circuit.

A number of factors contributed to the increase in the caseload of the federal courts in the first two decades of the Twentieth Century. As a result, the caseloads in some judicial districts grew and became unmanageable by the existing judges, especially in the Southern District of New York. After some efforts on the part of the senior circuit judge of the Second Circuit, Congress authorized the Chief Justice of the United States to send a district judge from any of the circuits to aid the district courts of New York. No judge could be forced to accept such an appointment.[99] The senior circuit judge, E.H. Lacombe, was optimistic that this would end for "all times" the congestion in the federal courts of New York.[100]

Before becoming Chief Justice of the United States, William Howard Taft urged the appointment of a group of judges which could be assigned freely to those district courts behind in their work. This group was described as a "flying squadron of judges" or as the "Light Horse Cavalry".[101] This proposal was never received with enthusiasm by members of the judiciary or members of Congress.

Judicial Salaries

Salaries are always a subject of controversy, and it was felt that at some periods, the salaries of federal judges were extremely low. The argument has often been advanced that qualified attorneys are deterred from taking an appointment to the federal bench because of low salaries. In fact, it has been said that some judges have left the bench for that reason.[102] One of the reasons for the resignation of Justice Benjamin R. Curtis from the Supreme Court was the low salary, in addition to the required absence from home.[103] Other judges who have resigned for this reason have gone to more remunerative practices. A classic example is George W. McCrary, judge of the Eighth Circuit, who accepted an offer as general counsel of the Atchison, Topeka and Santa Fe Railroad at a very large salary.[104] Many capable judges have remained on the bench who probably could have done as well if they had chosen to step down. Perhaps all judges do not have the same opportunity to leave the bench for bigger salaries.

Before 1891, salaries of the district court judges varied and were apparently determined by a perception of what the workload in that district would be. The salaries established in 1789 varied between a high of $1,800 for the judges in the Districts of Virginia and South Carolina and $800 for the judges in the Districts of Delaware and Rhode Island. Within five years, the salaries of these latter two judges were raised to $1,000 each.[105] At the same time, the salary of the justices of the Supreme Court was set at $3,500 and that of the Chief Justice at $4,000. At this period, the judges of the Supreme Court were expected to travel, but no provisions were made for travel expenses.[106]

Before the Civil War, no efforts were made to pay the judges for travel or for additional duties, except in the case of the district judge of Missouri, and later the judges in Michigan, Arkansas and Florida. In 1824, the district court judge in Missouri was allowed $800 extra per year for his work in settling conflicting land claims.[107] In 1846, Congress considered the suggestion that the salary of the deceased "circuit judge", who was really a justice of the Supreme Court, be divided among the district judges of the circuit. This proposal was rejected because district court judges were performing circuit court duties, and this would be extra compensation.[108] At times, the legislatures of the states petitioned Congress to increase the compensation of federal judges. In 1852, the legislature of California felt that the salaries of $3,500 for the judge of the Northern District and $2,800 for the Southern District were inadequate in view of the travel necessary to hold the sessions of the court.[109]

It is interesting to note that some congressmen objected to raising the salaries of judges on the basis of their travel needs. They objected because "when official duties are to be performed elsewhere, usually the courtesies known to railroad management come to the relief of the judge and enable him to travel through his district free of expense."[110] How widely "the courtesies known to the railroad management" were accepted by the federal judges is not known. At least one federal judge, Thomas Drummond, judge of the District Court of Illinois and later circuit court judge, before whom came railroad property in the hands of receivers worth millions of dollars, reported that he never accepted a present, not even a railroad pass.[111]

Impeachment charges were brought against Judge Charles Swayne of the Northern District of Florida, for he made use of a private car of a railroad company which was in the hands of a receiver in his court. The judge made a trip from Florida to his home in Delaware and from Florida to California, returning in this private car. His ingenious defense was that since the railroad property was in his possession, he believed that as head of the corporation, he had a right to use this private car, the same as any other official of the company. Some members of the congressional committee did not think this conduct was grounds for impeachment, but rather was a ground for censure.[112]

The district court judges in New York were singled out for special salary supplements. In 1873, the judge of the Eastern District was allowed $300 additional compensation for each term of the Circuit Court held in the Southern District for the trial of criminal cases.[113]

The compensation for federal judges during most of the Nineteenth Century received very little attention in Congress. As new district courts were established, the salaries of the judges were established, but very little thought was given to whether the salaries of other judges were adequate. In 1855, Congress passed its first comprehensive act defining the salaries of the various federal judges.[114] By this time, the highest paid judge was in the Northern District of California receiving $5,000 annually, followed by the judge of the Southern District of New York at $3,750 annually. Nine of the district court judges received an annual salary of $2,000.

A bill was introduced in the 49th Congress in 1886 to increase the salaries of all district court judges to $5,000 per year, thus making all salaries equal. However, it wasn't until 1891 that such a statute was adopted upon the recommendation of President Benjamin Harrison.[115] Preceding this enactment, a number of articles had appeared in the various legal publications urging an increase in the salaries of the federal court judges.[116] Some federal judges had supplemented their salaries in various ways. Since they were prohibited from practicing law, some organized law schools. Judge McDonald in Indianapolis charged each student forty dollars per session of four months, but this often required the judge to deliver a two hour lecture in the morning and preside in court during the other hours of the day.[117]

Since 1891, Congress has increased the salaries of federal judges at different periods but after much debate and consideration. In 1967, it enacted a far reaching statute by establishing a commission on executive, legislative and judicial salaries to make recommendations to the President quadrennially.[118] The recommendations could be considered by the President who would make his proposals to Congress with respect to the pay rate. The recommendations would become effective if Congress did not disapprove of them thirty days after receiving the President's suggestions. Presidents are free to ignore the recommendations, and some have done so.

The Constitution provides that the judge's salary shall not be reduced during his term of office, and this simple provision has raised interesting questions on at least two occasions. When the income tax was enacted in 1862, Chief Justice Taney wrote to the then Secretary of the Treasury, claiming that this tax reduced the salary of the federal judges and hence, was unconstitutional.[119] Later the Attorney General of the United States issued an opinion upholding this interpretation, but many judges had paid the tax and did not receive a refund. After the Revenue Act of 1918, this view was adopted by the Supreme Court.[120] In the Revenue Act of 1932, a provision was inserted that the compensation of judges of the courts of the United States taking office after June 6, 1932 would be liable for the tax. The provision was carried on in other revenue acts, and since that date, the salaries of all judges appointed have been subject to the federal income tax.[121]

Because of the constitutional prohibition against reduction of judicial salaries, judges escaped the reduction of the salaries of all government officials, including members of Congress, made in 1933.[122] Even though the judges escaped direct reductions in their salaries at that time, the effect of inflation in the decades following 1970 reduced the real value of the dollar as measured by the Consumer Price Index. For this reason, it was alleged in a suit in the United States Court of Claims that judges' salaries had been reduced. The decision went against this position.[123]

Until 1903, federal judges received their remuneration in quarterly payments.[124] The reason for this practice is found in the commercial practice of the day when the most common commercial paper was a sight draft which was a promise to pay upon its presentment at a designated place. Bank practices in the last century often required the actual transfer of funds for each transition.

Contributions of the Federal Judges to Literature

A number of federal judges have made significant contributions to the development of legal literature. The works of Justice Joseph Story on Bailments (1832), Constitutional Law (1833), Conflicts of Laws (1834), Equity Jurisprudence (1836), Equity Pleading (1838), Agency (1839), Partnership (1841), and Bills of Exchange (1843) are well known. These volumes were the first American legal texts. It is difficult to say whether the volume on conflicts of law or equity jurisprudence had the greatest impact, for both went through several editions.[125] Equity jurisprudence was last published in 1920.[126]

Another federal judge who contributed to the growing legal literature was Alfred Conkling, who wrote A TREATISE ON THE ORGANIZATION, JURISDICTION, AND PRACTICE OF THE COURTS OF THE UNITED STATES. Conkling's work was a standard practice book from the time of the first edition in 1842 until the last edition in 1864. In addition, Judge Conkling wrote another influential book entitled THE ADMIRALTY JURISDICTION, LAW AND PRACTICE OF THE UNITED STATES COURTS.

Other federal judges, too numerous to mention here, have made their contributions to legal literature through speeches and books. However, the pressure of work has prevented many of them from undertaking any work comparable to that of Justice Story.

A few judges have made contributions to general literature. Francis Hopkinson, the first district court judge for the District of Pennsylvania contributed to the literature of the Revolutionary movement as well as essays of literary criticism. He published a book of music which was the first such book published in America.[127] His son Joseph, who served on the same bench from 1828 to 1842, is famous for his musical composition, "Hail Columbia."

Judges were never used as primary characters in American novels during the Nineteenth Century. If they were portrayed at all, they were representative symbols of righteousness "whose behavior on and off the bench illustrated the moral certainties of the natural law."[128] The first novel in which the federal judge was the major character was entitled THE FEDERAL JUDGE by Charles J. K. Lust. The judge is portrayed in this novel as a sturdy and honest person who is elevated to the bench but subconsciously falls under the influence of his capitalist friend, a president of a railroad, and commits wrongs without losing his personal honesty. This story deals with the influence of the railroad tycoons on the law and the controversial use of the injunction in labor disputes. The significance of the novel is that it represents the turn-of-century attitude toward the appointment of federal judges. Generally, novels rarely represent accurately the law, but one review characterized this book thusly: "it may not be entirely good law, but it is good enough to fit the plot of the story."[129] Since THE FEDERAL JUDGE, the exploits of members of the federal judiciary have been the theme of a number of novels.

Probably the most amusing treatment of any federal courts in literature is the play by George S. Kaufman and Moss Hart, I'D RATHER BE RIGHT, first published in 1937. In this theatrical presentation, President Roosevelt attempted to help a young couple by passing some legislation, and at the mention of this, the nine justices cloned as Charles Evans Hughes jumped from behind the bushes and rocks to shout "Oh No! No you don't". In one scene, Roosevelt attempts to be conciliatory to the judges, but they reject his overtures after singing a jingle about "A little bit of constitutional fun". Roosevelt then muses, "You know, if I'd suggested putting six new girls on the bench, I'll bet they'd have said 'all right'."[130] This play enjoyed a run on Broadway, but it was not a significant musical. Since this play, other novels have considered the theme of appointment of federal judges.[131]

Federal Judges: An Appreciation

This brief survey only indicates some of the chief changes in the nature of the office of federal court judge since the first judges were appointed under the Judiciary Act of 1789. The judge at this particular time was responsible for the administration of his court, including the appointment of both the clerk and other court officials. There was no uniformity in the development of these lesser court officials, for the clerk or marshal would lend a member of their staff to become the court's messenger to perform other duties for the judge. By the end of the Twentieth Century, the federal judge had become the chief administrator of the hierarchy of court officials. During these two centuries, Congress gradually provided adequate quarters for the court rather than requiring the judge and marshal to make arrangements for meeting places in the local state courthouses or city halls or the local tavern. One need only survey the various statutes passed since 1945 regulating pensions, defense of judges for unauthorized acts, and many other provisions governing the activities of the office to experience the rapidly changing status of the federal judge. Indeed, the federal judge is no longer isolated in his own court, but now has contact with his colleagues through judicial councils, conferences and training sessions conducted by the Federal Judicial Center. Certainly, the first district court judge would be amazed at the change in functioning of the federal courts and the greater procedural requirements placed upon the judicial office.

Federal judges have played a significant role in the improvements in the administration of justice. The judges of the Twentieth Century have evidenced more interest in issues of judicial reform, and through the Judicial Conference of the United States, have contributed immeasurably to innovations in the operations of the federal courts. Chief Justice Taft was among the first who took an active part in mobilizing the federal judges and in urging Congress to take steps which streamlined the courts. Other federal judges such as John Parker of the Court of Appeals for the Fourth Circuit took up this work. Parker's efforts to establish the Administrative Office of the Courts and revise Title 28 of the UNITED STATES CODE in 1948 demonstrate this interest in judicial reform.

Other federal judges have stood up for unpopular causes such as civil rights and have used the federal courts to accomplish reforms in that area as well as in the area of prison conditions. These are dramatic actions which attract attention more than the judicial opinions which have more impact on the technical side of the law. It is difficult to determine outstanding opinions, and the judges on the federal bench who were respected for their learning have all been forgotten.

The function of the federal judge has changed during its two hundred years from a passive role in the development of the law to a more active role. Just how this evolution took place is difficult to ascertain, and its wisdom will be disputed for centuries to come.

FOOTNOTES TO CHAPTER 23

1. Great Charter of Liberties (Magna Carta), sec. 45.
2. Sydney Humphries, ed., BACON'S ESSAYS, "Of Judicature," p.299 (1912).
3. James D. Andrews, ed., THE WORKS OF JAMES WILSON, vol.II, p.159 (1896).
4. William F. Swindler, SOURCES AND DOCUMENTS OF UNITED STATES CONSTITUTIONS, vol.5, Mass. Constitution of 1780, pt.I, art.XXIX, p.96 (1975).
5. Act of September 24, 1789, sec. 8, 1 STAT. 76.
6. Sir William Blackstone, COMMENTARIES Introduction, p.69. This view is stated rather forceably in Henry Budd, "Reports and Some Reporters," 47 AMER. L. REV. 481 (1913).
7. Andrews, *supra,* note 3, p.159, 160.
8. Osborn et al. v. Bank of the United States, 9 Wheat. 739, 866 (1824).
9. Act of 12 and 13 William III, c.2, sec. III(7), 10 STAT. L. 360.
10. Leonard Woods Labaree, ROYAL GOVERNMENT IN AMERICA (1930), p.390.
11. James Kent, COMMENTARIES ON AMERICAN LAW, v.1, p.444 (14th ed. 1896).
12. The Farmers' Alliance of Illinois adopted a resolution at its annual meeting in 1890 urging election of federal judges. Note, 24 AMER. L. REV. 1003 (1890). This is but one illustration of attempts to change the tenure of federal judges.
13. THE FEDERALIST no.78.
14. Joseph Story, COMMENTARIES ON THE CONSTITUTION OF THE UNITED STATES (4th ed., 1873), pp.401-424; Kent, *supra,* note 11, p.445.
15. Erwin C. Surrency, "The Judges of the Federal Courts," 1 AMER. J. LEG. HIST. 76 (1957).
16. Burke Shartel, "Federal Judges — Appointment, Supervision, and Removal — Some Possibilities Under the Constitution," 28 MICH. L. REV. 487 (1930).
17. Joseph P. Harris, THE ADVICE AND CONSENT OF THE SENATE: A STUDY IN THE CONFIRMATION OF APPOINTMENTS BY THE UNITED STATES SENATE (1968), p.323.
18. Evan A. Evans, "Political Influences in the Selection of Federal Judges," 1948 WIS. L. REV. 330, argues that party affiliation has been important.
19. Harris, *supra,* note 17, p.314.
20. Donald O. Dewey, "Hoosier Justice: The Journal of David McDonald, 1864-1868", 62 INDIANA MAG. OF HIST. 179, fn.8, 189 (1966).
21. Executive Order 12097, November 8, 1978, 43 F.R. 52455.
22. Harris, *supra,* note 17, p.317.
23. For political implications in the appointment of federal judges, *see* J. Earl Major, "Federal Judges as Political Patronage," 38 CHICAGO BAR RECORD 7 (1956), and Evan A. Evans, "Political Influences in the Selection of Federal Judges," 1948 WISC. L. REV. 330. In 1965, President Johnson nominated Francis X. Morrissey as Judge of the District Court for the District of Massachusetts, who had come to the bar by attending a law school which had the diploma privilege. The American Bar Association's Committee reported "from the standpoint of legal training, legal experience, and legal ability, we have not had any case where these factors were so lacking." The nomination was withdrawn. For the mechanism of this procedure, *see* 87 A.B.A. REPTS. 601 (1962).
24. The Nominating Commissions created by President Carter have spawned a "learned" monograph and a host of articles. *See* Larry C. Berkson and Susan B. Carbon, THE UNITED STATES CIRCUIT JUDGE NOMINATING COMMISSION: ITS MEMBERS, PROCEDURES AND CANDIDATES (1980); Alan Neff, THE UNITED STATES DISTRICT JUDGE NOMINATING COMMISSIONS: THEIR MEMBERS,

PROCEDURES AND CANDIDATES (1980); Larry Berkson, "Carter's Judicial Selection System: How Well Does it Work?" 19 JUDGES J. 4 (Fall, 1980).

25. Griffin B. Bell, TAKING CARE OF THE LAW (1982), p.236. On page 40, Bell relates how some presidential advisors circulated judicial nominations to various pressure groups.

26. Harris, *supra,* note 17, p.302.

27. Charles Warren, THE SUPREME COURT IN THE UNITED STATES HISTORY, v.2, p.757 (Rev. ed. 1928).

28. Act of June 16, 1906, 34 STAT. 276.

29. Act of December 29, 1845, 9 STAT. 1.

30. Act of February 21, 1851, 11 STAT. 164.

31. For a history of the new cities where federal courts were held within each district, *see* Erwin C. Surrency, "Federal District Court Judges and the History of Their Courts," 40 F.R.D. 139 (1966).

32. Act of March 10, 1824, 4 STAT. 9; *see* Erwin C. Surrency, "The Appointment of Federal Judges in Alabama," 1 AMER. J. LEG. HIST. 148 (1957).

33. Act of February 6, 1839, 5 STAT. 315.

34. Act of August 2, 1886, 24 STAT. 213.

35. Act of March 3, 1911, sec. 1, 36 STAT. 1087.

36. Act of March 3, 1911, 36 STAT. 1123. For a complete history of the appointment of judges for each district, *see* Surrency, *supra,* note 31.

37. Act of June 22, 1936, 49 STAT. 1804-1806; four separate Acts for Missouri and Oklahoma, Kentucky, Washington, and West Virginia.

38. Act of February 24, 1910, 36 STAT. 202.

39. Act of September 14, 1922, 48 STAT. 837.

40. H.R. Rept. No. 308, 80 Cong. 1st sess., notes under sec. 133.

41. Act of February 10, 1954, 68 STAT. 8.

42. Since 1948, this has been 28 U.S.C. 133.

43. S. Rept. No. 117, 95th Cong., 1st Sess. 51 (1977).

44. Judge John C. Rose, JURISDICTION AND PROCEDURE OF THE FEDERAL COURTS (1926); p.76 comments on the practice of one judge to a district and how this practice was changing.

45. Act of April 29, 1812, 2 STAT. 719.

46. Act of April 9, 1814, 3 STAT. 120.

47. Act of February 4, 1903, 32 STAT. 795; Act of February 9, 1903, 32 STAT. 805.

48. Act of September 14, 1922, 48 STAT. 837.

49. Act of February 10, 1954, 68 STAT. 8. The Omnibus Judgeships Bills since 1922 are as follows; Act of August 19, 1935, 49 STAT. 659; Act of May 31, 1938, 52 STAT. 585; Act of March 24, 1940, 54 STAT. 219.

50. David S. Clark, "Adjudication to Administration: A Statistical Analysis of Federal District Courts in the Twentieth Century," 55 SO. CALIF. L. REV. 69 (1981); gives a table of the number of District Court judges including Circuit Court Judges and "District Court Judges" in the territories.

51. S. Rept. No. 117, 95th Cong., 1st sess. 11, 43 (1977).

52. Act of September 14, 1922, 48 STAT. 837.

53. Henry P. Chandler, "Some Major Advances in the Federal Judicial System," 31 F.R.D. 324 (1963).

54. S. Rept. No. 117, 95th Cong., 1st sess. 7-8 (1977).

55. S. Rept. No. 117, 95th Cong., 1st sess. 53 (1977).

56. Equity Rules, 1842, Rule LXXIII and those following.

57. Equity Rules, 1913, Rule 59.

58. *See* Jewelers' Circular Publishing Co. v. Keystone Publishing Co., 274 Fed. 932 (D.C. S.D. N.Y. 1921).

59. Act of April 30, 1790, sec. 21, 1 STAT. 117.

60. Act of May 8, 1792, sec. 11, 1 STAT. 278.

61. Act of March 3, 1821, 3 STAT. 643.

62. Act of December 18, 1812, 2 STAT. 788.

63. Leviticus 19:15; Deuteronomy, 1:17; 16:19; Proverbs 24:23 are but a few references.

64. 34 ABA REPTS. 88 (1909).

65. 49 ABA REPTS. 65 (1924).

66. "Symposium: Non-judicial Activities of Judges," 51 CHICAGO B. REC. 64 (Nov. 1969).

67. 34 ABA REPTS. 88 (1909); 42 ABA REPTS. 80 (1917).

68. Adopted June 6, 1925, 42 Ga. B. Assoc. Proc. 168 (1925).

69. 3 CALIF. STATE B.J. 82 (1928); STATE BAR OF CALIFORNIA v. SUPERIOR COURTS, 207 CALIF. 323, 278 Pac. 432 (1929).

70. U.S. Const. art. II, sec. 4.

71. Act of December 18, 1812, 2 STAT. 788.

72. Warren, *supra,* note 27, v.1, p.289.

73. Judicial Reform Act: Hearings on S. 1506 Before the Subcomm. on Improvements in Judicial Machinery of the Senate Comm. on the Judiciary, 91st Cong., 1st sess. 101 (June, 1969). *See* Joseph Borkin, THE CORRUPT JUDGE: AN INQUIRY INTO BRIBERY AND OTHER HIGH CRIMES AND MISDEMEANORS IN THE FEDERAL COURTS (1966). Jacobus Ten Brock, "Partisan Politics and Federal Judgeship Impeachments since 1903," 23 MINN. L. REV. 185 (1939), argues that most impeachment proceedings are politically motivated.

74. Judicial Discipline and Tenure: Hearings on S. 295, 522 and 678 Before the Subcomm. on Improvements in Judicial Machinery and the Subcomm. on the Constitution of the Senate Comm. on the Judiciary, 96th Cong., 1st sess. (1979).

75. National Law Journal, October 22, 1984, p.3.

76. Act of April 2, 1982, sec. 105(a), 96 STAT. 28.

77. Herman V. Ames, THE PROPOSED AMENDMENTS TO THE CONSTITUTION OF THE UNITED STATES (Annual Rept. American Historical Association for 1896), p.151.

78. Act of April 10, 1869, sec. 5, 16 STAT. 45; William S. Carpenter, JUDICIAL TENURE IN THE UNITED STATES (1918), p.186.

79. Act of June 23, 1910, 36 STAT. 1861.

80. Carpenter, *supra,* note 78, p.191.

81. Roosevelt's relation with the Supreme Court was a featured part of I'D RATHER BE RIGHT, a musical revue by George Kaufman and Moss Hart (1937).

82. Act of February 25, 1919, sec. 6, 40 STAT. 1158.

83. Act of September 2, 1957, 7 STAT. 586.

84. 89th Cong. 1st sess., House of Representatives. Committee on the Judiciary. Hearings, Federal Courts and Judges, September 29, 1965, p.272.

85. Peter Graham Fish, "The Circuit Councils: Rusty Hinges of Federal Judicial Administration," 37 U. CHICAGO L. REV. 203 (1970); J. Edward Lumbard, "The Place of the Federal Judicial Councils in the Administration of Justice," 47 A.B.A. J. 169 (1961).

86. John J. Gallo, "Removal of Federal Judges - New Alternatives to an Old Problem: *Chandler v. Judicial Council of the Tenth Circuit,*" 13 U.C.L.A. L. REV. 1385 (1966); Irving R. Kaufman, "Chilling Judicial Independence," 88 YALE L. REV. 681 (1979).

87. 28 U.S.C. 332.

88. U.S. Senate. Committee on the Judiciary. Subcommittee on Judiciary and Constitution. Hearings. Judicial discipline and tenure. 1979, p.44, for example.

89. U.S. Senate. Committee on the Judiciary. Subcommittee on Judiciary and Constitution. Hearings. Judicial discipline and tenure. 1979, p.45, in which Judge James Browning reported that during his 18 years on the Court of Appeals, the Council had not taken action by issuing a formal order.

90. Chandler v. Judicial Council of the Tenth Circuit, 398 U.S. 74, 86, note 7 (1970). *See also* Misc. Order, 382 U.S. 1003, 1005 (1966).

91. DEBATES IN THE SENATE OF THE UNITED STATES ON THE JUDICIARY DURING THE FIRST SESSION OF THE SEVENTH CONGRESS (Philadelphia, 1802), p.78.

92. Joseph Story, COMMENTARIES ON THE CONSTITUTION OF THE UNITED STATES (4th ed., 1873), v.2, p.428.

93. Felix Frankfurter and James M. Landis, THE BUSINESS OF THE SUPREME COURT (1928), p.172; James Willard Hurst, THE GROWTH OF AMERICAN LAW (1950), p.125.

94. Act of September 24, 1789, sec. 6, 1 STAT. 76.

95. James D. Richardson, A COMPILATION OF THE MESSAGES AND PAPERS OF THE PRESIDENTS 1789-1902 (1904), v.1, p.511.

96. Act of May 20, 1826, 4 STAT. 180.

97. Act of July 29, 1850, 9 STAT. 442.

98. Act of April 2, 1852, 10 STAT. 5.

99. Act of October 13, 1913, 38 STAT. 203.

100. Quoted in Peter Graham Fish, THE POLITICS OF FEDERAL ADMINISTRATION (1973), p.15. An anonymous note in a copy of this book read, "Boy, was *he* wrong!"

101. The efforts of Taft to get his bill enacted are recounted in detail in Fish, *supra,* note 100, p.24.

102. Albert Dickerman, "The Business of the Federal Courts and the Salaries of the Judges", 24 AMER. L. REV. 78, 85 (1890). The reason given for the resignation of William L. Day, judge of the United States District Court, Northern District of Ohio, was the "inadequacy of the salary." Judge Day's father was an associate justice on the Supreme Court and had been District Judge on this same Court. 16 LAW NOTES 36 (1915).

103. Benjamin R. Curtis, Jr., A MEMOIR OF BENJAMIN ROBBIN CURTIS (1879), v.1, p.244, 249.

104. Note: 24 AMER. L. REV. 661 (1890).

105. Act of February 27, 1795, 1 STAT. 423.

106. Act of September 23, 1789, 1 STAT. 72.

107. Act of May 26, 1824, sec. 13, 4 STAT. 56.

108. H.R. Rept. No. 113, 29th Cong. 1st sess., Vol. I, January 16, 1846.

109. Act of September 28, 1850, sec. 7, 9 STAT. 521; House Misc. Doc. 26, 32d Cong. 1st sess., Vol. I.

110. H.R. Rept. No. 1761, 49th Cong. 1st sess., Vol. VI, April 20 & 26, 1886, p.2.

111. Note, 24 AMER. L. REV. 660 (1890).

112. 8 LAW NOTES 441 (Feb. 1905).

113. Act of February 7, 1873, sec. 2, 17 STAT. 423; *See* Benedict v. United States, 176 U.S. 357 (1899).

114. Act of February 17, 1855, 10 STAT. 608.

115. Act of February 24, 1891, 26 STAT. 783; 24 AMER. L. REV. 107 (1890).

116. Dickerman, *supra,* note 102; "Salaries of Federal Judges," 14 LAW NOTES 25 (1910).

117. Dewey, *supra,* note 20, p.216, 222.

118. Act of December 16, 1967, sec. 216, 81 STAT. 638.

119. Printed in 157 U.S. 701 (1862).

120. Evans v. Gore, 253 U.S. 245 (1920).

121. O'Malley v. Woodrough, 307 U.S. 277 (1939). The dissenting opinion of Justice Butler reviews this history in detail.

122. Act of June 30, 1932, sec. 105, 47 STAT. 401.

123. Atkins v. United States, 556 F.2d 1028 (Ct. Cl. 1977).

124. Act of February 12, 1903, 32 STAT. 825.

125. Kurt H. Nadelmann, "Joseph Story's Contribution to American Conflicts of Law: A Comment," 5 AMER. J. LEG. HIST. 230 (1961); Lorenzen, "Story's Commentaries on the Conflicts of Laws — One Hundred Years After," 48 HARV. L. REV. 15 (1934).

126. Gerald T. Dunne, "Joseph Story's First Writing on Equity," 14 AMER. J. LEG. HIST. 76 (1970).

127. James D. Hart, ed., THE OXFORD COMPANION TO AMERICAN LITERATURE (4th ed., 1965), entry for Francis Hopkinson, p.382.

128. Maxwell Bloomfield, "Law and Lawyers in American Popular Culture," in Carl S. Smith, LAW AND AMERICAN LITERATURE; A COLLECTION OF ESSAYS (1982), p.143.

129. Charles K. Lusk, THE FEDERAL JUDGE (1896): *see* review in 1 LAW NOTES, p.125 (December 1897). Also, comment of Maxwell Bloomfield to author.

130. George S. Kaufman and Moss Hart, I'D RATHER BE RIGHT (1937), pp.58-63.

131. Professor Bloomfield supplied the following titles: Stephen Longstreet, THE PEDLOCK INHERITANCE (1972), and Steven Phillips, CIVIL ACTIONS (1983) as being of this genre.

Chapter 24

FEDERAL COURTS OF NATIONAL JURISDICTION

It is a common perception when federal courts are discussed to think in terms of the regular courts, ignoring those judicial bodies limited to a defined jurisdiction which function currently or have existed in the past. Whether these courts should be considered a part of the federal judiciary depends upon a consideration of the issue of constitutional versus legislative courts. It is strongly argued by judges and the legal profession that all judicial controversies should be resolved before a judge appointed under Article III of the Constitution. However, Congress has established a few courts with defined jurisdiction to resolve issues arising exclusively under federal law, such as patents and tariffs. With the establishment of such courts, a part of the jurisdiction was left with the regular federal courts, thus creating overlapping forums. Only recently has exclusive jurisdiction over all appeals in patent law been vested in a single court. Other courts were established in foreign countries under the provisions of a number of treaties. Judicial bodies established by the president in occupied territories constitute still another group. Issues arising in these courts have often found their way into the federal judicial system by various procedural devices.

A perceived need in the federal system is for a uniform resolution of issues arising under federal statutes — patents, social security and tax law are among those areas frequently cited — where there is a clear necessity for uniform application and administration of those programs. Originally, the mechanism providing for this desirable uniformity was furnished by the Supreme Court as the sole appellate court in the federal system. More recently, with the increase of population and other factors, it has become impossible for that Court to provide such guidance. Since specialized courts with a defined jurisdiction have never been favored in the federal judicial system, other solutions have been sought.

Regardless of the opposition to such courts, several courts with limited jurisdiction have become important judicial forums in the federal system, while others have ceased to exist after completing their work. Those still in existence may ascribe their success in part to the fact that so few lawyers practice before them, although all are aware of their existence. A first court with a defined jurisdiction was the Court of Claims, established in 1855.

Court of Claims

Under the theory of common law that the "sovereign can do no wrong", the state is usually immune from the liability arising from its own contracts and torts. If anyone had a claim arising under either of these branches of law against the federal government before the Court of Claims was established, he needed to lodge a petition for relief containing supporting evidence with Congress. These claims were referred to committees in both houses, which generally investigated them thoroughly. A bill would then be reported out of committee to proceed through the usual legislative process, ending with the signature of the President. Such a procedure for settling claims did not assure a rapid solution or justice for the claimant, for such bills could be defeated because of political opposition.

Partly to relieve Congress of this burden, an act was passed in 1855 establishing the Court of Claims, which would consist of three judges. This court would hear all claims "founded upon any law of Congress, or upon any regulation of an executive department, or upon any contract, expressed or implied", or any claim referred to it by Congress. The findings of the court were referred to Congress with a bill drafted for enactment to implement the judgment.[1]

The philosophy for founding this court was eloquently given by Charles O'Connor of New York, who stated that the court was the

> first-born of a new judicial era . . . henceforth our government repudiates the arrogant assumption [that the sovereign can do no wrong], and consents to meet at the bar of enlightened justice every claimant, how lowly soever his condition . . . but effectual progress has been made towards giving form and method to the administration of justice between the nation and the individual.[2]

It was generally assumed that Congress would not review these claims but would appropriate the necessary funds to pay the judgment. However, the committees of Congress fully considered the claims after the court had made its findings and passed upon them separately.[3] In 1863, at the urging of President Lincoln, Congress voted to give finality to the findings of the Court of Claims. An appeal was authorized to the Supreme Court when the amount exceeded $3,000. The judgment of the court would be paid out of general appropriations made for the purpose of satisfying private claims.[4]

When an appeal was first taken, the Supreme Court denied that it could hear appeals from the Court of Claims because its decisions were not judicial, since they could be revised by a member of the executive department, namely, the Secretary of the Treasury.[5] The review of the Secretary of the Treasury was finally repealed in 1866.[6] Since that date, the court has been assigned all types of claims against the government arising from Indian raids to claims for damages to oyster beds resulting from the dredging by the United States Corps of Engineers.[7]

The act creating the Court of Claims authorized three judges appointed during good behavior, reflecting the dignity with which the Congress intended to clothe this court. In 1863, two additional judges were authorized, bringing the total to five judges, which was the size of the court for over a hundred years.[8] In 1966, two more judges were authorized, and the court was permitted to sit in divisions of three judges.[9] The first judges of the court were John J. Gilchrist of New Hampshire, Isaac N. Blackford of Indiana, and George P. Scarburgh of Virginia, all of whom were distinguished jurists. Gilchrist had served on the Supreme Court of New Hampshire; Blackford had enjoyed a very distinguished career on the Supreme Court of Indiana, noted especially for his concise and lucid decisions; and Judge Scarburgh had served on a trial court in Virginia, as well as holding a professorship at William and Mary College. Indeed, the first bench on the Court of Claims was of the highest merit. The position of chief justice was created in 1863, and Joseph Casey, who was then a judge on the court, was appointed to this position and served in this capacity until 1870. On the whole, the judges of this court have been capable of deciding many difficult and perplexing cases.

The Court of Claims was originally established to hear claims referred to it by Congress. Generally, these referral cases were found in specific statutes. For example, in 1879, Congress authorized the court to "take jurisdiction of and adjudge the claims of officers and privates of the New Mexico Mounted Volunteers in the service of the United States during the war of rebellion, on account of losses of horses and equipment".[10] Some statutes entitled individuals to pursue a case in the Court of Claims for the settlement of property destroyed by Indians.[11] Many types of claims arising from the Civil War form a fascinating collection of decisions. In 1863, the Abandoned and Captured Property Act allowed former loyal owners of the seized property to recover the value of their property.[12] This statute was repealed in 1911.

With the adoption of the Bowman Act in 1883, Congress sought to simplify the procedure of referral by allowing any committee of either house whenever a claim was pending before it to refer the case to the Court of Claims. Heads of departments that had pending before them a controverted question of fact or law could transmit the issue with all necessary documents to the court for resolution. However, the court could not enter judgment; rather, it was required to report its findings to the department for guidance and action.[13] This act did not extend to claims growing out of damage by the Army or Navy during the Civil War. For the court to have jurisdiction, the person making the claim for supplies furnished to the Union forces had to aver that he "did not give any aid or comfort to said rebellion, but was throughout the war loyal to the government of the United States".[14] If the court found that such person had not been loyal, then it was without jurisdiction.

The court could not enter judgment in cases referred to it by a committee of Congress or by the head of an executive department. This was remedied several years later by an amendment which provided that when the court found that it had jurisdiction under the new act or under some previous act, it had the authority to render judgment and to report its proceedings to either house of Congress or to the department from which the case was referred.[15] This statute, known as the Tucker Act, extended the court's jurisdiction, becoming the basic statute under which the court has operated. The court could proceed to give judgment on any claims founded upon any regulation of the executive department, upon any contract for damages, or upon the Constitution or any law of Congress, except for pensions or cases in torts and those growing out of war claims of the Civil War, which were exempted from this act. The government was authorized to enter all defenses such as set-off in counter claims, which were available to the claimant.[16] Concurrent jurisdiction in these types of claims was granted the district courts where the amount claimed did not exceed $10,000, but was greater than $1,000. This statute limited the authority to refer cases to the Court of Claims to either house of Congress rather than to a committee.

Under the Tucker Act, the court has litigated a wide range of claims, including admiralty suits involving claims for salvaging a government steamer.[17] Another large area involves tax refunds, as well as the taking of property for water management projects and other work involving the country's navigable waters. Cases involving claims for pay for services performed are another large part of the court's business.

Another prolific source of cases in the Court of Claims has been the special status of the American Indian. Numerous special acts have given the court jurisdiction to hear claims for reparations for losses from Indian depredations. Although there have been numerous special referral statutes giving the court jurisdiction over such claims, the first general act was enacted in 1891.[18]

Since its founding in 1855, the Court of Claims has used commissioners to gather evidence.[19] Commissioners were appointed in each of the thirty states, and their chief duty was to take depositions. For this service, they were paid upon a fee basis.[20] By 1925, the business of the courts had increased to the extent where the existing judges were unable to hear all of the claims filed. Instead of providing new judges, the Court of Claims was authorized to appoint seven persons to be known as commissioners who would have the general powers of a special master in chancery.[21] The commissioners could conduct formal judicial proceedings at the trial level. With this provision, the court was separated into the appellate division, consisting of the judges, and the trial division, composed of the commissioners. The trial division could meet in various cities in the United States.

In 1948, the commissioners were given authority to make recommendations for conclusions of law, as well as findings of facts, when directed to do so by the court.[22] All Congressional referral cases were given to the trial division, and now are given to the United States Claims Court.

In the reference cases, Congress often provided for an appeal to the Supreme Court under existing law. The Act of 1863 provided that an appeal could be taken on behalf of the plaintiff to the Supreme Court where the amount in controversy exceeded $3,000 or where his claim was forfeited to the United States and in all claims adverse to the United States regardless of the amount.[23] Review by the Supreme Court was almost automatic, and appeals from the Court of Claims were numerous. In 1925, the number of appeals to the Supreme Court from the Court of Claims was limited to those accepted by certiorari. The same act gave to the Court of Claims the right to certify any questions of law desired for proper disposition of the case. However, this procedure is rarely used.[24]

The Court of Claims has been limited in its remedies to providing for money judgments only and has not had the authority to grant specific performance or to compel the issuance and delivery of a patent for land.[25] In all other situations, the court has acted on the common law principles of evidence and without a jury. The court was required to file a written opinion setting out the specific questions of law involved and the court's conclusion. The court could proceed in equity or admiralty according to its rules.[26]

Whether the Court of Claims was a legislative or a constitutional court was not decided until 1933, although the Supreme Court of the United States had in several cases implied that it was a constitutional court. A judge of the court brought an action to recover his salary which had been cut during the Depression years, but the Supreme Court held that the Court of Claims was not a constitutional court, and hence, the judges' salaries could be reduced during their tenure.[27] Obviously, the members of the court objected to this decision. In 1953, Congress specifically declared the court to be a constitutional court.[28] The House of Representatives Committee report argued that Congress had intended that it be a constitutional court since its creation and extensively reviewed the cases dealing with this problem.[29] The Supreme Court of the United States later bowed to the wishes of Congress.[30] In recognition of this status, the chief justice of the Court of Claims was authorized in 1956 to sit in the Judicial Conference of the United States. By virtue of this act, the budget estimate of the court would be approved by the Judicial Conference as with all other federal courts.[31]

Acceptance of the fact that the Court of Claims was a constitutional court ended the court's jurisdiction of Congressional reference cases, for under this doctrine, the court could only hear actual disputes and not suits referred for investigation and recommendation for settlement. Such suits were referred by either house of Congress to the chief commissioner of the court who appointed a commissioner to hear the matter and make a recommendation to the referring body, subject to a review by a panel of three commissioners.[32] This became known as the trial division of the court. In 1982, when the United States Court of Claims was abolished, these commissioners became the judges of the newly established United States Claims Court. This court has now succeeded to the colorful jurisdiction of the former Court of Claims.[33]

Court of Private Land Claims

Land titles of great economic value in those areas of the United States purchased from foreign countries were an abundant source of litigation in the Nineteenth Century. Under the principles of international law, such transfer of sovereignty only dissolved the relationship between the citizen and the former government and was never understood to be a cession of individual property to the new government unless the original inhabitants departed. Customarily, treaties provided for a two year period for the former inhabitants to dispose of their property and leave the country if they did not wish to become citizens of the new country.[34] All of these treaties required that the United States recognize these land grants that had been made prior to the date of cession and guarantee that the new citizens would benefit from the same privileges as those enjoyed by American citizens. Most of the disputes over land titles were settled by administrative bodies called Boards of Land Commissioners or Land Commissions, depending upon the area of the country in which the bodies were organized.[35]

A special commission was established in California and a Board of Land Commissioners was established in Louisiana and Florida to settle disputes of conflicting land claims in those areas. Otherwise, such disputes were settled by the Surveyor General, who was required to report to Congress. Appeals to the federal courts were authorized which brought many of these cases into the federal courts.[36]

Such boards worked well in Louisiana and Florida, but were as successful in California or in the other areas of the Western parts of the country. By 1890, Congress found that very few of the claims involving property in the areas of the country ceded by Mexico had been reported to it.[37] To settle some of these problems in a more judicious manner, Congress created the Court of Private Land Claims to settle land claims in the present states of New Mexico, Arizona, Utah, Nevada, Colorado and Wyoming.[38]

The jurisdiction of the court was exclusive "relative to the title to the land the subject of such case, the extent, location, and boundaries thereof, and other matters connected therewith fit and proper to be heard and determined".[39] The court was required to adjudicate claims "according to the law of nations" and the stipulations contained in two treaties with

Mexico. This required the court to consider "the laws and ordinances of the Government from which (the grant) is alleged to have been derived".[40]

The procedure before the court was to conform to the equity practice of the federal courts. The petition was required to set forth "fully the nature" of the claim with a thorough description of the grant. The federal government was represented by a United States attorney.[41] The commissioner of the General Land Office and all other officials having custody of land records were to produce these records at the request of either party.[42]

Appeals by both the claimant and the government were provided for in the statute. The Supreme Court recognized the Court of Private Land Claims as a constitutional court from which it could take appeals.[43] The Supreme Court was authorized to retry the cause and could take additional testimony, but the court never discussed this grant or exercised it.[44] Numerous appeals from the court were taken to the Supreme Court of the United States and involved many interpretations of Mexican law, ranging from questions of the official's authority to make the grant of land to issues of whether the claimant complied with the conditions of the grant.[45] The decisions of the Court of Private Land Claims were never collected and published.

The court held its first session in Denver on July 1, 1891 under Chief Justice Joseph R. Reid. The first session was for the purpose of organizing and adopting rules and preparing to receive cases for adjudication. The court met the following November in the same city and the next month in Santa Fe. The court found that 90% of its business was in Arizona and New Mexico where 30 million acres were claimed under Spanish grants.[46]

During its existence, the court litigated thousands of claims but the most remarkable case was that of Peralta Reavis, self-styled "Baron of Arizonac, Knight of the Colorados, Grandee of Spain", who claimed over 12 million acres under a grant from Philip V of Spain made in 1744. The claims had been held valid in several cases, but the grant was proven to be a forgery, and in 1896, the claimant and his wife were arrested and sentenced to imprisonment for conspiracy to defraud the government of public lands by a false claim. The United States Attorney General described this case as "one of the most remarkable and thoroughly prepared fraudulent claims which ever appeared in a court of justice".[47] The court had found invalid claims to 325,709 acres of 452,132 acres claimed in New Mexico, and similarly had found against the claimants of 155,467 acres of 202,163 claimed in Arizona.[48] The jurisdiction of the court was upheld on appeal, and only a few of its decisions were reversed.[49] The court was originally established for a four year period, but its life was extended several times, finally terminating June 30, 1904.[50] All unsettled claims had been earlier transferred to the General Land Office.[51]

Congress has considered numerous bills to create other courts of specialized jurisdiction, but generally the bills have met with little support. The creation of a Court of Patent Appeals was seriously considered.

Under the scheme urged by the American Bar Association, the court would consist of a chief justice and four other judges designated by the Chief Justice of the Supreme Court to serve for a stated period on this court. The court would have jurisdiction over all matters arising under the patent laws, and under some proposals, copyright and trademarks as well. This jurisdiction was exclusive of the Circuit Court of Appeals. Nothing as encompassing as this proposal was adopted until the creation of the Court of Appeals for the Federal Circuit.[52] Appeals from the Patent Office were given to the Court of Customs Appeals which partially met the demands of the patent bar.

In the 56th Congress (1899-1901), a bill was introduced to create a Court of Pension Appeals, but this bill died in committee. A Court of Indian Claims was proposed in the 59th Congress (1905-1907) to adjudicate claims between the federal government and the Indian tribes, but this proposal also failed. Congress has since received proposals to create a Court of Veteran's Appeals and an Administrative Court. In all probability, existing administrative agencies will evolve into adjudicative bodies to meet the perceived needs.[53] Such a development is illustrated by the creation of several boards which were later reorganized as courts, such as the Court of Customs Appeals.

Court of Customs Appeals

During nearly all of the first half of the Nineteenth Century, customs duties were the primary source of revenue for the federal government, and hence, it is not surprising to find a great deal of legislation on this matter. However, the merchants had to bring a common law action against the collector personally in the district or circuit courts to settle their grievances of excessive duties or high appraisal rates on goods.[54] The results of these law suits did not encourage the uniform application of the custom laws and led to a great deal of dissatisfaction as international trade developed. For this reason, in 1890, Congress provided for the appointment of nine members of a Board of General Appraisers before which these problems were to be litigated.[55] The number of members on the Board was not increased before its title was changed and neither was its jurisdiction.

Appeals from the Board of General Appraisers were taken to the Circuit Court of Appeals. Since the largest port in the country was located in the Second Circuit, the largest number of appeals from this Board were taken to the court in New York. In the Circuit Court of Appeals, new evidence could be introduced, and hence, the appeal was a trial *de novo,* not a review of the findings of the Board. The parties generally withheld testimony in the cases until they reached this stage.[56] This organization resulted in uneven application of the tariffs, which were expected to be uniformily administered.

The proposal to remove such appeals from the Circuit Court of Appeals to a specialized appellate court met with opposition. Some

Congressional leaders argued the move would lead to partiality among the judges, a charge which was made time and again against these specialized courts. However, the Court of Customs Appeals was created in 1909 to hear appeals from the Board of General Appraisers, with the result that all appeals in appraisal cases were removed from the Circuit Court of Appeals.[57]

In 1929, the jurisdiction of the Court of Customs Appeals was extended to appeals from the Patent Office, including both patents and trademarks, and became known as the Court of Customs and Patent Appeals.[58] Later, the court was given the authority to review appeals from the United States Tariff Commission on questions of unfair practices in import trade.

The court consisted of a chief justice and four associate justices. It was the first court created that had authority to hold its sessions in any location in this country fixed by rule of court.

In 1958, the court was declared to be a constitutional court by Congress and given representation in the Judicial Conference of the United States.[59] The court was reluctant to become a member of the Judicial Conference, for this would require the court's budget to be submitted to the Conference.[60]

The United States Court for Customs and Patent Appeals was abolished in 1982 and merged with the United States Court of Claims as the United States Court of Appeals for the Federal Circuit.[61]

The Commerce Court

The regulation of the railroads occupied the attention of the nation at the beginning of the Twentieth Century. The Interstate Commerce Commission was established in 1887, and appeals could be taken from this commission to federal courts. However, because of the then current backlog in the courts and the requirements of appellate procedure, appeals resulted in long delays, leading to the conclusion that this method did not adequately meet the needs of the nation. To remedy this, the suggestion was made that a specialized court be created to hear appeals from the Interstate Commerce Department.

President Taft in 1910 urged the creation of the United States Commerce Court, and this recommendation was enacted into law by a narrow margin in 1910.[62] The court consisted of five judges who were to be appointed from among judges of the Circuit Court of Appeals and designated to serve a given term on the court.[63] The court opened its sessions in Washington in February, 1911, and 36 cases were transferred to it from the Circuit Court of Appeals. The court reversed many of the decisions of the ICC, and was itself reversed on many of these issues by the Supreme Court. The court came under suspicion for favoring the railroads and immediately aroused strong political hostility. It was a source of controversy during its entire existence. The fact that one of the judges,

Robert W. Archbald, was impeached did not add to the court's popularity. With the change of administration in 1912, bills were immediately introduced in Congress to abolish the court, and in 1913, its demise was directed.[64]

The history of this court is well summarized by a writer who wrote that the Commerce Court

> was born in a political storm, almost at once became the object of political attack and bona fide opposition, was under congressional investigation almost continuously, was rescued from annihilation via the starvation route twice by the President's veto, and finally under a new administration was choked to death in an appropriation bill and so came to a tragic end after three years of violent experience.[65]

The experience with this court has probably influenced the thinking of the American bar about specialized courts more than any other event.

The Customs Court

In 1890, an attempt was made to bring uniformity in the administration of the tariffs act by removing the suits involving classification of goods and appraisal of tariffs from the federal courts invested in the Board of General Appraisers. The Board had exclusive original jurisdiction of all these questions and possessed the powers of a district court for preserving order, compelling the attendance of witnesses and the production of evidence, and punishing for contempt. The decisions of the Board were conclusive except when either of the parties, including the government, took an appeal to the Court of Customs and Patent Appeals.[66] As with any other court, the decisions of the Board were self-executing in that the importers had to pay the amount of duties found due immediately, except in the case of an appeal, and the Secretary of Treasury had to pay claims found by the Board. The difficulty that the Board encountered was that some foreign governments refused to honor commissions issued by the Board to take testimony within their boundaries. Because Congress felt that a change in title would end this confusion, in 1926, the title of the Board of General Appraisers was changed to the Customs Court.[67] This change in no way affected the jurisdiction of the Board, but was a recognition of its judicial functions.

Procedure before the Board or Customs Court has always been informal. The importer pays the duty and then files a protest specifically stating the classification claimed to be correct and the error committed by the Collector of Customs. The protest must clearly state that the classification is erroneous and that the matters relied upon by the importer are correct.[68] The procedure was compared to the common law action for money received. Since the procedure in the court was informal and without a jury, this facilitated the conclusion of cases very quickly. The court had its headquarters in New York, but a three-judge division could sit in any city which was a port of entry. In a revision of the Judicial Code of 1948, the statute pertaining to the Customs Court was incorporated within Title 28.[69]

In 1980, the Customs Court was completely restructured, and its title was changed to the United States Court for International Trade with significantly enlarged jurisdiction.[70] With the increase of multilateral negotiations which has led to a decrease in tariff duties and consequently a diminishing number of cases involving classification and valuation, the court lost some of its business. Other measures, such as countervailing duties and anti-dumping legislation, have created new problems. Many of these cases were being tried in the United States District Courts, and the purpose of the creation of the United States Court of International Trade was to bring these cases in one court. The Court of International Trade is a forum in which many interesting cases involving this country's relations with other nations are decided.

The Tax Court

With the increased complexities of the Internal Revenue Code and the growth of the dependence of the government on this source of revenue, a need was felt for a review of the decisions made by the Commissioner of Internal Revenue. As a result, in 1924, Congress created the Board of Tax Appeals.[71] Its jurisdiction was limited to hearing or reviewing the findings of the Commissioner. Its findings were determinative of the taxpayer's liability,[72] for the Commissioner could go into the district court and seek any additional tax the Bureau of Internal Revenue thought was due.[73]

The establishment of the Board was not greeted with enthusiasm for many conflicting reasons. Those charged with the collection of the income tax thought that the Board would unduly complicate their consideration of audits, while supporters wanted to give it a larger role in the determination of tax questions. The Board demonstrated its competency and surprised many of its critics.[74] In 1926, a number of significant changes were made in the Board. Direct appellate review of the Board's decisions could be taken to the Court of Appeals as determined by statutory venue rules.[75] Since then, the court has received additional jurisdiction and recognition.

Because of the dispute over the wisdom of establishing the Board of Tax Appeals, its nature was rather nebulous. The original proposal of the administration was to create a Board which was independent of the Bureau of Internal Revenue — the administrative body charged with the collection of the income tax — but not of the Treasury Department. The Board therefore was made an independent agency in the executive branch. The administration proposal underwent several changes in Congress, which specifically insisted that the decisions of the Board be published. It was further argued in Congress that the Board should be transformed into a court, but there was considerable opposition to this proposal.[76] This opposition came chiefly from the accountants who had been more involved in tax matters than the lawyers, and this professional competition has impacted the history of this judicial body.

After some evolution, some unique judicial administrative procedures were introduced. At first, the full Board had to review all decisions, but this procedure was changed. Now all opinions are forwarded directly to the chief judge who determines whether the opinion should be examined by the full court.

In 1942, the title of this body was changed to the Tax Court.[77] The name was changed for several reasons, chiefly to help the Board obtain facilities in federal court houses. The Congressional committee at the time was assured that this was not a step in the direction of establishing it as a judicial court. Proposals were made to incorporate the statutes pertaining to the court in the Judicial Code of 1948 and to make it a court of record. However, due to the objections of various members of Congress, this portion of the bill was withdrawn.[78] Although in name a court, this body has continued to function as an administrative agency, occasionally raising some sensitive issues.

Congress has considered several proposals to restructure the Tax Court system, but none of these proposals has been incorporated into law. Certainly one can agree that there is no area of federal law which demands uniform interpretation as does the administration of tax laws. Yet most tax issues are settled by the eleven Circuit Courts of Appeals, which often are in conflict. The practice of the Commissioner was to decide which decisions would be considered as precedent in the administration of the tax laws. For an administrator to make such a choice was considered most reprehensible by the majority of judges of the Courts of Appeals. Some inconsistency in the administration of the tax laws results from this process of appellate review by different Courts of Appeals.

In 1969, significant changes were made in the status and the procedure of the Tax Court. By declaring the Tax Court an Article I court, for the first time it had the same power as a district court, including the power to punish for contempt and to carry out its orders. A small claims division was established to handle cases where the deficiency or over-payment was less than $1,000. The court was authorized to appoint commissioners to try the cases in this division. The small claims procedure was flexible, and any evidence that had any value was admissable. This division could render a final ad hoc decision along with a brief summary of its reasoning.[79] The taxpayer could not appeal a decision, but motions for revision or reconsideration were available from the court itself.[80]

Directing Appeals to a Special Panel

The Congressional solution to providing for uniformity of the federal law where a national policy was necessary was the creation of special panels or courts consisting of judges appointed from the existing Courts of Appeals. This technique was first applied during World War II.

The United States Emergency Court of Appeals was created for the purpose of hearing all appeals under the Price Control Act of 1942.[81] The result of creating this special court was that all appeals were heard by one group of judges rather than being heard before each of the Courts of Appeals. The court consisted of three judges selected by the Chief Justice of the United States from among members of the federal judiciary. Fred M. Vinson was designated as the first Chief Judge of the court. When he left the bench, Albert B. Maris succeeded him and served until the court was terminated in 1962.[82] The court held its sessions any place in the United States for the convenience of the parties.

The court was given jurisdiction in 1948 to review the recommendations of the local advisory boards for the control or adjustment of maximum rents.[83] When price controls were inaugurated as a result of the Korean War, Congress was surprised to find that the court was in existence and still had a number of cases pending before it.

The Supreme Court upheld the Emergency Court's jurisdiction over cases after the expiration of the acts granting jurisdiction.[84] The court was given jurisdiction over appeals arising under the Defense Production Act of 1950.[85] The court continued functioning, hearing a limited number of cases per year. On December 6, 1961, the court met for the last time to render its opinion in *Rosenzweig v. General Services Administration.*[86] Since this was the final case on its docket, Chief Judge Maris terminated the court, although one member objected on the grounds that he knew of no principle which held that when the docket was cleared, the court would cease to exist.[87]

Congress has used this device of channelling appeals in a specialized area to a special court on several occasions since 1962. In 1974, in establishing the Council on Wage and Price Stability, the Congress provided for a Temporary Emergency Court of Appeals of the United States to hear appeals from the district courts in cases arising under that statute.[88] In the same year, in providing for a regional rail reorganization, a similar court was established entitled Special Court Regional Rail Reorganization.[89] The judges of these courts were appointed by the Chief Justice of the United States from among the judges on the United States Court of Appeals.

Bankruptcy Courts

In 1978, Congress undertook to upgrade the status of the referees in bankruptcy designating them as judges presiding over the Bankruptcy Court.[90] The Chandler Act of 1898 provided for referees who exercised certain summary jurisdiction and who oversaw the administration of the Bankruptcy Acts. The referees spent considerable amounts of time deciding whether a matter fell within the summary or the plenary jurisdiction. Most of the work of the referees was in the nature of a trial judge, since receivers were usually appointed to take charge of the property and administer it. The jurisdictional limitations imposed on the referees have embroiled the district courts and the parties in voluminous litigation where the sole issue was to determine whether the referee possessed the prerequisite summary jurisdiction to determine the merits of the issue. If the bankruptcy referee found that he did not have summary jurisdiction, the case was dismissed and the parties had to bring a suit in the United States District Court.[91] Congress sought to remedy these administrative defects by creating the bankruptcy courts.

When the question was presented whether these newly created bankruptcy courts could litigate such issues as interpretation of contracts involved in bankruptcy matters, the Supreme Court held that these bankruptcy courts were Article I Courts (legislative courts) and that such issues must be tried in an Article III Court.[92] This decision placed the administration of the bankruptcy laws into confusion as well as put into jeopardy any future attempts to implement any alternatives to expensive suits in the federal court.

The Supreme Court took the unusual step of postponing the effective date of its decision. Congress was faced with the alternative of establishing bankruptcy courts under Article III or continuing the old referee system. There was considerable opposition to increasing the number of the federal judges in this manner or to having essentially administrative matters handled by the equivalent of the district court judge. In 1984, Congress finally resolved the matter by providing for a bankruptcy judge with life tenure but with a lesser salary.

The bankruptcy judges were appointed by the judges of the Courts of Appeals for a term of five years. This unique method of appointment was adopted to prevent an apparent dominance of bankruptcy referees by the district courts.

> The appointment of bankruptcy judges by the district court has contributed significantly (1) to a real and apparent dependency on the part of the bankruptcy court and its judges upon the district courts which appoint and review the decisions of bankruptcy judges, and (2) to the image of the bankruptcy court as the stepchild of the district court.[93]

The jurisdiction was clearly defined by statute to avoid the constitutional objections created by the Supreme Court.

Court of International Trade

When the Customs Court was established in 1926, and for a time thereafter, its chief function was to agree or disagree with the decisions of customs officials as to the rate and amount of duty imposed. Following the conclusion of World War II, tariffs generally declined and certainly this was no longer a significant source of revenue. However, imports into the United States increased and there became a more aggressive attitude by American importers in challenging decisions of customs agents.[94] As a result, Congress significantly changed the procedure of the court and the procedure of the customs service. For example, the three-judge appellate panel was abolished.[95] The Trade Agreements Act of 1979 gave the court jurisdiction over international trade litigation, especially problems involving anti-dumping and countervailing duties. In that year, the court was authorized to grant injunctions in limited circumstances. This Act gave rise to some complexity in determining in which court such cases should be brought. Most of the federal district courts refused to entertain such suits, citing the constitutional mandate requiring uniformity in decisions relating to imports. As a result, some suits were divided for trial between two forums.[96]

In 1980, the Customs Court was changed to the Court of International Trade and was clearly made an Article III Court. The objective was to group into this court all matters pertaining to international trade and tariff laws of the United States. In addition to the jurisdiction formerly exercised by the Customs Court, the court could review decisions of the Secretary of the Treasury in denying or revoking a customs house broker's license, any suits against the government arising under the tariff acts, and any restrictions on importation of merchandise. By expanding the jurisdiction, the nature of the old Customs Court was changed significantly, for the court was given the same power "involving equity" as exercised by any district court, including the authorization to conduct jury trials.[97]

The Court of Appeals for the Federal Circuit

Congress has continued to study the problems of the judicial system. One result of this study was the merger of the Court of Customs and Patent Appeals and the United States Court of Claims into the United States Court for the Federal Circuit in 1982.[98] The purpose of this merger was to provide a court with national jurisdiction to render decisions in cases of national significance. Chiefly, this court was given jurisdiction over all matters of patent law which removed the forum shopping among the various Courts of Appeals. It is interesting that the committees of both houses of Congress stressed that this court was not a "specialized court", but that its docket would contain cases "spanning a broad range of legal issues in types of cases". It was argued "this rich docket assures that the work of the proposed court will be broad and diverse and not narrowly specialized".[99] The Congressional Reports argue that the creation of this court is "a sensible accommodation of the usual preference for generalist judges and the selective benefit of expertise in highly specialized and technical areas".[100] Whether this is a firm principle of federal judicial administration is very doubtful.

Claims Court

Abolishing the United States Court of Claims permitted the creation of a trial court for the purposes of adjudicating claims against the government. Prior to 1980, the United States Court of Claims had appointed commissioners who were assigned the trial jurisdiction of the court. The authority of the commissioners was limited; they could not enter dispositive orders since final judgments would be made only by the judges of the court. The status of these commissioners was upgraded and their independence assured by the fact that they were to be appointed by the President with the advice and consent of the Senate for a term of fifteen years. The United States Claims Court is designated as an Article I Court, as is the Tax Court. The Claims Court sits nationwide, and its organization and procedure resemble the Tax Court in many respects, except the Claims Court is included in Title 28 of the UNITED STATES CODE, unlike the Tax Court.

The National Courts Since 1948

Increasing interest has been centered on the specialized courts. The revisors of the Judicial Code of 1948 used the opportunity to bring the organization of these special courts into conformity with the other federal courts.[101] For example, the term chief judge was substituted for presiding judge as used in the United States Court of Customs and Patent Appeals and the Customs Court, but in the Court of Claims, this office was known as chief justice. This revision aided in restating the jurisdiction of these courts, making it possible to clarify overlapping jurisdiction. All of these courts had construed their jurisdiction very strictly.[102] Bringing these courts into the new Judicial Code focused attention upon these tribunals and set in motion the steps which incorporated them more closely into the federal judicial department, such as making them members of the Judicial Conference.

The need for an institution which could provide a uniform interpretation of certain federal programs such as the tax laws and social security has become more apparent. This can only be accomplished by directing all appeals to one particular court or panel. No longer can the Supreme Court be depended upon to resolve conflicts among the courts, for with its discretionary jurisdiction, it is far easier to take a case involving the scope of a school's authority in searching students rather than a case interpreting the tax law. On the other hand, the members of the American bar insist on generalist judges. The specialized courts are perceived as being weighted in favor of one group, for this was the perception left by the experience with the Commerce Court which left the general impression that it favored the railroads. It is further argued that there is a need for diversity and a guarantee from government excesses in a "diverse and independent judiciary".[103] Whether additional specialized courts will become accepted as a part of the federal judicial system is a matter that only future developments will resolve.

Consular Courts

Another interesting series of courts were the consular courts established in those countries where the United States was granted extraterritorial privileges. At one time or another, these courts functioned in Japan, China, areas in the Ottoman Empire, Abyssinia, Persia and other areas. Little is known of the function of these courts, for they have attracted scarce attention in the legal literature.[104] The jurisdiction of these courts differed in each country depending upon the provisions of the treaty and local law, but generally, a criminal jurisdiction and a limited civil jurisdiction were exercised in those cases involving an American citizen. Where and when these courts first began to function is not known, but Congress passed statutes governing these courts in 1848 and more importantly, in 1860.[105]

In addition to the judicial functions, the consuls exercised a legislative function as well. The statute provided that the consuls in these courts would apply the laws of the United States, the common law, equity and admiralty. If none of these furnished "an appropriate and sufficient remedy", the consuls should supply all defects by decrees and regulations.[106] The Attorney General of the United States had very early suggested that the phrase "common law" include the mass of law as applied by the courts of the states.[107] However, this left open the question of what federal statutes applied in these courts. This question was partially answered in the case of *Biddle v. United States*, in which the Circuit Court of Appeals held that laws passed by Congress applicable to the territories were equally applicable in the consular courts.[108]

The consular courts were not a part of the judicial system of the United States since appeals from consular courts were taken to the minister stationed in that country, whose decisions were final. Consular decisions could be attacked collaterally by such writs as habeas corpus, although such action was infrequent.[109] The only occasion when an appeal to a court from the minister occurred was in 1870 when an appeal to the Circuit Court for the District of California from the ministers in China and Japan was allowed.[110] The decision of the Circuit Court was final. The last consular court functioned in Morocco and was terminated in 1956.[111]

A consular court was established in China which did become a part of the judicial system. The consular courts in China exercised both civil and criminal jurisdiction when any American citizen was involved. In 1906, the United States Court for China was established to exercise civil jurisdiction formerly exercised by the consular courts where the amount in controversy exceeded $500 and in criminal cases where punishment was fixed at more than a $100 fine or 60 days in prison. The court had probate jurisdiction of American citizens. This separate court was established to relieve the consuls of this legal work, so they could "devote their whole energy to the legitimate functions of their office".[112] The consular courts in China were not replaced, but continued to function where the amounts fell below those of the China Court. Appeals could be taken from the consular courts to the Court for China.[113] Appeals could then be prosecuted, provided they met the jurisdictional requirements, to the Circuit Court of Appeals for the Ninth Circuit. A single judge was appointed to this post for a term of ten years and other court officials were authorized, including a commissioner, who, in addition to the duties of that office, held the consular court in Shanghai.[114] The court sat in several cities in China and had a bar of a number of American lawyers living in China.

The courts did not get off to an auspicious beginning, for within a year of his appointment, Judge Lebbeus R. Wilfley was investigated by the Judiciary Committee of the House. The charges against Judge Wilfley focused on his apparent discrimination among attorneys in Shanghai. When he arrived in China, the judge ordered all the attorneys who were then practicing in the consular courts to submit to an examination. The accusation was that this exam was purportedly a sham so that the judge could manipulate the results and allow particular attorneys (his acquaintances) to practice before the court.[115] Judge Wilfley later resigned.

The appropriations for the United States Court for China were included in the Department of State's budget, but in 1933, the judge and the staff of the courts were transferred to the Administrative Office of the Courts, and the district attorney and marshal were transferred to the Department of Justice by a Presidential Executive Order.[116]

Fortunately, decisions of this court were published and provide interesting insights into problems of such a court. The court was abolished by statute in 1948, although it ceased to function when the Japanese occupied Shanghai in 1941.[117]

Presidential Courts

It is usually thought that courts are only established by legislative action, but the President as the governor of occupied areas has the authority to establish courts. Such courts were usually created for a very limited period of time and usually passed into oblivion without having any impact upon the total federal jurisprudence except for individual suitors. The initial judicial system in territories such as Puerto Rico and the Phillipines were originally begun by the courts established by the President acting through the military, and from these bodies, developed the judicial systems in those islands.

During the Civil War and the Reconstruction period, several such courts were established in occupied areas despite Lincoln's hesitancy to set up temporary courts of summary justice.[118] In his first annual message in

1861, Lincoln stated that the courts had been closed in some areas which were in a state of insurrection and where there was no means for loyal citizens to collect their debts. He stated that he had "been urgently solicited to establish by military power courts to administer summary justice in such cases" but had been unwilling "to go beyond the pressure of necessity in the unusual exercise of power".[119] This was not the first occasion when such a course of action was suggested. During the Mexican war, the military authorities found it inconvenient to send to this country captured ships claimed as prizes for adjudication. The naval commander on station requested, and the President established, a Prize Court at Monterey. A chaplain was appointed judge and was given the authority to exercise admiralty jurisdiction in the case of capture, reporting his proceedings to and holding all prize-moneys for distribution upon the order of the Secretary of the Navy.[120] Lincoln later authorized the military authorities to establish such a court in Nashville, Tennessee, during the occupation by the Union forces. The jurisdiction of this commission was limited to all civil matters brought by loyal citizens.[121] The Supreme Court of Tennessee later declared the judgments of this court as nullities.[122]

The most famous of these courts established during the Civil War period was the Provisional Court of Louisiana. After the conquest of New Orleans on April 24, 1862, the city was governed by provost courts. The military commanders referred matters relating to policing the area to these courts, including crimes, and later, civil matters.[123] The military authorities began to have difficulties with French and British citizens and as a result, the President established the Provisional Court by proclamation.[124] The court had jurisdiction to hear "all causes, civil and criminal, including causes in law, equity, revenue and admiralty". The practice was to conform as nearly as possible to that which had been customary in the courts of the United States in Louisiana. The judgment of the court was final and conclusive, and there was no appeal from its decisions. Charles A. Peabody, a lawyer from New York, was appointed as judge of the court. After the reestablishment of the federal courts, the court continued to function until Congress terminated it in 1866.[125] The authority of the court was upheld by the Supreme Court in the case of *The Grapeshot*.[126] This is the only "court" established during this period in the United States according to available records. The military commissions established usually expired when civilian courts were reestablished.

Other courts have been established in the federal system which have attracted very little attention. Under the reconstruction program following the Civil War, a series of courts referred to as the "Cotton Courts" were established in the South to administer labor contracts between the plantation owners and the former slaves. The purpose of the court was to prevent exploitation of the new laboring class.[127]

Just before the Civil War, as a result of the treaty with Great Britain, a special court was established in New York to try any American seized by the navies of either country while participating in the slave trade. A judge was appointed for this court, but no record of its existence or function is known to exist due to the outbreak of the Civil War at that time.[128] To know of these courts is of antiquarian interest, but the important point is that they administered justice to a small group for a short period of time. In this sense, these judicial bodies did have significance!

FOOTNOTES TO CHAPTER 24

1. Act of February 24, 1855, 10 STAT. 612; George W. Atkinson, "The United States Court of Claims," 46 AMER. L. REV. 227 (1912).

2. Quoted in Hannis Taylor, JURISDICTION AND PROCEDURE OF THE SUPREME COURT OF THE UNITED STATES (1905), p.269.

3. Richardson, "History, Jurisdiction and Practice of the Court of Claims of the United States," 7 SO. L. REV. (n.s.) 787 (1882).

4. Act of March 3, 1863, 12 STAT. 765.

5. Gordon v. United States, 2 Wall. 561 (U.S. 1864). For an interesting account of this decision, *see* Wilson Cowen, "The United States Court of Claims: A History," 216 CT. CLAIMS REPTS., p.24, n.77.

6. Act of March 17, 1866, 14 STAT. 9.

7. *See* Newell W. Ellison, "The United States Court of Claims: Keeper of the Nation's Conscience for One Hundred Years," 24 GEO. WASH. L. REV. 256 (1956); Richardson, "History, Jurisdiction and Practice of the Court of Claims of the United States," 7 SO. L. REV. (n.s.) 796 (1882); James A. Hoyt, "Legislative History," 1 U.S. CT. CL. DIG. (1950); Harvey D. Jacob, "The United States Court of Claims," 22 CASE AND COMMENT 564 (1915).

8. Act of March 3, 1863, sec. 1, 12 STAT. 765.

9. Act of May 11, 1966, 80 STAT. 139.

10. Act of March 1, 1879, 20 STAT. 324.

11. Act of March 3, 1879, 20 STAT. 396.

12. Act of March 12, 1863, sec. 3, 12 STAT. 820.

13. Act of March 3, 1883, sec. 2, 22 STAT. 485.

14. Act of March 3, 1883, sec. 4, 22 STAT. 486.

15. Act of March 3, 1887, sec. 13, 24 STAT. 507.

16. Act of March 3, 1887, sec. 1, 24 STAT. 505.

17. Wilson Cowen, THE UNITED STATES COURT OF CLAIMS, A HISTORY (1978), p.43.

18. Act of March 3, 1891, 26 STAT. 851.

19. Act of February 24, 1855, sec. 3, 10 STAT. 613.

20. Cowen, *supra,* note 17, p.92.

21. Act of February 24, 1925, 43 STAT. 964.

22. Act of June 25, 1948, 62 STAT. 976.

23. Act of March 3, 1863, sec. 5, 12 STAT. 766; Act of June 25, 1868, 15 STAT. 75.

24. Cowen, *supra,* note 17, p.95.

25. Intermingled Cotton Cases, 92 U.S. 651 (1875).

26. Act of March 3, 1887, 24 STAT. 505.

27. Williams v. United States, 289 U.S. 553 (1933).

28. Act of July 28, 1953, 67 STAT. 226.

29. H.R. Rept. No. 695, 83rd Cong. 1st sess., found in 1953 U.S. CODE CONG. & ADM. NEWS 2006.

30. Glidden Co. v. Zdanok, 370 U.S. 530 (1962).

31. Act of July 9, 1956, 70 STAT. 497.

32. Act of October 15, 1966, 80 STAT. 957.

33. Act of April 2, 1982, 96 STAT. 42.

34. This point was made in United States v. Percheman, 7 Pet. 28, 68, 87 (1833), citing Vattel bk.2, c.17, a recognized writer in the field of international law.

35. *See* Notes in 2 STAT. 288, 324, 748 etc. Paul W. Gates, HISTORY OF PUBLIC LAND LAW DEVELOPMENT (Washington, 1968), p.87.

36. H.R. Rept. No. 675, 50th Cong. 1st sess., February 24, 1888, p.2.

37. George W. Rightmire, "Special Federal Courts," 13 ILL. L. REV. 17 (1918).

38. Act of March 3, 1891, 26 STAT. 854.

39. Act of March 3, 1891, sec. 7, 26 STAT. 857.

40. Act of March 3, 1891, sec. 7, 26 STAT. 857.

41. Act of March 3, 1891, sec. 2, 26 STAT. 855.

42. Act of March 3, 1891, sec. 4, 26 STAT. 856.

43. United States v. Coe, 155 U.S. 76 (1894).

44. Act of March 3, 1891, sec. 9, 26 STAT. 858.

45. A summary of those cases appealed to the Supreme Court are found in Taylor, *supra,* note 2, p.285.

46. 1891 ATT'Y GEN. ANN. REP., p.3-4.

47. 1896 ATT'Y GEN. ANN. REP. p.xxii. This adventure was made into a movie, BARON OF ARIZONA (1950) starring Vincent Price, Ellen Drew, and Bulab Bondi.

48. 1896 ATT'Y GEN. ANN. REP. p.xxii.

49. United States v. Coe, 155 U.S. 76 (1894).

50. Act of March 3, 1903, 32 STAT. 1144.

51. Richard Wells Bradfute, THE COURT OF PRIVATE LAND CLAIMS (1975), pp.53-54.

52. Rightmire, *supra,* note 37, p.15, 16.

53. Felix Frankfurter and James M. Landis, THE BUSINESS OF THE SUPREME COURT (1928), p.174.

54. *Ibid.,* p.148.

55. Act of June 10, 1890, sec. 12, 26 STAT. 136. This was a codification of the Tariff Acts and is popularly known as the McKinley's Acts or the Customs Administrative Act.

56. Frankfurter and Landis, *supra,* note 53, p.149.

57. Act of August 5, 1909, sec. 29, 36 STAT. 11.

58. Act of March 2, 1929, 45 STAT. 1475.

59. Act of August 25, 1958, 72 STAT. 848; Declared a constitutional court in Glidden Co. v. Zdanok, 370 U.S. 330 (1961).

60. 1956 U.S. CODE CONG. & ADM. NEWS 3023.

61. Federal Courts Improvement Act, April 2, 1982, 96 STAT. 25, 36.

62. Act of June 18, 1910, 36 STAT. 539.

63. The judges first assigned to the Commerce Court were as follows:
Hon. Martin A. Knapp, Presiding Judge (Designated to serve five years, Second Circuit).
Hon. Robert W. Archbald (Designated to serve four years, Third Circuit).
Hon. William H. Hunt (Designated to serve three years, Ninth Circuit).
Hon. John E. Carland (Designated to serve two years, Eighth Circuit).
Hon. Julian W. Mack (Designated to serve one year, Seventh Circuit) 188 Fed. iii, vi.

64. The fullest account of the history of this court is found in Frankfurter and Landis, *supra,* note 53, p.153-174; Rightmire, *supra,* note 37, p.97.

65. Rightmire, *supra,* note 37, p.97; *see* Jed Johnson, "The United States Customs Court — Its History, Jurisdiction, and Procedure," 7 OKLA. L. REV. 393 (1954).

66. H.R. Rept. No. 184, 69th Cong. 1st sess., February 3, 1926, p.2. *See* United States v. Kurtz, 5 Cust. App. 144 (1914).

67. Act of May 28, 1926, 44 STAT. 669.

68. George Stewart Brown, "The United States Customs Court II," 19 A.B.A.J. 417 (1933).

69. Act of June 25, 1948, c.646, 62 STAT. 907, as codified in 28 U.S.C. §451.

70. Customs Courts Act of 1980, Oct. 10, 1980, 94 STAT. 1727, as codified in 28 U.S.C. §251.

71. Act of June 2, 1924, sec. 900, 43 STAT. 336.

72. Dobson v. Commissioner of Internal Revenue, 320 U.S. 489 (1943).

73. Harold Dubroff, THE UNITED STATES TAX COURT: AN HISTORICAL ANALYSIS (1979), p.53. This is a definitive study of the Tax Court, and contains a detailed study of the development of the substantive law of the Court.

74. *Ibid,* p.102.

75. Act of February 26, 1926, sec. 1001, 44 STAT. 109.

76. Dubroff, *supra,* note 73, p.62, 111, 113.

77. Act of October 21, 1942, sec. 504, 56 STAT. 957.

78. 93 CONG. REC. 8552, 8613.

79. Tax Reform Act of 1969, December 30, 1969, sec. 957, 83 STAT. 487, 733. *See* 1969 U.S. CODE CONG. & ADM. NEWS 2343.

80. Anne S. Davidson, "Litigation in the Small Tax Case Division of the United States Tax Court — The Taxpayer's Dream," 41 GEO. WASH. L. REV. 538 (1973).

81. Act of January 30, 1942, sec. 204, 56 STAT. 32.

82. Proceedings of the Court's Final Session, 299 F.2d 1 (1962).

83. Act of March 30, 1948, sec. 204(e), 62 STAT. 97.

84. Woods v. Hills, 334 U.S. 210 (1948).

85. Act of September 8, 1950, sec.408(a), 64 STAT. 808.

86. Rosenzweig v. General Services Administration, 299 F.2d 22 (1962).

87. Proceedings of the Court's Final Session, 299 F.2d 1 (1962).

88. Act of August 24, 1974, 88 STAT. 750.

89. Act of January 2, 1974, 87 STAT. 998. Other examples where Congress directed that appeals be taken to a special "Temporary Court" are Emergency Petroleum Allocation Act, Act of November 27, 1973, 87 STAT. 627; Energy Policy and Conservation Act of 1975, Act of December 22, 1975, 89 STAT. 871; Emergency National Gas Act, Act of February 2, 1977, 91 STAT. 4.

90. Act of November 6, 1978, 92 STAT. 2657.

91. S. Rept. No. 95-989, p.17 (1978), 1978 U.S. CODE CONG. & ADM. NEWS (Legislative History) 5803.

92. Northern Pipeline Construction Co. v. Marathon Pipe Line Co., 458 U.S. 50 (1982).

93. S. Rept. No. 95-989, p.16 (1978), 1978 U.S. CODE CONG. & ADM. NEWS (Legislative History) 5802.

94. H.R. Rept. No. 91-267, p.3 (1970), 1970 U.S. CODE CONG. & ADM. NEWS (Legislative History) 3188, 3192.

95. Act of June 2, 1970, 84 STAT. 274.

96. H.R. Rept. No. 96-1235, p.19 (1980), 1980 U.S. CODE CONG. & ADM. NEWS 3137.

97. Act of October 10, 1980, 94 STAT. 1727.

98. Act of April 2, 1982, 96 STAT. 25.

99. S. Rept. No. 97-275, p.6 (1982), 1982 U.S. CODE CONG. & ADM. NEWS (Legislative History) 16.

100. *Ibid,* quoting Judge Jon O. Newman.

101. S. Rept. No. 1559, 80th Cong. 2d sess., June 9, 1948, p.1.

102. Eastpost S.S. Corp. v. United States, 178 Ct.Cl. 559, 372 F.2d 1002 (1967); United States v. Boe, 543 F.2d 151 (C.C.P.A. 1976); United States v. King, 395 U.S. 1 (1969) are but a few cases emphasizing this point.

103. S. Rept. No. 97-275, p.39 (1981), 1982 U.S. CODE CONG. & ADM. NEWS (Legislative History) 48.

104 *See* Hacksworth, DIGEST OF INTERNATIONAL LAW (1941), v.2, p.493, 569; Notes in 20 AMER. L. REV. 905 (1886), 15 AMER. L. REV. 537 (1881) and 22 AMER. L. REV. 125 (1888).

105. Act of August 11, 1848, 9 STAT. 276; Act of June 22, 1860, 12 STAT. 72; Act of July 28, 1866, 14 STAT. 322.

106. Act of June 22, 1860, sec. 4, 12 STAT. 73.

107. 7 OP. ATTY. GEN. U.S. 495 (1856).

108. Biddle v. United States, 156 F. 759 (C.C.A. 9th, 1907).

109. In re Ross, 140 U.S. 458 (1891).

110. Act of July 1, 1870, sec. 3, 16 STAT. 184.

111. Joint Resolution of August 1, 1956, 70 STAT. 774, authorized the President to terminate these courts by proclamation. Such a proclamation was never issued. Note in TREATIES IN FORCE (1967) under Morocco states that this jurisdiction was relinquished October 5, 1956.

112. H.R. Rept. No. 4432, p.2, 59th Cong. 1st sess., May 25, 1906; *See* S. Doc. No. 95, 58th Cong. 3d sess., January 13, 1905.

113. Act of June 30, 1906, 34 STAT. 816.

114. Act of August 7, 1935, 49 STAT. 538.

115. H.R. Rept. No. 1626, 60th Cong. 1st sess., May 4, 1908.

116 Executive Order 6166, June 10, 1933. *See* H.R. Doc. No. 124, 77th Cong. 1st sess., February 22, 1941.

117. Act of June 25, 1948, 62 STAT. 992; Erwin C. Surrency, "Records of the Court for China," 1 AMER. J. LEG. HIST. 234 (1957). H.R. Doc. No. 114, 78th Cong. 1st sess., February 22, 1943.

118. Daniel v. Hutcheson, 86 Tex. 51, 61 (1893); Scott v. Billgerry, 40 Miss. 119 (1866); Tharp v. Marsh, 40 Miss. 158 (1866); Myers v. Whitfield, 22 GRATT. 780, 782-783 (63 Va.)(1872).

119. James D. Richardson, A COMPILATION OF THE MESSAGES AND PAPERS OF THE PRESIDENTS 1789-1902, v.6, p.50 (1904).

120. *See* Jecker et al v. Montgomery, 13 How. 498 (U.S. 1851).

121. Hefferman v. Porter, 6 Coldw. 391 (Tenn. 1869).

122. Walsh v. Porter, 12 Heisk. 401 (Tenn. 1873).

123. "United States Provisional Court for the State of Louisiana," 4 AMER. L. REG. (n.s.) v.13, o.s. 65 (1864); "The Authority of the Provisional Court of Louisiana," 4 AMER. L. REG. (n.s.) 385, 534 (May 1865).

124. Proclamation is reprinted in 2 AMER. J. LEG. HIST. 86 (1958).

125. Act of July 28, 1866, 14 STAT. 344.

126. The Grapeshot, 9 Wall. 129 (U.S. 1869); Burke v. Tregre & Miltenberger, 19 Wall. 519 (1873). In Mechanics' & Traders' Bank v. Union Bank of Louisiana, 22 Wall. 276 (U.S. 1874), the jurisdiction of the provost courts was upheld.

127. Act of July 16, 1866, sec. 14, 14 STAT. 176. The records of these courts are in the National Archives, Records of the Bureau of Refugees, Freedman and Abandoned Lands, Record Group 105.

128. Treaty with Great Britain, April 7, 1862, 12 STAT. 1227; Act of July 11, 1862, 12 STAT. 531.

Chapter 25

COURTS IN THE DISTRICT OF COLUMBIA

The courts in the District of Columbia have been unique in that they have enforced laws applicable to the District in the same way as state courts would enforce state law within their jurisdictions; and at the same time, these courts have enforced federal statutes. Step by step, the courts in the District were given jurisdiction to review decisions of federal agencies as well as the local administrative agencies normally found in any other American city. In this century, exclusive jurisdiction over numerous federal administrative matters is vested in the district court in the district. In 1970, these two distinct jurisdictions were separated. The fact that these courts are located in the nation's capital gives them an importance over other federal courts of equal rank. But the history of acquiring this status begins with the establishment of the District of Columbia in 1801.

The courts in the District of Columbia were first organized under the Act of 1801 which established a Circuit Court and an Orphans' Court. The court of general trial jurisdiction was known as the Circuit Court, which was unique in the fact that it combined what would normally be state jurisdiction with federal jurisdiction. Any rights given by the local laws governing Washington and the District of Columbia that a citizen sought to enforce had to be brought in this court, including probate and criminal cases. The Circuit Court of the District of Columbia had the same national jurisdiction as the circuit courts of the United States as defined in the ill-fated Judiciary Act of 1801. Although the Act was repealed the following year, it was the basis for the jurisdiction of the Circuit Court in the District of Columbia until this court was abolished. Over a period of time, by practice and tradition, any distinctions between this Circuit Court and the circuit courts in the states exercising the complete jurisdiction of the federal courts disappeared. The Circuit Court of the District of Columbia consisted of one chief judge and two judges who would hold their offices during good behavior.[1] The District was not incorporated into a circuit until 1948.[2] The parts of the District in each of the two states were organized as separate counties and sessions of the court were held in each. In addition to the federal jurisdiction, the court was given jurisdiction over

all crimes and offences committed within said district, and of all cases in law and equity . . . and also of all actions or suits of a civil nature at common law or in equity, in which the United States shall be plaintiffs or complainants; and of all seizures on land or water, and all penalties and forfeitures made, arising or accruing under the laws of the United States.[3]

In addition to the Circuit Court, Congress provided for justices of the peace in the District of Columbia. The number of these officers would be determined by the President of the United States, and they would hold their offices for five years. Their jurisdiction extended to all matters civil or criminal relating "to the conservation of the peace, have all the powers vested in, and shall perform all the duties required of, justices of the peace, as individual magistrates" as prescribed by the laws of the states from which the District was formed.[4] Further, the justices had jurisdiction over "personal demands" which were less than $20. The jurisdiction of the justices of the peace was extended in 1823 to cases involving debts and damages which did not exceed the sum of $50 and they were to "give judgment, according to the laws . . . and the equity and right of the matter, in the same manner, and under the same rules and regulations, . . ." as the justice of the peace was authorized to do when the sum did not exceed $20.[5] The Circuit Court was denied jurisdiction of debts under this amount. This jurisdictional amount was enlarged in 1867 to $100 and extended to include both damages arising from contracts and injuries to persons, but excluded title to real estate, damages for assault and battery or for malicious prosecution.[6] In 1895, the justice of the peace was given concurrent original jurisdiction in these same areas with the Supreme Court of the District of Columbia where the amount did not exceed $300.[7]

An unusual feature of the justice system was the possibility of two trials before a jury. The statute of 1823 added that either party could, after the issue was joined, demand a jury trial before twelve jurors.[8] The same act provided for an appeal to the Circuit Court of the District of Columbia and provided that either party could demand a trial by jury. From the present perspective, this ability to have two jury trials on the same issue seems to be inconsistent with our present practice. This arose because of the Seventh Amendment to the Constitution which preserved the right to a trial by jury in suits at common law where the amount exceeded $20. It was held by the Supreme Court of the United States that a jury trial before a justice of the peace was not a jury trial in the sense of the constitutional requirements. A justice of the peace could not superintend the course of a trial or instruct the jury in matters of law, nor enter a verdict to arrest judgment, nor set aside or control the jury decision as is done in a court of record. This ability to have two jury trials on small claims continued into this century in all cases before justices of the peace, but a trial *de nova* in small civil cases has gradually disappeared as legally trained judges conducting a court of record have displaced the justices of the peace.[9]

The justices of the peace in the District of Columbia functioned as a small claims court until 1909 when they were organized collectively as the Municipal Court of the District of Columbia.[10] The justices of the peace were incorporated into the court as judges of the court. As their commissions expired, they could not be considered for reappointment unless they had been judges of the court for at least one year or had engaged in actual practice before the Supreme Court of the District of Columbia for five years before their appointment.

The first Chief Justice of the Circuit Court of the District of Columbia was William Kilty of Maryland. The associate judges were James Marshall, a brother of Chief Justice of the United States John Marshall, and William Cranch. When Kilty resigned in 1806 to become chancellor of Maryland, William Cranch became Chief Justice, a post he held until his death in 1855, having served on the court for over 54 years. Judge Cranch was described as a "benign, kindly old gentleman. . . . He was patient, painstaking and learned; but he became very deaf. . . ." For the last four or five years of his life he was unable to preside as judge. He enjoyed a great reputation as both a judge and as a reporter.[11] Cranch is better known as a reporter of the Supreme Court of the United States. He also prepared reports of the decisions of his own court, covering the period of 1801 to 1840, but these volumes were not published until 1852.

The Organic Act provided for the appointment of a register of wills and a judge of the Orphans' Court who would have the same duties and receive the same fees as the judges of the Orphan's Court in the state of Maryland. Appeals from the court were to be taken to the Circuit Court of the District.[12] This court was abolished in 1870 and its jurisdiction was transferred to the Supreme Court of the District of Columbia.[13]

Since the Act had made no provision for jurisdiction normally exercised by a federal district court, this defect was remedied the following year by an act requiring the Chief Justice of the Circuit Court of the District of Columbia to hold a district court twice a year which would exercise the same power and jurisdiction as the other district courts in the federal system.[14] Thus, a separate forum was created to exercise the jurisdiction of both the United States district courts and the state courts. This District Court continued until its termination in 1863.[15]

In 1838, the criminal jurisdiction exercised by the Circuit Court was transferred to the Criminal Court of the District of Columbia. For the purpose of holding the Criminal Court, the President of the United States was authorized to appoint one judge whose tenure was not stated. Terms of the court were to be held in both counties of the District, and the district attorney, marshal and clerk of the Circuit Court were to act in such capacity for the Criminal Court. Appeals were taken to the Circuit Court for the District.[16] This act was further amended to provide that the chief judge of the Circuit Court could hold this court in the event of the absence of the Criminal Court judge.[17] Judge Thomas H. Crawford of the Criminal Court had been ill for several months and died in 1863, at which time this court was abolished.[18]

In 1863, the judiciary system of the District was reorganized. The apparent motive for restructuring the courts was a suspicion of disloyalty among the judges on the Circuit Court.[19] The Circuit Court became known as the Supreme Court of the District of Columbia, consisting of four justices, one of whom was designated as the chief justice. These judges held their offices during good behavior. The Supreme Court succeeded to all the jurisdiction formerly exercised by the Circuit Court of the District of Columbia. The Criminal Court was abolished, but a Criminal Court was held by a judge of the Supreme Court. The district court was also abolished. The method of appeals was similar to the system used in New York where appeals were taken to the court in a general term. Review by writ of error or appeal could be sought in the Supreme Court of the United States from the general term in the same manner as from other circuit courts in the federal system. The Supreme Court in the District heard appeals from cases originating in the Justice of the Peace Courts.[20]

When the court was organized, President Lincoln did not reappoint any of the judges, but opted to appoint new personnel known for their loyalty. David K. Cartter of Ohio was named Chief Justice and the associate justices were Abraham B. Olin of New York, George P. Fisher of Delaware, and Andrew Wylie of the District of Columbia. The statute had changed the designation of the judges to that of justices. The first three of these individuals had been in Congress, and Justice Wylie had been practicing in Alexandria, Virginia. It was stressed in an editorial in the local paper that the nation had a deep stake in the affairs of the District, and it was therefore not "strange that in making these appointments [Lincoln] should have sought nominees known well to the whole country . . . rather than gentlemen of this community, who however well known and confided in at home, are unknown to the country in connection with the troubles of the times."[21]

Chief Justice Cartter was an extraordinary individual described as "imbued with a love of justice and fairness. . . ." He had an inventive mind, holding several patents on inventions he had created.[22] By all accounts, Judge Cartter was "an able judge, kind in his manner, grand in his presence, just in his judgments."[23]

The court was enlarged in 1870 when Justice Arthur McArthur was appointed to the bench. A sixth justice was added in 1879 with the appointment of Justice Walter S. Cox.[24]

With the increase in population during and following the Civil War, there was a correspondingly increased need in the District for courts exercising minor non-federal jurisdiction. In 1870, Congress authorized the creation of a Police Court with a judge learned in the law, appointed by the President for a term of six years. The jurisdiction of the court extended to all crimes deemed not capital or infamous, consisting of simple assaults and batteries, misdemeanors not punishable by imprisonment, and all the offenses against the ordinances of the city of Washington or the city of Georgetown or the laws of the Levy Court of the county of Washington. This Police Court was created to relieve the Supreme Court for the District of Columbia of this minor criminal jurisdiction.[25]

The next attempt to relieve the Supreme Court of the District of some of its functions was made in 1893 when its appellate jurisdiction was removed and given to a new court known as a Court of Appeals for the District of Columbia. The appellate court consisted of one chief justice and two associate justices, all appointed for life. Appeals could be taken from this court to the Supreme Court of the United States in matters exceeding $5,000. This court heard appeals from the Commissioner of Patents, a power previously exercised by the Supreme Court.[26] In 1934, the title of this court was changed to the United States Court of Appeals of the District of Columbia.[27] This change in name was necessary to correct a misconception of the nature of this court, since the old title implied that it was an appellate court for matters arising in the District of Columbia only. In addition to this local appellate jurisdiction, it had the same national jurisdiction as did the other federal courts. The court heard questions involving interstate commerce, mandamus proceedings in relation to Indian treaties, equity proceedings in relation to the public lands, and suits against the Federal Power Commission, the Civil Service Commission, the alien property custodian, and the Federal Trade Commission. It could also hear appeals from the Board of Tax Appeals without relation to the residence of the taxpayer. Interestingly enough, it held jurisdictional proceedings in relation to irrigation projects and the cancellation of mineral and oil leases on public lands. This does not exhaust the list of its jurisdiction.[28] Certainly this list of matters which fell within its jurisdiction entitled the court to greater recognition than simply a court to consider appeals of local matters within the District. This change was suggested by Judge D. Lawrence Groner, who served on this court from 1931 to 1948 and Judge Josiah A. Van Orsdel, who served on the court from 1907 to 1937. Both of these judges had seen this side of the jurisdiction of the court grow until it took up a greater part of the court's caseload.[29]

The caseload of the Court of Appeals for the District of Columbia grew rather rapidly as its jurisdiction expanded. As late as 1910, this court was handling many more cases with three judges than the other Circuit Courts of Appeals, with the exceptions of those in the Second and Eighth Circuits, which had four judges. The Attorney General suggested an increase from three to five in 1910, especially if Congress would give to this court jurisdiction over dispute entries on public lands on appeals from the General Land Office.[30]

At the turn of the Twentieth Century, questions arose whether the Supreme Court of the District of Columbia, the only trial court of record in the District, was a constitutional court. In 1901, Congress restated that the Supreme Court of the District of Columbia had the same jurisdiction as circuit and district courts of the United States and would be deemed a court of the United States.[31] The Supreme Court of the District of Columbia was held to be a constitutional court some years later.[32] Finally, in 1936, Congress changed the name of the Supreme Court of the District of Columbia to the District Court of the United States for the District of Columbia, but this in no way affected the jurisdiction of the court.[33] The statute governing the District Court and the Court of Appeals for the District of Columbia were included in the Judiciary Act of 1948, thus making them in all respects equal to corresponding federal courts in jurisdiction and powers.[34]

When the Supreme Court of the District of Columbia was established, one of the four judges was designated as the chief justice.[35] It was provided that one of the justices would hold a district court, but no statement was made that it was the duty of the chief justice to make this assignment. Certainly by creating the office of chief justice, it was intended that administrative functions be annexed to this office. The only occasion when the chief justice was given a specific statutory duty was in 1928 when he could appoint one of the judges to sit in condemnation of land cases and declare that this would be his primary duty.[36] During this period, the chief justice assumed gradually greater administrative functions. After the title of this court was changed to the District Court of the District of Columbia in 1936, the members of the court continued to be designated as associate justices and the chief justice, which were not titles used in other federal district courts. However, in 1948 when the District Court for the District of Columbia was incorporated into the judicial title of the UNITED STATES CODE, these titles were changed to conform with the titles in other federal courts.

Minor civil and criminal jurisdiction had been exercised by the justices of the peace commissioned by the president of the United States. The civil jurisdiction of the justices was raised several times, first to cases involving claims of less than $50 and finally to a $300 limit in 1867.[37] In 1895, exclusive jurisdiction of the justices of the peace was raised to cases with claims under $100 and their concurrent jurisdiction with the Supreme Court of the District of Columbia was raised to $300.[38]

In 1901, the justices of the peace were organized into an inferior court known as the Municipal Court of the District of Columbia. The jurisdiction formerly exercised by the justices of the peace was not changed upon the organization of this court. However, the office of the justice of the peace was abolished. The tenure of the justices of the peace on this court was changed to four years, and after the expiration of the terms of the justices of the peace, all those appointed to this court were required to be lawyers. An act of 1909 provided that the number of judges would be reduced to five and the jurisdictional amount of the courts raised to $500.[39] Other changes were made in the jurisdiction of this court.

In 1870, the criminal jurisdiction normally exercised by justices of the peace was transferred to the Police Court, which consisted of a single judge learned in the law. This judge had jurisdiction over all crimes of simple assaults and misdemeanors not punishable by imprisonment and all the offenses against the ordinances of the city of Washington and the laws of the Levy Court of the county of Washington. The judge of this court was a committing magistrate as well as a judge.[40]

In 1938, Congress established a unique branch within the Municipal Court of the District of Columbia known as the Small Claims and Conciliation Branch. The purpose of the statute was to provide for a speedy settlement of controversies where the claim or the value of personal property did not exceed $50, exclusive of interest, attorney's fees protest fees and cost. The jurisdiction of the court did not include actions for the recovery of possession of real property whether or not the action included claims for arrears of rent. The act stressed that the judges of the branch were to act as referees or arbitrators either alone or with others and not in the normal role of a judge.[41]

To further the administration of justice, several new methods of procedure were introduced. The statement of claims was required to be concise, and the clerk of the court, at the request of any individual, could help prepare this statement and other papers required to be filed. The statute permitted service of process by mail rather than personal delivery by a United States marshal. The judge could provide for the payment of claims over a period of time and upon such terms as were considered necessary.[42] The creation of this court was a part of a movement in the United States for the creation of a flexible court that could process small claims without the inconvenience or expense to the claimants. Nathan Cayton, a judge of the Municipal Court of the District of Columbia, is credited with being the author of this act as well as the first judge to serve in this branch.[43]

The next major change in the minor judiciary of the District was made in 1942 when the Police Court was merged into the Municipal Court for the District of Columbia, and the court was increased in the number of judges and its jurisdiction.[44] The new Municipal Court consisted of ten judges appointed by the president for a term of ten years. The court was organized into two branches, civil and criminal, and each branch succeeded to the jurisdiction exercised by the courts they were replacing. The civil jurisdiction was increased and made exclusive in civil actions involving personal property debts where the sum did not exceed $3,000.[45]

The same act established the Municipal Court of Appeals of the District of Columbia, which consisted of three judges appointed for terms of ten years. This court heard appeals from any final order or judgment of the Municipal Court of the District of Columbia or the Juvenile Court. One of the interesting provisions of this act was the fact that in a case where the amount in controversy was less than $50 or in an appeal from the small claims branch, the procedure was by a petition for the allowance of an appeal. If the appealing party was not represented by counsel, it was the duty of the clerk to prepare the application on his behalf. This court was created to relieve the workload of the United States Court of Appeals for the District of Columbia by removing appeals to it from the Municipal

Court. The Municipal Court of Appeals was given the usual authority to prescribe its own rules and procedure.[46] In 1962, the name of the Municipal Court was changed to the District of Columbia Court of General Sessions; and the Municipal Court of Appeals for the District of Columbia was designated as the District of Columbia Court of Appeals.[47] Eight years later, Congress would address itself again to a reorganization of the courts in the District, combining into one trial court several special courts.

Probate matters are administered by the state courts, so Congress had to provide for this in the District of Columbia. The Act of 1801 provided for an Orphans' Court presided over by a single judge. This court was abolished in 1870.[48] The term Orphans' Court was a name given to a court that handled the administration of the estates and other problems arising from the interpretation of wills in Pennsylvania and several other states. This title was borrowed from a court that existed in London to handle affairs of orphans.[49] The jurisdiction of the former Orphans' Court was transferred to a judge of the Supreme Court sitting in a special term for that purpose. In 1901, this court was designated the Probate Court. The probate of the wills and administration of the estates of many distinguished statesmen has been handled by the Register of Wills and the predecessor of the Probate Court, the Orphans' Court.[50]

A Juvenile Court in the District of Columbia was created in 1906. Its jurisdiction was enlarged in 1938.[51] The purpose of the statute was declared to be to secure for each child "such care and guidance, preferably in its own home, as will serve the child's welfare . . . to conserve and strengthen the child's family ties whenever possible".

This single-judge, autonomous Juvenile Court functioned well until 1960 when the backlog of cases began to increase significantly. It was during this period that some dramatic changes were forced into the law governing juveniles by decisions of the Supreme Court.[52] In 1961, two additional judges were authorized for the court although after serious studies, additional proposals for the reorganization of the court were made but not enacted by Congress at that time.[53] In 1970, the autonomous court was merged with the family division of the Superior Court which brought together other family matters into one division. The relation of the corporation counsel and the director of social services to the court was clarified.

In 1970, significant changes were made in the judicial system in the District of Columbia resulting in the separation of those courts exercising "state jurisdiction" from those exercising federal jurisdiction, surprisingly because of the increase in crimes committed in the District. The Supreme Court of the District of Columbia was replaced by the Superior Court of the District of Columbia. This court consisted of a chief judge and forty-three associate judges, which was a significant increase in the number of judges. The statute provided for a family division and a tax division, the latter having jurisdiction of all appeals for review of assessment of taxes and civil penalties in the District of Columbia. A small claims conciliation branch was continued and the jurisdictional amount was raised to $750, exclusive of interest, attorney's fees, protest fees and costs. The judges of this branch were given the authority to settle all cases, irrespective of the amount involved, by methods of arbitration and conciliation where the parties agreed. The Superior Court had jurisdiction in all criminal cases and in all civil cases arising in the District. As had become the practice in the structure of trial courts of this size, these two functions were organized into divisions.

The title Superior Court was adopted because Congress examined all of the titles used to describe the courts in the District and decided that this would be the most appropriate.[54]

The same statute established the District of Columbia Court of Appeals, consisting of a chief judge and eight associate judges who could sit in divisions consisting of three judges. The judges could sit *en banc* for a rehearing of a matter. This court had jurisdiction of appeals from all final judgments of the Superior Court of the District of Columbia as well as decisions of the commissioner of the District and several administrative agencies. The appeals court was given the usual powers of a court: to punish for contempt and to adopt rules to govern its business.[55] This court was declared to be the highest court in the District of Columbia, and its final judgment could be reviewed by the United States Supreme Court as could that of any other highest state court. By the creation of these two courts, the federal jurisdiction and the state jurisdiction in the District were finally separated.

One of the unique features of this statute was the gradual transfer of jurisdiction from the existing District Court of the District of Columbia to the new Superior Court. The statute gave precise instructions on what matters were to be transferred, beginning on February 1, 1971, and continuing through August 1, 1973. The most significant features of this act dealt with criminal practice reforms.[56] Another accomplishment of this statute was the appointment of a sizeable addition of judges to handle the increasing caseload caused by the litigation explosion in the last decades of the Twentieth Century.

The courts in the District of Columbia have played an unparalleled role in the development of administrative law. The first judicial review of an administrative agency assigned to the original Circuit Court and later to the Supreme Court was over certain decisions from the Commissioner of Patents. This jurisdiction was later exercised by the United States District Court for the District of Columbia until 1982, when all such appeals were transferred to the Court of Appeals for the Federal Circuit. This United States Court of Appeals for the District of Columbia was such a convenient forum that at times, Congress has vested appeals over other federal administrative agencies exclusively in this appellate court. By virtue of these appeals, the courts in the District of Columbia were not just another state or federal court but were courts that contributed materially to the development of federal administrative law.

FOOTNOTES TO CHAPTER 25

1. Act of February 27, 1801, sec. 3, 2 STAT. 105.

2. District of Columbia was first defined as a circuit in the Judicial Code of 1948, sec. 41, 62 STAT. 870. The Supreme Court had earlier spoken of the "eleven circuits forming the single Federal judicature." Commissioner of Internal Revenue v. Bedford, 325 U.S. 283, 288 (1944).

3. Act of February 27, 1801, sec. 5, 2 STAT. 106.

4. Act of February 27, 1801, sec. 11, 2 STAT. 107.

5. Act of March 1, 1823, sec. 1, 3 STAT. 743.

6. Act of February 22, 1867, sec. 1, 14 STAT. 401.

7. Act of February 19, 1895, sec. 1, 28 STAT. 668.

8. Act of March 1, 1823, sec. 15, 3 STAT. 746.

9. Capital Traction Co. v. Hof, 174 U.S. 1, 39 (1898).

10. Act of February 17, 1909, 35 STAT. 623.

11. Walter S. Cox, "Reminiscences of the Courts of the District," 23 WASH. L. REPT. 498, 500 (1895).

12. Act of February 27, 1801, sec. 12, 2 STAT. 107.

13. Act of June 21, 1870, 16 STAT. 160.

14. Act of April 29, 1802, sec. 24, 2 STAT. 166.

15. Act of March 3, 1863, sec. 3, 12 STAT. 763.

16. Act of July 7, 1838, c. 192, 5 STAT. 306.

17. Act of February 26, 1838, 5 STAT. 319.

18. Job Barnard, "The Early Days of the Supreme Court of the District of Columbia," 36 WASH. L. REPT. 30 (1908).

19. Theodore Voorhees, "The District of Columbia Courts: A Judicial Anomaly," 29 CATH. UNIV. L. REV. 922 (1980); F.L. Bullard, "Lincoln and the Courts of the District of Columbia," 24 A.B.A. J. 117 (1938).

20. Act of March 3, 1863, 12 STAT. 762.

21. Barnard, *supra,* note 18, p.30, 31.

22. *Ibid,* p.36.

23. "Chief Justice Carter," 15 WASH. L. REPT. 245, 247 (1887).

24. Act of July 15, 1870, 16 STAT. 160; Act of February 25, 1879, 20 STAT. 320.

25. Act of June 17, 1870, 16 STAT. 153.

26. Act of February 9, 1893, 27 STAT. 434.

27. Act of June 7, 1934, 48 STAT. 926.

28. S. Rept. No. 917, 73d Cong. 2d sess., April 26, 1934. Other areas of jurisdiction included titles to patented public lands, proceedings under the War Veterans' Act, proceedings in relation to irrigation projects, enrollment of Indians, suits under the antitrust laws and appeals from the Radio Commission.

29. H.R. Rept. No. 1748, 73d Cong. 2d sess., May 23, 1934.

30. 1910 ATT'Y GEN. ANN. REP. p.81.

31. Act of March 3, 1901, sec. 61, 31 STAT. 1199.

32. O'Donoghue v. United States, 289 U.S. 516 (1933).

33. Act of June 25, 1936, 49 STAT. 1921.

34. H.R. Rept. No. 308, 80th Cong., 1st sess.

35. Act of March 3, 1863, 12 STAT. 763.

36. Act of December 20, 1928, 45 STAT. 1056.

37. Act of March 1, 1823, 3 STAT. 748; Act of February 22, 1867, 14 STAT. 401.

38. Act of February 19, 1895, 28 STAT. 668. Supreme Court of the District of Columbia was authorized to make rules to govern its practice and procedure.

39. Act of February 17, 1909, 35 STAT. 623.

40. Act of June 17, 1870, 16 STAT. 153.

41. Act of March 5, 1938, 52 STAT. 103.

42. Frank H. Myers, "The Small Claims Court in the District of Columbia," 287 ANNALS OF THE AMERICAN ACADEMY OF POLITICAL AND SOCIAL SCIENCE, p.21 (1953).

43. Nathan Cayton, "Small Claims and Conciliation Courts," 205 ANNALS OF THE AMERICAN ACADEMY OF POLITICAL AND SOCIAL SCIENCES, p.57 (1939).

44. Act of April 1, 1942, 56 STAT. 190.

45. Act of April 1, 1942, sec. 4(a), 56 STAT. 192.

46. Act of April 1, 1942, sec. 6, 56 STAT. 194.

47. Act of October 23, 1962, 76 STAT. 1171.

48. Act of February 27, 1801, sec. 12, 2 STAT. 107; abolished by Act of June 21, 1870, sec. 4, 16 STAT. 161.

49. Coke's FOURTH INSTITUTE, p.248.

50. William Dennis, "Orphans' Court and Register of Wills, District of Columbia," 3 RECORDS OF THE COLUMBIA HISTORICAL SOCIETY, p.210 (1900).

51. Act of March 19, 1906, 34 STAT. 73; Act of June 1, 1938, 52 STAT. 596.

52. In re Gault, 387 U.S. 1 (1967); Harling v. United States, 295 F.2d 161 (D.C. Cir. 1961); Kent v. United States, 383 U.S. 541 (1966) 401 F.2d 408 (D.C. Cir. 1968).

53. H.R. Rept. No. 91-907, p.49.

54. H.R. Rept. No. 91-907, p.35.

55. Act of July 29, 1970, 84 STAT. 475.

56. Joseph D. Tydings, "District of Columbia Court Reform and Criminal Procedure Act of 1970," D.C. BAR J., August-December 1970, p.20.

Chapter 26

TERRITORIAL COURTS

Another group of federal courts was established in the territories and generally designated under decisions of the Supreme Court as "legislative courts". Since there are no American territories at the present, the importance of these courts has been passed over. But before Congress could establish courts in the territories, citizens often did so without legislative sanctions. The history of the territories is full of examples where local inhabitants undertook to establish regular judicial proceedings without formal sanctions of the law.[1] The vigilante and the lynching are part of the folklore of the West, but this should not lead to the conclusion that lawlessness prevailed. The miners' courts were the most famous of these extra-legal judicial bodies. At a later date, the actions of these courts were recognized in some territories by statute. Congress did establish courts as soon as an area was organized as a territory.

The Northwest Ordinance, the famous statute enacted by the Congress under the Articles of Confederation, set the pattern for judicial organization in the territories east of the Mississippi River by providing for courts consisting of three judges who would be appointed by the President and who would hold their offices during good behavior. This was a unique provision, for in those territories established later, the tenure of the judge was limited to a term of years. The court was not given a title immediately, but it later became known as the General Court. Sessions could be held by two of the three judges. This nameless court was given common law jurisdiction, and no mention is made in the Ordinance of granting appellate jurisdiction or chancery jurisdiction. An amendment in 1792, adopted by Congress under the Constitution, provided that a single judge could hold sessions of this General Court.[2]

These early judges, together with the governor, had the unusual authority to adopt laws that were in effect in existing states. As the judges and governors adopted laws of existing states, such courts as those held by the justices of the peace and the probate courts were established in the territories.[3] One authority has argued that the establishment of subordinate courts by the territories embraced in the Northwest was done in disregard of the provision of the Ordinance as an organic act.[4]

The first time Congress gave a title to a territorial court was in the organization of the Territory of Orleans, which later became the state of Louisiana. In this act, Congress provided for a superior court and "such inferior courts, and justices of the peace, as the legislature of the territory may from time to time establish."[5] The jurisdiction of this Superior Court extended to all criminal cases, with exclusive jurisdiction where the offense was capital, and original appellate jurisdiction in all civil cases where the value exceeded $100. The legislature of the Territory of Orleans later established an inferior court and justice of the peace courts. In the territories formed at this time, such as Illinois and later Florida, the term "inferior courts" was a favorite title. Generally, the legislative assemblies established probate courts.[6]

In the Territory of Orleans, Congress made an unprecedented move which was not to be repeated in any of the other continental territories by establishing a separate district court with full federal jurisdiction.[7]

In 1804, Congress organized all of the other parts of the Louisiana Purchase, excluding the Territory of Orleans, into the District of Louisiana and attached the area to the Indiana Territory. The judges were required to establish such courts as were needed and were required to hold two sessions in the new territory. The only sizeable city was St. Louis, where the courts held their first sessions. In the following year, the territory was reorganized with its own government and was designated as the Territory of Louisiana. The three judges appointed by the President exercised the same powers in the Territory of Louisiana as those in the Indiana Territory.[8]

The Act of 1812, establishing the Missouri Territory, was more complete in its provisions relating to the organization of the judiciary than previous territorial statutes.[9] The statute created and vested complete judicial power in a superior court. The court was to consist of three judges who had jurisdiction in all criminal cases and exclusive jurisdiction in civil cases of a value of $100 or more. The judges were to hold their courts at such time and place as prescribed by the General Assembly. The statute further authorized the legislative body to establish inferior courts. The legislature of the territory was given express authority to regulate the terms of these courts. It is apparent that Congress expected the superior court to be the highest court in the territory, exercising appellate jurisdiction from inferior courts which might be established by the territorial legislature. This structure was clarified by territorial statutes.

In creating the Alabama Territory in 1817, Congress first introduced a judicial organization which later became the standard for all future territories. Three judges were appointed by the President under this statute, and they were required to hold terms of the superior court separate from one another in such counties as were organized in the territory and at such time as the judges should agree among themselves.[10] In later territorial acts, the legislature was given the authority to establish the time and place of holding courts and to assign judges to a district. The same three judges were to meet in the state capitol as the General Court exercising both original and appellate jurisdiction. The General Court exercised full federal jurisdiction, a function that earlier, by a general statute, was assigned to the superior or district courts in the territories.[11] Some doubt arose as to whether the General Court could exercise admiralty and maritime jurisdiction, but this doubt was settled by a later act.[12]

Consistency was not a virtue of Congress at this date, for when the Florida Territory was organized in 1822, it was divided into two districts and a separate superior court was established in each. Appeals could be taken from either of these courts directly to the Supreme Court of the United States, and hence, no appellate court was organized in the territory at that time.[13] The Legislative Council of the territory complained to Congress about this omission, pointing to the tremendous power of a single judge from whose decision no appeal could be taken.[14] Two years later, a third superior court was organized, and the three judges were required to meet annually as the Court of Appeals.[15] This Court of Appeals held its first session on January 3, 1825.[16] Before Florida was admitted to the Union, Congress had established a total of five superior courts, including a special court in Key West — the largest number of courts for any territory except Dakota.

As Florida so aptly illustrated, different territories presented different judicial problems. A thriving shipping business between New Orleans and the East Coast existed at this period, and the routes followed by these ships took them close to the Keys of Florida where many were wrecked, thus giving rise to many admiralty problems. Since the nearest admiralty courts were those in St. Augustine and Pensacola, it became necessary to organize a special admiralty court in Key West. This court was called a superior court with the same jurisdiction as the other courts of that name established in the territory, but it was obvious that admiralty cases were to be its chief business.[17] This was a very interesting court and probably handled many interesting cases that have gone unreported in the admiralty and maritime fields. A provision of this statute which reveals the special admiralty jurisdiction in this court was the authority placed in this judge to license "wreckers" to salvage vessels. Florida was admitted as a state in 1845, with a single federal district court, but two years later the state was divided into two districts.[18] The United States District Court for the Southern District was located in Key West and was very active during the Civil War deciding admiralty cases. Key West served as a base for the Union fleet throughout the war years.

After the Wisconsin Territorial Act of 1836, the organization of the territorial courts became standard. This act provided for a supreme court consisting of a chief justice and two associate justices who would hold sessions in the state capital once a year. The territory was organized by the legislature into three districts presided over by one of the three judges. The courts were designated as district courts, a title which was to remain with the trial courts in these states. The statute organizing the territory, known as the Organic Act for Wisconsin, provided for probate courts and justice of the peace courts, but the jurisdiction of the latter was specifically limited by the Organic Acts. The legislative body could legislate on the jurisdiction of all courts as far as territorial matters were concerned.

The Organic Acts prohibited the justices of the peace from exercising jurisdiction where titles or boundaries of land were in dispute or where the sum involved exceeded a varying amount, beginning with $50 in the Wisconsin Act of 1836 and gradually rising to $300 in later acts.[19]

Three district courts were generally insufficient to supply the necessary judicial machinery in any territory; this fact became obvious to the inhabitants but not to Congress. To remedy this defect, several territorial legislatures began to expand the jurisdiction of the probate courts. In 1864, the Territory of Idaho established a probate court in each county and gave it concurrent civil jurisdiction in the enforcement of liens of mechanics and "in all civil actions where the amount in controversy shall not exceed $800". These courts were given concurrent jurisdiction with justices of the peace. Further, the probate judges were defined as "magistrates" for the purpose of issuing warrants for the arrest of those charged with a crime.[20] Congress did not usually concern itself with the problem of the jurisdiction of the inferior courts until 1847 when it legislated on the jurisdiction of these courts in the problem Territory of Utah. The jurisdiction of the district courts in the territory was defined as extending to chancery, actions of law where the sum exceeded $300, and where titles or possession of lands, mines or mining claims were in dispute. The probate court was confined to settlements of estates and matters of guardianship and was prohibited from hearing civil, criminal and chancery cases. For the first time, Congress provided for an appeal to the Supreme Court of the United States in a criminal case where the accused was sentenced to be executed or where a defendant was convicted of the crime of bigamy or polygamy.[21]

The justices of the peace were limited in the Organic Acts to amounts less than $50, but in later acts this amount was raised to $100. After 1870, this amount ranged from $100 to $300.[22] However, the territorial legislatures used various methods to encourage the use of the justice of the peace courts. The territories of Washington and Utah prohibited a plaintiff from recovering his costs when he brought an action in the district courts that could have been tried before justices of the peace.[23] This provision was struck down by the Utah courts on the grounds that the territorial legislature did not have the power to discriminate in matters of costs between two courts holding concurrent jurisdiction, one of which was established by Congress.[24]

One of the chief defects of the judicial organization found by the citizens was that the same judges traveled the circuit and rendered decisions which later were appealed to the Supreme Court consisting of the same judge and his two associates.[25] The Westerners suspected the judges of meeting and upholding each other's decisions on a reciprocal basis. The Supreme Court of Arizona became known as the "Supreme Court of Affirmance," and some members of the bar despaired of receiving justice through such judicial procedure.[26] When the number of judges was increased in a territory, it was possible for the judge who originally rendered the decision not to participate in the appeal.

The need for additional judges and courts in the various territories was obvious, and the Attorney General of the United States in 1882 recommended the creation of a fourth judge in each of the territories. The reason given by the Attorney General, Benjamin Harris Brewster, for this recommendation of the additional judicial manpower was based upon complaints from lawyers that the same judge who presided at the trial in the district courts was also sitting in the supreme court when their decisions were reviewed. Brewster concluded that "the justice of these complaints is so apparent that it seems unnecessary to enumerate the mischiefs growing out of the system."[27] In his report the following year, the Attorney General renewed his request on the same basis but added that the business in each of the courts was "sufficient to justify the appointment of another judge".[28]

Congress had authorized a third associate justice in the Dakota Territory in 1879. Strangely, Congress provided that the district court held by this fourth judge would not have jurisdiction to determine any case in which the United States was a party and that no United States grand or petit jury would be summoned in that court.[29] Why this limitation was placed upon that particular court is not clear. Congress continued to be generous to the Dakota Territory by increasing the number of judges by two in 1884. The jurisdiction of the judge of the Fifth District created in 1884 was limited in the same manner as the judge in the Fourth District.[30] The Congressional report suggested that there was little business in the new district "arising under the United States statutes, there being no real necessity for conferring on this court jurisdiction to hear and try United States cases."[31] The justification for another judge was that the First or Northern District was a huge territory, conducting "a large amount of United States business, which is entirely separate and distinct from the civil and Territorial business, and which form the great bulk of business of the court of that district."[32] These restrictions on the courts in the Fourth and Fifth Districts of the Territory of Dakota were abolished in 1888 when two additional judges were authorized, bringing the total number of judges to eight.[33] Congress had authorized more judges for the Territory of Dakota than it had for any other territory.

Congress, nevertheless, became more generous with the other territories, for in 1884, a fourth judge was authorized for the Washington Territory.[34] After this period, for all the territories left in the continental United States, the Supreme Court was to consist of one chief justice and three associate justices with a provision that no judge could participate in any case arising from his court.

One authority has written that probably the weakest link in the administration of justice in the West was the caliber of the judges.[35] They were not selected with respect to local needs or ability, but were selected from among party faithfuls, and hence, they looked upon the jobs as a political reward. Many of the judges considered the appointment as a stepping stone in their political careers. Very often, a judge who was appointed never went to the territory, and if he did make the trip from the East, he would stay only a short period and return. Traveling west by train and stage and then traveling a large circuit with the dangers of Indians and thieves was not to the liking of many Eastern lawyers who came West. However, a fair proportion of those who came West took their jobs seriously and were reappointed from time to time. Such a judge was Kirby Benedict, who was appointed by Lincoln as an associate judge in the Territory of New Mexico, which included both the states of New Mexico and Arizona.[36] The quality of the territorial judges began to improve when it became possible to make appointments from among the local bar. Some who came from the East found the local environment so inviting that they remained after they were removed from the court. Many of them came to play significant roles in the development of local law through such efforts as compiling the local statutes and drafting local laws. The territorial judges were not all bad and colorful, but neither did they all have outstanding legal talents.[37]

The judges appointed under the Northwest Ordinance received life tenure. This tenure was extended to the territories organized south of the Ohio[38] and later to the Mississippi Territory.[39] Beginning in 1804 with the division of the Louisiana Territory into two parts, the judges were given a tenure of four years.[40] The judge of the district court established under the Territory of Orleans enjoyed tenure during good behavior as provided in the Northwest Ordinance. However, only one territorial act after 1805 gave the judge tenure during good behavior and that was the Wisconsin Act in 1836.[41] It should be noted that Wisconsin was originally a part of the Northwest Territory, which may in part explain this difference in the tenure. In all the other territories, the term of the judge was limited to four years unless removed before that time.

The Supreme Court early defined territorial courts as legislative courts[42] and hence, the President had the power to remove any judge at his discretion.[43] The practice of removing territorial judges began under President Polk, but this power was greatly abused by President Grant. President Cleveland promised reform, although his record was not much better than his predecessor. He removed one of his own appointees, Chief Justice William A. Vincent of New Mexico. An editorial in the AMERI-CAN LAW REVIEW, probably the leading periodical of this date, strongly argued against the power of the President to remove territorial judges, suggesting that such power made the judges the puppets of the executive. However, Cleveland admitted his mistake in removing Vincent and later offered him another judicial appointment which Vincent declined.[44]

Usually the President gave no reason for removing a judge. In a letter to E. A. Thomas, Associate Justice in Wyoming, the Attorney General in 1875 asked for his resignation "for reason which the President deems important for public service".[45]

The conduct of the judge was often a source of complaints by the citizens. The judges were accused of being corrupt, and these charges were often substantiated. The judges in Nevada were reputed to be heavily interested in the mines involved in suits before them.[46] Eugene A. Tucker, judge of the District Court in the Territory of Arizona, was forced to resign after he agreed to hold court in Globe if the citizens furnished him with a residence.[47] These were but a few of the many complaints levied against the territorial judges.

The territories developed a method to deal with the unpopular judges through the technique of "sage-brush districting". Since the legislatures determined the districts in which the judges were to preside, if a judge proved too unpopular, the legislature would send him to a remote district. The legislature of Utah sent Charles B. Waite 350 miles from Salt Lake City with terms so arranged as to require two trips each year. The Wyoming legislature "sage-brush districted" W. W. Peck and, to add insult to injury, made a special appropriation to the other judges for their extra labors.[48] Finally, Congress was forced to take away the power of the legislatures to assign the judges in their respective districts in the territories of Montana, Idaho and Utah because of the random and discriminatory re-districting.[49]

The territorial judges conducted their business with the federal government through the attorney general. The most frequent cause of correspondence was the judge's desire to be absent from his district, and in this event, he made his request for a leave of absence through the attorney general. Judges were required to live in their districts and not to be absent without the consent of the President. Usually, if a judge was absent from his district, this meant that the other judges had to double up and hold his sessions of court.[50] One of the most frequent complaints levied against the judges was their long absences from their districts and failure to live in the district to which they were assigned. R. W. Stone, associate judge of the Colorado Territory, was accused of living in Denver rather than in his district, and several other judges were similarly derelict.[51]

In the early part of the century, the judges would rarely receive instructions from the federal government, but as the century progressed, and the Justice Department became an important part of the government, their problems received more consideration. The territorial judges in the last half of the Nineteenth Century recounted in considerable detail their activities and the many difficulties encountered in administering justice in their courts. They freely reported their efforts on behalf of the national administration.[52] The annual reports of the Attorney General of the United States reveal an increasing concern with the problems of the judges and the territorial courts. Congress' attention was directed to many inconsistencies which it had created.

The territorial courts served the same functions as state courts and federal courts and exercised the jurisdiction of both. In the early acts, the extent of the federal jurisdiction was not clear.[53] In 1805, Congress provided that the superior courts in all the territories in which a district court had not been established should "in all cases in which the United States are concerned, have and exercise, within their respected territories, the same jurisdiction and powers which are by law given to, or may be exercised by the district court of the Kentucky district".[54] The United States District Court in Kentucky was the first court in which the jurisdiction exercised by district and circuit courts was merged and hence, the superior courts could try any case within the federal jurisdiction. Later, territorial acts provided that the territorial district courts should use the first six days of their terms for the trial of cases arising under the federal law, and for this purpose, many courts kept separate dockets.

The Northwest Ordinance gave the judges a common law jurisdiction but omitted giving them chancery jurisdiction. The judges and governors of the Northwest Territory were fully aware of the omission of the word "chancery," and at no time did they attempt to give the courts equity jurisdiction. They assumed that chancery powers would be exercised through common law suits in the same manner as in Pennsylvania and Massachusetts. In 1802, the judges of the courts in Indiana petitioned Congress to give the courts chancery jurisdiction. Meanwhile, the governor of Indiana established a separate court of chancery. The omission of chancery jurisdiction was generally filled by local statutes. The inability of the courts in the Mississippi Territory to nullify Spanish land grants led to the establishment of a court of chancery there. In 1816, the territorial trial courts, supreme and district courts were given chancery as well as common law jurisdiction.[55]

When the Organic Acts began to give the supreme and district courts "chancery as well as common law jurisdiction," the question arose whether this jurisdiction was to be exercised separately or jointly. Several of the original states administered chancery jurisdiction through common law forms, and at least one state had established one form of action.[56] The territories of Washington and Montana enacted statutes establishing only one form of action and hence combined common law and equitable proceedings. This provision from the Montana Practice Act was challenged in the Supreme Court of the United States, and it was there decided that the territorial legislature could not combine the two proceedings. The Court reasoned that the territorial courts were subject to the same restrictions as the federal courts where the actions had been separate since the Process Act of 1792.[57] In 1874, Congress reversed the Supreme Court by granting the territories the authority to join the two forms of actions.[58] The question came before the Supreme Court again on an appeal from the Supreme Court of the Territory of Washington, and this time, without reference to the statute, the Court overruled its previous decision. The Court reviewed the Organic Acts again and decided that they did not direct the administration of "the jurisdiction of common law and chancery" separately as the federal courts had been directed.[59]

The extension of full federal jurisdiction in 1805 to the superior courts of the territories left the problem of admiralty jurisdiction unresolved.[60] In the Northwest Territory, the Superior Courts entertained libels to forfeit certain lumber under the revenue laws. These courts had established by rule an admiralty side, to use a contemporary term, which led to the courts designating certain days of their terms to hear maritime pleas.[61] However, some doubt arose as to whether these courts actually had admiralty jurisdiction. In 1818, Congress extended jurisdiction to the General Court of Alabama in all cases of admiralty and maritime jurisdiction.[62] In 1823, the territorial legislature of Florida gave a municipal court jurisdiction over maritime salvage. This grant was upheld by the Supreme Court of the United States.[63] The problem was definitely settled after 1836 when the territorial district courts were given "the same jurisdiction, in all cases arising under the constitution and laws of the United States as is vested in the circuit and district courts of the United States."[64]

The Northwest Ordinance was silent on the method of appeals from the trial courts in the territory. This defect was corrected in 1795 by Congressional legislation allowing a review by a writ of error to the General Court of the Northwest Territory consisting of the three trial judges.[65] A Mississippi Territorial Act established a court of appeals to be held by at least two of the superior court judges to hear appeals from all inferior courts.[66]

The first appellate court created by Congress in a territory was in Illinois in 1815.[67] This court was authorized to hear appeals from the circuit courts held by the individual superior judges as well as any other courts established in the territory.

In Florida, Congress had established two separate superior courts with complete federal jurisdiction. Appeals were taken from these courts to the Supreme Court of the United States where the amounts exceeded $1,000.[68] In 1824, a court of appeals was established for Florida consisting of the judges of the superior courts. The methods of appeal were left to the legislature to regulate.[69] When the establishment of a supreme court in each territory became a standard feature of the Organic Acts, appeals from the inferior courts of the territories were regulated locally, but appeals from the territorial supreme court to the Supreme Court of the United States were regulated by Congress.

At first, Congress failed to provide for an appeal from these territorial supreme courts. When an appeal was taken from the General Court of the Northwest Territory to the Supreme Court of the United States, the writ of error was dismissed because the Supreme Court could not exercise this jurisdiction unless specifically granted by an act of Congress.[70] An appeal was authorized in all cases to the Supreme Court of the United States "under the same regulations, as from the said district court of Kentucky district".[71] This limited judicial review only to those cases arising under federal law. From this period until 1836, Congress authorized judicial review of the various territorial supreme courts by the Supreme Court of the United States under the same limitation.

In the Organic Act for Wisconsin of 1836, the Supreme Court of the United States was granted appellate jurisdiction from the territorial supreme court in both federal and state jurisdiction. The amount involved had to exceed $1,000.[72] Special provisions were made for other types of appeals such as habeas corpus.

In 1885, Congress increased the jurisdictional amount to $5,000 for all territories, but made exceptions for certain cases including patents, copyrights or where the validity of a treaty or statute of the United States was involved.[73] When the Circuit Courts of Appeals were created in 1891, they succeeded to the appellate jurisdiction over the territorial courts. Most of these territorial courts were included within the Ninth Circuit, which at that period embraced all the states west of the Dakotas, including Kansas and Oklahoma.[74]

One question raised concerning the courts established by Congress in the territories was their status: were these judicial bodies courts of the United States in the constitutional sense or were they some other type of court? Congress had given the territorial courts the same jurisdiction over federal matters as exercised by the United States District Court in the District of Kentucky. The District Court in Kentucky was the only one in that state and, by the Judiciary Act of 1789, was given the jurisdiction normally exercised by both the district and circuit courts. For this reason, the territorial courts exercised full federal jurisdiction over matters in the territories as well as matters normally assigned to a state court. Chief Justice Marshall formulated the distinction between the Constitutional Courts established under Article III and the Legislative Courts established under Article IV. Under the Constitution,[75] Congress is given specific powers to govern territories, including the power to establish courts.[76] When the question arose whether these territorial district courts, in exercising federal jurisdiction, were bound by the laws of the territory or by federal law in jury selection, it was clear that these courts were not courts of the United States as were the district and circuit courts.[77]

Another source of confusion arose during the transition to statehood. To whom should the writ of error be directed after the state was admitted and before the regular United States District Court could be established? The records of the superior courts in Florida were transferred to the clerk of the state supreme court. The United States Supreme Court could not issue a writ under existing law; the records were in the hands of the clerk, not the territorial courts, and there was no appellate court to which a mandate could be directed to proceed further in the case or carry out the judgment pronounced by the Court.[78] Before Congress could establish a court in the state, an action in admiralty was brought to the court established in Key West. In 1845, Congress established a United States District Court, although it was not until July 8, 1846 that a judge was appointed to this court. The Supreme Court decided that the district court could try cases, for upon the admission of Florida as a state, the jurisdiction of these territorial courts ceased. In 1847, Congress provided for the transfer of cases from the territorial courts to the federal district court.[79]

One of the most unusual territorial courts was the United States Court in the Indian Territory. This area was not included in any organized territory because the area had been given to the Indians, who had established their own courts. However, these tribal courts did not have jurisdiction over any crime or action involving a white man. The United States District Court for the Western District of Arkansas had jurisdiction over this area for the purpose of trying white offenders, and it received its share of notoriety under Judge Isaac Parker, the "hanging judge". The Indian Territory was a convenient place for notorious outlaws to retreat and establish a base of operations. Going into the territory and arresting any of these individuals was certainly a dangerous undertaking. As a reaction to Judge Parker, who probably sentenced more individuals to hang than any other federal judge, in 1889 Congress established the United States Court in the Indian Territory.[80]

The jurisdiction of this court extended to all offenses against the laws of the United States except those offenses punishable by death or imprisonment at hard labor, which were reserved for one of the three district courts in other surrounding states. This statute had a number of interesting provisions, including the requirement that all procedure was to conform to and follow that of the Arkansas courts as prescribed in the MANSFIELD ARKANSAS DIGEST. Only Indians understanding English would serve as jurors. When a defendant was a citizen of the United States, only other citizens could serve as jurors. In passing this statute, Congress failed to provide for a grand jury, commissioners or other examining magistrates, and other defects were pointed out by the Attorney General.[81] In 1890, Congress organized the area now known as the state of Oklahoma into two territories, the Territory of Oklahoma and the Indian Territory.[82] Instead of extending the usual judicial organization to the Indian Territory, the original United States Court in the Indian Territory was organized into three divisions with a single judge. The jurisdiction of the court was extended to minor crimes and disputes between members of different tribes. The tribal courts continued to exercise jurisdiction over members of their own tribes except for certain crimes reserved for the federal government.

The first non-contiguous territory was Alaska, which was purchased from Russia in 1867. Knowing so little about the area, Congress could do little more than adopt a statute in 1868 which provided for the extension of the revenue laws to the area.[83] As far as courts were concerned, defendants were to be prosecuted in the district courts of California, Oregon or Washington. No mention was made of other types of judicial proceedings. The Army had taken over the territory, and much of the existing government remained in its hands, including the judicial system. Further, the local settlers administered justice among themselves when the need arose.[84]

In 1884, Congress passed a second act providing for the organization of the government of the Alaskan Territory.[85] A governor was authorized, but not a legislative body. A district court was created to exercise the usual jurisdiction of circuit and district courts of the federal system and "such other jurisdiction, not inconsistent with this act, as may be established by law." Appeals were to be taken from the District Court in Alaska to the Circuit Court in Oregon, which was then the closest state, since Circuit Courts of Appeals had not been created. The general laws of Oregon were made applicable to the territory. The attorney general of the United States was directed to furnish the necessary copies of these laws.[86] In addition to the usual judicial duties, the judge was required to collect license fees for bar rooms, select a site for the court house, and appoint commissioners. By 1900, it was clearly evident that one district court judge for the entire territory was inadequate.[87] In 1900, Congress organized Alaska into three divisions with a district court in each.[88] Nine years later, a fourth division was created which completed the basic judicial geographical organization of the territory until statehood.[89]

Congress provided legislation for the territory of Alaska more directly than for any of the other territories with the exception of the District of Columbia. In 1899, Congress enacted a criminal code and a code of criminal procedure for the territory and in 1900, a code of civil procedure and a civil code.[90] Special provisions applying to the territory were to be found in many general statutes not necessarily dealing with Alaska. This confused state of affairs led Congress to authorize, in 1912, the compilation of those Congressional statutes applicable to the territory.[91] Although this was not the first such compilation of laws applicable to the territory, it was the first one produced by Congress.

In no other area subject to the federal judicial system had the commissioner played such a leading role in the administration of justice. Since federal courts were the only form of judicial organization in the territory, and in view of the large areas embraced in a district, the commissioner was the only judicial officer for miles around. The commissioner performed the duties of a recorder of deeds, probate judge and justice of the peace, as well as the usual duties of a commissioner. The act of 1884 provided for four commissioners, a clearly inadequate measure.[92] The President was authorized in 1897 to appoint four additional commissioners.[93] The Civil Code enacted in 1900 authorized the judges to divide their districts into precincts, taking into account the size of the area, and to appoint a commissioner in each.[94] When Congress referred to the justice of the peace and the probate judge in this Civil Code and in the Code of Civil Procedure, these references were to the commissioners. Alaska was finally admitted as a state in 1959.[95]

In 1898, the United States came into possession of several territories acquired from Spain. These territories were occupied first by the military who were responsible initially for establishing courts. Within two years, the civilian authority established courts on a more permanent basis. In some areas, local judges were recruited, later to be supplemented by federal judges. In the Philippines, the civilian courts replaced the military courts in 1901. Three native Filipinos and four Americans were appointed to the supreme court.[96]

In 1898, Hawaii was accepted as a territory of the United States by Congress.[97] Since the Republic of Hawaii had an organized government with its own judicial system for most of the Nineteenth Century, the only court created by Congress was a district court to exercise federal jurisdiction.[98] A few years later, a second judge was authorized for this court.[99] The court was unique in that it resembled a district court established in the states rather than in the territories, and when admitted as a state in 1959, its jurisdiction was in no way affected.

Puerto Rico presented another unique situation. The courts in that area were originally established by orders of the military then occupying the island. The Organic Act providing the government for the island continued with the courts as they had been established by specific references to these military orders.[100] This statute established a United States District Court for Puerto Rico which had the full federal jurisdiction of both the circuit and district courts. Cases could be removed by the normal methods of appellate review to the existing Circuit Court of Appeals and the Supreme Court. This district court was the successor to the United States Provisional Court established by the military. Later, the legislative bodies of the island established other courts.[101]

In all the insular territories, a district court with federal jurisdiction was established with an appeal to the appropriate court of appeals. In none of these cases were these district courts considered constitutional courts in the sense that the judge received life tenure, but rather, they continued as territorial courts with federal jurisdiction.

It is easy to draw attention to the defects of the territorial judicial system because of the colorful judges and the faults emphasized in popular literature. The territorial courts did not function with the same dignity or on the same level as the Eastern courts, and certainly a lawyer from a well settled community going into this situation would suffer a cultural shock. However, much like the colonial courts in the early colonies, these courts matured to resolve complex legal issues such as mining and water rights which the Eastern states had not considered.

FOOTNOTES TO CHAPTER 26

1. IOWA CODE ANNOTATED, Constitutional volume (1949), p.4-5.
2. Act of May 8, 1792, sec. 4, 1 STAT. 286.
3. Northwest Ordiance, 1 STAT. 50, August 7, 1789.
4. Francis B. Philbrick, THE LAWS OF ILLINOIS TERRITORY, 1809-1818, p.xlii (1950).
5. Act of March 26, 1804, sec. 5, 2 STAT. 283.
6. *See* Pope's Digest, 1815, vol. 1, p.209-233, vol. 2, p.305-311 (1940); Francis S. Philbrick, THE LAWS OF INDIANA TERRITORY, 1801-1809, p.270-284 (1930).
7. Act of March 26, 1804, sec. 8, 2 STAT. 285.
8. Act of March 3, 1805, sec. 4, 2 STAT. 331.
9. Act of June 4, 1812, sec. 10, 2 STAT. 746.
10. Act of March 3, 1817, sec. 3, 3 STAT. 372.
11. Act of March 3, 1805, 2 STAT. 338.
12. Act of April 20, 1818, sec. 1, 3 STAT. 468.
13. Act of March 30, 1822, sec. 6, 7, 3 STAT. 654. This organization was continued under the Act of March 3, 1823, sec. 7, 3 STAT. 752.
14. 22 Carter, TERRITORIAL PAPERS 525.
15. Act of May 26, 1824, sec. 4, 4 STAT. 46.
16. 23 Carter, TERRITORIAL PAPERS 151.
17. Act of May 23, 1823, 4 STAT. 291.
18. Act of March 3, 1845, 5 STAT. 788; Act of February 23, 1847, 9 STAT. 131.
19. Earl S. Pomeroy, THE TERRITORIES OF THE UNITED STATES 1861-1890 (1947).
20. Act of December 19, 1864, sec. 620-624, LAWS . . . TERRITORY OF IDAHO, p.193-194.
21. Act of June 23, 1874, 18 STAT. 253.
22. Pomeroy, *supra,* note 19.
23. Act of December 2, 1869, LAWS OF WASHINGTON, 1869-70, p.123.
24. Hepworth et al v. Gardner, 4 Utah 439, 11 Pac. 566 (1886).
25. 1882 ATT'Y. GEN. ANN. REP. p.12. The attorney general comments on this defect and suggests that the Supreme Court should consist of unequal numbers of judges.
26. One Montana attorney wrote: "It would be better . . . to simply have mining or Justices courts." Quoted in Pomeroy, *supra,* note 19, p.52-53.
27. 1882 ATT'Y GEN. ANN. REP. p.12.
28. 1883 ATT'Y GEN. ANN. REP. p.14.
29. Act of March 3, 1879, 20 STAT. 473.
30. Act of July 4, 1884, 23 STAT. 101.
31. H.R. Rept. No. 753, 48th Cong., 1st sess., p.2 (March 11, 1884).
32. H.R. Rept. No. 753, 48th Cong., 1st sess., p.1 (March 11, 1884).
33. Act of August 9, 1888, 25 STAT. 399.
34. Act of July 4, 1884, 23 STAT. 101. A fourth judge was authorized in Montana, Act of July 10, 1896, 24 STAT. 138.
35. Pomeroy, *supra,* note 19, p.61.
36. Aurora Hunt, KIRBY BENEDICT FRONTIER FEDERAL JUDGE (1961).
37. John D. W. Guice, THE ROCKY MOUNTAIN BENCH, p.60 (1972).
38. Act of May 26, 1790, 1 STAT. 123.
39. Act of April 7, 1798, 1 STAT. 549; Blume and Brown, "Territorial Courts and the Law," 61 MICH. L. REV. 78 (1962).
40. Act of March 26, 1804, 2 STAT. 283.
41. Act of April 20, 1836, 5 STAT. 10; Wingard v. United States, 141 U.S. 201 (1890). This decision has a list giving the tenure of all territorial judges.

42. American Insurance Co. v. Canter, 1 Pet. 511 (U.S. 1828).

43. McAllister v. United States, 141 U.S. 174 (1890). In United States v. Guthrie, 58 U.S. 284 (1854), the point of the power of president to remove a judge was raised but not decided. The McAllister decision was reviewed in 21 AMER. L. REV. 1011 (1891).

44. 24 AMER. L. REV. 308 (1890). This editorial gives the details of the removal of Judge Vincent.

45. Letter of May 13, 1875, Edwards Pierrepont, Attorney General to E.A. Thomas, Book A, Letter Book of the Attorney General of the United States, National Archives.

46. Pomeroy, *supra,* note 19, p.17; 26 AMER. L. REV. 470 (1892).

47. 9 LAW NOTES 175 (Dec. 1905).

48. Guice, *supra,* note 37, p.81.

49. Pomeroy, *supra,* note 19, p.56-57.

50. *Ibid,* p.51.

51. Letter to R. W. Stone; Book A1, Letter Book of the Attorney General of the United States, p.176.

52. One such letter from Hiram Knowles to the Attorney General is reprinted in Guice, *supra,* note 37, p.154.

53. Act of March 26, 1804, sec. 8, 2 STAT. 285. The most complete article on this subject is Blume and Brown, "Territorial Courts and Law," 61 MICH. L. REV. 51-89 (1962).

54. Act of March 3, 1805, 2 STAT. 338.

55. Blume and Brown, "Territorial Courts and Law," 61 MICH. L. REV. 39, 54-59 (1962).

56. Beardsley, "Compiling the Territorial Codes of Washington," 28 PAC. N. W. QUART. 19 (1937).

57. Process Act, 1 STAT. 275, May 8, 1792. Orchard v. Hughes, 1 Wall. 77 (U.S. 1863); Dunphy v. Kleinsmith, 11 Wall. 610 (U.S. 1870).

58. Act of April 7, 1874, 18 STAT. 27.

59. Hornbuckle v. Toombs, 18 Wall. 648 (U.S. 1873).

60. Act of March 3, 1805, 2 STAT. 338.

61. Blume and Brown, *supra,* note 55, p.67-76.

62. Act of April 20, 1818, 3 STAT. 468.

63. American Insurance Co. v. Canter, 1 Pet. 511 (U.S. 1828).

64. Wisconsin Organic Act, sec. 9, 5 STAT. 10, April 20, 1836.

65. Theodore C. Pease, LAWS OF THE NORTHWEST TERRITORY 1788-1800 (1925).

66. Mississippi Historical Records Survey, Sargent's Code 1799-1800, p.7.

67. Act of March 3, 1815, 3 STAT. 238.

68. Act of March 3, 1822, sec. 7, 3 STAT. 656.

69. Act of May 26, 1824, 4 STAT. 46.

70. Clark v. Bazadone, 1 Cranch 212 (U.S. 1803).

71. Act of March 3, 1805, 2 STAT. 338.

72. Act of April 20, 1836, sec. 9, 5 STAT. 13.

73. Act of March 3, 1885, 23 STAT. 443.

74. Act of March 3, 1891, sec. 15, 26 STAT. 830.

75. U.S. CONST. art. IV, §3, cl. 2.

76. American Insurance Co. v. 356 Bales of Cotton, 1 Pet. 511 (U.S. 1828). This decision is often cited as American Insurance Co. v. Canter.

77. Clinton v. Englebrecht, et al, 13 Wall. 434 (U.S. 1871).

78. Hunt v. Palao, 4 How. 589 (U.S. 1846).

79. Benner v. Porter, 9 How. 235 (U.S. 1850); Act of February 22, 1847, 9 STAT. 128.

80. Act of March 3, 1889, 25 STAT. 783.

81. 1889 ATT'Y GEN. ANN. REP., p.xxii.

82. Act of May 2, 1890, 26 STAT. 81.

83. Act of July 27, 1868, 15 STAT. 241.

84. James Wickersham, OLD YUKON, TALES - TRAILS - TRIALS (1938), p.124-126.

85. Act of May 17, 1884, 23 STAT. 24.

86. Act of May 17, 1884, sec. 11, 23 STAT. 27.

87. 1889 ATT'Y GEN. ANN. REP., pp.41-42.

88. Act of June 6, 1900, sec. 2, 31 STAT. 322.

89. Act of March 3, 1909, 35 STAT. 839.

90. Criminal Code and Code of Criminal Procedure, March 3, 1899, 30 STAT. 1253, 1285; Code of Civil Procedure and Civil Code, Act of June 6, 1900, 31 STAT. 324, 334.

91. Act of August 24, 1912, sec. 19, 37 STAT. 518.

92. Act of May 17, 1884, sec. 5, 23 STAT. 25.

93. Act of June 4, 1897, 30 STAT. 56.

94. Civil Code of Alaska, sec. 1, 2, 31 STAT. 494, June 6, 1900.

95. Proclamation of January 3, 1959, 73 STAT. c.16; Act of July 7, 1958, 72 STAT. 348.

96. Arthur F. Odlin, "American Courts in the Orient," 47 AMER. L. REV. 321 (1917).

97. Joint Resolution, July 7, 1898, 30 STAT. 750.

98. Act of April 30, 1900, 31 STAT. 158.

99. Act of March 3, 1909, 35 STAT. 838.

100. Act of April 12, 1900, sec. 33, 31 STAT. 77.

101. DOCUMENTS ON THE CONSTITUTIONAL HISTORY OF PUERTO RICO (2d ed., June 1964).

Chapter 27

THE UNITED STATES COMMISSIONERS AND MAGISTRATES

The system of justices of the peace was an established feature of the judiciary in all the colonies by the time of the American Revolution. The need for such a system on the national level was recognized in the First Judiciary Act, which authorized the magistrates and justices of the peace in the different states, as well as mayors of cities, to act as committing magistrates for those accused of violating federal laws.[1] How well this system worked is not clear, although we have the testimony of a United States district judge for the Southern District of New York, Charles M. Hough, who stated "the early files of this court contain many commitments by local justices of the peace of the state of New York". The same judge indicated that "it did not take long for experience to demonstrate the difficulty and inutility of the borrowed and grudgingly given services of state officials".[2] Congress established the office of commissioners which gradually assumed many of these functions. Finally, the duties of this office were expanded and replaced by magistrates.

The commissioner system began in 1793 when Congress authorized the judges of the circuit court to appoint persons "learned in the law" to admit persons accused of a federal crime to bail.[3] No precise number of commissioners was authorized, and their appointment was left entirely to the discretion of the circuit court judges, who at that time were the justices of the Supreme Court. In determining the number of such appointments, the judge was admonished to consider "the extent of the district, and the remoteness of its parts from the usual residence"[4] of the federal judges or state judges of superior courts.

No salary was provided for this position, and it can only be assumed that the practice of adopting the local fee system as a basis of compensation was applied in the federal courts until 1812.[5] The first statutory recognition of fees as compensation appeared in the Act of 1812. The commissioners were authorized to receive the same fees as those allowed by state laws for admitting persons to bail and taking affidavits. This statute made some major changes in the office. The requirement that the person be "learned in the law" was omitted, and the duty of the office was extended to taking bail and affidavits in civil causes. This statute was the first to use the term "commissioner".

The appointment and number of commissioners were determined by the circuit court judges until 1968. Rarely did Congress urge the judges to appoint a sufficient number of commissioners, but in the Civil Rights Act of 1866, Congress directed that it "shall be the duty of the circuit courts of the United States and the superior courts of the Territories of the United

States, from time to time, to increase the number of commissioners, so as to afford a speedy and convenient means for the arrest and examination of persons charged with the violation of this act".[6]

The duties of the office were expanded both by statute and by local custom. At first, the authority of the commissioners to take bail and affidavits was limited to causes arising in the circuit court until extended to the district courts in 1817. The 1817 statute further authorized the commissioners to take depositions *de bene esse*.[7]

In addition to the duties given in the First Judiciary Act, of admitting individuals to bail, and in the Act of 1812 of giving commissioners authority to acknowledge affidavits, it soon became customary for the officers to issue warrants for the arrest of individuals charged with the violation of federal laws. In the First Judiciary Act, this duty was given to the federal judges and "any justice of the peace, or other magistrate of any of the United States."[8] This authority was specifically granted to the commissioners in 1842.[9] However, it can be presumed that commissioners were issuing warrants in some districts before this authority was formally acknowledged by statute.

Congress expanded the jurisdiction of the commissioners in 1846. Broad powers were conferred on them but in a very limited area. The commissioners were authorized, along with the district and circuit courts, to have full power and jurisdiction upon application of a consul requiring their assistance to carry into effect the award of arbitration or decree in disputes between captains and crews for any vessel belonging to the nation whose interests were committed to their charge.[10] This statute authorized the courts and the commissioners to issue all "remedial process, mesne and final," to carry these awards into effect and to enforce obedience by imprisonment until such awards were satisfied.[11] The effect of this statute was to confer judicial functions on the commissioners, but obviously, this type of proceeding was not wide-spread throughout the country and was chiefly confined to a few judicial districts.

It is interesting to note that this statute restated the position of the commissioner. The statute defines the commissioners as those

> appointed by the Circuit Court of the United States to take acknowledgements of bail and affidavits, and also to take deposi-tions of witnesses in civil causes, and to exercise the powers of any justice of the peace in respect to offenders for any crime or offence against the United States by arresting, imprisoning, or bailing, the same, under and in virtue of the laws of the United States.[12]

As these duties were added by previous statutes prior to 1846, the original duties were restated and expanded upon. The statute of 1846 is the last one which clearly restated the duties of the commissioner as an introduction to the assignment of a new task. A contemporary author observed that "the powers of these officers have been greatly enlarged, until at length the office has become one of considerable importance and responsibility."[13] This same author, in his original work published thirty years earlier, did not describe this office in these terms, which would indicate that it became increasingly significant during those three decades.

The Civil Rights Act of 1866 directed the circuit courts to "increase the number of Commissioners", and it also gave these officials the power to arrest, imprison, and bail any offenders defined in that statute. The commissioners were "required to exercise and discharge all the powers and duties conferred on them by this act, and the same duties with regard to offences created by this act, as they are authorized by law to exercise with regard to other offences".[14] Congress was determined that the Civil Rights statute would be enforced. The refusal of a marshal to execute a warrant or any other command was made a crime. The commissioners were authorized to appoint within their counties "any one or more suitable persons, from time to time, to execute all such warrants and other process as may be issued by them in the lawful performance of their respective duties".[15] This authorization was limited to this statute and was never repeated in subsequent civil rights acts.

Since there were so many statutory references relating the commissioner system to the justice of the peace system in the states, it apparently became a customary assumption that the roles were identical. This was an attitude which came to be resented by the commissioners in the Twentieth Century.[16] This resentment is understandable when the contemporary reputation of the justice of the peace system for its ineptness is considered. The Supreme Court had no doubts that the commissioners were under the supervision of the court to the same extent as masters in chancery or referees in bankruptcy.[17]

None of these statutes provided for any formal supervision, and the office grew in independence until these questions arose in the latter part of the Nineteenth Century. As early as 1844, in a case involving a marshal of the court, the Supreme Court ruled that "there is inherent in every court a power to supervise the conduct of its officers, and the execution of its judgments and process. Without this power, courts would be wholly impotent and useless."[18] Surely, this principle was applied to the commissioners who were probably removed from office by the judge of the court when he thought appropriate.[19] In other cases, those holding office were ignored, and their activities escaped any supervision.

The federal courts never exercised the prerogative of the Court of King's Bench of supervising inferior jurisdictions by the use of prerogative writs or by calling in the minor officials with their documents to render an accounting of their proceedings.[20] The Supreme Court decided that the issuance of a writ of certiorari by the circuit court to the district court to remove a matter for trial or examination was not supported by statute. The same principle was applied to the issuance of this writ by the district court or circuit court to the commissioner.[21] Since the function of a commissioner was ministerial and involved the exercise of discretion, no review was possible of any action he took. After the commissioner was given judicial functions, an appeal was provided to the district court.

No trial functions had been assigned to these commissioners by statute until the last decade of the Nineteenth Century, although they may have had such functions in a few circuits or districts. The commissioner became a logical official to try petty offenses which began to take up the time of the federal courts at this period. However, in 1888, the commissioners were authorized under the Chinese Exclusion Act to try offenders concurrently with the district court.[22] Apparently, the commissioners took an active part in the administration of this act, especially in California.

The commissioner was a useful officer to preside over petty offense trials in those areas governed by the federal government where no justices of the peace existed, such as Alaska and the Indian territory. The justice of the peace system operated in the other territories as they were established. An act of 1884 authorized the appointment of four commissioners in Alaska.[23] In 1897, four additional commissioners were authorized, bringing the total to eight.[24] The Civil Code of Alaska, enacted in 1900, authorized the judges to divide their districts into precincts and to appoint a commissioner in each. As in the earlier statutes, the Alaska Code authorized no particular number of commissioners. Although this Code speaks of justices of the peace and probate judges, these officers did not exist in Alaska at that time. The duties normally associated with these offices under the law of Oregon, which was the basis for the law in Alaska, were performed by commissioners who, in many areas, were the only judges in that particular region.[25] Travelling in the ice and snow from one settlement to another for trial of petty offenses conjures up more romantic and appealing visions than does travelling from the United States Courthouse in Brooklyn, New York, out to Fort Wadsworth for the same purpose.[26]

In the Indian Territory, which later became a part of the state of Oklahoma, the commissioners exercised the same powers as the justice of the peace under Arkansas law, which was the body of law made applicable to the territory. A number of these decisions are reported in the INDIAN TERRITORY REPORTS.

The federal courts had jurisdiction over federal enclaves, but for most of the Nineteenth Century, crimes committed on these areas were few and did not add any significant amount of work to the federal dockets. However, with the creation of national parks, the need existed for a minor judicial officer to enforce park regulations and to try petty offenses. Otherwise, such matters were taken before the district court judge. In 1894, Congress authorized the appointment of a commissioner for the Yellowstone National Park.[27] The commissioner was given authority to try individuals violating the rules promulgated by the Secretary of Interior and other statutes pertaining to the park. An office was established for the commissioner, which is the first time that a statute specifically provided for office space for a commissioner. Appeals from the commissioner were taken to the District Court of Wyoming and were governed by the laws of Wyoming relating to appeals from the justice of the peace. The Circuit Court of Wyoming could supply rules for the governing procedure before the commissioners.[28]

There is a tendency to consider the criminal jurisdiction of the federal courts as confined to those crimes so neatly arranged in a criminal code without realizing that other federal laws define many misdemeanors punishable by imprisonment not exceeding a year or by a fine less than $500. A 1966 list totaled over 750 such offenses.[29] Obviously, with the increased workload of the federal courts, especially after World War I, it was unproductive for a district court judge to try petty offenses in many districts. Several writers, including a United States district judge, suggested that Congress had the constitutional power to give the commissioners authority to deal summarily with petty offenses.[30] In 1940, the district court judges were authorized to designate certain commissioners to try and to sentence individuals charged with such petty offenses, with an appeal from the commissioner to the district court.[31]

Petty crimes such as speeding on the military reservations, killing migratory ducks out of season, and fishing illegally in the streams of the Great Smokey Mountains National Park began to fill the trial docket for many commissioners. These officials became more active as judges rather than as officials administering oaths and attesting documents. Because of the patchwork of statutes, some petty offenses committed on a federal enclave could be tried before a commissioner, whereas, if the same crime were committed elsewhere, it had to be tried by a district court judge.[32] The argument supporting trial by a district court judge was that those individuals who committed these crimes were entitled to the same privileges as those accused of more serious crimes.

The constitutional question of whether the commissioners can be assigned a trial function has been debated throughout the present century. The Commissioners to Revise and Codify the Criminal Laws of the United States suggested that this violated the constitutional provision of the guarantee of a trial by jury even for violation of penalties such as those prescribed by the Secretary of Interior for the Yellowstone National Park. On the other hand, some commentators relate this to the state practice of trying certain crimes by a minor official and have argued that the commissioners should have extensive trial functions.[33]

The question was raised whether the commissioners were judges, and at least one writer answered the issue in the negative. It was argued that the commissioner, even in a Chinese deportation case, could not punish a witness for contempt and refusing to testify, but had to report the matter to the district court for action. The conclusion was that the commissioners exercised certain judicial or quasi judicial duties but were not judges.[34]

Slight changes in practices had a profound impact on the nature of the office.[35] In at least one district after 1940, the committing hearing became an expanded preliminary hearing by virtue of rules of court providing that the district attorney and counsel for the defendant would exchange information.[36]

The early statute creating the office does not clearly define the title of the office other than "commissioner". For a time, they were known as the "commissioners to take affidavits," although the title most generally used was Commissioner of the Circuit Court. This title was changed in 1896 to that of the United States Commissioner, which was the first occasion when the title of the office was clearly stated.[37] The method of appointment was changed from selection by the circuit court judges (which had been the manner established in 1867) to selection by the United States district court judges. This statute considerably modified previous practices. The judge was free to appoint as many commissioners as he felt were necessary, but such appointments were to be entered in the records of the district court and notice given to the Attorney General of the United States. The commissioner formerly held his office at the pleasure of the appointing judge and could be removed for any reason, including the judge's preference to appoint another officer.[38] Upon the enactment of this statute, the appointment was for a term of four years, although the commissioner could be removed sooner.

Apparently, it had become the custom for the clerks and other officials of the district courts to be appointed to this office, a practice prohibited by the statute of 1896. Among the officials of the court who were disqualified to serve in the position were the jury commissioner, the clerk or the marshal, the bailiff, the janitor in any government building and any civil or military employee of the government.[39] The fee system, which was the basis of compensation, will explain why these minor functionaries enjoyed appointments to these responsibilities: appointment as a commissioner increased their compensation. The duties of the office were somewhat expanded by the fact that the commissioners could issue warrants for arrest of violation of internal revenue laws upon a sworn complaint of the United States district attorney. The commissioner and the clerk were authorized to administer oaths.

In reviewing the statute of 1896, Judge Charles M. Hough observed that the "effect of the statute of that year may be said to be no more than a change of title and of fee scale, plus the infusion of a supervisory power on the part of the Attorney General."[40] However, this assessment is only partially correct, for the statute placed requirements on recording appointments, expanded the duties, and generally upgraded the office. In the view of some writers, the beginning of the office dates from the enactment of that statute.

A gradual change appears to have taken place in the attitudes of some but not all judges in the removal of commissioners without cause. In a case involving the commissioners of the Western District of North Carolina, Judge Robert P. Dick indicated that the commissioners were authorized to exercise important judicial and ministerial functions and that they were entitled to the support of the court in the exercise of their functions. A commissioner should be fairly heard before his "official conduct is condemned by a peremptory removal from office."[41] In a concurring opinion, another judge indicated that these officers should not be capriciously removed but should "be assured that the faithful perform-ance of duty will be recognized and rewarded by continuance in office".[42] However, this high ideal was not uniformly applied.

During the period following World War II, the operations of the federal courts came under increased scrutiny as the backlog of cases mounted, new federal rights were created, and new problems were solved by statute. The commissioner system did not escape examination as a means of giving some relief to the federal courts. The commissioners themselves complained of the salary, for the increasing workload demanded more of their time for the same pay. The commissioner had been paid by fees limited to $10,500 per year until 1968. In some districts, the commissioner could earn the allowable fees in the first few months of the year which would require him to remit the balance of the year's fees to the federal treasury. The two most serious comments directed toward this group of officers were the lack of legal training and the fact that their remuneration continued to depend upon fees. For these officers to receive their income through fees was contrary to a decision of the Supreme Court of the United States, which held that where the presiding judicial officer depended upon collecting a fee from a convicted offender, the due process clause of the Fourteenth Amendment was violated.[44] In 1965, the commis-sioner system came under review, and Congress considered revamping the entire system by proposing to make the commissioners full-time salaried employees, requiring them to be members of the bar, and extending their trial functions over many other petty offenders.[45]

In 1968, under the leadership of Senator Joseph D. Tydings, Congress enacted the Federal Magistrates Act, which abolished the Office of United States Commissioner and substituted the system of magistrates, to be appointed by district court judges in such numbers as determined by the Judicial Conference of the United States.[46] The magistrates were required to be members of the bar, and if there were no qualified members of the bar, then a non-member could be appointed. A salary was substituted for the fee system. In addition to the trials of minor crimes, the district courts could assign additional duties in keeping with the require-ments defined by the Constitution and the laws of the United States. A magistrate could serve as a special master in a civil case or as an assistant in conducting pretrial or discovery procedures if empowered to act by a rule of court. The term of office was eight years, and the magistrate could be removed only for stated reasons by the majority of the appointing judges in the district.

Congress intended to create an officer to assist the district court judges by making the recommended finding of facts but leaving it to the court to issue the appropriate order.[47] In 1976, the authority of the district judge to assign matters to the magistrate and to dictate the procedure to be followed was clarified in an amending statute.[48] The purpose of this law was to make clear the authority of the magistrate to conduct evidentiary hearings, to screen the records, and to determine certain pretrial matters and motions. In 1979, the jurisdiction of the magistrates was extended to all federal misdemeanors with the reservation that the parties had to consent to such trials in writing. For the first time, the magistrate could conduct a hearing by a jury and allow the government to petition the district court to remove a particular case from the magistrate for a good cause shown.[49] Throughout the hearings, it was very clear that Congress intended to relieve the courts of some of their duties so that the cases could proceed more rapidly. The federal courts could not adjust to the new judicial officer, and several of the courts of appeals took a limited view of the role of the magistrate. The courts continued to question the authority of the magistrates to enter judgments. In 1983, the permission given to the magistrates to enter a judgment was declared unconstitutional.[50] This position was rejected by a number of the courts of appeals on the grounds that if the parties raised no objections, there could be no constitutional objection. This decision came as a result of declaring the bankruptcy courts unconstitutional.[51] Ultimately, the courts recognized the authority of the magistrates to act in a judicial capacity. The objective of Congress to give more judicial functions to this type of administrative officer will be realized gradually as the court learns to use this additional source of help.

This statute of 1968 ended the Office of the United States Commissioner and substituted a subordinate judicial office known as a magistrate. Since then, the role of the magistrate has continued to expand and in time will come to play a significant role in the administration of justice in the federal system.

FOOTNOTES TO CHAPTER 27

1. Act of September 24, 1789, sec. 33, 1 STAT. 91.

2. United States v. Maresca, 266 F. 713, 720 (1920).

3. Act of March 2, 1793, sec. 4, 1 STAT. 334.

4. *Ibid.*

5. Act of February 20, 1812, 2 STAT. 679.

6. Act of April 9, 1866, sec. 4, 14 STAT. 28.

7. Act of March 1, 1817, 3 STAT. 350.

8. Act of September 24, 1789, sec. 33, 1 STAT. 91.

9. Act of August 23, 1842, 5 STAT. 516.

10. Act of August 8, 1846, 9 STAT. 79.

11. *Ibid.*

12. *Ibid.*

13. Alfred Conkling, A TREATISE ON THE ORGANIZATION, JURISDICTION AND PRACTICE OF THE COURTS OF THE UNITED STATES (4th ed. 1864), p.90.

14. Act of April 9, 1866, sec. 4, 14 STAT. 28.

15. *Ibid., sec. 5.*

16. S. Rept. No. 1050, 89th Cong. 2d sess. p.18. Hearings Subcommittee on Improvements in Judicial Machinery. Committee on the Judiciary. U. S. Senate 1966, p.600 (J84/44.J89).

17. United States v. Allred, 155 U.S. 591, 595 (1895).

18. Griffin v. Thompson, 2 How. 244, 257 (U.S. 1844).

19. Judge Robert P. Dick observed: "I was reliably informed that some of the United States judges in other districts had peremptorily removed many commissioners without issuing against them formal rules to show cause why they should not be removed from office. I am also informed that there are some eminent lawyers who are now of opinion that United States judges, who are authorized to appoint commissioners of the circuit courts without any definite term of office, can remove them at pleasure, and may often do so properly without affording them any opportunity of explanation and defense, upon the ground that the best interests of the public service require prompt action." In re Commissioners of Circuit Court, 65 F. 314, 316-317 (C.C.W.D.N.C. 1894).

20. United States v. Ebb, 10 F. 369, 373 (D.C.W.D.N.C. 1881).

21. Patterson v. The United States, 2 Wheat. 221 (U.S. 1817); Ex parte Van Orden, 28 FED. CAS. 1060, 2 Blatchf. 166 (1854).

22. Act of September 13, 1888, 25 STAT. 476.

23. Act of May 17, 1884, sec. 5, 23 STAT. 25.

24. Act of June 4, 1897, 30 STAT. 56.

25. Erwin C. Surrency, "Federal District Court Judges and the History of Their Courts," 40 F.R.D. 159.

26. Hearings, Subcommittee on Improvements in Judicial Machinery, Committee on the Judiciary, U.S. Senate. U.S. Commissioner System, 1965, p.162.(Y4.J89/C73) This abolition of the commissioner system was based upon the argument that these officials should not be passing on affidavits for search warrants, or other sensitive issues.

27. Act of May 7, 1894, sec. 5, 28 STAT. 74.

28. *Ibid.*

29. This list is given in Hearings, Subcommittee on Improvements in Judicial Machinery, Committee on the Judiciary, U.S. Senate. Federal Magistrate Act, 1967. (J.84/Y4.J890), p.284.

30. John C. Rose, JURISDICTION AND PROCEDURE OF THE FEDERAL COURTS (3d ed., 1926), p.111.

31. Act of October 9, 1940, 54 STAT. 1058.

32. Hearings, Subcommittee on Improvements in Judicial Machinery, Committee on the Judiciary, U.S. Senate. Federal Magistrates Act, 1966.(J84/44.J89) p.600; Hearings, Subcommittee on Improvements in Judicial Machinery, Committee on the Judiciary, U.S. Senate. U.S. Commission System, 1965.(Y4.J89/C73), p.162. This abolition of the commissioner system was based upon the argument that these officials should not be passing on affidavits for search warrants, or other sensitive issues.

33. S. Doc. No. 49, 56th Cong. 1st sess., p.10; Rose, *supra,* note 30, p.111.

34. Rose, *supra,* note 30, p.131.

35. Blue v. United States, 342 F.2d 894 (C.A.D.C. 1964), is one of the first decisions to change the nature of the preliminary hearing from determining if the government had probable cause to permit discovery and to give the accused "a chance to learn in advance of trial the foundations of the charge and the evidence that will comprise the government's case against him." *Ibid* at 901.

36. S. Rept. No. 1050, 89th Cong. 2d sess., p.18. This was done in the District Court for the Eastern District of Michigan.

37. Act of May 28, 1896, sec. 19, 29 STAT. 184; Conkling, *supra,* note 13, p.89.

38. In re Commissioners of Circuit Court, 65 F. 314, 316 (C.C.W.D.N.C. 1894).

39. Act of May 28, 1896, sec. 20, 29 STAT. 184.

40. United States v. Maresca, 266 F.713, 720 (D.C.S.D.N.Y. 1920).

41. In re Commissioners of Circuit Court, 65 F. 314, 318 (C.C.W.D.N.C. 1894).

42. In re Commissioners of Circuit Courts, 65 F. 314, 318, 319 (C.C.W.D.N.C. 1894)(concurring opinion of Circuit Judge Charles H. Simonton).

43. H.R. Rept. No. 90-1629, p.4256.

44. Tumey v. Ohio, 273 U.S. 510 (1927).

45. Charles A. Linquist, "The United States Commissioner: An Evaluation of the Commissioner's Role in the Judicial Process," 39 TEMP. L. Q. 138 (1966).

46. Act of October 17, 1968, P.L. 90-578, 82 STAT. 1107.

47. H.R. Rept. No. 94-1609, pp.4, 7.

48. Act of October 21, 1976, 90 STAT. 2729.

49. Act of October 10, 1979, 93 STAT. 643.

50. Pacemaker Diagnostic Clinic of America v. Instromedix, Inc., 712 F.2d 1305 (9th Cir. 1983), 718 F.2d 971 (9th Cir. 1983), remanded 725 F.2d 537 (9th Cir. 1984).

51. Northern Pipeline Construction Co. v. Marathon Pipe Line Company and United States, 458 U.S. 50 (1982).

Chapter 28

COURT OFFICIALS

The judge is the center of attention in all court rooms, but it is difficult to appreciate that numerous officials had to arrange a vast number of details to bring the parties, jurors and court officials together at that particular time for the trial. Parties were notified, the jury was selected and made available, all the papers were properly arranged, served and preserved, and a host of other details were completed before the judge could begin the trial of the case. All this was made possible by supporting staff consisting of clerks, marshals, criers and court reporters. These officers rarely receive attention in the public press or official publication; but their efforts contribute to the efficiency in the court procedures. Slight changes in the record-keeping by the clerk have, step by step, changed the operations of the courts. Each successor in office takes up the methods of his predecessors and may make some changes of his own. Although these efforts defy incorporation in any general history of the federal courts, these officials deserve a place in that account.

The First Judiciary Act created the offices of clerk, marshal and district attorney in each judicial district. The marshals and district attorneys were appointed by the President, but the clerk was appointed by the judge of the district court. The American colonies had greatly simplified the staff of the courts, and none of the colonial courts had the elaborate staff of colorfully named court officials which were attached to the several English courts. A single clerk with deputies paid by fees earned from the litigants was more in keeping with the parsimonious tradition of compensating government officials in this country. The one innovation of the American experience was the creation of a public office for the purpose of prosecuting those charged with a crime in all courts. In England the prosecution of crimes was left to individuals, who shared in any fines, and to the initiative of citizens bringing matters either directly to the attention of the court or the grand jury. The offices of attorney general and solicitor general in England were advisory and represented the King in the civil courts, but did not represent the Crown in the criminal courts. The office of a prosecuting attorney originated through deputies appointed by the attorney general in each colony. If none were appointed, then the court made the appointment for that term of court. The office of district attorney combined these functions and was charged by statute "to prosecute in such districts all delinquents for crimes and offences, cognizable under the authority of the United States, in all civil actions in which the United States shall be concerned, except before the supreme court in the district in which that court shall be holden".[1] As contrasted to the prosecuting attorney in the states, the United States attorney was given the duty of representing the government in civil cases, which has resulted in this office representing the United States in all litigation.

These three offices in the federal system shared a number of common themes in their historical development, and the federal statutes often referred to them together, especially when establishing fees. From a common system depending upon fees allowed for similar services by state statutes, separate enactments during the subsequent century defined the fees for the different offices and, in some situations, for one of the officers in a specific judicial district. For these reasons, the fee system was never as simple in practice as it was in theory. Where the fees were dependent upon statutory allowance for similar services rendered by sheriffs in that state, an office in one district could be more profitable than in another. In some districts, a salary in addition to fees was attached to the office.

When these officers were required to account to the Treasury for the fees received, special allowances were authorized which began to create many exceptions. Did the reimbursements for travel and other expenses mean the most direct route or the route taken by the official? Could he collect two fees for travel when serving two writs to two different individuals on the same trip? A body of practice began to develop which is preserved in the decisions of the Solicitor of the Treasury and later the Comptroller of the Treasury. Some of these opinions were elaborate.[2] Later, based upon this experience, general instructions on interpretations of the statutes and administrative practices were issued. Certainly, this compensation system was never applied uniformly, for some fees were considered by the recipients as emoluments rather than fees that had to be reported. All these problems were eliminated by the adoption of a uniform salary.

Another theme that these offices shared was the degree of supervision they received from the nation's capital in the performance of their duties. When the three offices of the clerk, district attorney and marshal were created, no supervision was provided, for it was probably assumed that this function would be performed by the federal judge. As the administrative practices in the federal government developed, the Secretary of the Treasury was given supervision over the accounts of these officers. This function was later transferred to the Secretary of the Interior. This secretary had no power by statute to correspond or direct any of these offices and on several occasions recommended that their supervision, as well as the power of appointment, be transferred to the attorney general.[3] Each department in administering its area of governmental functions was able to call upon either of these three officers, but generally the marshal and the attorney for definite help. These departments could pass on their requests for action, but could exercise no further proctoring of these officers executing the requests.

One of the objectives of the Administrative Office of the Courts after its establishment in 1940 was to provide the courts with adequate staffs.

The Administrative Office took over supervision of the clerk and sought adequate salaries for those on the supporting staff. The offices of marshal and attorney were left under the supervision of the Attorney General. Under the auspices of the Administrative Office, money was appropriated to supply the courts with such essential services as secretaries, criers, court reporters and law clerks. When necessary, interpreters were authorized to assist the court in elucidating testimony of those witnesses unfamiliar with the English language. At present, a court staff serving a modern federal trial court consisting of several judges tends to be fairly large. In the years since the end of World War II, a number of factors have contributed to a greatly enlarged number of supporting staff. The judges in some districts need the assistance of an executive officer who will assist in the myriad details of the administration of the courts.

Only a minimal account of the developments in the offices of district attorney, the clerk and the marshal, is recounted here, which may fail to convey the true dimension of their role in the administration of justice.

Clerk

One court official essential for any lawyer to cultivate as a friend is the clerk, who, as a part of his unofficial duties, informs lawyers of proper procedures and alerts members of the bar to the filing requirements. These officers are generally the repository of local practice that will not be found in any formal set of rules.

The origin of the office is lost in the early histories of the English courts, but what is clear is that by the time of the settlement of the American colonies, large staffs of officials were attached to each English court under different titles, all entitled to certain fees and emoluments. In many of these offices, the appointee had a freehold interest, and it was his prerogative to dispose of the office as he wished. In the chancery courts, these clerks drafted the necessary documents to begin the cases, and no case could be filed in the court unless these preliminary matters were performed by them.[4] They acted as solicitors for the parties, and from this group developed the profession of solicitors who practiced exclusively before the chancery courts in England. The American colonies were well aware of the avariciousness of these officers in demanding fees, and probably sought to avoid that practice in the New World. A less noble explanation for this change was the lack of personnel in the colonies with good penmanship.

The official staff of the colonial courts consisted of a clerk and any deputies he cared to employ at his own expense. In the Royal Provinces, the attorney general appointed the clerks in the counties and shared in their fees. By the time of the establishment of the federal courts, the office of clerk was a recognized function associated with all courts.

In the First Judiciary Act, the Supreme Court and district court judges had the power to appoint their clerks.[5] It should be noted that the

appointment of the clerk of the United States Supreme Court was made by
the entire court rather than the Chief Justice of the United States. On the
third day of its first session, the Supreme Court by an order appointed
John Tucker of Boston as clerk. He was required to reside and keep his
office at the seat of the national government and not to practice law in that
Court while he continued to be a clerk.[6] In each district, the district court
judge appointed the clerk of his court, who would also serve as clerk of the
circuit court. No precise term of office was provided, and very early the
question arose whether the clerk could summarily be removed by the
judge. In 1839, the Supreme Court of the United States had to face this
issue. In removing the clerk, the judge wrote of his high regard for his
performance and the particular care he gave to the duties of his office, but
informed the incumbent that he was removed and another appointed in his
place. The Supreme Court ruled that the appointing judge could remove
the incumbent, and there was no appeal on the question of the abuse of
power.[7]

The clerk of the district court acted as a clerk of the circuit courts
until 1839 — an issue which proved to be a source of controversy.
Apparently, one justice felt he should have a part in this appointment, and
this dispute was important enough that it came to the attention of
Congress. In 1839, the circuit judge and the district judge jointly were
authorized to appoint a separate clerk for the circuit court.[8] In the event of
a disagreement between the judges, the appointment was made by the
presiding judge of the court, who at that period was the justice. This act
was understood to have been passed in consequence of a controversy
between the judges of the circuit court, which caused the interruption of
business, and was not intended to authorize a general practice of
appointing separate clerks for each court. However, under the general
provisions of the act, it became customary to appoint separate clerks for
both the circuit and the district courts.[9] Very often, the same individual
was appointed to both offices. When the office of circuit court judge was
established in 1869, the power to appoint the clerk for the circuit court
passed to this judge without the concurrence of the district court judge.[10]

The number of clerks in any particular judicial district became a
source of confusion, for Congress authorized clerks in locations other than
the seat of the court. When Arkansas was divided into two districts in
1851, the terms of the court in both districts were held by a single judge
who had the authority to appoint a clerk for each of the two districts.[11] In
1862, a clerk was authorized in Kentucky for every place that the district
court was held.[12] From a national perspective, it was confusing to find in
some judicial districts a single clerk with deputies in each city in which the
court met or, in other districts, clerks in each location with no supervision
except that offered by the judge. This confusion was ended in 1911 when
the circuit and district courts were combined. A clerk was authorized in
each judicial district, who was assisted by as many deputies as were

approved by the judge.[13] This authority to appoint additional personnel in the clerk's office later passed from the control of the judge, into the hands of the Attorney General, and finally, in 1948, to the Director of the Administrative Office of the Courts.

At the beginning of the federal judicial system, the clerk's office was required to be located where the sessions of the court were held, but in the event such sessions were held in two or more cities, the judge would designate where the office was to be permanently located.[14] In many, but not all, subsequent acts establishing judicial districts, the location of the clerk's office was specified. An examination of the acts shows no uniformity. By a series of acts beginning in 1887, the Southern District of Mississippi was separated into divisions. The clerk was to appoint a deputy at the location where the court was held in each division.[15] Three locations were established, and where the courts were to meet in the Western District of North Carolina, the judge was required to appoint three clerks, one in each of the cities where the court was held. The clerks were required to reside in those cities.[16] When North Dakota was split into divisions, the clerk was required to appoint deputies at each place where the court was held in the new divisions. These appointments had to be approved by the court, which could annul them at "its pleasure". The clerk, however, was made responsible for all the official acts and the negligence of all deputies.[17] The Judicial Code of 1911 provided that each of the district court judges would appoint a clerk, but all the incongruities were preserved.[18] Finally, the Judicial Code of 1948 ended this confusion by providing for one clerk in a district and giving authority to the district courts to designate the places within the district where the offices of the clerk or his deputies would be open.[19] In this organization, a single clerk in a judicial district was responsible for the operation of all offices in that district.

The duty most generally associated with the clerk is the maintenance of the records of the court. This duty required the clerk to be present at all sessions to enter the disposition of each case and keep additional records as may have been assigned by law. The First Judiciary Act summarized the clerk's obligations as faithfully to discharge the duties of the office, and reasonably to "record all the orders, decrees, judgments and proceedings of the said court" of which he was clerk.[20] The most essential record is the docket on which the cases are entered when first filed in the clerk's office. This docket also records the subsequent steps taken in the cases on file. During the early history of the national courts, minute books were kept in which were entered the orders and actions taken by the court each day. The clerk was enjoined by statute to keep many other types of records. A distinction has been drawn in judicial decisions between ministerial duties of the clerks and those duties which are actions of a court. Filing and keeping certain records are ministerial duties; sealing court's orders are actions of the court.

The federal courts were limited in their personnel and separated by some distances, so it became necessary for the clerks to perform functions which normally would have been performed by other officials. If Congress had created separate admiralty courts, another official would have been responsible for the clerical duties. In admiralty cases, if the counsel indicated to the court that he could not produce a witness to testify before the circuit court on the appeal from the district court, the clerk was to take down the testimony in writing. Such duties in other jurisdictions and at other times would have been performed by special commissioners. This procedure became unnecessary in 1803 when in admiralty and equity appeals, as contrasted to judicial review by writ of error, the evidence produced in the district court went with the case up to the circuit court and consequently had to be in writing.[21] The clerk could take special bail *de bene esse* in any action before the court where the judge was absent or disabled.[22] This, in effect, permitted a clerk to set bail when the judge was absent or disabled until this function came to be performed by others.

Interestingly enough, the First Judiciary Act provided that the marshal would adjourn the sessions of the circuit court from day to day until a judge was present. If neither of the judges attended by the close of the fourth day, the marshal was required to adjourn the court until the next regular term.[23] In 1840, if neither of the judges of the circuit court were to be present to open any regular or special session, a written order directed the marshal, and in his absence, the clerk, to adjourn the court until the next regular term.[24] However, in practice in some districts, the judges corresponded with the clerks who, one can assume, performed this function.

Upon the establishment of the federal courts, the clerk was compensated by the allowance of fees established by statute. In 1792, the clerk of the federal court was allowed the same fees as those normally charged by the clerks in the state where the court was located. In addition, he was allowed five dollars a day for attending any session of the court and ten cents per mile for his expenses in traveling from the place of his abode to the session of either court.[25] Where the clerk performed duties not normally covered by the fee of the state court, the judge was to allow "a reasonable compensation therefore".[26] A few modifications in these fees were made in 1799.[27] As new duties were given to the clerks, Congress would allow special fees for those purposes. In the various bankruptcy acts, the clerks were allowed certain fees similar to those allowed under the Copyright Act, where they accepted copyrighted materials on deposit. Trying to provide a satisfactory fee schedule was nearly impossible, and adopting the fee schedule of the state in which the court was located left many undesirable results. It was obvious that the central government did not know what the fees charged in a given state were, for in a 1794 resolution, Congress required the court to return true copies of the table of fees to the Attorney General from the state in which the court was located.[28]

There were many reasons for dissatisfaction with the collection of fees as a basis of compensation. In some judicial districts, this method of compensation could be very remunerative, with the recipient receiving a higher income than the judges. To remedy the inconsistency, in 1814, the clerks in certain states, including the Southern District of New York or Pennsylvania for either the district or circuit courts, were limited to one half of one per centum of all monies deposited in the courts.[29] This concept was made generally applicable in the Appropriation Act of 1841 when the clerk was allowed an annual salary of $1,500 payable from the fees received from the government. The clerk was required to continue to collect and return all payments exceeding this amount to the treasury.[30] The same statute provided that reasonable compensation should be paid to the deputies out of general appropriations. A few years later, this statute was revised, and the compensation allowed the clerk by the government was $3,500, in addition to his necessary office expenses and other fees which were allowed for special services. The fees collected from individuals and from filing under the Naturalization Acts were retained by the clerk. In some districts, the fees did not amount to a princely sum. In this event, if the fees did not exceed $500, the proper accounting officer of the Treasury was to pay the clerk such amount.[31] As early as 1878, the Attorney General complained that many of the clerks felt they did not have to include certain fees, such as those for copies and naturalization proceedings, in their reports.[32] The Attorney General recommended that where the same person held the office of clerk of both the circuit and district courts, that person should receive a limit of $5,000. The clerk of the District of Columbia had never been required to account for the fees received in his office, and for that reason, the attorney general recommended that this officer render an accounting as other clerks did.

The last comprehensive statute establishing fees was enacted in 1853, but Congress continued to attach fees for various purposes to different acts. Gradually, establishing fees became a function of the court. In the Bankruptcy Act of 1867 and 1898, the Supreme Court could set the fees by a general order.[33] The Courts of Appeals were allowed to prescribe their own fees, but later this was transferred to the Judicial Conference of the United States.[34]

In 1919, all clerks were paid a salary, as determined by the Attorney General of the United States, between $2,500 and $5,000, based upon the amount of business transacted. This was certainly a major change in the compensation of the office and had been urged for a number of years.[35] Interestingly, the Attorney General could allow the clerk to employ deputies and clerical assistants upon the clerk's recommendation, which was required to "state facts (as distinguished from conclusions) showing necessity for the same".[36] The effect of this law was to change the concept of financial support for the court officials. The litigants paid fees into the court for the general support of all administrators. The statute of 1853 continued to serve as the basis for the fees collected by the courts, along with its amendments, until 1925.[37] The term "filing fee" was substituted for the terminology used in the 1920 act "as full payment for all services to be rendered by the clerk".[38] Since 1896, the clerk's office has been responsible for collecting all fees allowed by law which are paid to marshals and attorneys as allowed for their services.[39]

Fiscal supervision of the clerks was transferred to the Department of the Interior in 1849 and later to the Attorney General upon the establishment of the Department of Justice.[40] Any other supervision the clerks received in the performance of their duties was exercised by the judge of the court. Few federal judges would have been versed in the administration of such an office and, for that reason, would have exercised very limited administrative control. Such control was provided with the creation of the Director of the Administrative Office of the Courts, who was charged with supervision of "all administrative matters relating to the offices of clerk and other clerical and administrative personnel of the courts".[41] This supervision has brought greater uniformity to the office and has made possible innovative techniques in handling this aspect of judicial administration.

As Congress established other courts, including the United States Circuit Court of Appeals, Commerce Court and the United States Court of Claims, a clerk for each of these bodies was regularly authorized. The appointment was vested in the court or, in rare cases, in the presiding judge. These officials played the same role in keeping the records for those courts as did the clerks of the United States district courts. These clerks have been dedicated to the performance of their duties and have been primarily responsible for its smooth operation.

United States Marshal

The United States marshal has been made famous through the fictionalized account of the exploits of these officers in bringing to justice the outlaws of the old West. The marshal of the Western novels traveled long distances to establish law and order, and indeed, some lost their lives in this endeavor. Unfortunately, the exploits of marshals in the territory of Alaska have never been popularized in this fashion, although their encounters with the forces of nature, including blizzards and wild animals, as well as outlaws, are equally dramatic. In fact, in nearly all the other areas of the country, the officer did not attract as much attention as he did in the West. The serving of a writ or the escorting of a prisoner to court or to prison in a more urbanized area does not capture the popular attention as easily.

In England and in America, the officer who enforced the judgment of the courts, served its writs and performed other administrative duties was the sheriff. This office had been established in all colonies prior to the break with England. Upon the establishment of federal courts, a similar position was provided in the office of the marshal for each United States district court.[42]

Of all the offices of the court defined in the First Judiciary Act, the provision governing the marshal is the most extensive. He was to be appointed by the President for a term of four years and could be removed from office at pleasure. He was required to attend the district and circuit court sessions within his own district and also the United States Supreme Court sessions when the terms of that court were held in his district. He was to execute throughout his district all the precepts issued by the courts, and he was to have the power as was common in England and the American states to command all the necessary assistance in the execution of this duty. The marshal was authorized to appoint deputies who could be removed by the district court judge; yet, the marshal was responsible for their performance.

The Judiciary Act of 1789 did not authorize the Supreme Court to have its own marshal, but rather required the marshal in the district where the Supreme Court met to serve the court.[43] This statute must have raised some confusion, for it was clarified four years later that the Judiciary Act did not require the attendance of the marshals of all the districts at the Supreme Court, but it was mandatory that the marshal in the district where the court met perform this duty.[44] When the Court moved permanently to Washington in 1801, the marshal in the District of Columbia served the Supreme Court in this capacity. This requirement generally did not inconvenience the Court, for during the first six decades of the Nineteenth Century, the justices came to Washington to hold sessions and were not permanently in residence there. In 1867, the Supreme Court was authorized to appoint its own marshal who was charged with the responsibility of taking care of all property belonging to the court and executing all processes and orders of the court.[45] It is interesting that this marshal was given a salary rather than fees and was required to render a true account of all court fees collected to the Secretary of the Interior. This marshal was allowed to appoint as many assistants and messengers as the Chief Justice approved in place of the crier and messengers then employed. Upon appointment by the President, the marshals were required to post a bond in the sum of $20,000 approved by the district court judge for the proper performance of their duties. This sum has survived into the Twentieth Century. The marshal had to take an oath in which he swore he would "true returns make, and in all things well and truly, and without malice or partiality, perform the duties of the office of marshal."[46] To prevent any lapses in the office, upon the death of the marshal, the deputies were to continue in office until specifically removed.

One of the duties associated with the office of marshal which is not mentioned in the First Judiciary Act is taking into custody any prisoners while executing the orders of the court. Since the federal government did not provide for jails, it became his responsibility to provide secure places to house prisoners. By permitting a prisoner to escape, the marshal or his deputy could be found guilty of a misdemeanor and fined a sum not exceeding $2,000 and imprisoned at the discretion of the court for a term not exceeding two years.[47] The marshal was not given the responsibility to investigate crimes during the Nineteenth Century, for his duties were essentially confined to making arrests upon the order of the court. The concept of investigating a crime to determine the offender developed after the establishment of police departments in the middle of the Nineteenth Century.

The full range of duties of the office were not comprehensively defined in the First Judiciary Act and had to be assigned by subsequent statutes and developed from practice. During the first decade, Congress proposed legislation for the office of the marshal on several occasions. Among the earliest duties given the marshal was the authority, in the absence of the district court judge, to adjourn the term of the court from day to day or until such time as the judge directed in a written order.[48] In 1792, he was given custody of all vessels and goods seized by an officer of the revenue service.[49] In 1795, in an act providing for the mustering of the militia to execute the laws of the United States, the marshals and their deputies were given "the same powers in executing the laws of the United States, as the sheriffs and their deputies, in the several states, have by law, in executing the laws of their respective states."[50] This definition of the office of marshal was considered as a general statute and has been kept in all revisions of the laws relating to the marshal. The same act provided that fines could be assessed against officers and members of the militia who failed to obey the orders of the President by a court martial, and the marshal was to collect the fines and turn the money over to the supervisor of the revenue in the district. Some of these provisions were found in a previous temporary act of 1792.[51]

The marshals were given a number of non-judicial duties not necessarily related to the historical functions of the office. Beginning in 1790, and until the Census Bureau was established in 1899, the federal marshals were in charge of taking the census in their judicial districts. For taking the first census, the majority of the marshals received $200 in addition to their regular salary. However, the marshal in Maryland was paid $300, while the marshal in New York was paid the normal $200 for these services. Congress must have thought it was easier to take the census in New York than it was in Maryland.[52]

Another duty associated with the office was in the capacity of the disbursing agent for the court. This became the marshal's responsibility in 1791 in the first statute providing for fees.[53] This statute provided for payment of jurors and witnesses and directed that the marshal disburse the funds. Further, he was to furnish the "fuel, candles, and other reasonable contingencies for holding a court".[54] From these humble beginnings emerged the process of this office acting as the administrator for the local federal courts.

After the first decade of the Nineteenth Century, Congress rarely mentioned the marshal in any statute except to regulate his fees or to assign special duties to a specific marshal in a given district. The marshal in the Southern District of New York was required to act in this capacity for the special court set up for the suppression of slave trade.[55]

Originally, the marshals were remunerated by fees, but Congress did not get around to prescribing the fees until 1791. Marshals were entitled to the fees prescribed by this statute from the time of their appointment in either of the first two years of the government.[56] Congress frequently took advantage of existing laws of the state by relating these fees to those charged by the sheriff in the state where the federal court was located. Where goods were taken on the writs of *fieri facias* and had to be appraised by state law, the marshal would select the appraiser and would be entitled to the same fees as the sheriff in that state.[57] Judging from the reports of 1793, the remuneration was not large, for few marshals received over $200, although John Skinner, marshal in North Carolina, received a total compensation of $606.47.[58] Beginning in 1817, Congress allowed the marshals of several new states a salary of $200 in addition to their fees. This was not done in every situation, for when Pennsylvania was split into two judicial districts, no salaries were authorized for the marshal of either district.[59] Prior to 1896, the marshals and their deputies were dependent upon fees, mileage charges and rewards as the basis for their income. The marshal was paid six cents per mile and only then if the proper receipts were kept. For performing any arrests, he received $2 whether the person arrested was a petty thief or a desperado who had to be pursued for hundreds of miles. It is said that the average marshal earned less than $500 per year.[60] Another quirk of the fee system was if a marshal killed a criminal during the pursuit, he forfeited all fees. Further, if friends or relatives of the deceased did not dispose of the body, the marshal was forced to bury the man himself at his own expense. In light of all these quirks in the fee system, there is no doubt that great temptations enticed marshals to generate as many fees as were permitted by statute.

An example of the abuse of the fee system involved the Indians. The deputy marshals in Oklahoma had a habit of arresting Indians by the wagon loads and taking them to the district court, charging them with introducing intoxicating liquors onto tribal lands. The marshal would take an Indian before the commissioner for arraignment under one name, collect a $25 fee, then remove the Indian and hold him elsewhere. After a proper period of time, another deputy would take the Indian before the Commissioner under another name and would then collect his fee for the same person. During the Nineteenth Century, Congress found great abuse of the fee system; tighter controls, including reporting to the Treasury, were instituted.[61] The marshals' accounts were approved by the judge in open court and paid by the Treasury. In 1896, the fee system was ended by the substitution of a salary for the marshals.[62]

During the Nineteenth Century, suits brought against the marshal generally concerned the fees charged, which is understandable when the incompleteness of the system is understood. From the beginning, there were gaps in the fee schedule, and in several instances, the Congress authorized the marshal to collect the same fee as the sheriff in his state.[63] These statutes did not fill all the gaps. It is not clear as to whether the marshal's fees were attached to the bills of costs or whether he had to present a separate bill to the litigants. It is clear that he could obtain an attachment to enforce the payment of his fees against the suitors in the court.[64]

George Washington, in selecting the first marshals, appointed many capable individuals who were well known in local politics. One author pointed out that out of the forty-five appointments under Washington and Adams, twenty-two are listed in the DICTIONARY OF AMERICAN BIOGRAPHY.[65]

By far the most famous marshals in the federal system were those in the Western territories, who are known in history for their gun duels and escapades with outlaws. The President was first authorized in 1813 to appoint a marshal in each territory for a term of four years.[66] In subsequent acts organizing the territory, the marshal was authorized to "execute all processes issuing from the said court when exercising their jurisdiction in the circuit and district courts of the United States".[67] It should be noted that this authorized the marshal to serve those processes which came before the territorial courts under their federal jurisdiction. Fiction has made it appear that these individuals undertook to solve crimes as police currently do, but if this was done, it was rarely true in fact. Like any other law enforcement official, the marshal could arrest any offender violating a federal law who came to his attention. Probably the Western marshals best known were those who rode with Judge Isaac Parker from the Western District of Arkansas. Judge Parker appointed some 200 deputy marshals; of these, 65 were slain in the performance of their duty. These men were better known as "men who rode for Parker". The marshals were responsible to the Department of Interior, as a part of the territorial government.

A special duty given to the marshals in several territories was the supervision of any federal penitentiary.[68] The establishment of these institutions and their operations form another interesting chapter in the history of the Old West.

It is not clear who exercised the supervisory powers over the marshals unless this was done by the judges of the federal courts. Nowhere is this function made clear. Congress directed that the marshals report to different federal agencies on matters coming before them. In 1820, the marshal was directed to execute the distress warrants of the officer of the Treasury Department. He was designated by the President as an agent to recover all money due the United States from officials having custody of government funds. The marshal was required to report within thirty days after the commencement of the term of the court upon what proceedings had taken place on all the writs of execution.[69] This was an interesting procedure in that this Treasury official would determine the arrears owed the government and then issue a distress warrant to the marshal to attach to the property. If the former government official challenged the amount due, he had to ask for an injunction to prevent the execution. Later, the office of Solicitor of the Treasury was established and these powers were transferred to him. This officer was given the authority to "instruct the district attorney, marshals, and clerks of the Circuit and District Courts of the United States, and all matters and proceedings, appertaining to suits in which the United States is a party, or interested, and cause them or either of them to report" from time to time.[70]

In 1861, the Attorney General was given general supervision of district attorneys and marshals, but this authority apparently did not extend to the territorial marshals.[71] This act was passed upon the commencement of the Civil War, and it can be presumed that the reason for its adoption was the anticipated new and important litigation growing out of this conflict. Since the Attorney General did not have a department or any sizeable staff, it would have been impossible for him to supervise closely these officers in the performance of their duties. In 1869, the Attorney General replied, to a Congressional resolution requesting that the head of each department list the number of clerks employed and what reduction in these staffs could be made, that he employed a total of ten clerks in various grades and one additional clerk to dispose of private land claims in California.[72] The Attorney General probably construed his supervisory powers to advise on interpreting points of law rather than a closer supervision of the marshals in execution of their offices.[73]

In conflict with the supervision of the Attorney General was an act of 1862 in which the marshals were directed to report to the Navy Department full particulars of the disposition of every prize vessel and cargo within their districts.[74] When the Justice Department was established in 1870, the only mention made of this power of supervision was the transfer of auditing the marshal's accounts from the Department of Interior to this newly created department.[75] Congress assumed that the Attorney General was exercising effective control, for how else could this omission of a stronger transfer be explained? Obviously, with the control by the Attorney General over law suits against the federal government, his concern with the marshals' performance continued to increase. Since 1870, the Attorney General has gradually assumed a complete supervision of the marshals' office.

The marshal was made liable for failure to perform certain acts, especially if these were the result of malfeasances. For example, under the Fugitive Slave Act of 1783, it was the duty of the marshal to capture slaves and to return them to their proper owner(s). If the marshals failed to capture the slaves, they were fined $1,000. Not only were the marshals reluctant to enforce this act in the North, but there were instances in the South when marshals or their deputies were disciplined for failure to seek out runaway slaves. In Brunswick, Georgia, a marshal was removed from office for refusing to pursue slaves that had escaped from a slave ship.[76] Generally, if the marshal failed to obey the writ issued by a court without a legal excuse or in violation of the rights of others, he was liable in an action by the injured party.[77]

After the Department of Justice was established, the Attorney General frequently commented on the tribulations of marshals. In 1890, he pointed out that the deputy marshal received the same fee for the arrest of a local, easily apprehended criminal as he did for one he had to pursue for weeks and capture only after a hard fight. The deputy was not allowed to recover for his expenses or time.[78]

The Attorney General sought greater protection for the marshals. The marshals found that it was not a crime to resist a federal officer acting in the line of duty, and this was not corrected until 1888.[79] This corrective measure, however, only applied to the resistance of federal officers in the Indian Territory. The statute was not made generally applicable until 1934 when it became a federal crime to kill, assault or forcefully resist a federal officer in the performance of his duties.[80] Prior to this date, cases for assaults on federal officers, including the marshals, were prosecuted in the state courts.

From the First Judiciary Act, the marshal had the authority to appoint as many deputies as he desired, but these deputies could be removed at pleasure by the judges of the district or circuit courts sitting within that district.[81] These deputies were to be compensated from the fees collected by the office. This was changed in 1896 when the marshals were given a salary in lieu of fees. At that time, two types of deputies were established, one of which was authorized by the Attorney General of the United States and paid a salary. The other group was called field deputies, who were appointed by the marshal and received three-quarters of the gross fees but not more than $1,500 a year. These field deputies could be removed by either the district court or the Attorney General.[82] In 1948, in the revision of the Judicial Code, this distinction was abolished and the duty was imposed upon the Attorney General to authorize the marshal to appoint as many deputies and clerical assistants as were needed. These deputy marshals could only be removed pursuant to civil service regulations.[83] The revisors note that since 1923 no deputy marshal had been removed by the district court.

Because the marshals were the enforcement arm of the federal courts, they were called upon to enforce injunctions in labor and civil rights actions and were required to perform many other unpopular duties. In an era when judicial proceedings are interrupted by "peaceful demonstrations", and threats are made upon the lives of officials, the duty of the marshal to protect the judge and the courtroom has vastly been enlarged. The professionalization of the deputy marshal service was recognized in 1969 when the United States marshal's service was officially established in the Department of Justice.

District Attorneys

The Judiciary Act of 1789 authorized the appointment by the President in each judicial district of "a person learned in the Law" to act as attorney for the United States in all criminal and civil cases in which the United States had an interest. Like the marshal, the district attorney was appointed by the President with the consent of the Senate for a term of four years.[84] The district attorney was to be compensated by fees that were "taxed therefor in the respective courts." Congress legislated for this office very rarely, which lead one authority to state "the scope and general nature of the duties of this office are sufficiently indicated by his official designation and the summary description of them contained in the original act above recited that little could be added".[85]

The First Judiciary Act did not give a title to this office, for it merely provided for the appointment of an attorney in each district. For this reason, this position was designated in statutes and court decisions often as "district attorney", "attorney", and the "United States attorney", often within the same decision and statute.[86] When the Justice Department was given supervision over these individuals in 1870, they became more commonly designated as United States attorneys. Finally, in revising the Judicial Code of 1948, the revisors adopted the title United States attorney and conformed all the statutes to this title.[87]

President Washington appointed a substantial number of individuals of ability and prominence "measuring up well to Washington's high standards". In 1796, a House Committee reported that these attorneys were men of reputation and integrity.[88] These early appointments in the original states set high standards for performance and were considered prestigious offices to be eagerly sought by ambitious attorneys. Probably the most prodigious duties confronting these offices were prosecutions for crimes and cases involving the customs and internal revenue laws. Prosecutions under the Embargo Act of 1794 and the Nonintercourse Act of 1798 did not endear these attorneys to the local population. The general practice was that when a customs agent found some reason to bring an action for the forfeiture of a bond or confiscation of goods, he referred the case to the district attorney who proceeded to prosecute.

No provision was made at the time the office was created for supervision of these individuals, and for a period, they acted independently as they thought proper. The Secretary of State did, on occasion, direct the district attorneys in matters pertaining to suits within the jurisdiction of his department as did the other department heads, but this was not a

continuing supervision of their conduct or direction in polcy.[89] The first
Attorney General, Edmund Randolph, urged Congress to give the Attorney General supervision of these government attorneys, but this was
not done until several decades later.[90] In 1817, the Treasury Department
was given statutory authority to superintend suits for the recovery of funds
due the United States. This included the authority to issue directions to the
district attorneys in collecting these debts.[91] The office of Solicitor of the
Treasury was created in 1830, and this officer was given power to direct
the attorneys, marshals and clerks in all actions pertaining to suits in
which the United States had an interest and to cause them to make a
periodic report to that officer.[92] In return, the attorneys were required to
give an account of all funds collected by them. When the Department of
Interior was created in 1851, supervision of the accounts of these offices
was transferred to that Department.[93] The Solicitor of the Treasury
continued to direct these officers in the performance of the duties relating
to that department. Other departments continued to refer suits in which
the United States was a party to the attorneys for prosecution. In 1861,
supervision over the attorney's accounts and proceedings were transferred
to the Attorney General.[94]

The Department of Justice supervised the accounts of the district
attorneys upon its establishment in 1870. At this time, the attorneys were
required to report on the proceedings in all legal matters to the Attorney
General and receive his directions.[95] Supervision and directions to the
district attorneys were not confined to the newly established Department
of Justice; many other officers, such as the Solicitor of the Treasury, who
had previously dealt directly with the district attorneys, continued to do
so. As late as 1924, the attorney was required to report directly to the
Solicitor of the Treasury and Commissioners of Internal Revenue on suits
handled for these agencies.[96] Only gradually, by executive orders and
custom, did the district attorneys come under the exclusive control of the
Department of Justice. The revisors of the Judicial Code of 1948 made it
clear that they were repealing all of those previous sections which required
the district attorneys to act at the direction of other officers.[97]

When the Department of Justice became responsible for the administration of the district attorneys throughout the United States, these offices
were in general disarray. Certain irregularities were regularly practiced
which would take decades to remedy. Correspondence between the district
attorney and the Attorney General was frequent, and gradually the
Department issued regular printed instructions which were circulated to
the marshals, attorneys, clerks and commissioners. The first such comprehensive document was issued in 1895 and gave general instructions about
reporting fees and other matters to the Department and general policies
governing the conduct of the district attorneys in carrying out their
duties.[98]

With an increase in the number of cases involving the United States,
the district attorneys often had to hire special assistants to help them in the

performance of their duties. The abuse of this practice was one of the contributing factors in convincing Congress to establish the Department of Justice. As early as 1861, the Attorney General was charged with the supervision of the district attorney and had the authority to employ additional help to assist in government cases.[99] After 1870, it is apparent that the attorneys continued to hire assistance when they thought it appropriate, without consulting the Attorney General. In 1896, before hiring any assistants, the district attorney had to demonstrate his need to the district judge and the petition had to contain "the facts as distinguished from conclusions, showing the necessity therefor".[100] Finally, in the revision of the Judicial Code of 1948, the authority was vested with the Attorney General to authorize any assistance that the United States attorneys needed in the performance of their duties.[101]

During the Nineteenth Century, the district attorneys were entitled to receive fees for their services. Generally when prescribing fees, Congress would apply the acts to the three offices of marshals, clerks and district attorneys. In 1792, the fees for the three offices were authorized, but in addition to those fees, the district attorney was entitled to those received by the state attorneys within the state where the district was located.[102] A few years later, the district attorneys were given an annual salary of $200 as full compensation for all extra services.

The compensation received from fees and salaries was not uniform throughout the country, for attorneys in different judicial districts would be the subject of special limitations or additions to their fees. The district attorney in the judicial district of Virginia was permitted such sums as the court considered "a reasonable compensation" where no fees were allowed for similar services in the state courts.[103] One part of the fee for both marshal and the district attorney was a *per diem* payment for attending the sessions of the court. The payment of such fees was prohibited in 1814.[104] This limitation was confined to certain districts including Massachusetts, Rhode Island, Pennsylvania and the Southern District of New York. This act was later repealed, creating equal compensation in all districts.[105] The district attorney was placed on a limited salary of $6,000 in 1842 when the secretary of Treasury was assigned the responsibility of receiving accounts of money received by the district attorney.[106] The proper accounting officers of the Treasury were responsible for allowing the necessary office expenses.

Although this statute seemed to have ended their fee compensation, the effect was quite different. Fees had been established for handling such matters as bankruptcy or examining land titles, and these fees were considered as extra compensation beyond the normal duties of the office. In later administrative practice, the fees for extra compensation became known as emoluments. This distinction is recognized in the REVISED STATUTES.[107]

Abuse is common to all offices which depend upon the fee system for compensation. This was true in the offices of the district attorneys. To increase the fees received from the office, the district attorneys were accused of bringing vexatious suits. For this reason, and because of other factors not discussed, the fee system was discontinued in 1896 when both the attorneys and marshals were given salaries in lieu of all fees.[108] The salary varied from $5,000 in a few districts, including the Western District of Arkansas, to a low of $2,000 in the District of Delaware. For comparison, the salary of all district court judges was raised to $5,000 in 1891.[109] An attempt was made to adjust the salary to the amount of work required in the office. The Commission to Revise and Codify the Criminal and Penal Laws recommended that the salaries of several attorneys be reduced. They noted that the salary of the United States attorney for the District of Kentucky was fixed at $5,000, but in 1901, the state was divided into two districts with an attorney in each. The salaries were continued at $5,000. The Commission concluded "if the salary of $5,000 was adequate when the state formed only one district, it is manifestly excessive since the division."[110] The Commission recommended a reduction of the salaries of the attorney for the Western District of Arkansas and the Eastern District of Texas, since the jurisidiction of these courts in the Indian Territory had been terminated, and for this reason, the allowance was out of line with the anticipated workload. Fortunately, Congress did not act on these recommendations.

Other Court Officials

From the three court officials created in 1789, the staff attached to the various federal courts has grown in number and significance. One of the first needs obviously was for an official who would remain in the court room during the trial of the case to attend to the wants of the court and the jury. The marshal normally was away from the court performing other duties. In 1799, all courts were authorized to appoint criers who were allowed two dollars per day for attending court.[111] In addition, the marshals were allowed to appoint up to three criers, if authorized by the judge, to attend to the grand and petit juries and for other necessary purposes. These appointees were allowed two dollars per day from the money held by the marshal.

A number of courts appointed criers before 1799, for one of the first actions taken by the United States Supreme Court even before appointing a clerk was to appoint Richard Wenman as "Cryer of this Court".[112] The numerous duties performed by this officer included overseeing the day to day functions of the court and the welfare of the judge and jury. During the Nineteenth Century, when this compensation was paid from the fees collected by the marshal, it was entirely within the authority of the local judge to approve the accounts and hence, allow these payments for any number as authorized by law. However, with a gradual shift to centralize control of all court funds and payment of salaries, funds for these minor officers had to be authorized through congressionally approved appropriations, and as a result, fewer officials could be appointed. The judges felt the need for a permanent officer who would maintain order while the court was in session and render personal assistance to the judge "in the performance of his duties both in the court room and in chambers". Because of this confidential relationship, the judges felt that they should appoint a crier.

The Great Depression impacted the federal courts in many ways, including limiting the number of supporting staff. Unfortunately, many courts had been without criers, since no appropriation had been made to pay them during the years after 1932.[113] The Judicial Conference recommended the establishment of a permanent crier which was accomplished in 1944.[114] The officers appointed by the marshal became known as bailiffs whose duty included attending to juries and guarding prisoners.[115] The crier was a full time position, whereas the bailiff was to be paid for his actual attendance on the court. An inadequate number of positions were funded for several years after 1944, but gradually the shortage was narrowed and criers became a regular part of all federal courts.[116] Later, it became permissible for the law clerk to act as a crier.

In the Nineteenth Century, it was incumbent upon judges to keep notes on evidence produced and testimony in trials before them, for it was their duty to certify a Bill of Exceptions taken out by the appellant. Stenographic records were known at the time the federal courts were established, but the service of those skilled in taking shorthand was not used in the federal courts until much later. As the Nineteenth Century progressed, in the federal courts in heavily populated areas such as New York and Philadelphia, the lawyers used stenographers to make a transcript of the testimony in order to expedite their preparation of a bill of exceptions. The Commission to Revise and Codify the Criminal and Penal Laws of the United States, when asked to draft a statute governing the courts, recommended that each district court be permitted to appoint an official stenographer.[117] The Commissioners argued "the value of shorthand notes of testimony and other proceedings in expediting trials and assuring accuracy in bills of exceptions and transcripts on appeal is abundantly established in experience".[118] It was asserted that these duties should be performed by a sworn officer of the court. By the beginning of the Twentieth Century, nearly all states provided for court stenographers. Unfortunately, in adopting the Judicial Code of 1911, the provision for the appointment of an official stenographer was omitted. In 1944, the federal courts for the first time were authorized to appoint official stenographers, but this was possibly recognizing a practice which had been prevalent.[119] These appointees were officially designated as court reporters.

Well into this century, the federal judges had no secretarial help in the performance of their duties. Judges in the Nineteenth Century wrote their own opinions which may explain why these decisions tended to be brief. Exactly when secretarial support was given to the judges is not clear, but certainly it was not until the present century that this was done officially. Often, judges had the services of a member of the clerk's staff who would make copies of documents since this was one function of that office. The transition was very slow and varied with the wishes of the judge. Under the auspices of the Administrative Office of the court, this situation began to improve as salaries were provided for secretarial support.

One additional supporting staff member for the judiciary is the law clerk. Although this office was first authorized in 1922, it is probable that the federal judges had used law clerks for a considerable period of time before that date when they were first authorized for the Supreme Court justices.[120] An ambitious young law student could easily be persuaded that time spent without pay in a judge's chambers, especially a Supreme Court justice, would be advantageous to his career. A law clerk was first authorized in 1922 in the Appropriation Act for each of the justices and chief justice of the United States Supreme Court. Each clerk was allowed a salary of $3,600 a year. These positions were made permanent in the enactment of the United States Code of 1924.[121]

In 1930, each of the circuit judges was allowed to appoint a law clerk with the approval of the attorney general.[122] The authorization of these law clerks came at the insistence of the Judicial Conference under Chief Justice Taft.[123] The value of having law clerks was recognized, and in 1936, a number of law clerks were authorized for the judges of the district court when approved by the senior judge of the circuit.[124] The number of clerks was limited to 35 throughout the United States which caused some confusion in administration, for more judges wanted clerks than were available. In 1940, Congress limited the number of law clerks to two in any one circuit. By 1945, a law clerk was provided for every district judge who desired one and whose need was certified by the senior circuit judge. The Director of the Administrative Office of the Courts optimistically predicted that "this is bound to increase the amount of judicial work which the judges can perform".[125] This is very true, but questions have been raised whether these law clerks are now performing judicial duties beyond the original concept of the office.

This has been but a brief survey of additional staff furnished the federal courts since their inception. Since 1945, the number of supporting staff has increased and each office is organized differently depending upon the size of the office. In the offices of the clerks and marshals, where a large staff is common, it is customary to divide the duties and make specific individuals responsible for given functions. In a small office, such specialization is not possible. No adequate historical account of the contributions made to the advancement of judicial administration in the federal courts by the supporting staffs, especially by the clerks, is possible except when limited to one district. This omission here in no way reflects on their true importance in the day to day operations of the courts. These individuals deserve more of a place in history.

FOOTNOTES TO CHAPTER 28

1. Act of September 24, 1789, sec. 35, 1 STAT. 92.

2. As one example, *see* Fees of District Attorneys - Keasbey's Case, 1 DEC. FIRST COMPTROLLER 172 (1880), and the digest of court opinions and decisions of the Treasury in Robert M. Cousar, DIGEST OF THE LAWS AND DECISIONS RELATING TO THE APPOINTMENT, SALARY AND COMPENSATION OF THE OFFICIALS OF THE UNITED STATES COURTS, H.R. Misc. Doc. No. 87, 53d Cong. 3d sess. (1895).

3. H.R. Ex. Doc. No. 95, 33d Cong. 1st sess. p.17 (April 25, 1854).

4. Sir William Holdsworth, A HISTORY OF THE ENGLISH LAW (1930), v.1, p.246, 421.

5. Act of September 24, 1789, sec. 7, 1 STAT. 76.

6. Erwin C. Surrency, ed., "Minutes of the Supreme Court of the United States," 5 AMER. J. LEGAL HIST. 69 (1961).

7. In re Hennen, 13 Pet. 230 (U.S. 1839).

8. Act of February 28, 1839, 5 STAT. 321.

9. Alfred Conkling, A TREATISE ON THE ORGANIZATION, JURISDICTION AND PRACTICE OF THE COURTS OF THE UNITED STATES (4th ed., 1864), p.89.

10. Act of April 10, 1869, sec. 2, 16 STAT. 45.

11. Act of March 3, 1851, sec. 4, 9 STAT. 595.

12. Act of May 15, 1862, sec. 7, 12 STAT. 387.

13. Act of March 3, 1911, sec. 3, 36 STAT. 1087.

14. Act of September 24, 1789, sec. 3, 1 STAT. 74.

15. Act of February 28, 1887, sec. 4, 24 STAT. 430; Act of April 4, 1888, sec. 4, 25 STAT. 79; Act of July 18, 1894, sec. 7, 28 STAT. 115.

16. Act of June 4, 1872, sec. 9, 17 STAT. 217.

17. Act of June 29, 1906, sec. 6, 34 STAT. 609.

18. Act of March 3, 1911, sec. 3, 36 STAT. 1087.

19. Act of June 25, 1948, sec. 751, 62 STAT. 920.

20. Act of September 24, 1789, sec. 7, 1 STAT. 76.

21. *Ibid,* p.89.

22. Act of May 8, 1792, sec. 10, 1 STAT. 278.

23. Act of September 24, 1789, sec. 6, 1 STAT. 76.

24. Act of July 4, 1840, 5 STAT. 392.

25. Act of May 8, 1792, sec. 3, 1 STAT. 277.

26. *Ibid.*

27. Act of February 28, 1799, sec. 3, 1 STAT. 624. For example, the 1799 statute provided for the circuit and district court clerks to receive an additional one-third of the fees over the amount allowed to state supreme court clerks. The federal clerks also received the minimal fees granted to clerks in admiralty courts, as established by the Act of March 1, 1793, 1 STAT. 332.

28. Resolution of June 9, 1794, 1 STAT. 402.

29. Act of April 18, 1814, 3 STAT. 133.

30. Act of March 3, 1841, 5 STAT. 427.

31. Act of February 26, 1853, sec. 3, 10 STAT. 165.

32. 1879 ATT'Y GEN. ANN. REP. 9.

33. Act of March 2, 1867, sec. 47, 14 STAT. 540.

34. H.R. Rept. No. 308, 80th Cong. 1st sess., p. A160 (April 25, 1947).

35. Act of February 26, 1919, 40 STAT. 1182.

36. *Ibid,* sec. 4, p.1182.

37. Act of February 11, 1925, 43 STAT. 857.

38. S. Rept. No. 1559, 80th Cong. 2d sess. (June 9, 1948). Revisor's note under section 1914.

83. Act of June 25, 1948, sec. 542, 62 STAT. 911.

84. Act of September 24, 1789, sec. 35, 1 STAT. 92.

85. Conkling, *supra,* note 9, p.211.

86. In re Neagle, 135 U.S. 1 (1890).

87. H.R. Rept. No. 308, 80th Cong. 1 sess., p.A57 (April 25, 1947).

88. White, *supra,* note 65, p.407.

89. *Ibid,* p.406-407.

90. Cummings and McFarland, *supra,* note 76, p.26.

91. *Ibid,* p.144.

92. Act of May 29, 1830, 4 STAT. 414.

93. Act of March 3, 1849, 9 STAT. 395.

94. Act of August 2, 1861, sec. 2, 12 STAT. 285.

95. Act of June 22, 1870, sec. 16, 16 STAT. 164.

96. 28 U.S.C. §436-88 (1924).

97. H.R. Rept. No. 308, 80th Cong. 1st sess., p.A60 (April 25, 1947).

98. These instructions were published in Digest of the Laws and Decisions Relating to Appointment, Salary and Compensation of the Officials of the United States Courts, edited by Robert M. Cousar. (Washington, Government Printing Office, 1895) H.R. Mis. Doc. No. 87, 53d Cong. 3d sess., p.201.

99. Act of August 2, 1861, sec. 2, 12 STAT. 285. Became REV. STAT. sec.363.

100. Act of May 28, 1896, sec. 8, 29 STAT. 181.

101. H.R. Rept. No. 308, 80th Cong. 1st sess., p.A63.

102. Act of May 8, 1792, sec. 3, 1 STAT. 277.

103. Act of February 28, 1789, sec. 5, 1 STAT. 626.

104. Act of April 18, 1814, 3 STAT. 133.

105. Act of March 8, 1824, 4 STAT. 8.

106. Act of May 18, 1842, item no. 167, 5 STAT. 483.

107. REV. STAT. (1874) sec. 834.

108. Cummings and McFarland, *supra,* note 76, p.179, 180.

109. Act of February 24, 1891, 26 STAT. 783.

110. S. Doc. No. 68, 57th Cong. 1st sess., p.24 (December 12, 1910).

111. Act of February 28, 1799, 1 STAT. 626.

112. Surrency, *supra,* note 6, p.70.

113. Henry P. Chandler, "Some Major Advances in the Federal Judicial System, 1922-1947," 31 F.R.D. 422 (1963).

114. Act of December 7, 1944, sec. 1, 58 STAT. 796.

115. *Ibid.*

116. 1950 REPT. DIR. ADMIN. OFFICE, p.42.

117. S. Doc. No. 68, 57th Cong. 1st sess., p.22 (December 12, 1901).

118. S. Doc. No. 68, 57th Cong. 1st sess., p.22 (December 12, 1901).

119. Act of January 20, 1944, sec. 1, 58 STAT. 5.

120. Act of June 1, 1922, 42 STAT. 614.

121. 28 U.S.C. §328 (1924).

122. Act of June 17, 1930, 46 STAT. 774.

123. Hearings before the Committee on the Judiciary, House of Representatives, February 3, and March 2, 1928, serial 23, p.55.

124. Act of February 17, 1936, 49 STAT. 1140.

125. 1945 REPT. DIR. ADMIN. OFFICE, p.31.

39. Act of May 28, 1896, sec. 8, 29 STAT. 181.

40. Act of March 3, 1849, sec. 4, 9 STAT. 395; Act of June 22, 1870, sec.15, 16 STAT. 164.

41. Act of August 7, 1939, 53 STAT. 1223.

42. Act of September 27, 1789, sec. 27, 1 STAT. 87.

43. *Ibid.*

44. Act of June 9, 1794, sec. 7, 1 STAT. 396.

45. Act of March 2, 1867, 14 STAT. 433.

46. Act of September 24, 1789, sec. 27, 1 STAT. 87.

47. Act of June 21, 1860, 12 STAT. 69.

48. Act of September 24, 1789, sec. 6, 1 STAT. 76.

49. Act of May 26, 1792, sec. 4, 1 STAT. 275.

50. Act of February 28, 1795, sec. 9, 1 STAT. 425.

51. Act of May 2, 1792, sec. 9, 1 STAT. 265.

52. Act of March 1, 1790, 1 STAT. 101, requiring the marshal to take the first census. The Census Bureau was established by Act of March 3, 1899, 30 STAT. 1014.

53. Act of March 3, 1791, 1 STAT. 216.

54. *Ibid.*

55. Act of July 11, 1862, 12 STAT. 531.

56. Act of March 3, 1791, sec. 1, 1 STAT. 216.

57. Act of March 2, 1793, sec. 8, 1 STAT. 335.

58. AMERICAN STATE PAPERS, MISCELLANEOUS, v.1, p.60.

59. Indiana, Act of March 3, 1817, 3 STAT. 391; Mississippi, Act of April 3, 1817, sec. 5, 3 STAT. 413; Illinois, March 3, 1819, 3 STAT. 503, are a few of the statutes authorizing a salary. Act of April 20, 1818, sec. 5, 3 STAT. 463, Pennsylvania was divided into two districts but no salary was authorized.

60. Shirley, LAW WEST OF FORT SMITH (1957), p.45.

61. H. R. Rept. No. 2164, 48th Cong., 1st sess. (1884), quoted in Leonard D. White, THE REPUBLICAN ERA — 1869-1901, A STUDY IN ADMINISTRATIVE HISTORY (1958), p.378.

62. Act of May 28, 1896, sec. 6, 9, 29 STAT. 179, 181.

63. Act of May 8, 1792, sec. 3, 1 STAT. 2776.

64. 2 Gallis C.C.R. 101.

65. Leonard D. White, THE FEDERALISTS, A STUDY IN ADMINISTRATIVE HISTORY (1961), p.414.

66. Act of February 27, 1813, 2 STAT. 806.

67. Act of March 2, 1861, sec. 10, 12 STAT. 213. This statute created the Territory of Nevada but this was rather typical of similar acts.

68. Act of January 1, 1871, sec. 2, 16 STAT. 398.

69. Act of May 15, 1820, 3 STAT. 592.

70. Act of May 29, 1830, 4 STAT. 414.

71. Act of August 2, 1861, 12 STAT. 285.

72. H.R. Ex. Doc. No. 11, 41st Cong. 2d sess.

73. Conkling, *supra,* note 9, p.200.

74. Act of July 17, 1862, sec. 12, 12 STAT. 608.

75. Act of August 2, 1861, 12 STAT. 285.

76. Homer Cummings and Carl McFarland, FEDERAL JUSTICE (1937), p.182.

77. Life and Fire Insurance Co. of New York v. Adams, 8 Pet. 306 (U.S. 1831).

78. 1890 ATT'Y. GEN. ANN. REP. p.13; 1893 ATT'Y. GEN. ANN. REP. p.20.

79. Act of June 9, 1888, 25 STAT. 178.

80. Act of May 18, 1934, sec. 1, 48 STAT. 780.

81. Act of September 27, 1789, sec. 27, 1 STAT. 87.

82. Act of May 28, 1896, sec. 10, 11, 29 STAT. 182.

INDEX